History of Artificial Intelligence

This book provides an overview of AI's historical development while understanding the cultural and scientific foundations that make today's AI possible. Through easy-to-understand explanations of complex ideas and a focus on both technological advances and ethical considerations, it provides an understanding of AI's past, present, and future.

History of Artificial Intelligence: From the Mathematics of Ancient Civilizations to Thinking Machines takes readers on a fascinating journey through the history of AI, showing how its origins can be traced back to ancient civilizations and their early advancements in mathematics, logic, and computation. It reveals the unexpected links between ancient calculation methods and the technologies that define modern life. By following AI's development, from the mathematical innovations of Mesopotamia, Egypt, and Iran to the revolutionary ideas of the European Renaissance and Enlightenment, readers will discover how human ingenuity over the centuries paved the way for the creation of intelligent machines. Each chapter takes readers step by step through major milestones, from the first mechanical calculators to the rise of modern computers and the development of TM. By exploring these key events and the contributions of diverse civilizations, the book offers fresh insights into AI's global history and its complex relationship with human thought. In the final chapters, the book also addresses the ethical and societal challenges AI presents today, giving readers a well-rounded understanding of how AI is shaping our future and what that means for all of us.

This book is written for a broad audience, including both general readers and academic audiences who are interested in the history, development, and ethical implications of AI. It is particularly suited for students, researchers, and professionals in fields such as computer science, AI, mathematics, history of science and technology, and digital ethics.

History of Artificial Intelligence

From the Mathematics of Ancient Civilizations to Thinking Machines

Abbas Tcharkhtchi, Hamid Reza Vanaei, and Sofiane Khelladi

CRC Press
Taylor & Francis Group
Boca Raton London New York

CRC Press is an imprint of the
Taylor & Francis Group, an **informa** business

Designed cover image: Abbas Tcharkhtchi, Hamid Reza Vanaei, and Sofiane Khelladi

MATLAB® and Simulink® are trademarks of The MathWorks, Inc. and are used with permission. The MathWorks does not warrant the accuracy of the text or exercises in this book. This book's use or discussion of MATLAB® or Simulink® software or related products does not constitute endorsement or sponsorship by The MathWorks of a particular pedagogical approach or particular use of the MATLAB® and Simulink® software.

First edition published 2026
by CRC Press
2385 NW Executive Center Drive, Suite 320, Boca Raton FL 33431

and by CRC Press
4 Park Square, Milton Park, Abingdon, Oxon, OX14 4RN

CRC Press is an imprint of Taylor & Francis Group, LLC

© 2026 Abbas Tcharkhtchi, Hamid Reza Vanaei, and Sofiane Khelladi

ISBN: 978-1-041-01199-6 (hbk)
ISBN: 978-1-041-01198-9 (pbk)
ISBN: 978-1-003-61363-3 (ebk)

DOI: 10.1201/9781003613633

Typeset in Times
by Deanta Global Publishing Services, Chennai, India

Contents

About the Authors

Abbas Tcharkhtchi is Distinguished Professor at Arts et Métiers Institute of Technology (ENSAM), Paris, France. He was previously the head of the Polymers and Composites Group of PIMM laboratory, the Head of the Processing, Mechanics, and Materials Department, and member of the research council of ENSAM. He was also the scientific manager of doctoral training at the Paris campus, where he was responsible for overseeing 70 PhD students. Currently, he is the president of the scientific and technical commission of the AFR association. He has published over 220 papers and contributed to the publication of several books.

Hamid Reza Vanaei is Associate Professor at Ecole Supérieure d'Ingénieurs Léonard de Vinci (ESILV), De Vinci Higher Education (DVHE) in Paris, France. He obtained his MSc and PhD in Mechanics of Materials from Arts et Métiers Institute of Technology (ENSAM) in Paris and works as Associate Researcher at the same institute. With six years of experience in Material Science, Mechanical Engineering, and Advanced Manufacturing, his primary research focuses on a multidisciplinary approach to optimizing Advanced Manufacturing techniques.

Sofiane Khelladi is Full Professor at Arts et Métiers Institute of Technology (ENSAM) in Paris, France, where he leads the Fluid and Energy Systems Engineering Laboratory (LIFSE). He also serves as a member of the ENSAM Research Council. His research activities center around three main themes with strong interactions: advanced numerical methods for fluid and energy systems, multiphase flows and multiphysics coupling, and aero-hydrodynamics and acoustics of turbomachines. His work focuses on modeling and analyzing fluid flows for the design of complex fluid and energy systems.

Foreword I

In the beginning, there was observation, measurement, and data. What we now call modern science would still have to wait. From the very start, humans created technology to master their natural environment and benefit from it. Later came the desire to go beyond the status quo, to break boundaries, to create what nature never intended like flying. And thus, engineering was born, driven by performance. Leonardo's dream was to fly, and wings became the necessary means to that end. As Theodore von Kármán once said: "Scientists study the world as it is; engineers create the world that has never been."

From the first scratches on cave walls to the earliest mechanical tools, from counting stones to astronomical observatories, the human quest to understand and shape the world has always relied on the subtle interplay between observation, abstraction, and invention. The Babylonian scribe calculating planetary movements, the Greek philosopher reasoning about geometry, the Persian astronomer refining astrolabes, and the Renaissance artisan forging clocks and automata, all were unknowingly laying the bricks of a long road toward science and engineering as we know them. With every new invention, from the Archimedean screw to Gutenberg's press, and with every theoretical leap, from Euclid's axioms to Newton's laws, our capacity to model, simulate, and ultimately transform reality has grown. Engineering emerged not suddenly, but as the natural heir to centuries of empirical crafts and scientific reasoning—a continuous evolution marked by dreams of flying, taming nature, and solving problems once considered unsolvable.

The First Industrial Revolution (water steam) transformed industry, and later, electricity gave rise to the Second Industrial Revolution, which enabled production to be more and faster. This revolution not only transformed industry but also society. Later, electronics joined the scene, and with it, automation. Welcome to the Third Industrial Revolution, which enabled not only faster production but also higher precision, improved quality, and the emergence of digital control systems.

However, despite all these advances, engineering remained product-based. Society is looking for performances; the product is a simple way to access those performances. When we buy a drill, we are in fact trying to buy a good quality hole, and despite these facts, engineering remained product-oriented. Why? Certainly, due to the fact that even if physics-based models are very rich (physically speaking), it was difficult both (i) to address the product in its environment, which is usually too large, too complex, too uncertain, and too fluctuating, and (ii) to solve them under the stringent real-time constraints needed for optimal decision-making in design or in operation, the ultimate goal of engineers and engineering. Engineering addressed these challenges by developing and mastering two major arts.

The art of modeling concerns all the physics throughout all the scales of description related to materials, processes, structures, and systems—a rich and holistic physics-based approach. The art of modeling was complemented by the art of simulation, addressing the solution of those models to better predict, which is compulsory for optimal design and optimal operation.

However, the potential accomplishments remained limited by the available computational resources as well as by the calculation characteristic times. Replacing product management with the management of performance requires faster predictions for quicker and better designs and for faster and better decisions …

The new engineering based on performances, at the beginning of the third millennium, needs processing faster, in real time and even faster, while ensuring highly accurate predictions. In some cases, it is, but in many others, in the vast majority, it is not the case, and significant deviations appear and grow over time, limiting predictive capabilities. An epistemic ignorance seems to persist in our conceptualization and description of physical reality. Models are models, but sometimes reality seems to contain something else, the so-called "ignorance" (the part of reality that our models ignore).

How to improve model predictability? The most natural and direct way consists of making measurements (collecting data) and comparing these measurements with the predictions based on the existing knowledge provided by the state-of-the-art models. Collecting abundant data is nowadays possible, and in many cases quite easy, in a fully interconnected global world. Then, artificial intelligence, which has entered our life, technology and social activities at the end of the second millennium, can learn predictive models from available or collected data, with the additional facility of performing that prediction in almost real time.

However, creating models from scratch, because the existing models based on physics are not accurate enough, is not the best choice. Creating a model based on data from scratch needs a lot of data, and in engineering and technology, data is synonymous with cost, and sometimes the data collection also implies considering an ethical dimension, fulfilling existing regulations, or addressing technical difficulties/limitations.

Today an appealing route advocates the alliance between both (i) the old analogic world of knowledge and physics-based models and (ii) the new digital world of data, manipulated by the more and more powerful (accurate, frugal, and explainable certifiable) techniques of AI.

This hybrid framework enables (i) making faster than usual physics-based simulations; (ii) making better by enriching the state-of-the-art physics-based models with data-driven models; (iii) making larger because data enables enlarging the domain of application of physics-based models; (iv) making safer because designs and decisions can be explained due to the physics-based foundations; (v) making cheaper because the data is only needed to enrich, and not for learning from scratch the already existing knowledge; and (vi) making different by using the recent generative capabilities of AI.

This is my personal story, but another much more documented, flowing from data and science to learning and engineering is reported in this excellent book of great relevance for undergraduate and postgraduate students, and more generally addressed to curious people looking for better understanding the articulation of the different arts that meet in modern science and engineering. It is written by recognized researchers, with a pedagogical dimension that remains present all along the book reading.

As for the models discussed above, by reading the book, I substantially reduced my amount of ignorance. As Stephen Hawking said: "The Greatest Enemy of Knowledge is not Ignorance, it is the Illusion of Knowledge." I strongly recommend reading it!

Francisco (Paco) Chinesta, Professor at the Arts et Métiers Institute of Technology (ENSAM), Director of the DesCartes program (CNRS@ CREATE), and Scientific Director of ESI Group

Foreword II

When I place a Babylonian cuneiform tablet beside a modern GPU, I witness the same human gesture repeated across four millennia: the urge to inscribe thought into matter. Clay, gears, vacuum tubes, silicon—every epoch chose its substrate and asked how far it could externalize intelligence. Even Hephaïstos, forging golden handmaidens and the bronze giant Talos, previewed our dream of artifacts that carry both toil and cognition. This book traces that dream with arresting breadth. Egyptian statues whose jaws opened during ritual, Aristotelian syllogisms in *Politique*, Hellenistic pneumatics, Leibnizian "calculus of reason," Babbage's engines, Turing's universal machine—each milestone shows that today's artificial intelligence is not a discontinuity but a fresh chapter in a very old story. The Dartmouth Workshop of 1956 merely baptized a trajectory already centuries in motion. I welcomed the invitation to write this preface because the authors refuse to treat AI as a purely technical novelty. Their narrative restores historical depth and anthropological texture, reminding us that the impulse to symbolize, organize, and automate reasoning has shaped cultures as surely as agriculture or metallurgy. By locating GPUs or generative artificial intelligence at the far end of that continuum, they dissolve the false drama of "machines versus humans" and replace it with a richer question: What kind of intelligence do we want to cultivate—both in silicon and in ourselves? The book's great strength is its insistence that AI is simultaneously technical, social, political, and economic. Standards, datasets, and loss functions always encode values—even when we pretend they are neutral. In foregrounding that ambivalence, the authors stand in a humanist tradition that treats technology as embedded in society, not floating above it.

My own work—Vice President and Director of R&D at IBM France—confirms the importance of that lens. From Deep Blue and Watson to responsible AI toolkits, we learned that algorithmic breakthroughs gain legitimacy only when paired with explanations, safeguards, and public debate. I personally defend a vision of AI as a tool in service of humanity. I believe in ethical, responsible, and explainable AI. I am convinced that technology must be accompanied by deep reflection, shared standards, and a strong commitment to transparency. This book fully aligns with that philosophy. It reminds us that innovation cannot be separated from public debate, ethical considerations, and societal challenges. It offers tools for building an AI that serves the common good. The pages ahead supply the historical context and conceptual scaffolding that such debate requires. Far from a retrospective museum tour, the final chapters confront the puzzles that keep today's labs awake at night: alignment of large-scale autonomous systems, interpretability when parameters outnumber neurons, and the leap from pattern completion to embodied agency. These open questions are presented not as crises but as invitations. Readers will see how centuries-old ideas—semantic clarity, logical provenance, and fairness—remain indispensable tools for tomorrow's breakthroughs.

The prose is accessible without dilution, rigorous without pedantry. Graduate students will gain a map that links theorems to myths; policymakers will find ballast against hype; curious citizens will discover that AI's dilemmas echo perennial debates about labor, representation, and power. Such plural address is rare and urgently needed. Beyond its analytic precision, the writing has moments of quiet poetry. Metaphors never outshine facts, yet they lodge the arguments in memory—an achievement as intellectual as it is literary. That balance ensures the book will endure well after today's model architectures are obsolete. In my view, this book should be required reading for anyone interested in AI. I believe the volume belongs in university curricula, professional-development programs, and civic reading circles. It equips us to steer technological momentum toward transparency, justice, and human flourishing—outcomes that will not arise by default.

I sincerely thank the authors for their outstanding work, their commitment to a topic as complex and sometimes divisive as AI, and their ability to build a bridge between academic insight and contemporary challenges. Their book is a precious compass for navigating the evolving landscape of AI. I hope this book will inspire vocations, spark meaningful debates, and illuminate decisions. May it help each of us to better understand the transformations underway, to better assess their scope, and to better shape our future choices. For if AI is a powerful force for transformation, it must remain a force in service of humanity. In a world where certainties are crumbling and reference points are often blurred, a book like this restores reflection to its rightful place. It invites us to be clear-eyed, cautious, and at the same time confident in our collective ability to steer progress toward greater justice, dignity, and freedom. Let me close where I began: the juxtaposition of tablet and GPU. One artifact captured grain tallies; the other drifts through vector spaces of language and protein folds. Both are mirrors. They reflect what we expect of intelligence and what we fear from it. May we use it not only to navigate the landscape of AI but to decide, deliberately, which futures are worth building.

Xavier Vasques,
Vice President and CTO, IBM Technology, France
Director of Research and Development, IBM France
Distinguished Data Scientist

Preface

Artificial intelligence today occupies an increasingly central place in our societies, our economies, and our daily lives. It is present in our phones, our search engines, our administrative services, our vehicles, our cultural recommendations, and our medical care. It is developing in all sectors of knowledge and production. Yet, despite this growing ubiquity, it often remains misunderstood, poorly defined, and sometimes fantasized. With this preface, we wish to present the spirit of this book, which we co-authored, with the aim of situating AI within the long trajectory of human development, and not to view it as a miraculous emergence or a radical break with the past. This book is neither a technical manual nor an ideological pamphlet: it is the result of an interdisciplinary reflection on the origins, mechanisms, uses, and social, political, and philosophical issues of AI.

Our approach is based on a simple but fundamental observation: AI was not born ex nihilo; it is the extension of a much older history, that of human intelligence itself. Since the dawn of time, man has strived to understand, explain, model, and organize the world around him. This desire to know was first translated into practical gestures, then into symbolic systems, languages, numbers, and calculations. Man has always combined thought and hand to create tools adapted to his needs: to survive, communicate, predict, transmit, and master the natural environment. This dynamic is at the heart of our evolution: each generation has inherited the ingenuity of those that preceded it, in turn bringing improvements, bifurcations, and innovations.

Thus, AI appears as a point of arrival (or rather, a milestone) in this long history of thought embodied in devices. One could even say that it mirrors our collective capacity to transform abstract intelligence into operational intelligence. Writing, calculation, algorithms, machines, and programs are not ruptures but different expressions of the same historical movement. Since Antiquity, we have seen the emergence of forms of algorithmic reasoning, attempts to mechanize thought, reflections on the rules of deduction, the conditions of truth, and the possibilities of prediction. From Egypt to Mesopotamian civilizations, from Ancient Greece to Ancient India and China, and from medieval Persia to Renaissance Europe, we find traces of this collective intelligence seeking to organize and objectify itself. What we call "AI" today is simply the contemporary name for this desire to systematize reasoning and expand human cognitive abilities. It is because mathematics has progressed, because logic has been formalized, and because mechanics and then electronics have made it possible to build structures with rapid and repeatable execution that we have been able to design programs capable of imitating certain aspects of our thinking. It is therefore essential not to detach AI from its historical and cultural foundations. It is inseparable from science, and also from philosophies of mind, theories of knowledge, and conceptions of machines and living things, of work and technology.

Our book emphasizes this continuity. We wanted to show that AI should not be approached as a technical oddity or an external threat, but as a human creation, shaped by very ancient needs and increasingly sophisticated tools. It is both a technological advance and a cultural construct. It extends our desires for simplifica-tion, automation, forecasting, and delegation. It is neither good nor bad in itself: it is what we make of it, what we choose to do with it, collectively and politically. This is the stance we have sought to adopt throughout our work, avoiding as much as pos-sible triumphalist discourses and apocalyptic prophecies.

This book also adopts a critical perspective. We affirm that AI, although a product of human intelligence, must not be left solely in the hands of its designers. It involves ethical choices, economic trade-offs, and social consequences. History teaches us that every major technological transformation is accompanied by profound upheav-als, sometimes beneficial, and sometimes destructive. AI is no exception. It can be used to improve medical care, accelerate scientific research, optimize energy con-sumption, and facilitate access to knowledge. But it can also be used to control, monitor, impose standards, exclude, or manipulate.

In this permanent tension between progress and domination, between liberation and instrumentalization, we affirm that AI is a powerful tool that must be harnessed for the common good. It should not be conceived as an economic weapon for the benefit of the strongest, nor as a substitute for human thought, but as a lever of col-lective intelligence. To achieve this, it is essential to develop democratic regulatory frameworks. Laws, conventions, and international agreements must govern the uses of AI and guarantee their transparency, accessibility, and respect for fundamental human rights. Regulation must not stifle innovation, but rather ensure its ethical and social purpose.

What we want to emphasize is that AI reveals as much as it transforms our way of being in the world. By creating systems capable of imitating cognitive functions, we also question what it means to "think," "decide," "act," and "learn." AI thus becomes a revealer of our own mental and social functioning. It forces us to redefine fundamental notions: intelligence, autonomy, responsibility, and consciousness. It challenges our institutions, our economic models, and our educational systems. It redraws the line between human and non-human.

As editors, we have chosen an accessible yet demanding style of writing. We wanted to offer a text that would be readable by non-specialists, yet based on solid knowledge, precise references, and structured thinking. This book is aimed at stu-dents, teachers, researchers, and anyone interested in the major issues of our time. We believe that AI cannot be left to engineers or businesses alone: it concerns soci-ety as a whole, and as such, it must be the subject of an informed public debate.

Our ambition is modest: to contribute to this debate by offering a rigorous analyti-cal framework, a historical perspective, and an opening to related disciplines. We do not provide definitive answers, but rather elements of understanding, benchmarks for reflection, and avenues for action. We know that AI is evolving rapidly, that technolo-gies are constantly transforming, and that boundaries are shifting. This is precisely why we believe in the importance of in-depth reflection, of taking a step back, and of being anchored in long-term history.

We take a committed but non-partisan position. We believe that the development of AI can be an opportunity for humanity, provided it is guided by clear principles: inclusion, justice, solidarity, transparency, and autonomy. We also believe that this opportunity can turn into a threat if we abandon critical thinking, collective action, and civic vigilance. It is this dual movement, hope and fear, that we have attempted to accurately and nuancedly capture.

Finally, we dedicate this book to all those who, in history as well as in the present, have contributed to the advancement of human knowledge. AI is not the work of a few isolated geniuses, but the product of an immense collective effort, often invisible, sometimes painful. It is in this sense that we say it is the result of the efforts and sacrifices of humankind since its appearance on Earth. Every advance, every tool, and every new idea is a response to a vital need, to a desire to live better, to understand better, and to communicate better. This book is a modest continuation of this shared work.

The Authors

1 Introduction
Parallel Evolution of Civilizations and Intelligence

1.1 ARTIFICIAL INTELLIGENCE TODAY AND LESSONS FROM ITS HISTORY

Artificial intelligence (AI), far from being a recent breakthrough, is the result of a long and evolving process rooted in centuries of mathematical, logical, and philosophical thought. In its modern form, AI is defined by its ability to perform tasks requiring cognitive functions such as learning, reasoning, perception, or decision-making. With the advent of machine learning (ML) and deep learning (DL), AI systems can now improve their performance autonomously, handling vast amounts of data and adapting to new contexts without explicit programming. This capability has revolutionized multiple fields, including industrial efficiency, healthcare diagnostics, self-driving technology, and the creative industries. Yet, as these systems grow more powerful, they also raise major challenges: interpretability of complex models, generalization beyond training data, and the sustainability of computation-intensive methods. Furthermore, as AI is increasingly deployed in high-stakes areas like healthcare, finance, and justice, concerns about trust, transparency, and fairness become central. The use of probabilistic models, graph-based reasoning, and optimization algorithms illustrates how AI stands on a deep mathematical foundation while seeking to simulate intelligence in systems that interact with a dynamic, uncertain world.

To understand the current landscape of AI (and to guide its future), it is essential to reflect on its history. According to the timeline shown in Figure 1.1, the evolution of AI has not been linear but marked by alternating periods of optimism and stagnation, known as *AI winters*, where technological limits defied initial ambitions. Early attempts to automate reasoning and perception often fell short, revealing the need for stronger theoretical models, more data, and scalable computational frameworks. These historical setbacks offer valuable lessons: the danger of overpromising, the importance of transparency, and the ethical implications of automated decisions. Debates about bias, responsibility, and algorithmic justice today echo issues already raised decades ago. By studying the history of AI, researchers and policymakers can avoid past mistakes and better assess the societal consequences of deploying intelligent systems. In the end, AI's development should be seen not just as a technical advancement, but as a continuation of humanity's long-standing effort to systematize thinking, anticipate actions, and create tools that enhance our mental capabilities.

DOI: 10.1201/9781003613633-1

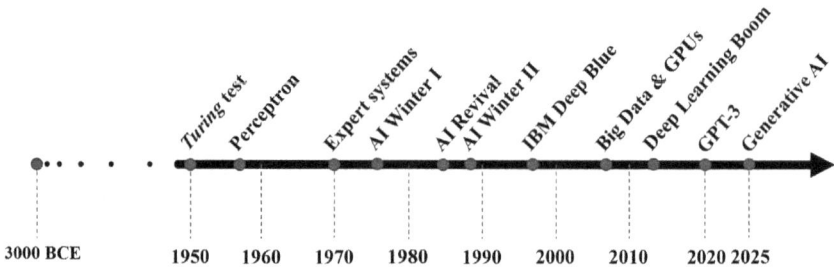

FIGURE 1.1   Timeline of key events in AI history.

1.2   FROM MEASUREMENT TO ARTIFICIAL INTELLIGENCE

Since ancient times, humans have always sought to meet their fundamental needs: measuring distances, managing agricultural lands, constructing buildings, and predicting natural phenomena. To achieve this, they have relied on measurement tools and mathematical methods. Measurement and calculation are, therefore, fundamental skills that enable humans to interact with their environment and solve practical problems. One might wonder, as societies became more complex, how to manage massive amounts of data, solve complex equations, or analyze systems with numerous parameters. In response to these difficulties, people developed tools for computation, starting with basic devices and eventually creating computers that could handle data with extraordinary speed and accuracy.

Today, with the exponential accumulation of data and the increasing complexity of problems to be solved, AI has emerged as a natural extension of this quest. AI allows for the modeling, analysis, and resolution of problems once considered unsolvable by automating complex processes, learning from data, and proposing optimal solutions. The evolution of mathematics, from mechanical tools to intelligent machines, illustrates humanity's continuous progress in harnessing the power of computation and logic. To help illustrate this progression, Figure 1.2 presents a simple flowchart of the logical and chronological steps with further details as follows:

- Step 1: Basic Needs

Since ancient times, fundamental survival needs have led humans to measure, count, and calculate. These activities help solve essential practical problems, such as calculating land for agriculture or constructing monuments and infrastructure. To achieve this, humanity has relied on basic mathematics, such as arithmetic and geometry, which laid the foundation for the first technical solutions.

- Step 2: Increasing Complexity of Problems

As societies developed, the problems to be solved became more complex, involving the management of multiple parameters in fields such as commerce, astronomy, and engineering. To address these challenges, more advanced tools and methods were invented. Among them were the abacus, used for practical calculations, and the first algorithms developed by civilizations like the Babylonians and Greeks. These innovations helped rationalize calculations and improve their accuracy.

- Step 3: Rationalization of Calculations

The increasing volume of data and the growing complexity of calculations required new means to perform them efficiently. This period saw the invention of mechanical machines that partially automated calculations. Mechanical calculators, designed by thinkers, greatly simplified arithmetic operations. At the same time, calculation tables were created for specific applications, particularly in astronomy and finance. These tools laid the groundwork for more advanced automation.

- Step 4: Automation

The advent of computers revolutionized the way large and complex datasets were processed. This stage of automation enabled the resolution of extremely complex equations and the execution of simulations in fields such as science and engineering. Computers far exceeded human capabilities in terms of speed and accuracy, ushering in a new era for computation and modeling.

- Step 5: The Creation of AI

The creation of AI represents a major breakthrough in automating intellectual processes. AI enables the analysis of highly complex systems and decision-making based on massive amounts of data. Through ML, it can learn from data and propose optimal solutions. Applications of AI include big data analysis, automation of complex tasks such as robotics, and content generation through generative AI. This stage illustrates the continuous evolution of computation, from rudimentary tools to intelligent machines.

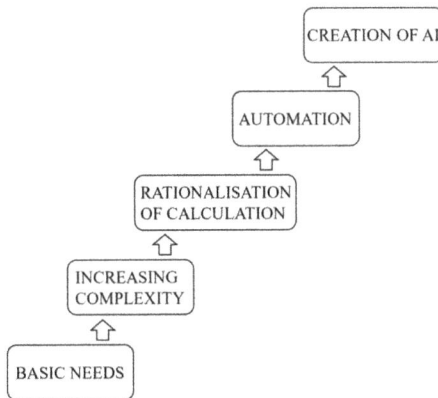

FIGURE 1.2 Chronological steps from basic needs to AI creation.

1.3 AI AS THE CULMINATION OF A MILLENNIA-LONG QUEST FOR HUMAN INTELLIGENCE

AI is often considered a recent technological advancement, but in reality, it is part of a millennia-old human quest to understand and replicate intelligence. This aspiration has transcended ages and cultures, taking different forms depending on the beliefs and knowledge of each era.

In Mesopotamia, the earliest known civilizations, such as the Sumerians and Babylonians (c. 3000–500 BCE), developed intricate systems of logic, divination, and mechanized rituals using water clocks and gears, suggesting an early interest in the predictability and automation of nature. Their cuneiform tablets also recorded mathematical and astronomical procedures that laid the groundwork for rule-based reasoning. In Egypt, the polymath Imhotep (c. 27th century BCE), considered one of the earliest known scientists and engineers, integrated architecture, medicine, and knowledge systems in ways that prefigured the rational organization essential to later technological systems. Egyptian priests also used mechanical devices, such as hidden temple doors and automaton-like statues operated by steam or water, which astonished worshippers and symbolized divine intelligence. In India, thinkers like Panini (c. 6th–4th century BCE) developed a formal system of grammar in his Ashtadhyayi, employing meta-rules and transformations that anticipate modern computational linguistics. Around the same time, Pingala (c. 3rd century BCE) introduced a binary number system while analyzing Sanskrit prosody link to digital computation. In Ancient Iran, during the Achaemenid era (c. 550–330 BCE), advancements in mechanical and hydraulic engineering were employed in the royal gardens (paradises) with complex water-lifting and animation systems. Some Zoroastrian accounts mention mechanical figures crafted by priests for astrological or ritual purposes, reflecting a symbolic union of cosmology and machinery. In Greece, mythical and philosophical representations of intelligence took mechanical form, such as Hephaestus' self-moving statues and golden servants, and later, Archytas of Tarentum (c. 428–347 BCE), who is said to have built a steam-powered wooden bird. These illustrate how Greek thinkers conceptualized reason and motion together, setting the stage for future automata and AI fantasies. In China, the legend of Yan Shi, an engineer of the Zhou dynasty, tells of an artificial man capable of moving and behaving like a real person, as recorded by Liezi (c. 4th century BCE). This story demonstrates how ancient Chinese philosophy also explored artificial life through mechanical ingenuity and metaphysical speculation.

These examples illustrate that the desire to understand and create AI dates back to ancient times, long before technology made it possible. Each culture projected its own concerns and hopes onto these representations of AI, shaping the ways AI is perceived today.

The earliest attempts to understand or replicate intelligence often manifested through mechanical constructions or philosophical theories. In Ancient Iran, devices such as automated fountains in royal gardens or astronomical mechanisms linked to temples already demonstrated technical ingenuity and an interest in imitating natural or human phenomena. During the Islamic Golden Age, several Iranian polymaths made foundational contributions that connected mechanics, mathematics, and theories of cognition. Khwarizmi (c. 780–850), of Persian origin, introduced systematic methods of calculation and the concept of algorithm, a basis of modern computing. Razi (865–925) promoted empirical observation and rational analysis in science and philosophy. Farabi (c. 872–950) developed a classification of the sciences and proposed a hierarchical model of the intellect, linking logic, metaphysics, and mental processes. Avicenna (Ibn Sina) (980–1037) developed a comprehensive model of the soul and thought, distinguishing between sensation, imagination, and rational thought, concepts that remain relevant in discussions of AI. Later, Nasir al-Din Tusi (1201–1274) refined logical systems and introduced early ideas of motion and transformation that foreshadowed dynamic modeling in AI.

Thinkers like Aristotle (384–322 BCE), through his formal logic, and René Descartes (1596–1650), with his dualistic view of mind and body, also sought to describe the underlying principles of human thought, shaping Western philosophical frameworks that would later influence cognitive science and AI. The desire to replicate intelligent behavior also took mechanical forms. The automatons of antiquity and the Middle Ages, such as those designed by Al-Jazari (1136–1206) in the Islamic world, incorporated water-driven systems and programmable features to simulate human and animal actions. Later, during the Renaissance, Leonardo da Vinci (1452–1519) conceptualized and built mechanical devices resembling humanoid figures, blending anatomy, mechanics, and artistry.

These early efforts, whether through speculative philosophy or mechanical invention, laid the basis for what would later become modern AI. The emergence of modern AI would not have been possible without contributions from multiple academic disciplines. Philosophy, by addressing fundamental questions about the nature of the mind and knowledge, provided the theoretical framework necessary to consider the possibility of non-human intelligence. Advances in biology and neuroscience allowed for a deeper understanding of brain mechanisms, paving the way for AI models inspired by neural structures. However, it was mathematics and computer science that truly enabled AI's development, through the evolution of formal logic, information theories, and early algorithms. Figures such as Alan Turing (1912–1954), who laid the theoretical foundations of computing, played a decisive role in transitioning from philosophical speculation to technical realization. Ultimately, AI is the product of a long intellectual evolution, blending philosophy, biology, and mathematics, which has gradually transformed an ancient quest into a technological reality.

1.4 DEFINITIONS: LOGIC, COMPUTATION, MATHEMATICS, INTELLIGENCE, AND AI

To fully understand the topics discussed in this book, it is essential to understand the meaning of certain key terms that form the foundation of the explored concepts (as summarized in Figure 1.3). These terms, often used across various disciplines such as philosophy, mathematics, and computer science, help clarify fundamental notions related to intelligence, reasoning, and the underlying mechanisms of AI. A clear and precise understanding of these concepts is essential for following the discussions, analyses, and applications presented in this work.

Logic is a philosophical and mathematical discipline that studies the principles of valid reasoning and argumentation. It aims to define the rules and structures that allow drawing correct conclusions from given premises. As a formal tool, logic includes systems such as propositional logic and predicate logic, which are used to model statements and relationships between them. Logic is foundational to many fields, including mathematics, computer science, and philosophy, providing rigorous frameworks for analyzing ideas, verifying consistency, and constructing proofs.

Computation, in its broadest sense, refers to any systematic process of processing information, often through algorithmic or arithmetic means. In mathematics, it includes basic operations such as addition, subtraction, multiplication, and division, as well as advanced concepts like differential and integral calculus, which help study variations and areas under curves. In the context of computer science, computation also refers to the execution of algorithms by machines, making it a fundamental component of AI and information sciences.

Mathematics is a formal science that studies structures, relationships, quantities, and changes. It is based on abstract concepts such as numbers, geometric shapes, algebraic structures, and functions. Mathematics is divided into several branches, including arithmetic, geometry, algebra, and analysis. It serves as a universal language for expressing physical laws, modeling natural or social phenomena, and solving complex problems across various domains, including science, engineering, and economics.

Intelligence is a complex mental ability that enables a living being or system to observe, understand, reason, and solve problems. It includes multiple dimensions, such as memory, logic, creativity, adaptability to changing environments, and the

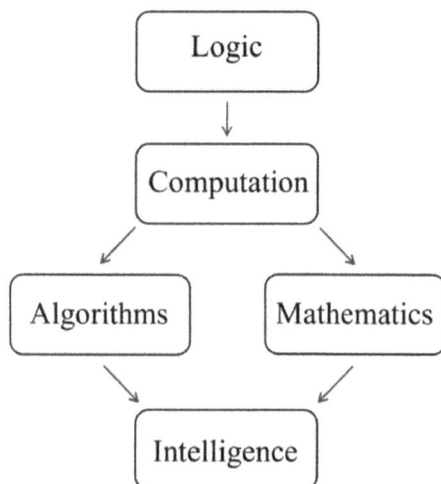

FIGURE 1.3 Mind map interlinking the five concepts: logic, computation, mathematics, algorithms, and intelligence.

capacity to learn new information. In humans, intelligence manifests in various forms, including emotional, linguistic, logical-mathematical, and social intelligence. In a broader sense, intelligence can also be attributed to groups, organizations, or even machines capable of performing complex mental tasks.

AI is fundamentally positioned at the intersection of mathematics, logic, and computation, as depicted in Figure 1.4. These three pillars collectively provide the theoretical and practical frameworks necessary for the development of intelligent systems. AI refers to a broad research field and a set of technologies aimed at creating systems capable of simulating behaviors traditionally associated with human intelligence. Such behaviors include, but are not limited to, pattern recognition, decision-making, problem-solving, and natural language interpretation. The domain of AI encompasses several major subfields, including ML, natural language processing (NLP), computer vision, and expert systems. These subfields influence mathematical modeling, algorithmic design, computational theories, and, increasingly, large-scale data sets to achieve their objectives. Beyond the technical sphere, AI introduces profound ethical and societal considerations, particularly concerning its impacts on employment, privacy, security, and human rights. These issues underscore the importance of responsible AI research and application. Examples of AI applications in contemporary society include autonomous vehicles, virtual personal assistants, healthcare diagnostics, financial fraud detection, and intelligent recommendation systems.

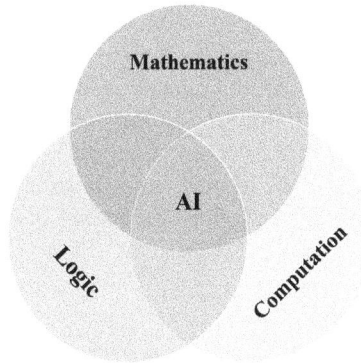

FIGURE 1.4   Venn diagram illustrating the foundational disciplines of AI.

1.5   FUNDAMENTAL ELEMENTS OF MATHEMATICS

Mathematics is a system composed of numerous interdependent elements. Initially, this system was relatively simple, but it gradually became more complex over time. Throughout this evolution, the foundational concepts gained sophistication, enabling the emergence of new elements. The history of mathematics thus reflects the development and transformation of these essential components. The fundamental elements of mathematics include several core concepts that serve as the foundation of this discipline. In what follows, the most important ones are summarized to provide a better understanding of them.

1.5.1 NUMBERS AND NUMERATION SYSTEMS

Numbers (integers, rational, real, complex, etc.) and numeral systems trace their origins back to the earliest human civilizations, approximately 5,000–6,000 years ago. The first numeral systems emerged to address practical needs such as trade, agriculture, and resource management. The Sumerians in Mesopotamia developed one of the earliest known numeral systems, based on the sexagesimal system, which still influences modern timekeeping and angle measurement. Later, the Egyptians used a rudimentary decimal system, followed by the Babylonians, who perfected the positional system.

The history of the evolution of numbers and numeral systems, from antiquity to the modern era, is closely tied to the practical needs of civilizations over time (Figure 1.5). In ancient times, the choice of numeral systems reflected the daily concerns and observations of different societies. For example, the Babylonians used a sexagesimal system primarily because of its divisibility, which allowed for simpler calculations in fields such as astronomy and time measurement. This system has persevered in modern society through hour divisions, with 60 minutes in an hour and 360° in a circle. Other civilizations adopted different numeral systems based on their culture and needs. The Romans, for instance, developed a numeral system using fixed symbols (I, V, X, etc.), which was well-suited for managing dates, military organization, and commercial transactions but did not include a place-value system as used today.

The Egyptians, on the other hand, used a base-10 system for calculations. This decimal system became widely adopted worldwide due to its natural alignment with the number of human fingers, making counting and number management more intuitive. The modern decimal numeral system, with the introduction of zero as a distinct digit, has its roots in ancient India, where mathematicians such as Brahmagupta in the 7th century made significant contributions. This system was further developed and refined by scholars of the Islamic world. It gradually became the dominant numerical system worldwide, largely due to the contributions of medieval Iranian

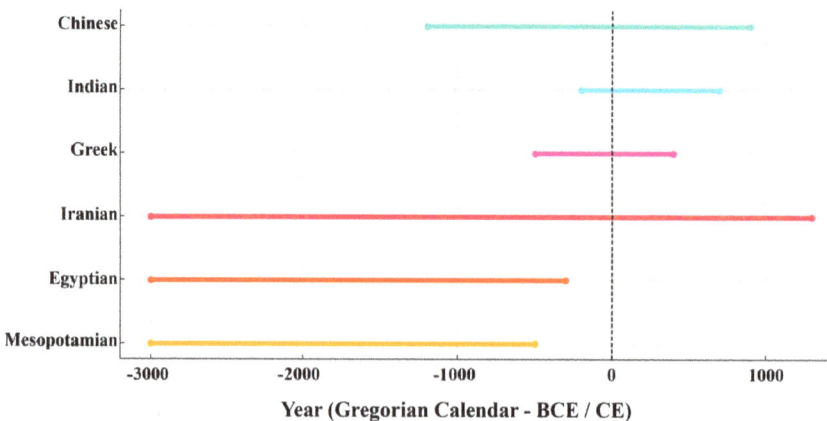

FIGURE 1.5   Timeline of contributions to historical number systems.

mathematicians, who transmitted Indian numerals and the base-10 concept to the Western world. The numerals used by these mathematicians, far more practical than Roman numerals, allowed for a simpler representation of large numbers and facilitated calculations. These advances were essential for the growth of trade and the economy in Europe during the Renaissance, as well as for the progress of science and mathematics.

However, in the 17th century, more complex systems were developed to meet the growing demands of new technologies. The German mathematician Gottfried Wilhelm Leibniz (1646–1716) was one of the first to formalize the idea of the binary system, based on the two digits 0 and 1. Although this system was not immediately applied on a large scale, it became essential in the era of modern computers. Today's computers, which are at the core of modern technology, operate entirely on binary principles. The electronic circuits of computers, including processors, are designed to recognize and manipulate two states: active (1) or inactive (0), which perfectly corresponds to the binary system.

The shift to base 2 fundamentally transformed information processing. Each unit of information in a computer, called a bit, can take one of these two values: 0 or 1. These bits are organized into bytes (groups of 8 bits) that represent data such as numbers, text, or images. Modern computing systems are entirely based on this binary representation of information, enabling extremely fast and efficient calculations at the processor level. Thus, base 2 is the foundation of all computational and information processing systems. Every program, algorithm, and operation in AI ultimately relies on manipulating these 0s and 1s. For instance, in neural networks (NNs) and DL, which are at the heart of AI, the computations performed by computers to learn and make predictions are carried out using binary processes on massive datasets.

With the rise of computers in the second half of the 20th century, another system emerged: base 16 (the hexadecimal system), which is used to represent binary values in a more compact form more efficiently. Each hexadecimal digit represents four binary digits, making it easier for programmers to work with and manage data in computing systems. This system has become fundamental in programming languages and computer interfaces, particularly for color representation, memory addressing, and binary file management. Thus, the evolution of numeral systems, from the Babylonians' base-60 system to the base-16 system used in modern computing, illustrates civilizations' advancements in mathematical understanding and their application to technology. Numeral systems have played an essential role in organizing societies, facilitating trade and science, and laying the foundation for complex technological systems used today. From the simplicity of the decimal system to the complexity of binary and hexadecimal systems, each numeral base has found its place in an ever-evolving world where practical and technological needs dictate mathematical choices.

1.5.2 ARITHMETIC OPERATIONS

The basic arithmetic operations (addition, subtraction, multiplication, and division) date back to prehistory when humans began counting and manipulating quantities.

The first evidence of the systematic use of these operations appears in the Sumerian and Egyptian civilizations between 3000 and 2000 BCE. Cuneiform tablets from Mesopotamia reveal that the Sumerians employed methods for addition and subtraction to manage goods and solve practical problems related to resource allocation. The Egyptians, for their part, used multiplication and division techniques based on processes of doubling and addition.

Over the centuries, these operations were formalized with the development of numeral systems. The Greeks studied the properties of numbers, but it was in ancient India, with the introduction of the decimal system and zero, that these operations became more systematic and universal. These concepts were transmitted to Europe through the Islamic world starting in the 9th century, particularly thanks to the work of Khwarizmi. In the modern era, the standard symbols for addition (+), subtraction (−), multiplication (× or ·), and division (÷ or /) emerged in Europe during the 15th and 16th centuries, standardizing their use. Today, these operations are not only fundamental to school mathematics but are also at the heart of algorithms and complex calculations that power computers and AI.

1.5.3 ALGEBRA

Algebra, one of the fundamental branches of mathematics, has its origins in ancient times, although in rudimentary forms. The Babylonians (around 2000 BCE) laid the foundations of algebra by developing methods to solve quadratic and linear equations using geometric and arithmetic techniques. However, their approach was concrete and based on specific cases, without the abstract formalization of concepts. The Greeks, notably Euclid (around 300 BCE), used algebraic methods in their geometric works, but algebra had not yet been distinctly separated from geometry.

The decisive turning point came with the Iranian mathematician Khwarizmi (780–850) in the 9th century. In his work Kitab al-Mukhtasar fi Hisab al-Jabr wal-Muqabala, he systematized the rules for manipulating equations and introduced terms and methods that gave birth to algebra as an independent discipline. The word "algebra" comes from the term al-jabr used in his book. Khwarizmi also laid the foundations for solving quadratic equations and developed general procedures applicable to abstract problems.

Over the centuries, algebra evolved to encompass the study of polynomials, functions, and abstract algebraic structures such as groups, rings, and fields. Influential figures such as René Descartes (1596–1650) and François Viète (1540–1603), active in Europe during the 16th and 17th centuries, introduced modern notations and the concept of variables, which helped establish the connection between algebra and geometry. In the 19th century, mathematicians like Évariste Galois (1811–1832) advanced the study of abstract algebra, laying the foundations for many modern mathematical structures. Today, algebra extends far beyond classical equations, playing a central role in fields like cryptography, AI, and theoretical physics, where it allows for modeling complex systems and solving global problems.

1.5.4 GEOMETRY

Geometry is the study of shapes, sizes, positions, and properties of space. It includes points, lines, angles, surfaces, volumes, and geometric theorems. Geometry is one of the oldest branches of mathematics, having emerged from the practical need to measure land and construct structures. Its origins date back to early civilizations, particularly in Egypt and Mesopotamia, around 4,000 years ago. The Egyptians used geometric principles for land surveying after the Nile's floods and for building monuments such as the pyramids. The Babylonians, on the other hand, recorded geometric calculations related to surfaces and volumes on clay tablets. These practical applications laid the foundation for the early concepts of plane and solid geometry. Geometry reached a new level of formalization in Ancient Greece with figures like Thales (624–546 BCE) and Pythagoras (570–495 BCE), who introduced axiomatic and deductive approaches. Euclid (300 BCE) played a central role by compiling and structuring geometric knowledge in his work *Elements*, which remained a fundamental reference for over 2,000 years. In this work, he defined fundamental concepts such as points, lines, and planes and established theorems like the Pythagorean theorem. Meanwhile, mathematicians like Archimedes (287–212 BCE) extended geometry to the study of volumes and solid surfaces.

Before the Renaissance, geometry experienced significant development in the Islamic world, notably through mathematicians and astronomers like Omar Khayyam (1048–1131). In the 11th century, Khayyam made notable contributions to geometry and algebra. He is famous for his work on solving polynomial equations, particularly cubic equations, which he approached using geometric methods. Khayyam demonstrated that these equations could be solved through geometric constructions involving conic sections, marking a significant advancement in geometric algebra. Additionally, he applied geometry to develop the Persian calendar, using geometric principles to calculate the solar year's length with remarkable precision based on Earth's rotation around the Sun. His work, combining geometry and astronomy, played a key role in advancing medieval science and led to the creation of a highly accurate calendar, still in use today in Iran.

Over the centuries, geometry has evolved to include new dimensions and perspectives. During the Renaissance, Descartes combined algebra and geometry by developing analytic geometry, enabling the representation of geometric figures through equations. In the 19th century, the works of Gauss (1777–1855), Lobachevsky (1792–1856), and Riemann (1826–1866) led to non-Euclidean geometries, expanding geometry's applications to physics, particularly in Einstein's theory of general relativity. Today, geometry remains a foundation of mathematics, with applications in diverse fields such as computer graphics, robotics, theoretical physics, and AI.

1.5.5 TRIGONOMETRY

Trigonometry is the study of the relationships between angles and sides of triangles, as well as trigonometric functions such as sine, cosine, and tangent. Its roots trace back to ancient Mesopotamia and Egypt, where early geometers used rudimentary

concepts to solve practical problems such as land measurement and the construction of pyramids. However, trigonometry emerged as a distinct discipline in Ancient
Greece around the 3rd century BCE, with the works of Hipparchus of Nicaea (190–
120 BCE), often regarded as the father of trigonometry. Hipparchus introduced the
first chord tables in a circle, which were the precursors of modern trigonometric
functions. Ptolemy (100–160 CE) refined these concepts in his Almagest, a foundational work that established essential principles for studying the relationships
between angles and arcs in a circle.

During the Islamic Golden Age, trigonometry underwent significant advancements. Scholars such as Al-Battani (858–929), Abū Rayḥān Bīrūnī (973–1048), and
Nasir al-Din Tusi (1201–1274) systematized Greek methods and expanded upon them.
Al-Battani introduced the sine function as a separate entity, and Tusi developed the
law of sines, a fundamental result for spherical triangles used in astronomy. These
contributions were compiled into manuals that influenced medieval Europe through
Latin translations. The introduction of tangent, cotangent, secant, and cosecant functions in Arabic texts laid the basis for modern formulations. From the Renaissance
onward, European mathematicians such as Regiomontanus (1436–1476), François
Viète (1540–1603), and Leonhard Euler (1707–1783) further advanced trigonometry,
particularly by unifying circular and angular approaches. With the introduction of
modern notation, trigonometric functions became a central tool for analyzing peri-
odic phenomena in fields such as physics, engineering, and modern sciences. Today,
trigonometry remains a cornerstone of applied mathematics, with applications ranging from navigation and medical imaging to signal analysis and space exploration.

1.5.6 INFINITESIMAL CALCULUS (DIFFERENTIAL AND INTEGRAL CALCULUS)

Infinitesimal calculus, encompassing differential and integral calculus, is the study
of rates of change and infinite sums. This includes differentiation, integration, limits,
and infinite series. Infinitesimal calculus emerged in the 17th century as a mathematical revolution. It was developed independently by Isaac Newton (1643–1727) and
Leibniz, although their approaches differed. Newton used calculus to solve problems
in physics, particularly to describe the laws of motion and gravitation. Leibniz, on
the other hand, introduced a more systematic notation (such as $\int$ for integration and
d for differentials), which is still in use today.

Following their work, infinitesimal calculus was refined by mathematicians
such as Leonhard Euler (1707–1783), Joseph-Louis Lagrange (1736–1813), and
Carl Friedrich Gauss (1777–1855). The 19th century saw the rigorous formalization of the concept of limits, thanks to Augustin-Louis Cauchy (1789–1857) and
Karl Weierstrass (1815–1897), establishing a solid foundation for calculus. Today,
infinitesimal calculus remains central to numerous scientific fields, from differential
equations in physics to optimization in AI.

1.5.7 SET THEORY

It is the study of sets, the relationships between them, and the operations that can
be performed on these sets (such as union, intersection, and difference). Set theory

emerged in the late 19th century as a fundamental branch of mathematics. It was primarily developed by the German mathematician Georg Cantor (1845–1918), who introduced the concept of sets to formalize ideas such as infinity and the relationships between collections of objects. In 1874, Cantor demonstrated that some infinities are "larger" than others, laying the foundation for the hierarchy of infinities and cardinal numbers. He also established key principles such as the notion of bijections, subsets, and axioms for comparing the sizes of infinite sets.

In the 20th century, set theory became a formal framework for most modern mathematics. The Zermelo-Fraenkel axioms (ZF), supplemented by the axiom of choice (forming ZFC), were developed to avoid paradoxes such as Russell's paradox. These axioms remain at the core of set theory, serving as the foundation for various branches of mathematics, from algebra to analysis. Set theory continues to be an active field, influencing areas such as logic, model theory, and constructive mathematics.

1.5.8 Probability and Statistics

Probability and statistics, while closely related, have distinct yet converging origins. Probability theory emerged in the 17th century, primarily through the work of Blaise Pascal (1623–1662) and Pierre de Fermat (1607–1665), who laid its mathematical foundations while addressing questions related to games of chance. Their discussions led to the concept of probability as a mathematical measure of uncertainty. Other notable contributions include those of Christiaan Huygens (1629–1695), who wrote the first systematic work on probability, and Jakob Bernoulli (1654–1705), who introduced the law of large numbers in his book Ars Conjectandi (The Art of Conjecturing), published later in 1713. Although formal probability theory was developed in early modern Europe, several scholars from the Islamic world, particularly between the 8th and 14th centuries, had already explored related concepts such as uncertainty, empirical observation, and estimation. Iranian thinkers like Razi (865–925), Avicenna (980–1037), and Biruni (973–1048) applied reasoning about likelihoods in medical, astronomical, and philosophical contexts, though not in the form of a mathematical theory. Their work reflects an early engagement with probabilistic thinking, even if not formalized in the same way as later European approaches.

Statistics, on the other hand, has its roots in the collection and analysis of demographic and economic data as early as the 18th century. Early statistical tools were rudimentary and often used for administrative or political purposes, such as censuses. In the 19th century, statistics took a scientific turn with the work of Adolphe Quetelet (1796–1874), who introduced concepts such as the "average man," and Carl Friedrich Gauss (1777–1855), who developed the normal distribution (or bell curve). Later, Francis Galton (1822–1911) and Karl Pearson (1857–1936) introduced concepts such as correlation and regression, laying the foundation for modern statistics.

In the 20th century, the fusion of probability and statistics led to the development of a rigorous mathematical framework for modeling and analyzing uncertainty. Andrey Kolmogorov (1903–1987) formalized probability theory using set theory, while figures such as Ronald Fisher (1890–1962) and Jerzy Neyman (1894–1981) transformed statistics into a fully developed scientific discipline with applications ranging from biology to economics. Today, probability and statistics are omnipresent, underpinning fields such as AI, big data analytics, and complex system modeling.

1.5.9 MATHEMATICAL LOGIC

Mathematical logic is the study of reasoning and formal structures, including propositions, logical connectives, proofs, and theorems. It has its origins in antiquity, where Greek philosophers such as Aristotle (384–322 BCE) laid the foundations of formal logic. He introduced the concept of the syllogism, a structure of deductive reasoning that remained the basis of logic for centuries. His work was further developed by medieval thinkers like Farabi (872–950), Avicenna (980–1037), and Nasir al-Din Tusi (1201–1274), who extended Aristotelian logic within rich philosophical frameworks. In the Latin West, Thomas Aquinas (1225–1274) also adapted Aristotelian concepts to theological and philosophical contexts. Logic took a mathematical turn with the work of Leibniz, who envisioned a calculus ratiocinator, a universal system for representing and manipulating reasoning. However, it was in the 19th century that mathematical logic truly emerged as an independent discipline. George Boole (1815–1864) developed Boolean algebra, establishing a link between logic and mathematics by introducing logical operators (AND, OR, NOT). These concepts were refined by Augustus De Morgan (1806–1871) and became fundamental tools in mathematics and computer science.

In the 20th century, mathematical logic underwent a revolution thanks to figures such as Giuseppe Peano (1858–1932), who formalized mathematics using logic, and David Hilbert (1862–1943), who proposed a program to prove the consistency of mathematics. However, Kurt Gödel (1906–1978) demonstrated the limitations of this program, revealing that any sufficiently powerful formal system contains undecidable propositions. Modern mathematical logic encompasses diverse fields such as model theory, set theory, and automated theorem proving, playing an important role in AI, databases, and the philosophy of mathematics.

1.5.10 GRAPH THEORY AND COMBINATORICS

Although they were initially driven by practical concerns, they emerged as formal mathematical fields in the 19th century. Combinatorics, which comprises counting and studying the arrangements of objects in finite sets, has ancient roots in the works of Euclid and his successors.

Between the 8th and 14th centuries, Iranian mathematicians made significant contributions to early combinatorial thinking, particularly in relation to algebra, enumeration, and geometric problems. In the 9th century, Karaji (c. 953–1029), of Persian origin, explored binomial coefficients and laid the groundwork later formalized in Pascal's triangle. His algebraic treatment of powers and combinations prefigured key aspects of combinatorics. Omar Khayyam (1048–1131), known for his work on the classification of cubic equations, also engaged in geometric arrangements that touched on combinatorial ideas. Later, Sharaf al-Din Tusi (1135–1213) and Nasir al-Din Tusi (1201–1274) contributed to the logical and structural understanding of mathematical relationships, indirectly influencing the evolution of discrete mathematics. However, it was in the 17th century, with the early works of Blaise Pascal (1623–1662) and Pierre de Fermat (1607–1665), that the foundations of probability theory and combinatorics were laid, particularly through developments in combinations and arrangements. Graph theory originated in 1736, with the resolution of the famous Königsberg bridge problem by Leonhard Euler (1707–1783). This problem, which involved crossing every bridge in the city of Königsberg without passing over the same bridge twice, led Euler to define the concept of a graph composed of vertices (or nodes) and edges (or arcs) connecting these vertices. Euler thus laid the groundwork for graph theory, but it was not until the 20th century, with more formal work by mathematicians such as Paul Erdős and László Lovász, that the field experienced significant growth. The study of graphs quickly became a fundamental tool in diverse areas such as chemistry, computer science, and network theory. In combinatorics, a major advancement was the formalization of counting methods for combinatorial objects in specific structures, such as permutations, partitions, and graphs. In the 20th century, combinatorics gained prominence with the emergence of coding theory and communication network theory. Today, graph theory and combinatorics are essential in modern research on optimization, theoretical computer science (notably for shortest path algorithms and network optimization), and the analysis of large data sets, graph algorithms, and game theory applications.

The fundamental elements of mathematics from its origin are summarized in Table 1.1.

TABLE 1.1
Mathematical Branches and AI Applications

Branch	Historical Period	Modern Application in AI
Numbers and numeration systems	Ancient Mesopotamia, Egypt, Ancient Iran	Data encoding, digital representation (binary, hex)
Arithmetic operations	Ancient Sumerians, Egyptians	Computational algorithms, processor operations
Algebra	9th c. (Khwarizmi)	ML models, symbolic AI
Geometry	Egypt, Ancient Greece, Iran	Computer vision, robotics
Trigonometry	Greece (Hipparchus of Nicaea), Islamic Golden Age (Biruni, Tusi)	Signal processing, 3D modeling
Infinitesimal calculus	17th c. (Newton, Leibniz)	Optimization, backpropagation in DL
Set theory	19th c. (Cantor)	Neural network architecture, formal language theory
Probability and statistics	17th–19th c. (Pascal, Gauss)	Bayesian learning, uncertainty modeling, data science
Mathematical logic	Ancient Greece, Iran (Farabi), 19th–20th c.	Automated reasoning, knowledge representation
Graph theory and combinatorics	18th c. (Euler) onward	Network analysis, graph-based ML
Branch	Historical period	Modern application in AI

1.6 MATHEMATICAL METHODOLOGIES

Mathematical methodologies refer to the various approaches and techniques used to solve problems, prove theorems, or explore mathematical concepts. To fully understand the evolution of mathematics throughout history, it is essential to comprehend how these methodologies have developed over time. Indeed, the methods used in different historical periods reflect the intellectual advancements and discoveries that have shaped the discipline. Some of the key methodologies that have marked this evolution are summarized as follows.

1.6.1 RIGOROUS PROOF

Rigorous proof is a defining characteristic of mathematical thought, distinguishing it from empirical or intuitive reasoning. Its roots can be traced back to Ancient Greece, particularly to the monumental work of Euclid (c. 300 BCE), whose *Elements* became a foundational text for centuries. Euclid's axiomatic method, based on postulates, definitions, and logically derived theorems, set the stage for a tradition of deductive reasoning that continues to this day. Through this framework, he established a vision of mathematics as a system of knowledge built on incontestable principles, where truth is guaranteed by the structure of logical inference. This vision deeply influenced later civilizations, especially those that translated and preserved Greek texts while expanding upon them through new techniques and perspectives.

During the 8th–14th centuries, the Islamic Golden Age saw the flourishing of science and mathematics across a vast territory from Spain to Central Asia. It is within this context that the Greek heritage was not only preserved through translations but profoundly transformed. In particular, the methodology of proof evolved significantly thanks to the work of scholars in Baghdad, Nishapur, Ray, Isfahan, Bukhara, and beyond. These mathematicians not only reproduced Greek theorems but also expanded the scope of mathematical research, introducing new methods and new areas of application, notably in algebra and trigonometry. Among the earliest was Al-Kindi (801–873), an Iraqi philosopher and polymath who emphasized the use of logical structure in the treatment of numbers and proportions, integrating philosophical logic into the foundations of mathematical exposition.

In the 10th and 11th centuries, Iranian mathematicians played a particularly central role in advancing proof-based mathematics. Karaji (c. 953–1029) made significant contributions to algebra, including the proof of results involving binomial coefficients and sequences. He is one of the first to employ mathematical induction in an informal way, a technique that would later become standard in mathematical reasoning. His student Ibn al-Haytham (965–1040), though born in present-day Iraq, also built on this approach, offering formal arguments in optics and geometry, and even attempting early versions of what would now be called the method of exhaustion, akin to integral approximation.

The most emblematic figure of rigorous algebraic proof in the Islamic world remains Omar Khayyam (1048–1131), the Persian mathematician, astronomer, and philosopher. While often celebrated for his poetry, Khayyam's mathematical work is of remarkable depth. In his Treatise on Demonstration of Problems of Algebra, he sought geometric solutions to cubic equations using conic sections, but unlike the intuitive approaches of earlier scholars, he insisted on full, rigorous geometric demonstrations. His approach synthesized algebra and Euclidean geometry in a way that respected the axiomatic structure of the Greeks while advancing algebraic practice. Khayyam's work is notable for its demand for logical completeness and its philosophical awareness of the foundations of mathematics.

Another great Persian scholar, Sharaf al-Din Tusi (1135–1213), continued this heritage by analyzing algebraic equations using both algebraic and geometric techniques. In his treatise on cubic equations, he introduced methods to determine the number of positive roots, reflecting a growing concern for completeness and rigor in algebraic solutions. Later, Nasir al-Din Tusi (1201–1274) made significant contributions to both mathematics and logic. In particular, his development of non-Euclidean geometrical concepts and his attempt to revise and critique Euclid's fifth postulate marked a turning point in the understanding of mathematical foundations. Tusi's approach emphasized clarity of definitions, careful logical development, and the precise use of terminology, all hallmarks of rigorous mathematical reasoning.

Elsewhere in the Islamic world, scholars such as Thabit ibn Qurra (826–901) and Al-Maghribī (1220–1283) enriched the tradition of formal proof. Thabit expanded upon Euclidean geometry with original propositions and precise demonstrations, while Al-Maghribī's algebraic works displayed a deep understanding of symbolic manipulation and proof verification. The emphasis on method, structure, and clarity in these works reflects the Islamic world's assimilation and refinement of Greek methods. The use of structured, step-by-step demonstrations became a defining feature of mathematics, often accompanied by commentaries that clarified each logical transition—a precursor to the style seen in modern mathematical proofs. The transition to modern mathematical rigor in the West owes much to this rich heritage. While Fermat (1607–1665), Pascal (1623–1662), and Newton (1642–1727) are credited with introducing proof by contradiction, mathematical induction, and early forms of calculus, their developments were built upon layers of knowledge transmitted from Islamic world scholars. Many of their key sources were based on Latin translations of Iranian and Arabic texts, often originally authored by Iranian or Arab thinkers. The spirit of rigor that had animated Khayyam, Karaji, Biruni, and Tusi was reborn in a new intellectual environment, now linked to the scientific revolution. However, it would take the 19th century to bring full formalism and abstraction to the fore.

In the 19th century, mathematicians such as Richard Dedekind (1831–1916) and David Hilbert (1862–1943) led a movement toward the complete formalization of mathematical proofs. Dedekind introduced set-theoretic definitions of numbers, while Hilbert followed a grand project to ground all mathematics on a consistent, complete axiomatic system. Their work represents the conclusion of a long tradition, stretching from Euclid through Khayyam to Hilbert, in which rigor, clarity, and structure have been progressively refined. Today, the demand for formal proof is not only a mathematical requirement but also a philosophical one, to the enduring heritage of centuries of intellectual effort across cultures, with the Islamic and especially Iranian mathematical traditions forming a vital bridge in that evolution.

1.6.2 MATHEMATICAL MODELING

The emergence of mathematical modeling is deeply rooted in the long history of human attempts to understand and predict natural phenomena. Even in antiquity, scholars sought to represent aspects of the world through numbers and geometric forms. In Mesopotamia and Ancient Egypt, mathematical techniques were employed for land measurement, architecture, and calendar construction, reflecting a primitive form of modeling tied to practical needs. Greek thinkers, notably Ptolemy (c. 100–170 CE), developed geometric models to explain planetary motion, as seen in his Almagest, which remained authoritative for over a millennium. At the same time, Indian astronomers like Aryabhata (476–550 CE) and Brahmagupta (598–668 CE) used trigonometry and arithmetic to model celestial events. In the Islamic Golden Age, scholars such as Al-Battani (c. 858–929) and Tusi (1201–1274) refined astronomical models and introduced methods of approximation, iteration, and geometric transformations to describe planetary trajectories. These contributions laid a conceptual and technical foundation for later developments, particularly during the European Renaissance, where the revival of classical knowledge met with experimental inquiry and the rise of mechanistic philosophy.

The Renaissance marked a pivotal shift toward a more systematic use of mathematics in the natural sciences. Influenced by the rediscovery of Greek, Iranian, and Arabic works, figures such as Niccolò Tartaglia (1499–1557) and Galileo Galilei (1564–1642) began applying mathematical equations to study motion, falling bodies, and the behavior of projectiles. Galileo, in particular, championed the idea that the universe is written in the language of mathematics, and his kinematic equations represented some of the earliest formal models of physical systems. A major leap occurred with Johannes Kepler (1571–1630), who used observational data from Tycho Brahe to derive his three laws of planetary motion. Kepler's laws, expressed mathematically, demonstrated that the motion of celestial bodies could be described not through philosophical speculation, but through precise geometric and algebraic relationships. Meanwhile, in the Islamic world, Persian polymaths such as Omar Khayyam (1048–1131) had earlier developed mathematical techniques that combined algebra and geometry to analyze complex relationships, paving the way for the kind of analytical thinking seen in Kepler's and Galileo's work.

During the 17th and 18th centuries, mathematical modeling gained further momentum as it became central to the emerging physical sciences. Isaac Newton (1642–1727), with his Philosophiæ Naturalis Principia Mathematica, provided a unified mathematical framework to model motion and gravitation using differential equations. His laws of motion, expressed through calculus, allowed scientists to predict the behavior of bodies under various forces, establishing a model that connected mathematics directly to the real world. Leibniz, developing calculus independently, laid the groundwork for symbolic and systematic modeling techniques. Later,

Leonhard Euler (1707–1783) and Joseph-Louis Lagrange (1736–1813) expanded the scope of mathematical modeling into mechanics, elasticity, and celestial dynamics. Their formulation of equations to model dynamic systems further entrenched the use of mathematics as a universal descriptive and predictive tool. These advances set the stage for a new way of thinking, where mathematics was no longer just a computational aid but a central language of scientific theory and explanation.

It was in the 19th century, however, that mathematical modeling emerged as a distinct and centralized methodology, deeply embedded in both theoretical and applied sciences. With the rise of thermodynamics, electromagnetism, and fluid dynamics, modeling became essential to describe increasingly complex natural systems. Pierre-Simon Laplace (1749–1827) used probabilistic models and differential equations to study celestial stability and physical determinism, while Joseph Fourier (1768–1830) introduced series expansions to model heat distribution. James Clerk Maxwell (1831–1879) developed a set of partial differential equations (PDEs) to unify electricity and magnetism, producing a model that not only explained electromagnetic phenomena but also predicted the existence of electromagnetic waves. These models were not merely theoretical, and they had immense practical consequences, influencing the development of technologies such as radio, engines, and electrical circuits. The success of mathematical modeling in capturing physical reality with such precision reinforced the idea that mathematics was not only descriptive but also deeply explanatory. By the end of the 19th century, the integration of mathematics and physics had become so profound that scientific progress was increasingly measured by the power and elegance of its models.

1.6.3 Numerical Analysis

Numerical analysis, as a distinct branch of mathematics, began to take shape with the development of numerical approximations aimed at solving problems too complex for exact solutions. In the 17th century, the growth of astronomy and mechanics created a pressing need for reliable computational tools. Mathematicians began using interpolation methods, finite differences, and early forms of series expansion to approximate functions and tabulate astronomical data. The use of Taylor series allowed for the local approximation of functions by polynomials, providing a powerful tool to estimate values when exact expressions were unavailable or difficult to manipulate. These techniques were essential not only for astronomers like *Kepler* and Newton but also for navigators, engineers, and physicists who required accurate predictions of planetary positions, trajectories, and mechanical behavior. Even at this early stage, numerical methods were recognized as crucial instruments for translating theoretical insight into practical computation.

The 18th and especially the 19th century observed significant progress in both the theory and application of numerical methods. One of the innovative developments was Isaac Newton's (1642–1727) formulation of the Newton-Raphson method, an iterative algorithm for finding roots of equations that remains widely used today. This method introduced the concept of successive approximations, iteratively refining an initial guess to converge toward an accurate solution, which lies at the heart of modern numerical computation. Simultaneously, mathematicians explored numerical solutions to systems of linear equations, eigenvalue problems, and differential equations, laying the groundwork for what would later become standard numerical procedures. The increasing complexity of scientific and engineering problems demanded efficient and reliable approximations, leading to the formalization of error analysis and convergence criteria. These topics have since become central to the field of numerical analysis. During this period, algorithms began to emerge not merely as mechanical tools but as structured mathematical constructs that required proof of validity, stability, and performance.

The true transformation of numerical analysis, however, occurred in the 20th century with the advent of digital computers. The capacity to perform massive, repetitive computations with speed and precision opened the door to entirely new classes of problems and solution strategies. Complex differential equations modeling heat transfer, fluid dynamics, or electromagnetic fields could now be solved numerically with techniques such as finite element methods and finite difference schemes. Simultaneously, advances in linear algebra, interpolation theory, optimization, and numerical integration flourished as computing resources grew. The field evolved into a fully developed discipline, bridging pure and applied mathematics, computer science, and engineering. Today, numerical analysis is indispensable not only in traditional scientific domains but also in ML, climate modeling, structural design, and financial forecasting. Its power lies in its ability to produce approximate solutions where analytical expressions fail, thereby bringing the abstract precision of mathematics into direct contact with the complex and often messy realities of the physical and technological world.

1.6.4 GEOMETRY AND VISUALIZATION

Geometry has a long history, dating back to Egypt, Iran, and Ancient Greece, with Euclid (around 300 BC), who codified geometric principles in his work *Elements*. Between the 8th and 14th centuries, scholars in the Islamic world played a vital role in advancing geometry. For example, Ibn al-Haytham (965–1040), also called Alhazen, developed work on geometric optics in his famous book Kitab al-Manazir (Book of Optics), exploring the geometry of light rays and spherical mirrors. Omar Khayyam (1048–1131), on the other hand, worked on the geometric foundations of cubic equations and introduced ideas on parallels that foreshadowed non-Euclidean geometries. These contributions were essential in transmitting and enriching geometric knowledge during the Renaissance. After advancements in the Middle Ages, geometry underwent a revolution in the 17th century with the introduction of analytic geometry by René Descartes (1596–1650), which allowed the linking of geometry and algebra. In the 19th century, non-Euclidean geometry, developed by Carl Friedrich Gauss (1777–1855) and Bernhard Riemann (1826–1866), opened new perspectives in mathematics, and in the 20th century, 3D visualization, associated with modern technologies, transformed the way geometric concepts are understood.

1.6.5 SIMULATIONS AND EXPERIMENTATION

Numerical simulations experienced a true revolution in the 20th century with the emergence of computers, which allowed for solving complex equations that were previously unsolvable by analytical means. These simulations became essential in fields such as physics, engineering, and even social sciences, where they allow modeling of various phenomena, from fluid dynamics to wave propagation. For example, the first meteorological simulations based on PDEs, developed in the 1950s, marked a key milestone in understanding and predicting complex systems. The advent of computers transformed calculation methods, replacing manual techniques with sophisticated algorithms capable of handling large volumes of data. The Monte Carlo simulation method, developed in the 1940s by John von Neumann (1903–1957) and Stanislaw Ulam (1909–1984), was another major milestone in the evolution of numerical simulations. This method relies on probabilistic procedures to explore systems with many random variables. Initially used to solve problems related to nuclear physics within the Manhattan Project, it quickly found applications in diverse fields such as optimization, finance, and industrial process modeling. Monte Carlo simulations are particularly powerful in situations where deterministic solutions are inaccessible, and they play a key role in decision-making and risk management. Concurrently, the consideration of errors and uncertainty in simulations has improved their reliability and accuracy. After World War II, the rise of supercomputers, such as the Cray-1 developed in 1976, accelerated these advancements. These progressions were supported by mathematicians and engineers like Richard Hamming (1915–1998), who introduced error-correction techniques, and Donald Knuth (born 1938), who contributed to modern algorithms. These efforts helped quantify error margins and better understand the limits of simulations. Thus, modern numerical tools, by integrating error and uncertainty analysis, have become indispensable instruments for predicting, analyzing, and optimizing complex systems in a wide range of scientific and industrial fields.

1.7 THE RELATIONSHIP BETWEEN MATHEMATICS AND AI

1.7.1 MATHEMATICAL FOUNDATIONS OF AI ALGORITHMS

The relationship between mathematics and AI is essential and fundamental, as mathematics provides the theoretical tools and models necessary to design, understand, and optimize intelligent systems. AI, in essence, relies on algorithms and processes designed to mimic human intelligence by processing data and making decisions. These algorithms, whether used for ML, pattern recognition, or decision-making, are built on solid mathematical concepts, including statistics, optimization, linear algebra, and probability theory. For example, in ML, statistical models are used to estimate parameters and make predictions from data. Regression, whether linear or logistic, is a classic example of using statistics to link a dependent variable to independent variables and make forecasts.

1.7.2   Linear Algebra and Optimization in Model Construction

Mathematics, and particularly linear algebra, also play a significant role in manipulating data and parameters in AI models. Matrices and vectors are fundamental objects for representing and processing data, especially in fields like deep neural networks (DNNs), where data is transformed through multiple layers of computation. Matrix operations, such as matrix multiplication, are used to perform complex calculations, allowing NNs to process large amounts of data and extract relevant features. Additionally, optimization, a key area of mathematics, is central to supervised learning (SL) and AI model optimization. Techniques like gradient descent are used to find the best parameters for a model by minimizing the error between the model's predictions and the actual data. Optimization is also used to solve more complex problems, such as those encountered in big data processing or the analysis of complex networks, like social networks or recommendation systems.

1.7.3   Probability and Graph Theory for Uncertainty and Structure

In these contexts, graph theory and associated algorithms are used to analyze and optimize the relationships between different elements of a network. For example, graph traversal algorithms are used to determine optimal paths or identify communities within a network. Furthermore, probability plays a fundamental role in managing uncertainty and variability in data. Probabilistic models, such as *Bayesian* networks or *Markov* models, are used to predict future behaviors from past data, taking into account the uncertainties inherent in real-world systems. Thus, AI relies on a multitude of mathematical concepts to process, analyze, and make decisions from data. Statistics are used to analyze and describe data, while linear algebra and optimization enable the design of powerful algorithms capable of handling large amounts of information. Probability, graph theory, and other branches of mathematics are also used to model uncertainties, complex relationships, and optimize the performance of intelligent systems. In short, mathematics is the language and the tools that allow AI to function and solve complex problems across various fields, from image recognition to economic trend forecasting.

To provide a clearer perspective, Figure 1.6 illustrates how different areas of mathematics contribute to the development of AI.

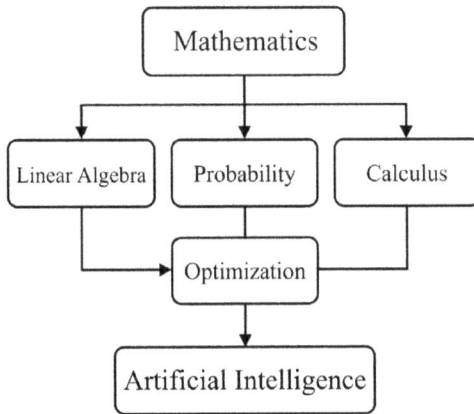

FIGURE 1.6   Different mathematical areas that contribute to AI.

1.8   MAJOR TRANSITIONS IN THE HISTORY OF MATHEMATICS AND THEIR IMPACT ON AI

The progress in mathematics has been marked by several major transitions that have profoundly influenced the way mathematics is understood, applied, and taught. Each of these transitions took place at specific periods in history, in various regions of the world. These transitions were not limited to the evolution of mathematical concepts but also laid the foundations for modern computational methods, leading to the emergence of AI.

1.8.1   FROM PRACTICAL ARITHMETIC TO THEORETICAL ARITHMETIC

The transition from practical to theoretical arithmetic between approximately 3000 BCE and 300 BCE marks a profound evolution in human cognition and mathematical abstraction. In early civilizations such as Mesopotamia and Egypt, arithmetic was primarily utilitarian, serving purposes such as managing land, collecting taxes, counting goods, and building infrastructure. Scribes and officials developed efficient methods for performing calculations with basic tools like clay tablets and papyri, creating rudimentary algorithms based on repeated addition, subtraction, or proportions. These techniques, while practical, laid the groundwork for more advanced thinking. Over time, the growing complexity of social structures, trade, astronomy, and engineering demanded not only efficient calculation but also a deeper understanding of the logic behind the operations. In this context, the intellectual horizon began to shift: numbers were no longer seen solely as tools but also as abstract entities deserving of study for their own intrinsic properties. This conceptual leap was initiated by thinkers such as Thales of Miletus (c. 624–546 BCE) and Pythagoras (c. 570–495 BCE), who sought to uncover harmony and order in the universe through the study of numerical relationships, inaugurating the era of theoretical arithmetic and geometry. Their work laid the foundation for mathematical logic, pattern recognition, and symbolic abstraction that remain essential in the development of algorithms, including those behind modern AI. This evolution toward abstract reasoning and formal arithmetic was not confined to the Greek world; parallel and complementary developments were also taking place in other great civilizations, particularly in the East. In Ancient Iran, early scientific figures played a key role in bridging practical knowledge with speculative reasoning. One of the most remarkable is *Astanes* (a Persian chemist and scholar from the Achaemenid period, likely before the 5th century BCE, said to have influenced Democritus), who may have contributed to early atomic theory through Iranian traditions of natural science. During the Sassanid era, Furghan (3rd century CE; architect of the monumental Taq Kasra in Ctesiphon, a masterpiece of Persian imperial engineering) exemplified the application of geometric and mathematical knowledge in large-scale architecture. These contributions illustrate that the development of theoretical arithmetic was not a linear or isolated phenomenon, but rather a dynamic, multicultural process. Iranian thinkers, often overlooked in dominant historical narratives, played a fundamental role in expanding mathematical reasoning. By combining technical skill with abstract thought, they helped shape an intellectual legacy that continues to resonate in contemporary computational logic and theoretical models.

1.8.2   FROM PRACTICAL GEOMETRY TO THEORETICAL GEOMETRY

Between approximately 2000 BCE and 300 BCE, geometry evolved from a set of empirical practices aimed at solving concrete problems, such as construction, land division, and water management, into a systematic, abstract discipline grounded in logical reasoning. In Mesopotamia, the development of large-scale urban structures such as ziggurats, walled cities, and ceremonial temples reflected a deep familiarity with geometric planning. Irrigation systems composed of rectilinear canals and intersecting levees, used to regulate the fertile plains between the Tigris and Euphrates rivers, were not only technical feats but also spatially organized structures based on consistent measurements and orientations. Clay tablets recovered from this region show geometric computations used for surveying land, establishing right angles, and calculating areas—practices crucial for organizing labor, resolving land disputes, and sustaining agriculture. In Egypt, geometry found its most emblematic expression in the construction of the pyramids, where symmetry, alignment with cardinal directions, and proportion were employed with astonishing precision. Beyond pyramids, temples, tombs, and obelisks were laid out on geometric grids, often aligned with celestial phenomena. Egyptian agricultural life depended on remeasuring plots of land after the annual Nile flood, reinforcing a tradition of applied geometry intimately tied to seasonal rhythms. Meanwhile, in Ancient Iran, particularly during the Elamite, Median, and Achaemenid periods, geometry emerged in the architectural coherence of palatial complexes such as those of Pasargadae and Persepolis, which were designed with orthogonal layouts, modular construction elements, and axial symmetry. The royal gardens were not only aesthetic marvels but also mathematical compositions, with quadrilateral subdivisions, intersecting water channels, and proportional walkways suggesting a geometrical representation of cosmic harmony. Hydraulic infrastructures, including qanats, bridges, and stepped irrigation channels, were deployed across complex terrains with precise control of gradient and flow, demonstrating practical geometric mastery on a territorial scale.

From this rich foundation, geometry gradually evolved into a formal and theoretical science. The Greeks, building upon earlier knowledge from Mesopotamia, Egypt, and Iran, systematized geometric principles through axioms, logical deduction, and demonstrative proofs. This transition marked a radical shift: geometry was no longer merely a tool for building and measuring—it became a discipline based on abstraction, universality, and reasoning. This new perspective enabled thinkers to generalize spatial principles beyond the material world and to formalize them in symbolic terms. Such formalization was essential not only to the progress of mathematics but also to the emergence of algorithmic thinking. Indeed, the capacity to represent space, shape, and transformation through abstract logic laid the groundwork for the automation of calculations—a critical step toward the development of symbolic systems and, eventually, the foundations of AI.

1.8.3 FROM CELESTIAL CYCLES TO MATHEMATICAL ABSTRACTIONS: HOW ASTRONOMY SHAPED MATHEMATICS

Between 300 BCE and the 8th century CE, astronomy became the most sustained and fertile scientific discipline, acting as a bridge between ancient traditions and new intellectual frameworks across civilizations. Its continuity was not only ensured by its practical applications (e.g., timekeeping, navigation, religious rituals) but also by its demand for increasingly precise and abstract tools, which profoundly shaped the evolution of mathematics. While geometry and arithmetic had already reached a level of theoretical organization among the Greeks, it was the needs of astronomy that pushed these fields into new territories of reasoning, accuracy, and abstraction. The sky provided a constant, measurable domain, and its observation required tools and models that far exceeded empirical estimation. To calculate the positions of the sun, moon, and planets, scholars needed to refine numerical algorithms, develop new geometric constructs, and manipulate cyclical time, turning astronomy into a powerful engine for mathematical innovation.

In Mesopotamia, Babylonian astronomers had already built sophisticated arithmetic models to track lunar and planetary cycles, establishing early forms of prediction through tables and regular patterns. These methods required the manipulation of large numbers and complex periodicities, setting the stage for algorithmic thinking. The Greeks, particularly through Ptolemaic astronomy, introduced geometric models to describe celestial motion (e.g., epicycles, deferents, and spheres), which demanded spatial reasoning and theoretical consistency. But it was in India and Iran that astronomy became an active driver of mathematical creativity. Indian astronomers developed trigonometric functions such as sine and cosine to model planetary paths, creating tables of values and rules for their calculation. These functions were essential not only for astronomy but would later be generalized in geometry and calculus. In Sassanid Iran, astronomers preserved and used multiple systems, including the Zoroastrian solar calendar, which divided the year into 12 months of 30 days, with 5 epagomenal days. Maintaining this calendar with seasonal accuracy required knowledge of the solar year and the equinoxes, which in turn encouraged observations and geometric modeling of the sun's path. Institutions like Gundishapur became centers where Greek, Indian, and Persian methods were compared and refined, with mathematics serving as the common language of synthesis.

By the 7th and 8th centuries, as the early Islamic world began translating scientific texts, astronomy was already a discipline rich in computational tables, symbolic systems, and conceptual models in which all were deeply mathematical. Trigonometry, originally tied to celestial measurement, was formalized into a general mathematical tool. Arithmetic evolved beyond basic calculation into structured algorithms used for astronomical prediction. Geometry was extended from static figures to dynamic planetary paths, leading eventually to the study of conic sections and spherical geometry.

1.8.4 FROM RHETORICAL ALGEBRA TO SYMBOLIC ALGEBRA

From the 8th to the 17th century, algebra underwent a profound transformation from rhetorical formulations written entirely in words to the emergence of symbolic algebra using abstract notation. In its earliest form, algebra was a verbal discipline, where operations, quantities, and unknowns were expressed in sentences, making the process of manipulation lengthy and restricted to specific cases. However, the need for greater generality and efficiency gradually pushed algebra toward abstraction and structural reasoning. A major milestone in this shift was the systematization introduced by Khwarazmi, whose work laid the foundation for algebra as a general method for solving equations, independent of specific numbers. His approach introduced algorithmic procedures that could be applied in a repeatable and logical manner (procedures that later gave rise to the very concept of algorithms). Over the centuries, algebra evolved further into a symbolic language capable of representing unknowns, constants, and operations through concise and universal symbols. This development dramatically increased the power of algebraic reasoning, allowing mathematicians to handle increasingly complex problems, manipulate abstract entities, and develop general rules governing mathematical structures.

The impact of this evolution on the eventual development of AI is fundamental. The shift from rhetorical to symbolic algebra introduced a new paradigm in which mathematical reasoning could be encoded, processed, and formalized independently of human language or intuition. This symbolic framework made it possible to design procedures that could be executed systematically and, later, by machines. The abstraction and modularity introduced by symbolic algebra provided the conceptual groundwork for programming languages, logical inference systems, and formal methods, all of which are central to AI. Whether in ML models, where variables and functions are manipulated in high-dimensional spaces, or in symbolic AI, where logical relationships are encoded and solved automatically, the influence of algebra is omnipresent. Without the formalism that emerged during this period, it would have been impossible to define the structured representations and operations required for automated problem-solving. Thus, the historical journey from spoken arithmetic reasoning to symbolic algebra was not merely a mathematical evolution. It was a necessary precondition for the birth of AI as a field rooted in logic, abstraction, and computation.

1.8.5 FROM EUCLIDEAN GEOMETRY TO NON-EUCLIDEAN GEOMETRY

During the 19th century, geometry underwent a radical conceptual shift that challenged assumptions considered absolute for over two millennia. Until then, the foundations of geometry were based on Euclid's postulates, especially the fifth, which defined the nature of parallel lines. For centuries, this postulate resisted proof, leading scholars to explore what would happen if it were altered or replaced. This intellectual experiment led to the development of non-Euclidean geometries, in which space could be curved rather than flat, and where the rules governing lines, angles, and distances varied from those of classical geometry. These new geometries revealed that Euclid's framework was only one among many logically consistent possibilities. Rather than being a universal truth, geometry became a branch of mathematics with multiple valid structures depending on the underlying assumptions. This expansion transformed not only mathematics itself but also our conception of physical space, paving the way for entirely new ways of thinking about form, structure, and motion.

The implications of non-Euclidean geometry extended far beyond mathematics and physics. In modern computational sciences and AI, these geometries offer powerful tools for modeling complex, nonlinear, and multidimensional systems. The ability to conceive of curved or distorted spaces enabled the representation of real-world phenomena that could not be captured within flat, Euclidean frameworks. For example, in ML, data often lies on high-dimensional manifolds that require non-Euclidean treatment to be effectively analyzed or visualized. Similarly, in graph theory, knowledge representation, and NNs, relationships between entities may follow paths that defy linear or classical spatial intuitions. Non-Euclidean concepts allow AI systems to operate in flexible mathematical spaces where proximity, connection, and transformation can take richer and more adaptive forms. Thus, the departure from Euclid was not only a mathematical revolution but also redefined the very structures through which machines understand, navigate, and reason about the world.

1.8.6 FROM ARITHMETIC TO NUMBER THEORY

From the 17th century onward, arithmetic, originally focused on the manipulation and calculation of numbers, gradually evolved into a much deeper and more abstract field known as number theory. Whereas classical arithmetic dealt with operations like addition, subtraction, multiplication, and division applied to whole numbers, number theory sought to explore the hidden structure, properties, and relationships among these numbers. Concepts such as divisibility, primes, congruences, modularity, and the distribution of primes became central themes. This transition marked a profound shift from utilitarian computation toward mathematical curiosity and theoretical insight. Initially considered a purely abstract pursuit with little practical use, number theory eventually revealed connections to algebra, geometry, and logic, forming bridges between discrete mathematics and continuous structures. The exploration of patterns within numbers and the development of formal proofs became foundational tools not only for mathematicians but for the emerging field of algorithm design. The influence of number theory on the rise of computer science and AI has been both fundamental and far-reaching. In particular, the development of cryptographic systems, essential for data protection, authentication, and secure communication in AI systems, relies heavily on principles derived from number theory. Modern cryptographic protocols are based on the difficulty of solving certain number-theoretic problems, such as factoring large integers or computing discrete logarithms, which remain computationally hard even for powerful machines. Furthermore, number theory has shaped algorithmic thinking by introducing the idea that problems can be encoded and solved through sequences of logical steps constrained by numerical properties. Many AI applications, from encryption in communication between agents to integrity in data validation, rely on algorithms grounded in number theory. Even more abstractly, the rigorous mindset fostered by this branch of mathematics, which combines structure, proof, and pattern recognition, parallels the logical foundations upon which AI systems are built. In this sense, the journey from elementary arithmetic to advanced number theory has provided not only mathematical tools but also conceptual frameworks that continue to guide the logic of intelligent machines.

1.8.7 FROM GEOMETRY TO GEOMETRIC ALGEBRA

In the 17th century, a major conceptual shift occurred in mathematics with the unification of algebra and geometry, giving rise to what is now known as geometric algebra or analytic geometry. This transformation allowed geometric figures, such as curves, lines, and surfaces, to be described not just visually or intuitively, but through equations and coordinate systems. By translating spatial problems into algebraic expressions, mathematicians gained a powerful new toolset for analyzing complex geometric phenomena with precision and generality. The ability to represent geometric entities in algebraic terms meant that properties like intersection, tangency, curvature, and distance could be computed, manipulated, and generalized systematically. This synthesis not only revolutionized the study of geometry but laid the groundwork for numerous applied fields, including physics, engineering, and later, computer science. In AI, this legacy is particularly evident in areas such as geometric modeling, computer vision, robotics, and spatial reasoning, where systems must interpret, reconstruct, or simulate real-world shapes and environments. Whether in the form of 3D object recognition, motion tracking, or the simulation of environments in virtual agents, the algebraic encoding of geometry remains central. The transition from pure spatial intuition to symbolic geometric representation thus marks a pivotal moment in the history of mathematics, one that continues to shape the way intelligent systems understand and interact with space.

1.8.8 FROM DIFFERENTIAL AND INTEGRAL CALCULUS TO MATHEMATICAL ANALYSIS

Between the 17th and 19th centuries, the evolution of differential and integral calculus into the more rigorous and comprehensive framework of mathematical analysis marked a major turning point in the formalization of mathematical thinking. Originally devised to understand motion, change, and accumulation, calculus provided powerful tools to describe rates of variation and areas under curves. However, these early formulations relied on intuitive notions that lacked precision. Over time, the concepts of limit, continuity, convergence, and differentiability were rigorously defined, giving birth to mathematical analysis as a formal discipline capable of handling both finite and infinite processes with accuracy. This transition allowed mathematicians to model and study not just physical systems in mechanics and physics, but also abstract mathematical objects and functional spaces. In the context of AI, mathematical analysis offers essential methods for modeling systems that evolve over time or react to changing inputs. Whether analyzing speech signals, forecasting economic trends, controlling robotic movements, or training NNs, the capacity to represent and manipulate dynamic processes through continuous mathematical structures is crucial. Tools from analysis (e.g., differential equations, function approximation, and stability analysis) enable AI systems to make predictions, learn from time-dependent data, and adapt in real time. Thus, the formalization of calculus into analysis not only advanced the rigor of mathematics but also became an indispensable pillar for modern computational intelligence.

1.8.9 FROM CLASSICAL GEOMETRY TO TOPOLOGY

Emerging between the late 19th and 20th centuries, topology marked a conceptual revolution by extending the boundaries of classical geometry. While traditional geometry focused on precise measurements of angles, lengths, and areas, topology shifted attention toward the intrinsic properties of spaces that remain unchanged under continuous deformation, such as stretching, twisting, or bending without tearing or gluing. This new mathematical lens emphasized connectivity, continuity, and structure over metric properties, allowing shapes and spaces to be analyzed based on their fundamental form rather than their exact dimensions. The abstraction introduced by topology opened entirely new fields of inquiry in mathematics, including the study of complex surfaces, higher-dimensional spaces, and qualitative properties of dynamical systems. In AI, these topological concepts have had a growing influence, especially in domains that involve complex data structures and DL. NNs, for instance, operate in high-dimensional, nonlinear spaces where the relationships between inputs, layers, and outputs cannot always be described using traditional geometric tools. Topology provides a framework to understand the global behavior of such systems, including how data clusters, how features persist across transformations, and how different layers of a network interact. Tools derived from algebraic and computational topology are increasingly used to analyze the shape of data, identify hidden structures, and improve the robustness and interpretability of AI models. As a result, the transition from classical geometry to topology not only enriched pure mathematics but also offered powerful methods for reasoning about the structure and behavior of intelligent systems operating in abstract and complex environments.

1.8.10 FROM CONTINUOUS TO DISCRETE MATHEMATICS

In the 20th century, a profound transformation took place in mathematics with the growing emphasis on discrete rather than continuous structures. While classical mathematics had long been dominated by concepts tied to continuity (e.g., as real numbers, differential equations, and smooth curves), the rise of logic, set theory, combinatorics, graph theory, and finite structures marked a paradigm shift. Discrete mathematics focuses on entities that are countable, distinct, and often finite, such as bits, graphs, logical propositions, and integers. This shift provided the essential foundations for the emerging field of computer science, allowing for the formalization of algorithms, data structures, and information processing. Problems that involve decision-making, classification, optimization, and communication began to be framed in terms of logical operations, binary states, and symbolic manipulation rather than continuous equations. This perspective proved especially crucial for AI, where systems must operate through sequences of well-defined steps, reason through symbolic structures, and process digital information. The efficiency and scalability of modern AI, from rule-based reasoning to NNs, from search algorithms to data encoding, depend fundamentally on discrete methods. The ability to represent knowledge, actions, and learning processes in discrete terms enables AI to function within digital architectures, interact with data efficiently, and solve complex problems in finite time. Thus, the shift from continuous to discrete mathematics not only opened a new realm of theoretical exploration but also made possible the computational frameworks that drive contemporary intelligent systems.

1.8.11 FROM ANALYTICAL TO NUMERICAL APPROACHES

In the 20th century, the advent of computing technology marked a turning point in the way mathematical problems were approached, leading to a shift from purely analytical methods toward numerical ones. Traditional analytical techniques aimed to find exact, closed-form solutions to equations using symbolic manipulation, often requiring high levels of abstraction and idealized conditions. However, as real-world problems became more complex, featuring nonlinearity, uncertainty, and massive datasets, exact solutions were often unattainable or impractical. Numerical mathematics emerged to address these challenges by focusing on approximate solutions obtained through algorithms and iterative procedures. These methods made it possible to solve large systems of equations, simulate dynamic processes, and model high-dimensional phenomena with acceptable precision and computational efficiency. The rise of programmable machines provided the perfect medium for implementing such techniques, as computers could perform thousands or millions of calculations per second, updating estimates step by step until convergence. In AI, this transition was transformative: modern AI algorithms, particularly in areas like ML, rely heavily on numerical methods for training models, optimizing parameters, minimizing error functions, and processing continuous data streams. Gradient descent, matrix operations, Monte Carlo simulations, and differential approximations are grounded in numerical mathematics. This computational approach allows AI systems to learn from data, adapt to changing environments, and operate effectively in uncertain or complex conditions. The move from analytical to numerical thinking thus enabled the practical realization of ideas once confined to theory, and it remains one of the pillars upon which the power and flexibility of modern AI rests.

1.8.12   FROM DETERMINISTIC TO PROBABILISTIC APPROACHES

Between the 19th and 20th centuries, a major conceptual shift occurred in mathematics and science with the transition from deterministic to probabilistic approaches. Deterministic models operate under the assumption that, given complete information and fixed rules, outcomes are fully predictable. While this framework was effective for many physical systems, it proved inadequate for dealing with phenomena characterized by randomness, incomplete data, or uncertain environments, situations frequently encountered in real-world contexts. The development of probability theory introduced a new language for reasoning under uncertainty, enabling the quantification of likelihoods, the modeling of random events, and the analysis of distributions over possible outcomes. This probabilistic framework became essential in disciplines ranging from physics and biology to economics and information theory. In AI, the integration of probabilistic reasoning allowed machines to deal with ambiguity, noise, and variability in data. Algorithms could now estimate the most likely classifications, infer hidden variables, and update beliefs as new information arrived. Applications such as ML, NLP, robotics, and computer vision rely heavily on probabilistic models to make predictions, adapt to uncertain inputs, and optimize decisions under risk. Rather than seeking certainty, modern AI systems embrace uncertainty as a core feature of intelligent behavior, using probability to navigate complex and dynamic environments. The shift from deterministic to probabilistic thinking thus marked a crucial evolution not only in mathematics but also in the very foundations of artificial cognition.

1.8.13   FROM CLASSICAL LOGIC TO NON-CLASSICAL LOGIC

In the 20th century, the field of logic underwent a significant expansion with the development of non-classical systems that went beyond the rigid true/false dichotomy of traditional formal logic. While classical logic had long served as the foundation of deductive reasoning, its binary structure proved insufficient for modeling the nuances, ambiguities, and partial truths encountered in natural language, human reasoning, and real-world decision-making. The emergence of alternative logical frameworks (e.g., multi-valued logic, fuzzy logic, modal logic, and intuitionistic logic) introduced more flexible tools capable of capturing gradations of truth, context-dependence, and uncertainty. These innovations redefined the scope of logic from a rigid formalism into a dynamic and expressive system applicable to a wide range of disciplines, including linguistics, epistemology, and theoretical computer science. In

AI, the shift to non-classical logic enabled the design of systems that could operate under incomplete or contradictory information, reason about possibilities and beliefs, and make inferences in uncertain environments. Such systems are especially useful in natural language understanding, knowledge representation, autonomous decision-making, and human–machine interaction, where strict binary logic falls short. By embracing complexity and ambiguity, non-classical logic brought AI closer to the richness of human reasoning, offering a more realistic and adaptable framework for intelligent behavior. This evolution not only enriched the foundations of logic itself but also provided essential tools for building AI systems capable of nuanced judgment and contextual understanding. The successive transitions that have marked the history of mathematics are not merely internal shifts within the discipline; they have profoundly influenced the emergence and structuring of artificial intelligence. Table 1.2 summarizes the principal mathematical transitions and their impact on the concepts and methods employed in AI.

TABLE 1.2
Major Mathematical Transitions and Their Impact on AI

Transition	Historical Period	Impact on AI
From practical arithmetic to theoretical arithmetic	Antiquity → Renaissance	Formalization of numbers and operations; basis of algorithms.
From Euclidean to non-Euclidean geometry	19th century	Spatial modeling in robotics and geometric reasoning.
From classical to non-classical logic	20th century	Uncertainty modeling, fuzzy logic, non-binary reasoning in AI.
From continuous to discrete mathematics	19th—20th century	Machine learning, graph-based algorithms, digital systems.
From rhetorical algebra to symbolic algebra	9th—16th century	Symbolic computation and formal reasoning in AI.

2 Artificial Intelligence at Its Origin

2.1 EVOLUTION OF MATHEMATICS AND LOGIC IN ANCIENT CIVILIZATIONS

Ancient societies used mathematics in innovative ways to solve a variety of practical problems, addressing both everyday life and large engineering projects. Mathematics was not just a theoretical activity, but an essential tool for meeting the concrete needs of these civilizations. In Ancient Egypt, for example, mathematics was very important for administration, especially in the management of agricultural lands. With the Nile flooding every year, it was necessary to regularly reevaluate and redefine land plots. The Egyptians used geometry for these tasks, calculating areas and volumes to fairly distribute arable land and collect land taxes. They also developed methods for calculating the volumes of structures such as silos and pyramids, demonstrating a sophisticated application of geometry and arithmetic. In Mesopotamia, mathematics was used for trade and astronomy. They applied this knowledge to create accurate calendars, essential for agriculture, and to predict celestial movements. Large-scale trade in this region also led to the development of accounting and measurement techniques, including algorithms for solving quadratic equations, which helped manage complex transactions and commercial exchanges.

In Ancient Iran, mathematics also played a major role, especially in irrigation. The Ancient Iranians used the qanat system (as schematically shown in Figure 2.1), an underground irrigation network, to transport water over long distances, and their understanding of mathematics was essential for designing and building these systems. Iran was also an important center for the construction of monuments, such as Persepolis, where mathematical techniques were applied to design and build impressive palaces and temples with calculated proportions and symmetries.

DOI: 10.1201/9781003613633-2

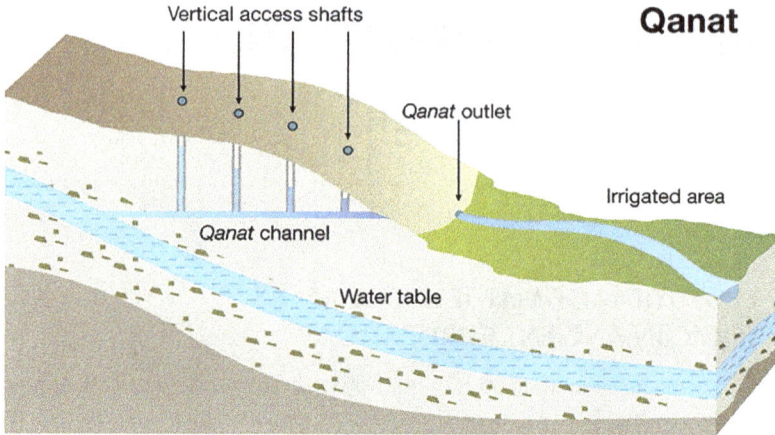

FIGURE 2.1   Ancient Iranian qanat system (Adapted with permission from [1]).

In India, mathematics also played a central role in solving practical problems. Ancient Indians developed the concepts of zero and infinity, as well as numerical systems that simplified commercial and astronomical calculations. These concepts were essential for large irrigation projects and the construction of complex religious structures.

The Ancient Greeks, for their part, took mathematics to more theoretical heights while maintaining practical applications. They developed Euclidean geometry, which allowed them to solve architectural problems, such as the construction of temples and theaters, where proportions and symmetry were essential. Archimedes, one of the greatest mathematicians of antiquity, used geometric methods to calculate complex surfaces and volumes that were applied in engineering and construction.

In Ancient China, mathematics was applied to many practical fields, including astronomy, cartography, and construction. The Ancient Chinese developed precise measurement systems and calculation methods for large engineering projects, such as the construction of irrigation canals and fortifications. Their approach to mathematics was also influenced by a philosophical view of the cosmos, where mathematical principles were used to understand the harmony and balance of the universe.

Mathematics in ancient societies was much more than a mere academic discipline; it was an essential tool for managing land, building monuments, developing trade systems, and understanding the cosmos. These practical applications not only allowed these civilizations to thrive but also laid the foundations for modern mathematical developments. The mathematical approaches of different civilizations varied significantly based on their cultural contexts, practical needs, and the notation systems they developed. These differences reflect not only the diversity of these civilizations' practical concerns but also their philosophical perspectives on mathematics and the world. A summary is presented in Table 2.1.

TABLE 2.1
Chronological Evolution of Mathematical and Logical Thought in Ancient Civilizations

Era/Period	Civilization	Key Contributions
~3000 BCE	Sumerians (Mesopotamia)	Counting, base-60 system, early algebra, cuneiform writing
~2500 BCE	Egyptians	Practical geometry, fractions, early algebra for administration
~2000–1500 BCE	Babylonians	Algebraic equations, quadratic solutions, tables of reciprocals
~1200–500 BCE	Ancient Iran (Elam, Medes, Persians)	Astronomical mathematics, calendars, early logical organization of knowledge
~1000–300 BCE	Chinese (Zhou dynasty)	Decimal system, counting rods, early algorithmic thinking
~600–300 BCE	Greeks	Deductive reasoning, geometry (Euclid), formal logic (Aristotle), number theory (Pythagoras)
~500–200 BCE	Indians (Vedic period, early classical age)	Zero concept, infinity, formal systems of logic (Nyaya Sutra)

2.1.1 THE FIRST TRACES OF CALCULATIONS IN MESOPOTAMIA

2.1.1.1 The Major Civilizations of Mesopotamia

Mesopotamia, meaning land between the rivers in Greek, is a historical region located between the Tigris and Euphrates rivers, corresponding mainly to present-day Iraq and partially to areas of Syria, Turkey, and Iran. It is considered the cradle of many ancient civilizations. The main civilizations shaping the region could be categorized as follows.

- **The Sumerians** (3500–2000 BC): The Sumerians are often regarded as the first great civilization in human history. They founded city-states such as Ur, Uruk, Eridu, and Lagash. Known for inventing cuneiform writing, they also developed complex urban management systems, agricultural irrigation, and made advancements in mathematics and astronomy.
- **The Akkadians** (2334–2154 BC): Under the reign of Sargon of Akkad, the Akkadians established the first empire in history, unifying several Sumerian city-states. Their language, Akkadian, became a lingua franca in the region, gradually replacing Sumerian.
- **The Babylonians** (2000–539 BC): Babylon became a major cultural and political center under the reign of Hammurabi, known for his famous code of laws. Later, under Nebuchadnezzar II, the Babylonians reached their

peak, with architectural achievements such as the Hanging Gardens and the Ishtar Gate.

- **The Assyrians** (2500–609 BC): Primarily located in northern Mesopotamia, the Assyrians built a powerful military empire. Their capital, Nineveh, was a center of learning and culture. They are known for their engineering feats, extensive libraries (such as that of Ashurbanipal), and military campaigns.
- **The Chaldeans** (626–539 BC): Sometimes referred to as the Neo-Babylonians, the Chaldeans succeeded the Assyrians and restored Babylon as their capital under Nebuchadnezzar II. This period was marked by significant astronomical advancements and cultural achievements.
- **The Elamites** (2700–640 BC): Although located on the eastern periphery of Mesopotamia (in present-day southwestern Iran), the Elamites had a significant influence on the Mesopotamian region. They maintained trade and military relations with the Sumerians, Akkadians, and Babylonians.
- **The Hittites** (1600–1200 BC): Primarily based in Anatolia (modern-day Turkey), the Hittites briefly influenced Mesopotamia through military and cultural interactions with the Babylonians and Assyrians.
- **The Kassites** (1600–1155 BC): The Kassites ruled Babylon after the fall of the Old Babylonian Empire. Their rule lasted several centuries, bringing a period of political and cultural stability.

2.1.1.2   The Impact of Mesopotamian Mathematics on Science and Society

The inhabitants of Mesopotamia used their mathematical skills to solve a variety of practical problems essential to their daily life, economy, and cultural and scientific activities. The main types of problems that the Mesopotamians (particularly the Babylonians) sought to solve through their calculations are listed as follows.

- **Agricultural and Land Management**: Agriculture was at the heart of the Mesopotamian economy, and managing agricultural lands was very important. The Mesopotamians used their mathematical knowledge to measure and divide land, calculate field areas, and manage irrigation. They had to determine the quantities of seeds needed for planting and predict crop yields. These calculations involved the use of geometry to estimate the areas of irregular plots, which was essential for the fair distribution of land and tax collection.
- **Trade and Economy**: Trade was a prosperous activity in Mesopotamia, and mathematics played a major role in managing commercial transactions. The Mesopotamians calculated prices, interest rates on loans, and conversions between different units of measurement. They developed techniques to solve arithmetic problems related to the exchange of goods, contracts, and loans. For example, they used multiplication tables and inverse tables to simplify complex commercial calculations.
- **Astronomy and Celestial Predictions**: The Mesopotamians were deep observers of stars and planets, developing advanced mathematical methods to predict celestial movements. They used their knowledge to calculate lunar phases, eclipses, and planetary positions. These predictions were

essential for establishing agricultural, religious, and administrative calendars, as well as for astrological purposes. Their sexagesimal (base-60) system was particularly well-suited for astronomical calculations, allowing them to divide circles into 360 degrees, which is still in use today.

- **Construction and Engineering**: Mathematics was also used in the construction of Mesopotamian infrastructure, such as temples, ziggurats, and irrigation canals. They applied geometry to ensure structures were properly aligned and to calculate the volumes of construction materials needed. Mathematics also helped them design complex irrigation systems to channel river water to farmlands, which was crucial for survival in Mesopotamia's arid environment.
- **Solving Algebraic Problems**: The Mesopotamians were among the first to develop algebraic techniques for solving linear and quadratic equations. They tackled problems involving unknowns, often related to the distribution of goods, trade exchanges, or dimensional calculations.

The Mesopotamian numeral system, based on a combination of a sexagesimal and decimal (base 10) systems, had a significant influence on other cultures, particularly in the fields of astronomy, time measurement, and geometry. One of its most enduring legacies is its impact on how we measure time today. The Mesopotamians divided an hour into 60 minutes and a minute into 60 seconds, a convention later adopted by other civilizations, which remains in use worldwide. This system became a universal standard due to the ease with which 60 can be divided by multiple numbers, making calculations practical and conversions relatively simple.

In addition to timekeeping, Mesopotamian mathematics, especially their sexagesimal calculation methods, influenced Greek geometry and astronomy. Greek scholars, such as Hipparchus and Ptolemy, adopted the division of the ecliptic into 360 degrees, a practice derived from the Mesopotamian system. This approach facilitated complex calculations in astronomy and geometry and laid the foundation for the method still used today to divide a circle into 360 degrees. The transmission of this knowledge through Greek scholars ensured its integration into later mathematical traditions. Beyond Greek influence, the Mesopotamian sexagesimal system was also preserved and developed by Islamic scholars during the Middle Ages. Iranian mathematicians, such as Biruni and Khwarizmi, played a fundamental role in expanding and refining Mesopotamian knowledge, particularly in astronomy and trigonometry. These advancements were later transmitted to Europe through translations of Arabic and Iranian texts during the Renaissance, shaping the mathematical work of European scholars and contributing to the development of various scientific disciplines.

The influence of the Mesopotamian numeral system extended beyond mathematics and timekeeping, playing a crucial role in cartography and navigation. The division of the Earth's circumference into 360 degrees became a fundamental principle for cartographers and navigators, enabling precise measurements of latitude and longitude. This convention facilitated significant progress in maritime exploration, the development of accurate maps, and the establishment of global trade routes. Through its contributions to time measurement, geometry, astronomy, and navigation, the

Mesopotamian numeral system left a profound and lasting impact on many later civilizations. Its innovations have endured for millennia and continue to be essential in scientific and practical applications today.

2.1.1.3   Advanced Mathematical Tools of the Babylonians

Among the various civilizations of Mesopotamia, the Babylonians played a significant role. They used several mathematical tools to perform their calculations, some of which were remarkably sophisticated for their time. Their numeral system, clay tablets, and mathematical methods were at the core of their practices.

The Babylonians used clay tablets as a medium for recording their calculations. These tablets, inscribed with cuneiform symbols (━ ✕━ ⊐: *cuneus* meaning wedge, and *forma* meaning shape) using a stylus, have been discovered in large numbers by archaeologists. They contain multiplication tables, division tables, squares, and square roots, as well as solutions to algebraic problems. These tablets served both for everyday calculations and educational purposes, providing reference tools for merchants, scribes, and astronomers. One notable example (as shown in Figure 2.2) is a 3,700-year-old Babylonian clay tablet known as Plimpton 322, which has reshaped the history of mathematics. It displays a set of numbers corresponding to trigonometric patterns used to calculate the sides of right-angled triangles.

FIGURE 2.2   The clay tablet, known as *Plimpton 322*, was discovered in the early 1900s in southern Iraq (Adapted with permission from [2]).

The Babylonian numeral system was a sexagesimal system with a decimal influence, allowing for great flexibility in calculations. They used symbols to represent numerical values in a positional structure, similar to our modern decimal system but based on 60. This system made division easier due to its many divisors (1, 2, 3, 4, 5, 6, 10, 12, 15, 20, 30), which was particularly useful in astronomical and commercial calculations. The Babylonians developed multiplication tables that often extended up to 20, as well as inverse tables (multiplication by fractions) to facilitate division (Figure 2.3). These multiplication tables helped speed up complex calculations by simplifying the multiplication process, which was especially important for commercial transactions and astronomical computations. They used inverse tables for division. Since division in a sexagesimal system could be complex, they preferred multiplying by the inverse of a number rather than dividing directly. These tables listed the inverses of common numbers, simplifying calculations. They also had tables listing the squares and cubes of numbers, which allowed them to solve algebraic problems, including quadratic and cubic equations. These tables were particularly useful in geometric and astronomical calculations.

FIGURE 2.3   Division table and fraction conversion (Image by M0tty, licensed under CC BY-SA 3.0 via Wikimedia Commons).

In addition to multiplication tables, the Babylonians used exponentiation tables (squares and cubes) as well as square root tables. These tools were essential for solving geometric problems, particularly in construction and surveying, as well as for solving complex algebraic equations. Their algebraic techniques, though rudimentary compared to modern algebra, enabled them to solve linear and quadratic equations. While their methods were not symbolic like modern algebra, they relied on rigorous procedures and practical formulas. For example, they could solve problems that translated into second-degree equations, often related to geometry, such as calculating the areas of rectangles or the volumes of solids. They also employed approximation methods to solve complex problems. For instance, they used iterative techniques to find square roots. A famous tablet, known as the Yale tablet (YBC 7289), shows an extremely precise approximation of the square root of 2, demonstrating their ability to find solutions with remarkable accuracy. They developed practical algorithms recorded on their tablets for tasks such as land distribution, crop volume management, and unit conversions. These algorithms allowed them to address real-world problems, such as fairly distributing land among farmers or calculating interest on loans. Although their understanding of trigonometry was not as advanced as that of later Greek or Islamic civilizations, some researchers believe that the Babylonians used rudimentary trigonometric approaches to solve problems related to astronomy and angle measurement. However, their methods were not yet formalized into theories like those developed by later cultures. The Babylonians had a variety of sophisticated mathematical tools for their time, ranging from numerical tables inscribed on clay tablets to practical algorithms for solving everyday problems. These tools, combined with their sexagesimal system, enabled them to handle complex calculations in diverse fields such as agriculture, commerce, construction, and astronomy.

2.1.2 Geometric Foundations by the Egyptians

Ancient Egypt, the cradle of a fascinating civilization, played a key role in the development of mathematics, particularly geometry. Practical needs related to agriculture, such as measuring land after the Nile floods, and architectural achievements, notably the pyramids, stimulated an advanced understanding of geometric principles. Valuable documents, such as the Rhind Papyrus (1650 BCE), attributed to the scribe Ahmès, and the Moscow Papyrus (1850 BCE), reveal the methods used to solve problems related to areas, volumes, and monumental alignments. Egyptian mathematical knowledge also influenced other cultures through exchanges and travels. Thales of Miletus (624–548 BCE), famous for his theorem and geometric explorations, is said to have traveled to Egypt to learn their techniques. Similarly, Pythagoras (570–495 BCE), whose work on triangles is legendary, was influenced by Egyptian and Mesopotamian geometry. These figures represent the transmission of knowledge that enriched the foundations of Western mathematics. Their mathematical legacy reflects profound ingenuity and practical understanding of numbers and shapes. Besides Ahmès, who contributed to preserving this knowledge in his writings, other anonymous scribes left traces of an advanced mathematical tradition that would inspire generations of thinkers around the world. These cultural exchanges and practical applications demonstrate how Egyptian geometry laid the foundations for many theories still used today. The Egyptians used geometry in a sophisticated manner in their architectural projects, especially in the construction of the pyramids, which remain among humanity's most impressive achievements. They were particularly attentive to the alignment of the pyramids. For example, the Great Pyramid of Giza is aligned with remarkable precision to the cardinal points. The Egyptians used geometry to orient the sides of the pyramid toward the four cardinal directions, probably by observing the stars and using geometric instruments like the gnomon (shadow stick) to trace angles and align the square base. The base of the Great

Pyramid is an almost perfect square, with each side measuring about 230.4 meters, with an error of less than 0.1%. This geometric precision was essential for ensuring the stability of the structure and was achieved using precise measuring techniques, likely based on stretched ropes and stakes.

The Egyptians used a specific ratio to determine the slope of the pyramid's faces, which is about 51.5 degrees. This ratio is related to the height of the pyramid and half the length of the base, which is equivalent to the inverse tangent of the angle, reflecting a practical understanding of the geometric relationships between lengths and angles. This not only ensured the stability of the pyramid but also achieved the desired pyramidal shape. An interesting example is the rhomboidal pyramid of Dahshur, which features two different inclinations. The base starts with a steeper slope (about 54 degrees) before changing to a gentler slope (about 43 degrees) toward the top. This change may have been a correction during construction to stabilize the structure, showing how the Egyptians used and adjusted geometry to address practical challenges. They used geometry to estimate the volumes of materials needed to construct the pyramids. For example, the total volume of the Great Pyramid is about 2.6 million cubic meters. Calculating this volume would have involved knowledge of the formula for the volume of a pyramid ($V = 1/3 \times$ base $\times$ height). Even if the exact formula was not used in this form, the Egyptians certainly understood the relationship between the base size, height, and the amount of materials required. These calculations allowed them to plan the work, especially for the transport and extraction of limestone and granite blocks. They also had to estimate the size of the ramps and platforms used to lift the blocks as the pyramid rose, which required an understanding of space and weight.

They also used triangles for various measurements, including determining angles and slopes. For example, the 3:4:5 triangle, a right triangle with side lengths of 3, 4, and 5 units, may have been used to ensure right angles were maintained at the pyramid corners and other structures. They also used simple ratios to ensure proportions were respected. For example, the slope of the Great Pyramid roughly corresponds to the ratio 14:11, a ratio that may be linked to the golden ratio, although this relationship remains a subject of debate among historians. The Egyptians understood that the geometry of the pyramids, particularly the angle of their faces, played a crucial role in distributing weight and thus in the structural stability of the building. Errors in the angle could compromise the pyramid's integrity, as seen with the rhomboidal pyramid. On the other hand, Egyptian geometry deeply reflects the Ancient Egyptians' understanding of space and measurements, particularly through their architectural achievements, land management, and artistic representations. This understanding, while practical and empirical, demonstrates a remarkable mastery of geometric principles tailored to the specific needs of their civilization. The construction of the pyramids, temples, and other monuments shows that the Egyptians possessed advanced knowledge of space and geometry. For example, the precision with which the pyramids are aligned with the cardinal points reveals a sophisticated understanding of terrestrial space in relation to celestial bodies. They were able to design structures with nearly perfect square bases and precise angles, illustrating their ability to apply geometric principles to organize space rigorously. This geometric mastery is also evident in the symmetry and harmonious proportions of temples, where each spatial element is carefully measured and positioned to create a balanced whole.

Egyptian geometry played a crucial role in land management, particularly for the agricultural plots flooded by the Nile. Every year, after the floodwaters receded, the land had to be remeasured and redistributed. Egyptian surveyors, called rope stretchers, used ropes knotted at regular intervals to measure the land and restore the boundaries of the fields. This method reflects a practical approach to geometry, where measuring angles and distances was essential to ensure fair and effective management of agricultural resources. Their understanding of geometry allowed them to calculate the areas of plots, even when they had irregular shapes, ensuring a fair distribution of land. They applied geometric principles in their artistic representations, particularly in the proportional systems used for sculpting statues and painting human figures. The Egyptian "canon of proportions" divided the human body into standardized units, typically measured in fists or cubits, thus creating harmonious and proportionate figures. This use of geometry to represent space and proportions in art shows that the Egyptians had a structured and systematic view of space, which they applied not only in architecture but also in visual art.

In the construction of the pyramids and other monuments, they had to calculate the volumes of materials needed, such as the amount of stone to be extracted and transported. Their ability to estimate these volumes shows that they understood the geometric relationships between different shapes, such as cubes, rectangles, and pyramids. They likely used empirical formulas to estimate volumes and plan the work effectively. This practical application of geometry reflects their understanding of space in terms of quantity and resource management. The emphasis on precise alignment and symmetry in their constructions shows that the Egyptians had a conception of space based on order, regularity, and harmony. The precise alignment of the pyramids with the cardinal points, as well as the perfect symmetry of the temples, indicates that the Egyptians saw geometry as a means of reflecting a cosmic order in terrestrial space. This geometric view of space also symbolized stability and eternity, essential concepts in Egyptian culture, especially in relation to funerary monuments.

Given the above-mentioned explanations, Egyptian geometry reflects a pragmatic and symbolic understanding of space and measurements, tailored to the needs of their civilization. Whether for building monuments, managing agricultural lands, or creating works of art, the Egyptians used geometry as an essential tool to organize, measure, and give meaning to their environment. This approach not only enabled remarkable architectural and artistic feats but also contributed to shaping a culture deeply imbued with the concepts of order and proportion.

Furthermore, Egyptian mathematics is primarily known through several documents and artifacts that have survived over the centuries. These sources offer valuable insight into how the Ancient Egyptians used mathematics in their daily lives, administration, and architectural projects. There are several documents and artifacts representing Egyptian mathematics. The Rhind Papyrus (or Ahmès Papyrus) is one of the most famous Egyptian mathematical documents (as shown in Figure 2.4). Dating back to 1650 BCE, it is a copy made by the scribe Ahmès of an older document. This papyrus measures about 5.25 meters in length and contains 87 mathematical problems. It presents a variety of mathematical problems, ranging from arithmetic to geometry. It covers topics such as the division of grain, calculations of field areas, proportions, and granary volumes. It also includes calculation methods, such as the Egyptian method of multiplication by duplication and addition, as well as approximations of fractions. This document is essential for understanding Egyptian mathematical techniques and their practical application.

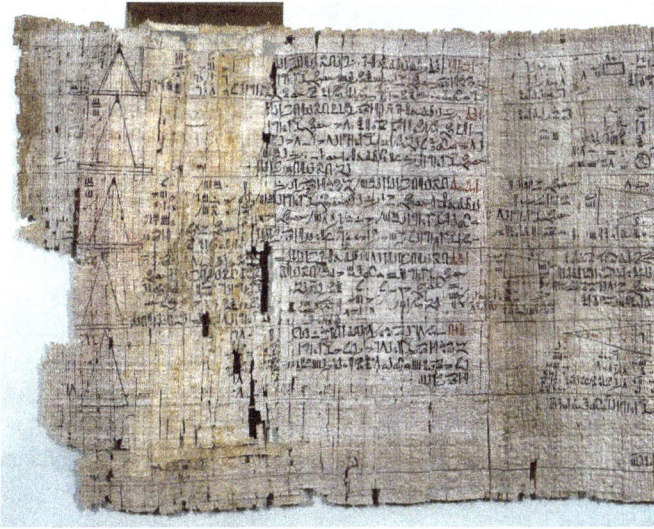

FIGURE 2.4 Rhind Papyrus (or Ahmès Papyrus) (https://curiosmos.com/ancient-egypts-rhind-mathematical-papyrus-explained-in-10-interesting-facts/).

The Moscow Papyrus, dated around 1850 BCE, is another major mathematical document. It is kept at the Pushkin State Museum of Fine Arts in Moscow. This papyrus contains 25 mathematical problems, several of which concern geometry. Notably, it presents calculations for finding the area of a semicircle, the volume of a truncated pyramid, and the area of a curved surface. These problems demonstrate a sophisticated understanding of geometry, particularly in practical contexts such as construction and resource management.

Wooden tablets and ostraca (fragments of pottery or stone used for writing) have also revealed information about Egyptian mathematics. These objects were often used for school exercises or administrative calculations. The tablets and ostraca contain examples of arithmetic calculations, fractions, and area measurements. They show how scribes and students were trained in mathematics and how these skills were applied in daily life, particularly for land administration, tax calculation, and resource management.

Inscriptions found on various monuments, temples, and tombs provide clues about the use of mathematics in architecture and engineering. These inscriptions may include precise measurements of dimensions, material volumes, and angles used in construction. For example, architectural plans found in some tombs demonstrate the practical application of geometry to design harmonious and aligned structures, reflecting a deep understanding of geometric principles.

The Egyptians used knotted ropes to perform geometric measurements, particularly to delimit fields after the annual flooding of the Nile. These ropes were divided into standard length units (cubits), allowing surveyors to take precise measurements. The cubits themselves, often made of wood or stone, were standardized units of measurement, engraved with precise divisions. These tools reveal how the Egyptians applied geometry in practical contexts, such as surveying and construction.

2.1.3   THE ROLE OF ANCIENT IRAN

Ancient Iran, before the arrival of Islam, played a fundamental role in the history of science, influencing fields as varied as logic, mathematics, medicine, astronomy, and natural sciences. As a cultural crossroads between East and West, it integrated, synthesized, and transmitted knowledge from surrounding civilizations, Babylonian, Greek, Egyptian, and Indian, while developing its own innovative ideas. This position made Persia a major hub for scientific and philosophical thought from the Achaemenid period onward. One such example of early scientific contribution is Estanas (c. 500 BCE). Estanas conducted research on the composition and properties of matter and played a key role in transmitting chemical and natural knowledge to the Hellenistic world. His legacy laid the foundation for the development of natural philosophy in Greece and later influenced medicine and pharmacology. His contributions exemplify how Ancient Iran not only preserved and refined earlier knowledge but also exported original insights that shaped global intellectual traditions.

Logical and rational thinking in Ancient Iran has its roots in Zoroastrianism, founded by Zoroaster. This belief system, based on a dualistic view of the world, opposing Ahura Mazda (Good) and Angra Mainyu (Evil), shaped how philosophical and ethical questions were approached. It laid the groundwork for structured, systematic reasoning that would inspire thinkers like Plato. Under the Sassanids, Iran remained a center of rational inquiry, particularly at the Gundishapur School, where Greek, Indian, and Syrian scholars collaborated on disciplines such as logic, medicine, and mathematics. These interactions provided the intellectual foundation for the Islamic Golden Age. In the Sassanid period, a golden age of engineering and architecture emerged. Barazeh (c. 220 CE), an innovative engineer during the reign of Ardashir I, revived the city of Firouzabad. He designed it with a radial layout, advanced water distribution, and solid defensive structures, creating not just a military stronghold but a cultural and economic hub. Meanwhile, Baranoush (c. 260–320 CE) built the Shadorvan of Shushtar, a sophisticated hydraulic system composed of dams, canals, and irrigation devices—an outstanding example of ancient water management. These projects showcase the advanced application of engineering principles and sustainable design in Ancient Iran. Architectural excellence was further exemplified by figures like Farghan (c. 280–340 CE), the builder of the majestic Taq Kasra in Ctesiphon. This vaulted hall, with the largest brick arch of the ancient world, symbolized imperial power and engineering mastery. Jahan Barzin (c. 290–350 CE) contributed to royal ideology through his design of the Throne of Taghdis, a ceremonial and symbolic centerpiece of Sassanid authority. Similarly, Sheydeh (c. 300–360 CE) created the Palace of Khawarnaq in Al-Hirah, blending aesthetics, engineering, and political symbolism. These architectural marvels reflected not only cultural grandeur but also the depth of technical knowledge that later influenced Islamic palace and urban design.

Mathematics held a crucial place in the administrative and infrastructural systems of Ancient Iran. Inheriting Babylonian techniques, Iranians refined numerical systems and geometric principles for constructing qanats, underground water channels that exemplify an advanced understanding of hydraulics. These structures required precise calculations for gradient, flow, and stability, and their success also supported taxation systems and agricultural planning. Such practices laid the practical and theoretical groundwork that later fed into the development of algebra and trigonometry.

Astronomy was another domain in which Ancient Iran excelled. The Persians inherited Babylonian knowledge and adapted it to meet practical and religious needs. The Zoroastrian calendar, based on precise observations of solar and lunar cycles, is an example of this mastery. Divided into 12 months of 30 days, with extra days to align the solar year, it influenced the Egyptian and Greek calendars. Persian astronomical observations were also used to predict the movements of celestial bodies, aiding navigation and the synchronization of religious rituals. These insights, integrated with Indian and Mesopotamian traditions, were transmitted to the Islamic world and later to medieval Europe.

In medicine, Ancient Iran made significant advances. Zoroastrian texts, such as the Vendidad, contain descriptions of plant-based remedies, surgical practices, and hygiene rules. These insights were enriched under the Sassanids through exchanges with Greek and Indian traditions. The Gundishapur School, though more developed during the Islamic period, has Sassanid roots and enabled the synthesis of these medical traditions. A fascinating discovery attests to the beginnings of restorative medicine in Ancient Iran, at Shahr-e Sukhteh, an archaeological site dating from the Bronze Age. The world's first and oldest artificial eye belongs to a woman aged between 25 and 30 (Figure 2.5). This eye was discovered during archaeological excavations in the city of Shahr-e Sukhteh, located in the Sistan and Baluchestan province of Iran. The artificial eye of Shahr-e Sukhteh is approximately 4,800 years old. It is considered the first ocular prosthesis made by humans, with a semi-spherical shape and a diameter slightly greater than 2.5 cm (1 inch). The materials it is composed of are very light, and it was likely made from a bitumen paste. Furthermore, a thin layer of gold leaf covers the surface of the artificial eye. At the center of this eye, a circle (representing the iris) is engraved, and a series of golden lines, representing the blood vessels of the eye, is visible. Additionally, there are small holes on each side of the eye, allowing the prosthesis to be secured in place with a gold thread.

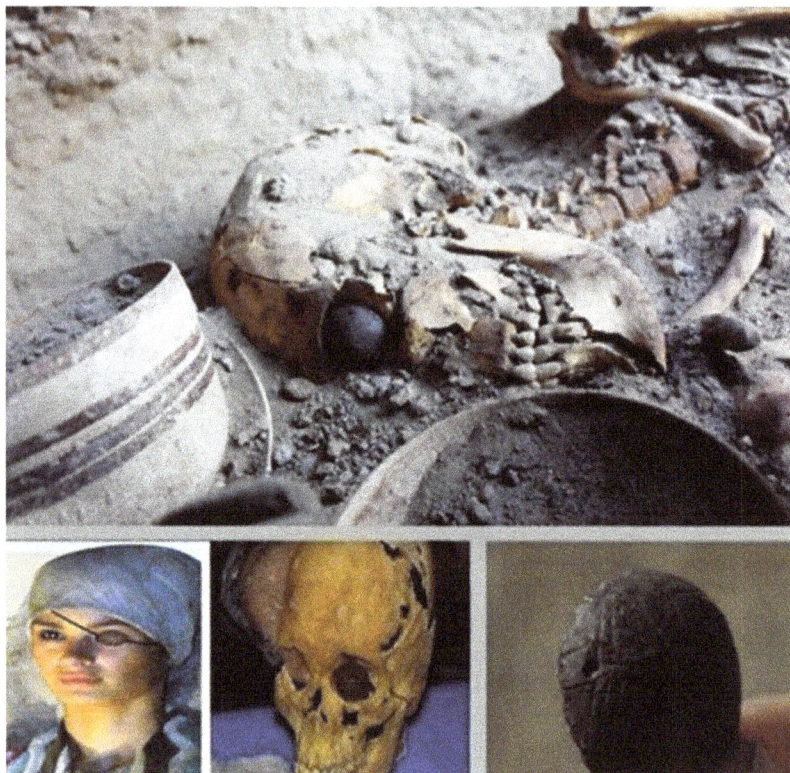

FIGURE 2.5   The artificial eye of Shahr-e Sukhteh (in Iran) is approximately 4,800 years old.

The natural sciences also flourished in Ancient Iran, particularly in resource management and the philosophy of nature. Zoroastrianism emphasized the balance between man and nature, a vision reflected in the agricultural and hydraulic practices of the Persians. The design of the qanats illustrates this harmony: these underground channels allowed water to be transported over long distances while conserving water resources. This technology, exported to the Middle East, North Africa, and even Spain, reflects an advanced ecological understanding. The preservation of land, water, and air was incorporated into Zoroastrian rituals and laws, thus influencing later environmental thinking. Chemistry and alchemy also benefited from Persian contributions. Ostanes, the legendary alchemist, transmitted chemical knowledge to the Hellenistic world, influencing Hermetic traditions. Persian artisans were masters in the production of perfumes, dyes, and precious metals, using sophisticated chemical techniques for their creations. These artisanal practices laid the foundations for experimental chemistry, later enriched by Islamic scholars. They also played a central role in the transmission of knowledge between civilizations. Under the Achaemenids, the royal libraries and administrative archives of Persepolis are evidence of a rigorous management of knowledge. Exchanges between Persian and Greek philosophers and scholars, notably under Darius and Xerxes, facilitated the diffusion of ideas. This cultural transmission laid the foundations for later intellectual traditions, influencing figures like Pythagoras and Plato. By integrating these local and foreign knowledges, Ancient Iran became a bridge between civilizations, uniting the Greek, Mesopotamian, Indian, and Egyptian worlds. This role as a cultural crossroads allowed Persia to establish lasting foundations in the fields of rational thought, mathematics, medicine, astronomy, and the natural sciences. The scientific and intellectual legacy of Ancient Iran has been transmitted through the ages and left a lasting imprint on the history of science, forever marking the evolution of human thought.

2.1.4 PROGRESS OF MATHEMATICS IN GREECE

Thales of Miletus (c. 624 BCE—c. 546 BCE) is considered one of the first thinkers to introduce a rational approach to understanding the world. Originating from Miletus, he was a philosopher, scientist, engineer, and geometer. He sought to explain natural phenomena based on universal principles, breaking away from traditional mythological explanations. For example, he considered water to be the fundamental element from which everything originated. By laying the foundations of scientific thinking, he played a crucial role in the emergence of philosophy and natural sciences.

Thales is also recognized for his remarkable contributions to geometry. He is especially famous for what is now called Thales' theorem, which establishes proportional relationships in triangles, although its formalization came later. He used geometric techniques to solve practical problems, such as measuring the height of Egyptian pyramids or estimating the distance of ships at sea. He is also credited with fundamental works in geometry, including proving that every angle inscribed in a semicircle is a right angle. These accomplishments show his pioneering role in applying mathematics to real-world problems. His impact is immense and has profoundly impacted the development of mathematics in antiquity. His approach, based on logic and demonstration, influenced major figures like *Pythagoras* and Euclid, laying the foundations for classical geometry. His rational approach not only transformed Greek mathematics but was also passed down through the centuries, influencing scientific development in the Arab and European worlds. By combining theory and application, Thales remains a key figure in the history of science and rational thought.

Western mathematical thought is structured by Greek mathematicians like Euclid (c. 325 BCE—c. 265 BCE). His work, mainly embodied in his magnum opus *Elements*, profoundly shaped Western mathematical thinking by establishing a model of rigor and logic that lasted for over two millennia. *Elements* is not just a treatise on geometry but a foundational corpus that gathers and systematizes the mathematical knowledge of the time, organizing it according to a rigorous deductive framework. This text served as the foundation not only for geometry but also for the way mathematics as a whole would be developed, taught, and applied.

At the heart of the *Elements* is the axiomatic approach, where Euclid begins with clear definitions, postulates (or axioms), and common notions to deduce a series of propositions or theorems. This method, which involves building new knowledge from truths considered self-evident, not only structured geometry but also established a standard of logical rigor that became the pillar of Western mathematical thought. The systematic demonstration of each statement from basic principles instilled a spirit of method and intellectual discipline that became characteristic of the scientific approach.

The diffusion and teaching of Euclid's *Elements* also played a central role in shaping mathematical thought. For nearly 2,000 years, this work remained the reference manual for teaching geometry in Europe until the 19th century. The way mathematics was taught was deeply influenced by the logical structure of the *Elements*. Students learned to think deductively, to value rigorous proof, and to understand the importance of postulates and axioms. This education forged generations of thinkers capable of reasoning methodically and precisely, a quality indispensable not only in mathematics but also in philosophy, physics, and other scientific disciplines.

Euclid's influence extended beyond geometry to other branches of mathematics, including algebra and number theory. His axiomatic method was adopted in the study of arithmetic, influencing mathematicians like Diophantus and, later, in the modern era, Carl Friedrich Gauss. The concept of deductive construction from axioms was thus transposed into diverse fields of mathematics, creating uniformity in the way mathematical problems were addressed and theories established. This uniformity fostered the emergence of a coherent mathematical tradition in the West, where logical rigor became an unalterable norm.

The impact of Euclid's work was also felt in philosophy, where his deductive approach influenced thinkers like René Descartes. He, for example, sought to apply a geometric method to philosophy, thus creating a link between mathematics and philosophy that endures to this day. Modern philosophy, particularly formal logic, owes much to this Euclidean tradition of rigor and systematic demonstration. By drawing on Euclid's methods, Descartes and others contributed to establishing the foundations of Western rationality, where every argument must be supported by logical proof.

Euclid's influence in physics is evident in the work of Isaac Newton. In his Principia Mathematica, Newton structured his laws of nature in a manner similar to the Euclidean method, establishing axioms and then deducing the laws of motion and gravitation. This approach allowed for the formulation of universal laws with the same rigor used for geometric theorems. Euclidean geometry was also at the heart of the conception of physical space until the revolution of general relativity, when space was reconsidered under the influence of non-Euclidean geometries.

The mathematical and scientific revolution of the 19th century, with the emergence of non-Euclidean geometry, showed the limitations of Euclid's work, but it did not diminish its influence. In fact, the questioning of Euclid's postulates opened the door to an even broader expansion of mathematical thought. Euclid's ability to structure geometry axiomatically served as the starting point for alternative geometries, such as those of Lobachevsky and Riemann, thus demonstrating that even the most established structures could be revisited while still adhering to rigorous logic.

Another highly influential scientist is Archimedes (287 BC–212 BC). He made major contributions to both physics and mathematics, profoundly shaping the evolution of these disciplines. In physics, one of his most famous contributions is the discovery of Archimedes' principle, which states that any object submerged in a fluid experiences an upward buoyant force equal to the weight of the displaced fluid. This principle, fundamental to hydrostatics, helped to understand the mechanisms of flotation and determine the conditions of equilibrium for submerged bodies, thereby paving the way for practical applications in shipbuilding and hydraulic engineering. Archimedes laid the foundations of the statics and dynamics of rigid bodies in mechanics. He is famous for his work on the lever, summarized in the statement, Give me a place to stand, and I will move the world. Archimedes formulated the fundamental laws of levers, describing how forces can balance weights on a lever based on their respective distances from the pivot point. This understanding led to significant advances in the design of simple machines, and his work is still foundational to the modern study of mechanics.

He was also a pioneer in the field of hydrostatics, in addition to the principle that bears his name. He explored the conditions of equilibrium for floating bodies, deepening the study of centers of gravity and pressure. His work on the stability of ships, in particular, demonstrated how physical principles could be applied to practical problems, ensuring the safety and efficiency of maritime constructions. His work, On Floating Bodies, is a testament to his contributions to this branch of physics, where he developed concepts that would be rediscovered and further developed much later.

Archimedes is recognized in mathematics for his innovative methods in calculating areas and volumes. He accurately calculated the volumes and areas of spheres, cylinders, and paraboloids. One of his most remarkable achievements was determining the area under the parabola, which he obtained using a method that foreshadowed integral calculus, centuries before its formal development by Newton and Leibniz. This method of exhaustion, involving approximating an area or volume by a sum of increasingly smaller geometric figures, laid the foundations for infinitesimal calculus.

Archimedes is also famous for approximating the value of π with unmatched precision for his time. By inscribing and circumscribing regular polygons around a circle, he succeeded in bounding π between two rational values, thus demonstrating a geometric approximation method that is still taught in mathematics courses today. This innovative approach established a standard of rigor in calculations that was crucial for the subsequent development of geometry.

In addition to his contributions to geometry and mechanics, Archimedes also innovated in the field of applied mathematics, particularly by combining theory and practice. He designed war machines such as catapults and complex pulley systems, using his mechanical knowledge to defend Syracuse against the Romans. These inventions demonstrate how he applied his theoretical discoveries to real-world problems, illustrating the close link between pure science and its practical applications.

Archimedes' legacy in the history of science is undeniable. His methods and discoveries not only marked his era but also inspired generations of scientists and mathematicians after him. His writings, rediscovered during the Renaissance, played a key role in revitalizing scientific studies in Europe, laying the foundations for the development of modern mathematics and physics. His impact is felt in many fields, from fluid mechanics to mathematical analysis, consolidating his status as a giant in the history of science. Thus, Archimedes' specific contributions to physics and mathematics are numerous and varied, covering areas from hydrostatics and mechanics to geometry and applied mathematics. His ability to combine rigorous theoretical thinking with practical applications demonstrates his versatile genius. The methods and concepts he developed continue to influence modern science, making Archimedes a central figure in the history of mathematics and physics. It should be noted that, in its evolution, mathematics has influenced other scientific fields. For example, Pythagoras' theorem (Pythagoras: 570 BC–495 BC), which states that in a right triangle, the square of the hypotenuse is equal to the sum of the squares of the other two sides, has had a profound influence well beyond mathematics, impacting various scientific fields. In geometry, this theorem is a cornerstone that has allowed the development of Euclidean geometry and, by extension, the formulation of more complex geometric concepts. Its use has solved problems related to distances, areas, and volumes, thus paving the way for applications in cartography, architecture, and astronomy.

The Pythagorean theorem has played a crucial role in physics in formulating the laws of motion and mechanics. For example, in the context of kinematics, it is used to calculate the resultant distance when objects move simultaneously in two perpendicular directions. This application is particularly useful for describing projectile motion, where the vertical component of gravity and the horizontal component of initial velocity are related in a Pythagorean manner to determine the trajectory of the projectile. Optics is another area where the Pythagorean theorem has had a notable influence. It is used in analyzing phenomena of reflection and refraction, where the angles of incidence, reflection, and refraction are often related by geometric relationships involving right triangles. In the design of optical instruments such as telescopes and microscopes, the theorem helps calculate focal distances and optimize the performance of these devices, ensuring that light rays are correctly focused. In astronomy, the Pythagorean theorem is fundamental for determining the distances between celestial bodies. For example, it is used to calculate distances within the solar system and beyond, combining angular measurements with linear distances to determine the positions of planets and stars. This application has been essential in the development of spherical trigonometry, which is used to map the celestial sphere and navigate at sea. Engineering sciences have also greatly benefited from the Pythagorean theorem. In designing structures and machines, this theorem is used to ensure the stability and balance of constructions. For example, in civil engineering, it helps determine the forces acting on bridges and buildings by analyzing force vectors and moments of inertia. In fluid mechanics, it is used to model fluid flows in pipes, where differences in pressure and velocity can be linked by Pythagorean relationships.

Modern computer science also makes use of the Pythagorean theorem, particularly in the field of graph theory and computational geometry. It is used to calculate distances between points in multidimensional spaces, which is essential for search, sorting, and visualization algorithms. Pythagorean methods are also applied in digital image processing, where they help analyze and manipulate shapes and patterns for various applications, from facial recognition to virtual reality. Music and acoustics have been influenced by the Pythagorean theorem, which has enabled the mathematical analysis of harmonics and musical intervals. Pythagoras himself observed that the lengths of vibrating strings and the frequencies of the sounds they produce could be related by simple ratios, often expressed in terms of squared lengths. This observation led to the formalization of the theory of musical harmony, influencing not only music but also the study of sound waves and the construction of musical instruments, thus connecting the science of numbers with the art of music.

2.1.5 ROMAN PRACTICAL SCIENCES AND MATHEMATICS

The Romans, while important in certain practical fields, did not develop or theorize mathematics and science as extensively as the Greeks or other civilizations such as the Persians or Egyptians. The Romans were primarily known for their pragmatism and their ability to apply scientific and mathematical knowledge to solve concrete problems in fields such as engineering, architecture, and administration. Mathematics was used for practical purposes, notably for administration and taxation. It helped in collecting taxes, managing public finances, and organizing censuses. Tools like the abacus facilitated these calculations. The Romans also standardized systems of measurement and weight for trade and construction, reflecting a solid understanding of practical mathematics.

The Romans excelled in geometry for designing their impressive infrastructures, such as aqueducts, roads, and monumental buildings like the Colosseum and the Pantheon. However, these geometric principles were often inherited from the Greeks, and the Romans showed little interest in abstract theorization. In the sciences, the Romans were masters of application rather than fundamental research. They were exceptional engineers, designing aqueducts capable of transporting water over long distances, durable bridges, and paved roads that have withstood centuries. These accomplishments reflect a profound understanding of the principles of physics and mechanics, even if they were not always scientifically formalized. In medicine, they enriched practices with infrastructure like military hospitals (valetudinaria) and writings from authors like Celsus and Galen. These advancements, however, were largely inspired by Greek and Egyptian traditions. In astronomy, the Romans employed rudimentary knowledge to organize calendars and religious events. The Julian calendar, adopted under Julius Caesar, was based on precise astronomical calculations, but these came mostly from Egyptian and Greek knowledge. Their contribution to agriculture excelled through practical texts, such as those by Varro and Columella, which described agricultural techniques based on empirical observation of nature. Generally, the Romans did not develop abstract scientific theories but preferred to rely on Greek discoveries and adapt them to their needs. The works of Euclid, Archimedes, and Hippocrates were widely respected and taught in Roman schools, though few new theories were added to these bodies of knowledge.

The true genius of the Romans lies in their pragmatism and their ability to effectively apply the knowledge inherited from the Greeks, Egyptians, and other cultures to build an empire of unprecedented scope and longevity. Their interest in science was focused on practical goals, and their advancements in engineering, administration, and architecture have left a lasting legacy. Although their contribution to mathematical theory or fundamental scientific research was limited, they skillfully utilized available knowledge to meet the needs of their society and solidify their dominance over much of the ancient world. Compared to the Greeks, who made fundamental contributions to geometry, astronomy, and natural philosophy, or to the Egyptians and Babylonians, who excelled in practical mathematics and astronomy, the Romans were more like ingenious users of existing knowledge. At the same time, the Persians and Indians were developing advanced approaches in astronomy, algebra, and natural sciences. While the Romans were exceptional in their technical and organizational achievements, they did not produce major figures in mathematics or abstract science comparable to those of these civilizations.

2.2 ADVANCES IN DIFFERENT FIELDS OF MATHEMATICS IN THE EAST

2.2.1 LOGICAL AND ARITHMETIC THOUGHT AMONG THE INDIANS

2.2.1.1 The Influence of Indian Mathematical Concepts on Modern Numeral Systems

Indian mathematical concepts played a crucial role in the development of modern numeral systems, profoundly influencing how numbers are represented, calculated, and understood today. One of the most significant contributions of Indian mathematicians is the invention of the decimal numeral system, which is based on the use of ten digits (from 0 to 9) and the position of the digits to determine their value. This system, often called the Iranian-Arabic numeral system, forms the foundation of nearly all numeral systems used in the modern world. The decimal numeral system was revolutionary because it introduced a key concept: place value. Unlike earlier numeral systems, such as the Roman or Egyptian systems, where each symbol had a fixed value, the Indian system allowed the same digit to represent different values depending on its position in the number. For example, in the number 342, the digit 3 represents three hundreds, the digit 4 represents four tens, and the digit 2 represents two units. This innovation greatly simplified arithmetic calculations and made possible the development of more advanced algebraic methods.

Another fundamental contribution of Indian mathematicians is the introduction of the zero, a concept that did not exist in earlier numeral systems. Zero, called *ś ūnya* in *Sanskrit*, was initially used by Indian mathematicians to indicate the absence of value in a given position. This invention not only simplified the writing of large numbers but also enabled the development of more abstract mathematical concepts, such as negative numbers and complex algebraic operations. Zero quickly became an indispensable tool for mathematicians worldwide, and it remains one of the cornerstones of modern computation.

The Indian numeral system was transmitted to the Islamic world, where it was adopted and refined by mathematicians like Khwarizmi. He wrote treatises on arithmetic and algebra that were translated into Latin in the 12th century, thereby introducing the Iranian-Arabic numeral system to Europe. Europeans quickly recognized the advantages of this system over the Roman and Greek numeral systems, and it gradually supplanted these systems in commercial, scientific, and administrative practices. The influence of the Indian numeral system on European mathematics cannot be overstated. The adoption of the decimal system transformed methods of calculation in Europe, enabling rapid advancements in areas such as accounting, navigation, and engineering. Arithmetic methods based on place value and the use of zero facilitated the development of algebra, analytic geometry, and infinitesimal calculus. Without these innovations, the scientific progress of the Renaissance and the modern period would have been much slower and more limited.

Their numeral system also influenced how numbers are taught and used in education. Learning the basics of arithmetic, as practiced in schools around the world today, relies on Indian concepts of numeration. Basic operations such as addition, subtraction, multiplication, and division are all carried out according to the principles of the decimal system, demonstrating the continuing importance of this invention in everyday life and mathematical education. The introduction of zero and the decimal numeral system also had profound repercussions in the fields of philosophy and logic. The concept of zero raised questions about emptiness, infinity, and the nature of existence, which were explored by philosophers and theologians in different cultures. In India, zero was already linked to metaphysical concepts in the context of Buddhist and Hindu philosophy, and its adoption in mathematics allowed these ideas to be integrated into logical and arithmetic frameworks, influencing the development of mathematical logic.

Furthermore, the Indian numeral system influenced numeral systems beyond Europe. When European explorers spread the Iranian-Arabic system worldwide during colonization and trade, it was adopted in regions as diverse as the Americas, Africa, and East Asia. Today, this system is universally used in business, science, technology, and even in cultural contexts where other numeral systems once prevailed.

Another aspect of the influence of Indian mathematical concepts on modern numeral systems is their impact on digital technologies. The binary system used in computers, which relies on the digits 0 and 1, is indirectly derived from the Indian positional numeral system. The ability to represent the absence or presence of value using zero enabled the development of binary logic, which is the basis of all modern electronic computing systems. Thus, the impact of Indian mathematical innovations continues to be felt in cutting-edge technologies. The legacy of Indian mathematics in modern numeral systems is a powerful example of how scientific and technological ideas can transcend cultural and geographical boundaries. The concepts developed by Indian mathematicians more than a thousand years ago have transformed the way the world thinks, calculates, and understands numbers. Their influence is evident in the daily lives of billions of people and continues to be a cornerstone of numerical systems and mathematics globally.

2.2.1.2 The Main Theorems or Discoveries of the Indian Mathematical School

The Indian mathematical school produced many fundamental theorems and discoveries that had a lasting impact on the development of mathematics worldwide (Table 2.2). Among the most notable contributions are works on infinite series, approximations of π, number theory, Diophantine equations, as well as advanced methods of calculation and geometry. One of the most famous theorems from the Indian mathematical school is the work of Madhava of Sangamagrama (c. 1340—c.

1425) on infinite series, particularly in the context of calculating the value of π. Madhava is considered the founder of the Kerala School of Mathematics, and he developed series for trigonometric functions, including sine, cosine, and arctangent. These series, known as Madhava's series, foreshadow what are now called Taylor and Maclaurin series, which were discovered in Europe several centuries later. In particular, Madhava developed a series for arctangent that was used to calculate π with great precision, long before similar developments in Europe.

An additional significant contribution of the Indian mathematical school is Brahmagupta's formula for calculating the area of a cyclic quadrilateral (a quadrilateral inscribed in a circle). This formula, which relates the area of the quadrilateral to the lengths of its sides, is a remarkable example of the mathematical ingenuity of Indian scholars. Brahmagupta also formulated rules for solving certain quadratic equations and proposed methods for solving Diophantine equations, polynomial equations where the solutions sought are integers. His work laid the foundation for later developments in algebra and number theory. Aryabhata (476—550), another major Indian mathematician, made important contributions to trigonometry and algebra. He was one of the first to introduce the concept of sine and cosine, although he used different terms to describe them. He also formulated a remarkably accurate approximation of π, describing it as nearly 62832/20000, which is equivalent to 3.1416, very close to the modern value of π. In addition, Aryabhata worked on quadratic and linear equations, proposing methods for solving them that were used for centuries.

Bhaskara II (1114—1185), another giant in Indian mathematics, developed what is now called Bhaskara's rule for solving quadratic equations, a method that remains a fundamental part of algebra. He also worked on complex problems in geometry, such as determining areas and volumes, and improved methods for solving Diophantine equations. His work Lilavati is a treatise on mathematics that served as a textbook for centuries and is famous for the clarity of its explanations and the way it made mathematics accessible and interesting.

The work of Indian mathematicians on Diophantine equations is particularly notable. They developed specific methods for solving these equations, especially those of the Pell type, long before these methods were rediscovered in Europe. The Indian approach to these problems, which involved integer solutions for quadratic equations, was a precursor to European developments in number theory and influenced mathematicians such as Fermat and Euler.

In addition to these specific contributions, the Indian mathematical school was also a pioneer in the development of fast and efficient calculation techniques. Indian mathematicians developed algorithms for basic arithmetic operations such as addition, subtraction, multiplication, and division, which are still taught today. They also devised methods for calculating square and cube roots, as well as techniques for handling large numbers, all using the decimal number system they invented. They also worked on astronomical problems and used mathematics to develop accurate models of planetary motion, eclipses, and other celestial phenomena. Their work in astronomy not only contributed to the development of this science but also stimulated new mathematical discoveries, as the challenges posed by astronomy required advanced mathematical tools.

TABLE 2.2

Major Contributions of Indian Mathematicians

Mathematician	Contribution	Field
Aryabhata	Approximation of π, trigonometric functions	Algebra, astronomy
Brahmagupta	Cyclic quadrilateral, rules for zero and negatives	Geometry, algebra
Madhava	Infinite series for sine, cosine, arctangent	Analysis
Bhaskara II	Quadratic equations, arithmetic techniques	Algebra

2.2.1.3 The Approach of Indian Mathematicians to Solving Complex Problems

Indian mathematicians approached the solving of complex problems with a remarkable combination of intuition, algorithmic rigor, and theoretical innovations. Their approach was characterized by a deep respect for systematic methods and efficient algorithms, as well as the ability to explore abstract concepts with a clarity that was often ahead of their time. One of the most striking aspects of their method was the use of systematic algorithms to address mathematical problems. Instead of relying solely on geometric proofs, as was often the case in other ancient mathematical traditions, Indian mathematicians developed algorithmic procedures that allowed for repeatable and structured problem-solving. For example, in algebra, they developed precise rules for solving quadratic, cubic, and even complex Diophantine equations. These methods were often presented in the form of verses or prose, making the algorithms easy to memorize and transmit.

Another fundamental aspect of their approach was their ability to work with infinite series and understand approximations in a sophisticated way. Madhava of Sangamagrama's work on infinite series is an early example of this type of innovation. By developing series for trigonometric functions such as sine and cosine, Indian mathematicians were able to approximately represent complex functions and calculate values like π with unprecedented precision. This approach allowed for the solving of problems that would have been inaccessible with simpler methods.

Indian mathematicians also approached complex problems by relying on innovative concepts such as zero and negative numbers. The introduction of zero as a fully fledged digit in their numeral system simplified and generalized calculations, paving the way for solving more difficult problems. For example, they were able to handle equations where one of the solutions could be zero or negative, an idea that greatly expanded the possibilities for solving equations. In geometry, their mathematicians demonstrated their ability to solve complex problems through the clever application of theorems and constructions. For example, Brahmagupta formulated methods to calculate the area of cyclic quadrilaterals (quadrilaterals inscribed in a circle), generalizing earlier results and applying them to more complex cases. These results not only solved practical geometric problems but also laid the foundation for future developments in geometry and trigonometry. They also made significant contributions to number theory by addressing complex problems like Diophantine equations.

Their approach often involved breaking these problems into simpler steps, using algebraic techniques to find integer solutions to polynomial equations. This progressive and systematic problem-solving method not only enabled the resolution of complex equations but also influenced generations of mathematicians in other traditions, particularly in Europe.

In astronomy, Indian mathematicians applied their skills to solve problems related to the prediction of planetary motions and eclipses. These calculations, often highly complex, required an advanced understanding of astronomical cycles and the ability to manipulate data over long periods. Thanks to their algorithmic approach and their use of mathematics to model natural phenomena, they developed highly accurate astronomical tables that were used for centuries.

The transmission and teaching of these methods were also an essential part of the Indian approach. Indian mathematicians often codified their discoveries in the form of sutras (*verses*) or slokas (*stanzas*) in their texts, facilitating the memorization and dissemination of these complex ideas. This way of structuring and transmitting mathematical knowledge allowed for the widespread diffusion of these techniques and ensured that future generations could learn and apply them. Thus, Indian mathematicians approached the solving of complex problems by combining rigorous algorithmic methods with a profound understanding of abstract mathematical concepts. Their ability to generalize, explore new ideas like zero, and apply mathematics to concrete problems, while effectively transmitting this knowledge, has left a lasting legacy that continues to influence modern mathematics (Figure 2.6).

FIGURE 2.6 Aryabhata, pioneer of Indian mathematics, notable for advances in astronomy, algebra, and the approximation of π.

2.2.2 THE CHINESE SCHOOL OF MATHEMATICS AND LOGIC

2.2.2.1 The Mathematical Challenges of Ancient China

Chinese mathematicians, throughout history, focused primarily on practical and concrete problems directly related to the needs of Chinese society, such as administration, agriculture, astronomy, architecture, and resource management. Their pragmatic approach to mathematics is reflected in the types of problems they sought to solve and the methods they developed to achieve this. One of the main problems addressed by Chinese mathematicians was land management and taxation. With a growing population and complex agricultural systems, it was crucial to measure land accurately, calculate areas and volumes, and manage taxes fairly. Texts such as the *Jiuzhang Suanshu* (*The Nine Chapters on the Mathematical Art*), one of the oldest Chinese mathematical treatises, clearly illustrate this concern. This text presents methods for calculating the areas of irregular fields, the volume of grain piles, and solving problems related to the distribution of harvests and taxes. These techniques were essential for imperial administration and for maintaining economic order in the empire.

Another key domain was astronomy and the creation of calendars. Chinese mathematicians developed methods to observe celestial movements and predict eclipses, moon phases, and the positions of planets. The development of accurate calendars was vitally important for religious rites, agriculture, and state affairs. For example, mathematicians sought to solve problems related to the 60-year cycle of the Chinese calendar, harmonizing lunar and solar cycles. They developed techniques for calculating the intervals between celestial events, leading to advancements in trigonometry and arithmetic. Architecture and engineering were also areas where Chinese mathematicians had to solve complex problems. The construction of large structures, such as pagodas, bridges, and especially the Great Wall of China, required precise calculations of forces, materials, and volumes. Mathematicians developed techniques for calculating slopes, angles, and proportions of buildings, using advanced geometric concepts. This knowledge was crucial for ensuring the stability and durability of constructions and optimizing the use of resources. Solving equations, particularly systems of linear equations, was another major problem for Chinese mathematicians. They developed algebraic methods, such as those described in the *Jiuzhang Suanshu*, to solve systems of simultaneous equations, often in the context of resource distribution or solving fiscal problems. One of the most well-known methods is the Gaussian elimination method, used to solve systems of equations long before it was rediscovered in Europe. This method highlights the importance of algebra in Chinese mathematics and their ability to solve complex problems with systematic techniques.

Chinese mathematicians were also interested in numbers and arithmetic theories, especially in the context of numerology and mathematical games. They explored problems related to arithmetic and geometric progressions, as well as magic numbers, such as magic squares. These studies, though often motivated by mystical beliefs, led to important mathematical developments, particularly in number theory. Another area of interest was flood management and hydraulics, a crucial problem in a country traversed by many rivers. Mathematicians developed techniques to calculate river flows, reservoir capacities, and the dimensions of irrigation canals. These calculations were essential for the construction of dams, dikes, and for managing water resources to prevent devastating floods and ensure a regular water supply for agriculture. They were also concerned with economic and commercial problems.

They developed methods to calculate interest, prices, and profit shares in business transactions. These calculations were often complex, involving percentages, proportions, and the rule of three, and they were essential for financial management in an increasingly sophisticated economy. A summary of the contributions of Chinese mathematicians is presented in Table 2.3.

TABLE 2.3
Key Practical Problems Solved by Chinese Mathematicians

Domain	Problem Type	Example
Land management	Measurement of irregular fields	Agricultural taxation
Astronomy	Eclipse prediction, calendar harmonization	Lunar–solar calendar
Engineering	Construction of bridges, pagodas, the Great Wall of China	Calculation of slopes and forces
Algebra	Solving systems of linear equations	Gaussian elimination method
Number theory	Magic squares, progressions	Numerology studies
Hydraulics	River flows, irrigation calculations	Flood control systems
Commerce	Profit and interest calculation	Rule of three

2.2.2.2 Transmission of Chinese Mathematical Discoveries

Chinese mathematical discoveries were transmitted to other cultures through various means, including trade, cultural exchanges, text translations, and diplomatic missions. As summarized in Table 2.4, these channels allowed Chinese mathematical innovations to spread beyond China's borders and influence distant civilizations, contributing to the global enrichment of mathematical knowledge. One of the primary vectors for the dissemination of Chinese mathematics was the Silk Road, a network of trade routes connecting China with Central Asia, the Middle East, and Europe. Along this route, not only were goods exchanged, but also ideas and knowledge. Merchants, travelers, and scholars who traveled the Silk Road carried books, manuscripts, and oral knowledge, facilitating the spread of Chinese mathematical concepts. For example, Chinese techniques in arithmetic and geometry were transmitted to Persian scholars, who then adapted and integrated them into their own mathematical traditions. Diplomatic missions and cultural exchanges also played a crucial role in the transmission of Chinese mathematical discoveries. Throughout different historical periods, Chinese emperors sent envoys to other countries, bringing gifts, books, and scientific documents. These exchanges allowed Chinese knowledge, including mathematics, to reach royal courts and centers of learning in regions such as Korea, Japan, Southeast Asia, and even the Middle East. For instance, the Chinese decimal numeration system and calculation methods were adopted and adapted in Japan and Korea, where they became part of local educational systems.

The transmission of Chinese mathematics was further facilitated by the translation of texts. During the Tang and Song dynasties, China maintained close relations with the Islamic and Buddhist worlds, leading to the translation of many Chinese texts into Iranian, Sanskrit, and other languages. Chinese mathematical works, such as those compiled in the Jiuzhang Suanshu, were thus disseminated in the Islamic world. Iranian scholars, such as Khwarizmi, incorporated some of these methods into their own work, contributing to the later transmission of Chinese mathematics to Europe through Latin translations.

Foreign missionaries and scholars in China also played a significant role in the transmission of Chinese mathematical discoveries. During the Ming and Qing dynasties, Jesuit missionaries, in particular, were key figures in translating Chinese texts into Latin and sending them to Europe. These missionaries, often scholars and mathematicians themselves, not only introduced European science to China but also brought Chinese knowledge back to Europe. Chinese calculation methods, trigonometry, geometric concepts, and innovations in astronomy found their way to the West, where they were studied and sometimes integrated into the European scientific tradition. Another means of disseminating Chinese mathematical discoveries was interaction with neighboring Asian cultures, especially Korea, Japan, and Vietnam. These regions maintained close ties with China for centuries, adopting and adapting many Chinese innovations, including in mathematics. For example, the Chinese methods for constructing magic squares, trigonometric calculations, and solving equations were transmitted and refined in these cultures, contributing to the development of their own mathematical traditions.

The influence of Chinese mathematics also extended to Central Asia and the Middle East through Mongol conquests. In the 13th century, the Mongol Empire established a vast network of communication and trade connecting China to the West. Under the Yuan dynasty, Chinese mathematicians interacted with Persian and Arab scholars, promoting the exchange of mathematical ideas. Chinese concepts and techniques, such as those used in astronomy and geometry, were assimilated and further developed by Islamic scholars, enriching the Islamic mathematical tradition. Their discoveries were transmitted to other cultures through multiple channels, including trade, cultural exchanges, text translations, and scholarly interactions. These transmissions allowed Chinese innovations to enrich the mathematical traditions of other civilizations, contributing to the global evolution of mathematics. The reach of Chinese influence is evident in how concepts such as calculation methods, trigonometry, and geometry were integrated and developed in diverse cultures, including those of the Middle East, Europe, and East Asia.

TABLE 2.4

Major Channels of Transmission for Chinese Mathematics

Channel	Example
Trade	Silk Road exchanges
Cultural diplomatic missions	Envoys to Korea, Japan, Persia
Text translations	Arabic translations of Jiuzhang Suanshu
Foreign scholars	Jesuit missionaries (Ming and Qing dynasties)
Mongol conquests	Knowledge spread to Middle East and Europe

2.2.2.3   The Originality of Chinese Mathematical Approaches

Chinese mathematical approaches were distinguished by several unique characteristics that set them apart from methods used in other civilizations, such as those of Ancient Greece, India, or the Islamic world. These specificities resulted from the way mathematics was integrated into the culture, society, and practical needs of Ancient China, as well as how Chinese mathematicians conceptualized and applied mathematical principles. One of their most distinctive characteristics is their highly pragmatic and utilitarian orientation. Unlike Greek mathematicians, who often focused on abstraction and the search for universal truth through logical demonstrations, Chinese mathematicians approached mathematics primarily as a tool for solving concrete problems related to administration, agriculture, engineering, and astronomy.

Another unique feature of Chinese mathematics is the extensive use of algebraic methods to solve equations. Chinese mathematicians developed sophisticated techniques for solving systems of linear equations long before these methods were rediscovered in Europe. Gauss's method, for example, was already practiced in China under the name of the pivot method. This algebraic approach, in which equations are systematically manipulated to find solutions, contrasts with the Greek emphasis on geometric demonstrations and visual constructions.

Furthermore, they stood out in their approach to arithmetic calculations and series. They developed advanced techniques for operations on large numbers and fraction calculations, using devices such as the abacus, which was a fast and efficient calculating tool. The Chinese also explored sequences and series long before other cultures, with work on arithmetic and geometric sequences as well as magic squares. These magic squares, which involve arranging numbers in a grid to obtain the same sums in all directions, are an example of the originality and creativity of Chinese mathematicians in exploring numerical properties. Geometry in China was also unique in that it was often linked to practical applications rather than theoretical abstractions. Chinese mathematicians focused on applied geometry, used to solve problems in engineering, construction, and urban planning. For example, they used geometric methods to calculate the areas and volumes of complex structures, such as pagodas or dikes, and to determine the correct proportions in architecture. This approach contrasted with that of the Greeks, for whom geometry was more of a study of perfect shapes and abstract relationships. Astronomy and trigonometry in China also had distinctive characteristics. The Chinese developed unique methods for observing stars and planets and for creating accurate calendars. Their trigonometry was often used in conjunction with complex arithmetic calculations to solve problems related to astronomical cycles, eclipse prediction, and time measurement. Unlike the Greeks, who used circles and spheres to model the cosmos, the Chinese directly integrated mathematical concepts into their astronomical observations, producing calendars that were both mathematically rigorous and culturally significant. However, another distinctive aspect of Chinese mathematics is the integration of mathematical concepts with philosophy and cosmology. Mathematics in China was not merely a technical field; it was often linked to philosophical concepts such as yin and yang, the five elements, and natural cycles. For example, Chinese mathematicians could use mathematical concepts to model cycles of time, seasons, or dynasties, reflecting a worldview in which mathematics served to understand and harmonize the universe.

2.2.3 Contribution of Iranians and Arabic-Speaking Countries (Middle Age)

2.2.3.1 The Iranian Mathematicians

   i. Khwarizmi (780–850)

The journey of Iranian mathematics begins with Abu Jafar Muhammad ibn Musa Khwarizmi, who merged Greek and Indian traditions in his works, notably Mukhtasar fi Hisab al-Jabr wa al-Muqabala. This book, translated multiple times into Latin under the title Liber Alghoarismi, is the origin of the English term algorithm.

Khwarizmi's works played a fundamental role in structuring and developing algebra, to the extent that his name is often associated with this branch of mathematics. Living in the 9th century in Iran, he wrote a major work titled Kitab al-Jabr wa-l-Muqabala, which is considered the foundational text of algebra. This treatise systematized methods for solving equations that were previously known but not rigorously formalized, thus laying the foundation for algebra as a mathematical discipline distinct from geometry. One of Khwarizmi's most significant contributions was the introduction of a clear and systematic method for solving linear and quadratic equations. Before him, mathematics was dominated by Greek geometric methods, where equations were solved primarily through geometric constructions. In contrast, Khwarizmi proposed a symbolic and arithmetic approach, manipulating the coefficients and terms of equations to simplify and solve them. This algebraic method allowed for the generalization of equation solving, making it applicable to a wide range of mathematical problems. He also introduced technical terms that shaped the language of algebra. The word "algebra" itself comes from the Arabic word al-jabr, meaning "reunion of broken parts," referring to one of the operations he described for solving equations. By clarifying and naming these operations, Khwarizmi enabled the standardization of mathematical language, facilitating the transmission and teaching of these concepts in the Islamic world and later in Europe.

The structure of Khwarizmi's work also influenced how algebra was taught for centuries. His methodical approach, explaining step by step the resolution of equations and illustrating each method with concrete examples, served as a model for later algebra textbooks. This pedagogy, combining theory and practice, allowed students to understand and apply algebraic concepts effectively, contributing to the dissemination and adoption of algebra in the Islamic world and, later, in Europe.

The influence of Khwarizmi's work extended to how mathematics was perceived and practiced. Before him, mathematics was often seen as a branch of natural philosophy, closely linked to geometry and the study of proportions. By focusing on algebraic solutions, Khwarizmi paved the way for a more abstract form of mathematics, where relationships between numbers could be studied independently of geometric considerations. This abstraction allowed for the development of new theories and techniques that enriched the mathematical discipline as a whole.

Beyond algebra, Khwarizmi's work also structured the development of arithmetic in Europe, particularly through the introduction of Arabic numerals and the decimal numbering system. While these elements were originally developed in India, it was through Khwarizmi's works and those of other Islamic world scholars that these concepts were transmitted to the West. This arithmetic revolution not only facilitated calculations but also laid the groundwork for later algebraic developments by providing a numerical framework suited to equation manipulation. His book was translated into Latin in the 12th century under the title Algoritmi de numero Indorum, allowing his ideas to spread widely in Europe. This translation was a key factor in the revival of mathematics in Europe, marking the beginning of algebra as a central discipline in university education. European mathematicians of the Middle Ages and the Renaissance, such as Fibonacci and later Vieta, were strongly influenced by the concepts introduced by Khwarizmi, which they further developed and expanded, ultimately giving rise to modern algebra. To understand his role in the creation of the algorithm, it is essential to revisit his fundamental contributions to mathematics and algebra. His name, Latinized as Algoritmi, is the origin of the word "algorithm," which today refers to any sequence of instructions used to systematically solve a problem. Khwarizmi revolutionized mathematical thought by introducing precise and reproducible methods for solving complex calculations, particularly in algebra. His book, Kitab al-Mukhtasar fi Hisab al-Jabr wal-Muqabala, laid the foundation for modern algorithms by describing rigorous procedures for solving equations.

An algorithm is a finite sequence of steps that leads to a solution by following a structured and logical reasoning process. In mathematics, it often involves solving an equation or performing calculations in an ordered manner. One of Khwarizmi's most famous contributions is his algorithm for solving quadratic equations, based on the method of completing the square. This technique transforms a quadratic equation into a form that makes it easier to extract the unknown variable. Consider the equation $x^2 + 10x = 3$. Khwarizmi first takes half the coefficient of x, which is $10/2 = 5$, then squares it, obtaining $5^2 = 25$. He then adds this squared value to both sides of the equation, resulting in $x^2 + 10x + 25 = 39 + 25$, which simplifies to $(x + 5)^2 = 64$. Taking the square root of both sides, he finds $x + 5 = 8$, and by isolating x, he determines that $x = 3$. This step-by-step reasoning follows a structured process characteristic of a well-defined algorithm. Figure 2.7 illustrates this solution using the method of completing the square. This algorithmic principle, developed by Khwarizmi, extends far beyond mathematics. By structuring calculations into systematic rules, he laid the groundwork for modern numerical methods. His influence even extends to the fields of computer science and AI, where algorithms play a crucial role in optimizing calculations and processing large amounts of data. Khwarizmi's approach, based on rigor and logical sequencing, continues to shape modern sciences.

Starting equation: $X^2 + 10X = 39$

↓

Divide the coefficient of X by 2 and Square it: $5^2 = 25$

↓

Add this term to both sides: $X^2 + 10X + 25 = 64$

↓

Rewrite as a perfect square: $(X + 5)^2 = 64$

↓

Extract the square root: $X + 5 = 8$

↓

Find X: $X = 3$

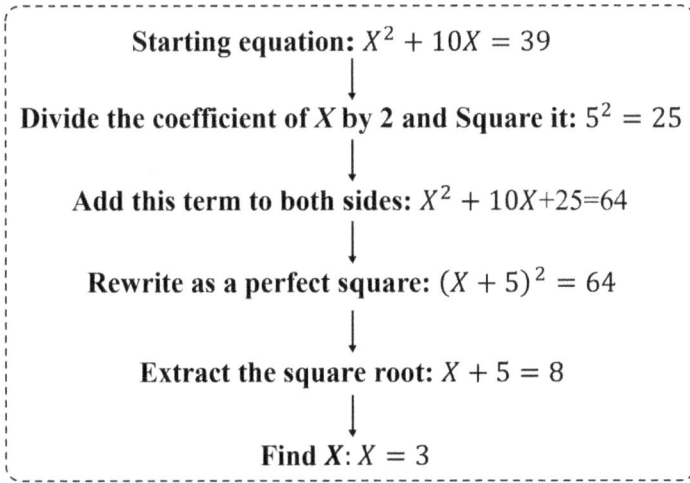

FIGURE 2.7   The algorithm for solving the equation $x^2 + 10x = 39$.

In addition to his technical contributions, he also influenced how mathematics was culturally perceived. By integrating algebra into the corpus of Islamic sciences, he contributed to the idea that mathematics was a powerful tool for solving practical problems, whether related to administration, commerce, or astronomy. This utilitarian vision of mathematics encouraged scholars to continue developing algebra and other branches of mathematics, seeking to apply them to an increasingly diverse range of fields. Khwarizmi's structuring of algebra had a lasting impact that is still felt today. The foundations he laid enabled the development of new branches of mathematics, such as abstract algebra and group theory, which have become key areas of modern mathematics. His methodology, combining logical rigor with pedagogical clarity, remains a model for mathematics education, and his influence continues to shape how we approach equation solving and algebraic symbol manipulation.

ii. Abu'l-Abbas Fadl ibn Hatim Nayrizi (865–922)

Abū ʿAbbās Fazl ibn Ḥātim Nairīzī, commonly known as Nayrizi, was a Persian mathematician and astronomer of the 9th century. He is best known for his commentaries on Euclid's *Elements*, a work that played a crucial role in the transmission of geometric knowledge in the Islamic world and, subsequently, in Europe. He wrote detailed commentaries on Books I–X of the *Elements*, clarifying Euclid's geometric concepts and theorems, making them more accessible to his contemporaries. His work on the *Elements* played a pivotal role not only in preserving Greek geometric knowledge but also in adapting and expanding it within the Islamic world. His commentaries became essential for understanding foundational geometric concepts and theorems, and were instrumental in making Euclid's geometry more accessible.

These contributions were eventually transmitted to medieval Europe through Latin translations, particularly by Gerard of Cremona in the 12th century. Nayrizi's insights thus significantly influenced the revival of mathematics in Europe at the end of the Middle Ages.

Among his most remarkable contributions is his critical engagement with Euclid's fifth postulate, also known as the parallel postulate. Unlike the other postulates, this one was considered less intuitive. In modern form, it states: If a straight line intersects two other lines and the sum of the interior angles on the same side is less than 180°, then the two lines, if extended indefinitely, will meet on that side. Many mathematicians, including Nayrizi, attempted to derive this postulate from the others or propose equivalent formulations.

Nayrizi reformulated the postulate using the concept of equidistance. He defined two lines as parallel if the perpendicular distance between them remains constant. Using modern notation, if we consider two lines AB and CD, and a perpendicular EF such that for every point $x \in AB$, the distance $d(x, CD) =$ constant, then $AB \parallel CD$. This idea forms the basis for our current understanding of parallel lines in terms of constant separation. He illustrated this concept with practical geometric examples. For instance, let a line EZ be perpendicular to both AB and GD. If $EZ \perp AB$ and $EZ \perp GD$, then, according to Nayrizi, $AB \parallel GD$. He formalized this result as a proposition: "If the same line is perpendicular to two other lines in the same plane, then those two lines are parallel." While seemingly obvious today, this was a significant conceptual innovation at the time. He also proposed alternative criteria for parallelism based on the angles formed by a transversal. One such criterion states that if a line ttt intersects two lines AB and CD, and creates equal alternate interior angles (e.g., $\angle ABC = \angle DCE$), then $AB \parallel CD$. This criterion, now standard in geometry, was originally treated by *Nayrizi* as a theorem intended to replace or support the fifth postulate. He went further to show that if the sum of the interior angles on the same side of a transversal is exactly two right angles (i.e., $\angle A + \angle B = 180°$), then the lines are parallel. This approach reverses Euclid's original assumption: instead of assuming that less than 180° implies intersection, he claimed that equal to 180° implies no intersection, hence, parallelism.

To strengthen these arguments, Nayrizi frequently used reductio ad absurdum. He would assume that two lines are equidistant, then construct multiple perpendiculars between them. If the lines were not parallel, those perpendiculars would produce inconsistent distances (e.g., $d_1 \neq d_2$), violating the definition of equidistance, and thus leading to contradiction. He also implicitly formulated what would later be known as Playfair's axiom: Given a point A not on a line d, there exists exactly one line d' through A that is parallel to d. Though formalized much later, this concept appears clearly in Nayrizi's thought and illustrates his deep engagement with the logical structure of Euclidean geometry.

Nayrizi did not limit himself to two-dimensional geometry. He applied his geometric understanding to spatial (3D) interpretations as well. For example, he explained that in a rectangular parallelepiped (a 3D box), opposite faces are bounded by parallel lines because they maintain constant separation and never intersect, offering a concrete physical sense of what it means for lines to be parallel in space. He referenced Greek philosophers such as Simplicius but improved upon their arguments with greater logical clarity. He pointed out missing assumptions in prior demonstrations and laid the groundwork for a more rigorous, axiomatic method, prefiguring developments that would only emerge in modern mathematics centuries later. He also emphasized that all attempts to prove the fifth postulate from the others essentially restate it in another form, suggesting an early awareness of its logical independence. This idea anticipated the revolutionary insights of Lobachevsky and Bolyai in the 19th century, who formally established the validity of non-Euclidean geometries.

Beyond his work on geometry, Nayrizi also made important contributions to astronomy. He authored treatises on the astrolabe, describing its construction, use, and applications in celestial calculations. His explanations helped refine the instrument and enhance the accuracy of astronomical observations, making it a vital tool for medieval astronomers. Though not as well-known in this domain as Biruni or Tusi, Nayrizi helped integrate Euclidean geometry with early trigonometric methods to solve astronomical problems more efficiently, thus participating in the early development of analytical techniques. Ultimately, he stands as a remarkable figure in the history of science. As a mathematician, commentator, and innovator, he exemplifies the Iranian scholarly tradition's depth and intellectual rigor. His work on parallel lines, the fifth postulate, and Euclidean geometry paved the way for future discoveries and helped sustain the continuity of mathematical thought from antiquity to modernity.

iii. Razi (865–925)

Abu Bakr Muhammad ibn Zakariya Razi was a prominent Persian physician, chemist, and philosopher, born in Rey, Iran. Known for his advancements in medicine and chemistry, he profoundly influenced science during the Middle Ages. One of his major contributions was the compilation of Kitab al-Hawi, a medical encyclopedia that gathered the knowledge of his time. His work in chemistry, particularly on substances and distillation processes, earned him recognition as a pioneer in pharmaceutical production and drug research. He also made notable discoveries in the preparation of acids and bases. However, his impact extends far beyond medicine and chemistry, with significant contributions to mathematics, particularly in the fields of logic and reasoning.

Although Razi is not often cited among the great mathematicians of his time, he played a crucial role in developing scientific methods and mathematical reasoning. His work on logic, methodology, and demonstration helped structure the scientific approach in natural and experimental sciences. He proposed rigorous methods for studying scientific phenomena and emphasized the importance of experimentation and systematic observation that are fundamental to modern scientific methodology. His logic, though influenced by Greek philosophy, was innovative in its focus on practical and verifiable reasoning, a fundamental principle in mathematics and science in general.

In mathematics, Razi used arithmetic and algebraic concepts in his research. Although he did not leave behind works directly related to complex mathematical theories, he actively contributed to the evolution of mathematical thought through his philosophical writings. His methodical approach and rigorous logic refined the way mathematics was applied in experimental sciences. For example, his reflections on the classification of natural phenomena contributed to the advancement of applied mathematics, particularly in geometry and astronomy, where he integrated mathematical principles to better understand the laws of nature. Razi's legacy endures through his influence on subsequent generations of scientists and mathematicians. His ability to integrate mathematics into his practical research, combined with his emphasis on empirical methods, paved the way for advancements in fields as diverse as medicine, chemistry, and natural sciences. While his name is primarily associated with medicine, his impact on scientific methodology and his indirect contributions to mathematics marked a turning point in the history of science, with his principles continuing to resonate in modern scientific approaches.

iv. Farabi (872–950)

Abu Nasr Muhammad ibn Muhammad Farabi, known as the Second Master after Aristotle, was a Persian philosopher, logician, and mathematician. Born in Farab, he is often regarded as one of the greatest philosophers of the Islamic world. While his contributions to mathematics are less well-known, they are nonetheless significant, particularly in the fields of logic and music theory. Farabi used mathematics as a tool to understand other sciences, especially logic and music. He studied proportions and musical intervals, linking these concepts to mathematical principles. In his book Kitab al-Musiqa al-Kabir, he demonstrated how musical dimensions could be described using numerical ratios. For example, he showed that certain musical intervals, such as the octave, perfect fifth, and perfect fourth, could be expressed through simple ratios of natural numbers:

$$\text{Octave} = \frac{2}{1}, \text{Perfect Fifth} = \frac{3}{2}, \text{Perfect Fourth} = \frac{4}{3}$$

These ratios explain why some musical intervals sound more harmonious. He also analyzed the relationship between the length of a vibrating string and the frequency of the produced sound, expressed based on Equation (2.1):

$$f = \frac{v}{2L} \tag{2.1}$$

where f is the produced frequency, v is the wave velocity in the string, and L is the length of the vibrating string.

Farabi also wrote extensively on logic, a field in which he sought to apply mathematical methods to clarify reasoning processes. He was among the first to attempt to formalize Aristotle's logic in mathematical terms, contributing to the evolution of logic as a more structured and rigorous discipline. He explored probability concepts and syllogistic reasoning, showing how quantitative rules could be used to analyze the validity of logical arguments. For instance, if the probability of an event A occurring is $P(A)$, and the probability of event B occurring given that A has occurred is $P(B \mid A)$ then the probability of both events occurring simultaneously is given by Equation (2.2):

$$P(A \cap B) = P(A) \cdot P(B \mid A) \tag{2.2}$$

This formula demonstrates how mathematical principles can be used to assess the correctness of logical reasoning. In fact, Farabi's efforts in this field significantly influenced the development of mathematical logic and reasoning theories in both Islamic philosophy and Western thought.

In addition to his work in logic and music, Farabi wrote about more directly mathematical topics, though his contributions in this area are often underestimated compared to his philosophical works. Nevertheless, he demonstrated a deep understanding of mathematics, which he regarded as an essential tool for comprehending both the physical world and abstract concepts. His view of mathematics as a fundamental science necessary for all other disciplines had a lasting impact on how mathematics was perceived in the Islamic world. Farabi's legacy extends far beyond his mathematical contributions. As a philosopher, he laid the foundations of Islamic philosophy, and his influence has endured throughout history. However, his work in mathematics, particularly in applying mathematical principles to logic and music, shows that he viewed mathematics as a central discipline in the pursuit of knowledge. This perspective shaped scholars of the Islamic world and had lasting repercussions on the development of science in general.

v. Mahani (820–880)

Abu-Abdullah Muhammad ibn Īsa Mahani, a Persian mathematician and astronomer, was born in Mahan, in the Kerman province, and passed away in Baghdad. His work marked a significant milestone in the history of Islamic sciences and their influence on the later development of mathematics in Europe.

He conducted precise observations in astronomy using an astrolabe from Baghdad, studying lunar and solar eclipses as well as planetary conjunctions. These studies, carried out between 854 and 866, were later utilized by Ibn Yunus in his famous Al-Zij al-Kabîr al-Hâkimi, contributing to the refinement of astronomical tables of the time. In mathematics, Mahani distinguished himself through his contributions to geometry and algebra. He commented on several books of Euclid's *Elements*, exploring concepts such as quadratic equations and irrational numbers, and studied complex problems like the duplication of the cube. He is best known for his work on a problem posed by Archimedes, which involved dividing a sphere into two parts of given volumes. This led him to formulate a cubic equation ($x^3 + c^2b = cx^2$), known as Mahani's equation. Although he did not find a complete solution, his work paved the way for further research on cubic equations by scholars such as Omar Khayyam. Additionally, Mahani contributed to the transmission of Greek knowledge by improving Ishaq ibn Hunayn's translation of The Spherics by Menelaus of Alexandria, a key text on spherical trigonometry. He also wrote original treatises, including works on azimuth and mathematical ratios, demonstrating his interest in both theoretical and practical problems. The impact of his work, combining innovation and rigor, made him a central figure in medieval Islamic science, laying the groundwork for major advances in mathematics and astronomy.

vi. Abu Sahl Wajjan ibn Rustam Quhi (940–1000)

Abu Sahl Wajjan ibn Rustam Quhi, also known as Abu Sahl Kuhi, was a prominent Persian mathematician and astronomer of the 10th century. He is particularly recognized for his work in geometry, where he tackled complex problems related to conic sections and geometric constructions. Kuhi explored topics such as angle trisection, the duplication of the cube, and the geometric construction of conics, following in the tradition of Greek mathematicians like Apollonius of Perga.

One of Kuhi's notable achievements is his method for constructing a parabola using purely geometric techniques, without relying on algebraic equations. This work demonstrates his mastery of advanced geometric concepts and his ability to extend classical Greek geometry methods. His research on conic sections also contributed to a better understanding of these curves and their applications in both geometric and astronomical contexts. In addition to his contributions to geometry, he was also a skilled astronomer who worked on the design and improvement of astronomical instruments. He wrote about the use and construction of the astrolabe, an essential instrument for observing stars and planets. Notably, Kuhi enhanced the stereographic projection, a method used in the construction of the astrolabe, which increased the accuracy of astronomical observations. Kuhi also made contributions to spherical trigonometry, which is crucial for astronomy. He explored the relationships between the angles and sides of spherical triangles, which are used to calculate the positions of stars and planets on the celestial sphere. Kuhi developed a mathematically rigorous method to determine the distance between a meteorite and the Earth's center. In this method, he proposed that two observers, located in two distant cities, should record the meteor's trajectory at the exact moment it appears and disappears. To ensure accuracy, the locations of these observers needed to be precisely known in terms of latitude, longitude, and azimuth. Each observer noted the apparent path of the meteor in the sky, the angle of elevation at the start and end of its visibility, and the exact time of appearance and disappearance. By combining these independent observations, it was possible to trace the two lines of sight and determine the meteor's actual position in space by their intersection. His work in trigonometry not only helped refine astronomical calculation methods but also laid the groundwork for future developments in mathematics and astronomy.

His legacy is evident in his contributions to geometry and astronomy, which had a lasting impact on the development of these disciplines in the Islamic world. His work influenced later scholars, and his geometric approach to mathematical problems served as a model for future generations. He exemplifies how Persian mathematicians not only preserved classical knowledge but also enriched and expanded it, paving the way for new scientific discoveries.

vii. Kushyar Gilani (971–1029)

Kushyar ibn Labban Gilani, originally from the region of Gilan in Iran, was a distinguished mathematician, astronomer, and geographer whose work represents a crucial chapter in the development of mathematical and astronomical sciences during the Islamic Golden Age. His influence extended across generations, impacting both the Islamic world and later European scholars.

His major work, titled al-Zij al-Jami wa al-Baligh ("The Comprehensive and Refined Astronomical Tables"), served as a comprehensive synthesis of Greek and Indian astronomical traditions, meticulously corrected and extended. In this treatise, he presented detailed astronomical tables to facilitate calculations of planetary positions, eclipses, and the timing of celestial risings and settings. He also addressed the computation of the qibla direction and prayer times, thus linking theoretical astronomy with practical religious observance.

Gilani was also a pioneer in adopting and promoting the Indian numeral system. In his treatise Kitab fi Usul Hisab al-Hind (The Book on the Principles of Indian Arithmetic), he elaborated the decimal positional system using the digits 1–9 and the concept of zero. He clearly explained the rules for the fundamental arithmetic operations (addition, subtraction, multiplication, and division) as well as more advanced procedures like the extraction of square and cube roots. His explanation of the square root algorithm, inspired by Babylonian methods, is especially noteworthy:

This iterative formula for approximating the square root of a number is an early precursor to modern numerical analysis and is still studied today.

His arithmetic work is pedagogically exceptional for its clarity and methodological precision. He presented practical examples using step-by-step decompositions that helped popularize positional arithmetic across the Islamic world. This approach showcased the power and simplicity of the decimal system, allowing more efficient computations and making arithmetic more accessible to scholars and merchants alike. In astronomy, his tables were not only theoretical instruments but also practical tools for daily religious life, as they were used to determine the direction of Mecca (qibla) and the precise times for daily prayers. His application of spherical astronomy and geometric methods enabled these calculations with increased accuracy, which further underlines the functional integration of science and faith in the Islamic intellectual tradition.

Gilani was also one of the early teachers of the renowned polymath Avicenna (Ibn Sina), which further attests to his stature and influence in the scholarly world. His style of writing was logical, structured, and accessible, indicating a deep concern for clarity in the transmission of knowledge. Moreover, his methodical and analytical approach helped transition the heritage of Indian and Greek mathematics into a distinctly Islamic framework. He did not merely transmit earlier knowledge but actively reorganized and expanded it, setting the stage for further advancements in algebra, trigonometry, and astronomical modeling. His works were eventually translated into Latin and contributed to the corpus of knowledge that would later fuel the scientific developments of the European Renaissance. His emphasis on numerical procedures, positional notation, and geometric logic planted seeds that would later grow into the foundations of algorithmic thinking and mathematical abstraction. Through his efforts, he played a pivotal role at the crossroads of ancient and modern science. His legacy is one of precision, synthesis, and innovation, making him a foundational figure in the historical evolution of science and mathematics across civilizations.

viii. Abū Rayḥān Birūni (973–1048)

Abū Rayḥān Birūni was a brilliant Iranian scholar, born in the region of Khwarazm, now part of modern-day Uzbekistan or Turkmenistan but historically within the Persian cultural and scientific sphere. He is widely regarded as one of the most distinguished and versatile intellectuals of the Islamic Golden Age. A true polymath, Birūni's contributions extended far beyond mathematics, reaching into astronomy, physics, geography, philosophy, history, pharmacology, and linguistics. Deeply rooted in the intellectual traditions of Persia, he approached knowledge not merely as a body of facts to be preserved but as a dynamic and interconnected domain to be rigorously questioned, tested, and expanded. His interdisciplinary mindset and empirical method influenced generations of scholars both in the Islamic world and beyond.

In mathematics, Birūni made foundational contributions, particularly in trigonometry, which he helped establish as an independent scientific discipline rather than just a tool for astronomy. He systematically used all six trigonometric functions, sine, cosine, tangent, cotangent, secant, and cosecant, and compiled highly accurate tables that served both theoretical and practical purposes. He introduced the concept of the radius in trigonometric calculations, simplifying computations and laying the groundwork for modern trigonometric methods. His work extended into spherical trigonometry, crucial for solving astronomical and geographical problems. One of the key formulas he applied in spherical triangle calculations was the spherical law of sines:

One of the key formulas he used in spherical triangle calculations is the spherical law of sines, as shown by Equation (2.3):

$$\frac{\sin(a)}{\sin(A)} = \frac{\sin(b)}{\sin(B)} = \frac{\sin(c)}{\sin(C)} \tag{2.3}$$

where a, b, c are the arc lengths (sides) of the spherical triangle and A, B, C the corresponding angles.

This identity allowed him to determine the positions of stars, calculate geographic coordinates, and solve other complex problems on a spherical surface.

Birūni's contributions to geodesy, the science of measuring the Earth, were particularly groundbreaking. One of his most celebrated accomplishments was the calculation of the Earth's radius and circumference using a geometric and trigonometric method that did not require traveling long distances. He climbed a mountain and measured its height h, along with the angle of depression θ from the summit to the horizon. Using these two quantities, he derived Equation (2.4) to estimate the Earth's radius:

$$R = \frac{h}{1 - \cos(\theta)} \tag{2.4}$$

This method, both elegant and practical, revealed his ability to apply theoretical geometry to real-world measurements. His result, approximately 6339.6 km, was astonishingly close to the modern value of 6371 km, a remarkable achievement given the limited tools available in the 11th century. In his geographic studies, Birūni also addressed the problem of calculating distances between cities using latitude and longitude. He applied spherical trigonometry to derive Equation (2.5) for the angular distance D between two locations on a sphere:

$$\cos(D) = \sin(\varnothing_1)\sin(\varnothing_2) + \cos(\varnothing_1)\cos(\varnothing_2)\cos(\Delta\lambda) \tag{2.5}$$

where ϕ_1 and ϕ_2 are the latitudes of the two locations, and $\Delta\lambda$ is the difference in their longitudes.

This formula allowed him to compute distances with a level of mathematical sophistication that would not be matched again until the modern era of global navigation and geospatial science. He also excelled in numerical analysis by using interpolation techniques to estimate values between known data points. This approach was essential for constructing detailed astronomical and trigonometric tables. One of the most basic yet powerful tools he employed was linear interpolation, expressed based on Equation (2.6):

$$f(x) \approx f(x_0) + \frac{f(x_1) - f(x_0)}{x_1 - x_0} \cdot (x - x_0) \tag{2.6}$$

This method enabled him to achieve a high degree of precision in his calculations and made his tables indispensable tools for scholars of his time.

Beyond mathematics, Birūni was a pioneering astronomer who conducted meticulous observations and calculations of celestial phenomena. He measured the obliquity of the ecliptic, studied the apparent motion of the Sun, tracked planetary positions, and charted the lunar phases with remarkable accuracy. He even discussed the possibility of the Earth's rotation on its axis—an idea far ahead of his time. His treatises compiled and critiqued knowledge from Greek, Indian, and Persian sources, while also proposing original insights. He developed and improved astronomical instruments such as the astrolabe and the armillary sphere, and emphasized the role of empirical observation in validating theoretical models of the cosmos. In geography, he revolutionized the measurement of time zones, latitudes, and longitudes. He collected data on the coordinates of hundreds of cities, analyzed the Earth's surface, and studied climate zones, mountains, and rivers with a detail that foreshadowed modern physical geography. He also addressed religious and practical questions, such as calculating the correct qibla (direction of prayer) and prayer times based on local solar time. His work in physics was equally impressive as he conducted studies on mechanics, hydrostatics, optics, and thermodynamics. He measured the specific weights of various substances and explained physical phenomena like tides, winds, and the formation of mountains through observation and logical reasoning. He explored the behavior of sound and light, including their speed, reflection, and refraction. In pharmacology and mineralogy, he compiled an encyclopedic collection of knowledge on the properties, classifications, and applications of hundreds of natural substances. He categorized minerals by physical attributes such as color, hardness, and density and provided detailed descriptions of their uses in medicine and industry. His scientific methodology in this domain anticipated Renaissance taxonomic practices.

He was also a respected historian and cultural scholar. In his renowned work *Kitāb al-Hind* (meaning *The Book of India*), he documented Indian philosophy, religion, astronomy, and mathematics with a remarkable level of objectivity and respect. Unlike many of his contemporaries, he approached foreign knowledge not with superiority or prejudice, but with a desire to understand and compare systems of thought. This cross-cultural intellectual engagement is one of the hallmarks of his legacy. Fluent in Persian, Arabic, Sanskrit, and Greek, he acted as a bridge between civilizations. He translated numerous Sanskrit texts into Arabic and Persian, critically evaluated them, and integrated their insights into broader scientific discourse. His linguistic capabilities were not merely tools for communication, but the instruments of comparative analysis and knowledge synthesis. He believed that truth could emerge from any culture and that rational inquiry was universal.

Birūni's unwavering commitment to observation, verification, and reason made him a pioneer of the empirical method, centuries before the formalization of the scientific method in Europe. He questioned established ideas, proposed alternative explanations based on evidence, and refused to accept claims without testing them. His ability to combine clarity of thought with scientific precision and his conviction that mathematics and logic were keys to unlocking the mysteries of the natural world mark him as one of the greatest minds in the history of science. His legacy is not confined to any one discipline or region. Through his vast and rigorous body of work, Birūni demonstrated that knowledge is a universal endeavor, one that transcends borders and epochs. His life and writings remain a timeless reminder that science flourishes not through dogma but through curiosity, humility, and reason.

ix. Abū ʿAlī Ḥusayn ibn ʿAbd Allāh ibn Sīnā (980–1037)

Abū ʿAlī Ḥusayn ibn ʿAbd Allāh ibn Sīnā, known in the West as Avicenna, was a renowned Iranian polymath, born in 980 in Afshana, near Bukhara (in present-day Uzbekistan), and he died in 1037 in Hamadan, Iran. He is recognized as one of the most influential scholars in the history of science and philosophy. From a very young age, Avicenna demonstrated an extraordinary aptitude for learning. He began his education early and rapidly progressed through studies in logic, mathematics, astronomy, philosophy, and medicine, eventually mastering all the major fields of knowledge of his time before reaching adulthood. He lived in a flourishing intellectual period where Persian, Greek, and Indian scientific traditions were actively translated, synthesized, and advanced within the Islamic world. By the age of 17, he had already gained a reputation as a brilliant physician after successfully treating the Samanid ruler of Bukhara. As a result, he was granted access to the royal library, which was one of the richest in the region, providing him with the resources needed to begin composing his first significant works.

Avicenna is credited with authoring around 250 works across various fields. Two of his most influential books are *The Book of Healing* (*Kitāb al-Shifā*), a vast philosophical and scientific encyclopedia, and *The Canon of Medicine* (*al-Qānūn fī al-Ṭibb*), a monumental medical text that remained a central reference in European universities until the 17th century. These texts are testaments to his ability to bridge theoretical knowledge and practical application.

In *The Canon of Medicine*, Avicenna established a systematic approach to diagnosing and treating diseases. He refined and expanded upon the works of earlier physicians such as Galen and Hippocrates, integrating them with his own observations. He provided accurate descriptions of diseases such as diabetes, linking symptoms like sweet urine to kidney dysfunction, and emphasized empirical evidence in the diagnostic process. He also pioneered aspects of mental health, offering early forms of classification for psychological disorders. His approach combined physiological, psychological, and ethical treatments. In his work on fevers, for example, he proposed a typology based on the pattern and periodicity of temperature fluctuations, identifying continuous, intermittent, and tertian fevers with remarkable precision for his time. He developed a quantitative perspective in pharmacology, analyzing drugs by their qualities, potency, and dosage. He introduced Equation (2.7) to model the therapeutic impact of a substance:

$$\text{Total Effect} = \text{Quality} \times \text{Potency Degree} \times \text{Dosage} \qquad (2.7)$$

This early attempt at quantifying medical outcomes highlights his inclination toward mathematical reasoning even in biological contexts. He also made important contributions to mathematics, which he viewed as essential for scientific and philosophical reasoning. In *The Book of Healing*, he presented mathematics as comprising four core branches: arithmetic, geometry, astronomy, and music. For him, these disciplines formed the foundation of rational thought and scientific inquiry. In arithmetic, he examined the nature of numbers and numerical relationships. He discussed perfect numbers, such as 28, whose proper divisors (1, 2, 4, 7, and 14) sum to the number itself ($1 + 2 + 4 + 7 + 14 = 28$). He viewed such numerical harmony as a reflection of deeper cosmic order and philosophical significance.

In geometry, Avicenna adopted and expanded on Euclidean concepts, applying them to philosophical and metaphysical contexts. He explored continuity, the infinite divisibility of space, and the structure of geometric entities. He explained that a line consisting of an infinite number of points could be expressed based on Equation (2.8):

$$\text{Line} = \lim_{n \to \infty} \sum_{i=1}^{n} \text{Point}_i \qquad (2.8)$$

This intuition, while not formalized in modern terms, reveals his deep engagement with the foundations of space and geometry.

In astronomy, he proposed modifications to the Ptolemaic model to address observed irregularities in planetary motion. Though he maintained a geocentric worldview, he introduced intermediate spheres to correct inconsistencies, laying conceptual groundwork later taken up by Islamic astronomers like *Tusi*. He also analyzed music mathematically, following the Pythagorean tradition. He described musical intervals using numerical ratios, as presented previously. This musical theory reflected his broader vision of mathematics as the language of harmony, order, and metaphysical truth. Mathematics was more than a technical discipline for him, and it was a gateway to certainty. He believed that the demonstrative power of mathematics trained the intellect to reach metaphysical understanding. He famously stated that mathematical clarity leads the mind toward philosophical truth, reinforcing its importance in education and inquiry.

In logic, which he considered a branch of mathematics, he developed an advanced system of syllogisms. He created rigorous classifications of deductive reasoning. For example, the classical syllogism "All men are mortal; Socrates is a man; therefore Socrates is mortal" can be represented based on Equation (2.9):

$$\forall x \in \text{Humans, Mortal}(x) \rightarrow \text{Mortal}(\text{Socrates}) \qquad (2.9)$$

His approach to knowledge was holistic. He rejected the compartmentalization of disciplines and saw medicine, mathematics, logic, and astronomy as interconnected parts of a unified intellectual framework. To him, each science illuminated the others, and together they revealed the rational structure of the universe. His works were translated into Latin and studied in medieval European universities. *The Canon of Medicine* became a medical textbook in centers like Montpellier and Padua, while his writings on logic and metaphysics deeply influenced Scholastic philosophers such as Thomas Aquinas and Albertus Magnus. He continued to write, teach, and practice medicine until his death in 1037. His intellectual legacy shaped both the Islamic East and the Christian West for centuries. He is remembered not only as a physician but also as a mathematician, astronomer, philosopher, and logician.

x. Omar Khayyam (1048–1131)

Omar Khayyam is primarily known in the West for his poetry, but he was first and foremost a distinguished mathematician and astronomer. Born in Nishapur, Iran, Khayyam worked on various aspects of mathematics, making significant contributions to algebra. He is particularly famous for his classification of cubic equations and for developing geometric methods to solve them. Indeed, in this period, the increasing number of problems that resulted in cubic equations highlighted the growing necessity of finding general solutions for their roots. Given this necessity, Omar Khayyam's contributions gained special significance. He sought to categorize cubic equations and provide a comprehensive method for solving them. Although the roots of these equations were found through geometric solutions, and despite the fact that Khayyam was unable to develop an algebraic or numerical solution for them, he firmly believed that in the future, others would succeed in doing so.

It is no exaggeration to say that Khayyam's valuable contributions to mathematics played a fundamental role in the advancement of this field, particularly in the 19th century. His book on algebra, titled Treatises on Algebra and Muqabala, is an invaluable work that has had a significant impact on the evolution of this discipline. In this book, he systematically categorizes and classifies equations, including cubic equations, and provides methods for finding their roots. To solve a cubic equation, Khayyam transformed it into a homogeneous equation. For instance, to solve the equation $x^3 + ax = b$, he first rewrote it as $x^3 + p^2x = p^2q$. He then used two quadratic equations as $x^2 + y^2 = qx$ and $x^2 = py$ to find the root. Then, by plotting these two curves (as shown in Figure 2.8), he identified their intersection point, D. He then rigorously demonstrated that the x-coordinate of point D is the root of the given cubic equation.

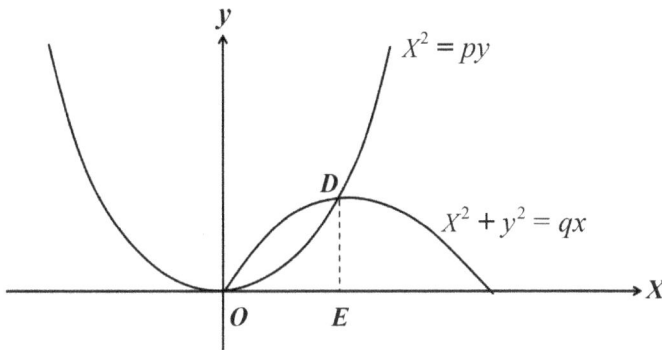

FIGURE 2.8   Geometric solution of the equation $x^3 + p^2x = p^2q$.

Khayyam also made important contributions to the theory of parallels. In another of his works, he critiqued Euclid's fifth postulate (the parallel postulate) and explored alternatives, thus anticipating certain aspects of non-Euclidean geometry. Although his attempts to prove the parallel postulate were not entirely successful, his ideas laid the groundwork for later developments in this field, which would only be fully realized several centuries later.

In addition to his work in algebra and geometry, Khayyam also made significant contributions to astronomy. In 1079, under the direction of the Seljuk Sultan Malik Shah, he participated in the reform of the Persian calendar, creating the Jalali calendar, renowned for its accuracy. This calendar, which corrected some of the flaws of the Julian calendar, is still used in Iran today in a slightly modified form, known as the Persian calendar. Khayyam was also a respected philosopher and physician. His approach to mathematics and science was deeply influenced by his philosophical worldview, which combined rationality with mysticism. This perspective allowed him to develop a rigorous method of inquiry while maintaining an open-mindedness that led him to question the foundations of the science of his time. Despite his major scientific contributions, Khayyam was long better known for his poetry, particularly

The Rubaiyat, which was popularized in the West by Edward FitzGerald's 19th-century translation. However, modern scholars increasingly recognize his role as a mathematician and scientist, rediscovering the breadth of his work and its lasting impact on mathematics and astronomy.

xi. Nasir al-Din Tusi (1201–1274)

Nasir al-Din Tusi, born in 1201 in Tus, in present-day Iran, was one of the greatest scholars of the Islamic Golden Age. Despite living during the turbulent period of the Mongol invasions, he left a deep mark on intellectual history through major contributions in astronomy, mathematics, philosophy, and the natural sciences. With the support of Hulegu, grandson of Genghis Khan, Tusi founded the Maragha Observatory in 1259, which soon became one of the most advanced centers for scientific research of the medieval world. The observatory, equipped with an immense library, enabled Tusi to gather, translate, and develop knowledge drawn from Greek, Indian, and Islamic traditions.

Tusi's work in trigonometry represents one of his most fundamental contributions. Prior to his efforts, trigonometry was not considered an independent discipline; it was seen merely as a tool for astronomy. Tusi was the first to treat it as a distinct branch of mathematics. In his treatise on plane and spherical figures, he defined the six basic trigonometric functions: sine, cosine, tangent, cotangent, secant, and cosecant. He explored their properties and relationships in both plane and spherical geometry. One of his most famous achievements was the formulation of the spherical law of cosines as presented in Equation (2.10):

$$\cos(c) = \cos(a) \cdot \cos(b) \cdot + \sin(a) \cdot \sin(b) \cdot \cos(C) \qquad (2.10)$$

where a, b, and c denote the lengths of the arcs (i.e., sides) of the spherical triangle, and C is the angle at vertex C, opposite side c.

This relation is essential for navigation, astronomy, and the study of curved surfaces. It applies in contexts where space is not flat, such as on Earth's surface or the celestial sphere. At Maragha, Tusi led a team of scholars who made precise astronomical observations and compiled the Ilkhanic Tables. These tables corrected many errors in earlier astronomical models and served as a reference for centuries. They even influenced the later work of European astronomers, including Copernicus. Tusi's geometrical precision and observational rigor laid the foundations that would reverberate through the development of heliocentric theories in the Renaissance.

Tusi also made significant contributions to algebra, building upon and transforming the work of Khwarizmi. While he focused on solving quadratic equations using geometric methods, Tusi began to move toward a more abstract and symbolic approach. He classified second-degree equations based on their structure, such as $ax^2 = bx$, $ax^2 = c$, and $ax^2 + bx = c$. He solved them systematically using methods that can be seen as precursors to modern algebraic techniques. Although he still regarded negative roots as having no physical reality, as was common at the time, his generalizations hinted at a deeper algebraic understanding. His work helped algebra evolve from a collection of procedural techniques into a logically structured science.

In geometry, Tusi wrote an important commentary on Euclid's *Elements*, in which he clarified and expanded upon classical geometric theories. His critique of Euclid's fifth postulate aligns with the ideas of other medieval mathematicians like Khayyam. He also explored regular polygons and polyhedra, thereby extending the reach of Euclidean geometry. These explorations were not just mathematical but also philosophical, reflecting his training as a theologian and philosopher. He often linked mathematical reasoning to metaphysical and ethical reflections, embodying the integrated view of knowledge characteristic of the Islamic intellectual tradition. Perhaps one of his most original inventions was the Tusi Couple, a geometric mechanism that transforms two circular motions into a linear oscillation. Designed to address flaws in the Ptolemaic model while preserving the circular nature of celestial motion, the Tusi Couple consists of a smaller circle of radius r rotating inside a larger circle of radius *2r*. A point on the circumference of the smaller circle traces a straight line along a diameter of the larger circle. Equations (2.11)–(2.14) describing the motion of this point are:

$$x(t) = R \cos(t) - r \cos(2t) \tag{2.11}$$

$$y(t) = R \sin(t) - r \sin(2t) \tag{2.12}$$

Setting $R = 2r$, we obtain:

$$x(t) = r(2\cos(t) - \cos(2t)) \tag{2.13}$$

$$y(t) = r(2\sin(t) - \sin(2t)) \tag{2.14}$$

This motion results in an exact linear oscillation, and this model was later used by Copernicus in his heliocentric theory. The Tusi Couple exemplifies Tusi's ability to merge geometric rigor with physical insight and creative innovation. Tusi's influence extended beyond the Islamic world. His treatises were translated into Latin and reached European scholars during the Renaissance. His work in trigonometry, algebra, and astronomy contributed to solving practical problems in navigation, geography, and timekeeping. He demonstrated that, even in a politically unstable era, the pursuit of science could flourish and provide the foundation for future discovery.

The enduring legacy of Tusi lies in his capacity to formalize and abstract mathematical reasoning. His integration of geometry, algebra, and astronomy paved the way for a deeper understanding of natural phenomena. This synthesis of disciplines contributed to the long-term evolution of mathematics from its ancient roots to its modern forms. Through his innovations, he helped bridge the gap between ancient Greek theories and the scientific advancements of Renaissance Europe.

Tusi's work also reflects a broader movement in intellectual history, formalization, and systematization of thought. These developments laid the groundwork for later advances in logic, computation, and ultimately AI. By organizing algebra into a coherent structure, defining trigonometric relationships with precision, and modeling complex motion using geometry, Tusi contributed to a tradition of reasoning that could be encoded into symbolic systems.

This process of transforming intuition into symbolic logic is at the heart of AI. The mathematical tools used today in AI-algebraic structures, logical inference, and algorithmic manipulation owe much to centuries of development beginning with thinkers like Tusi. His legacy, passed through the hands of Renaissance scholars and Enlightenment thinkers, quietly shaped the foundations of modern computation and reasoning systems. As such, Tusi's contributions represent more than scientific achievements. They mark a pivotal moment in the intellectual journey from observing the cosmos to modeling the mind. His work embodies a continuity in human thought that connects the study of stars to the architecture of algorithms, and the exploration of numbers to the design of machines capable of learning. In this light, Tusi is not only a towering figure of medieval science but also a distant forerunner of the modern digital age. His holistic vision, rigorous logic, and inventive spirit continue to inspire, reminding us that every breakthrough in AI rests on the shoulders of centuries of cumulative insight, and among those shoulders, Tusi stands firm.

xii. Kashi (1380–1429)

Ghiyath al-Din Jamshid Mas'ud Kashi, often simply called Kashi, was a Persian mathematician and astronomer of the late Middle Ages. Born in Iran, Kashi is best known for his work on decimal fractions and his highly precise calculation of π (*pi*). He managed to calculate π with an accuracy of up to 16 decimal places, long before modern numerical computation methods were developed. This achievement was crucial for the evolution of numerical analysis, a fundamental branch of modern mathematics. He also wrote several works on arithmetic and astronomy, the most famous being *The Key to Arithmetic* (*Miftah al-Hisab*). In this book, he laid the foundations for decimal computation and introduced methods for performing calculations with high precision. This treatise had a lasting influence on mathematics in Persia and beyond, particularly by facilitating the complex calculations required for astronomy and architecture.

In astronomy, Kashi contributed to improving astronomical tables and designing more precise astronomical instruments. He worked at the Samarkand Observatory, founded by Ulugh Beg, where he collaborated with other scholars to refine astronomical models and calculations needed to predict the positions of planets and stars. His work at Samarkand helped correct errors in previous astronomical tables and significantly improved the accuracy of astronomical observations. Kashi also worked on solving algebraic equations, particularly cubic and quartic equations. His methods, which combined geometric and algebraic approaches, laid the groundwork for future developments in algebra and analysis. Although his work on equations was not as widely disseminated as his contributions to arithmetic and astronomy, it demonstrates his deep understanding of advanced mathematics. Kashi's legacy is widely recognized in the Islamic world and beyond. His innovations in computational methods and his scientific rigor have had a lasting impact on mathematics and astronomy. His work contributed to the emergence of numerical analysis, which has become a central field in modern mathematics, and his contributions to astronomy helped refine the precision of astronomical observations for centuries. An illustration of major Iranian Mathematicians is included in Figure 2.9.

FIGURE 2.9 Major Iranian mathematicians.

2.2.3.2 The Mathematicians of Other Countries in the Islamic World

i. Al-Kindi (801–873)

Abū Yūsuf Ya'qūb ibn Isḥāq al-Kindī, known as Al-Kindi, was born in Kufa into a noble family of the Kindah tribe. He grew up in an intellectual environment and pursued his studies in Basra and Baghdad, two major centers of knowledge during the Abbasid era. Under the patronage of rationalist caliphs such as al-Ma'mūn and al-Mu'tassim, he worked at the House of Wisdom, where he participated in the translation and study of Greek texts. Although he did not master Greek directly, Al-Kindi collaborated with translators to enrich and comment on the works of Greek philosophers such as Aristotle and Plotinus. He also enjoyed the support of the court elite, though his career was temporarily disrupted by a period of disgrace under Caliph al-Mutawakkil, before regaining his status shortly before his death in 873.

Al-Kindi played a pioneering role in integrating Greek philosophy into Islamic thought. He believed that scientific truth and revealed truth were in harmony, which led him to defend rational inquiry against critics. In metaphysics, he adapted Aristotelian and Neoplatonic concepts to study the First Cause, which he identified with an immutable divine principle. He also contributed to various disciplines such as physics, astronomy, music, and medicine, striving to create a universal synthesis of knowledge. His systematic and encyclopedic approach influenced later genera-tions of Muslim scholars, notably Ibn Sina, and laid the foundation for a scientific philosophy that integrated multiple fields of knowledge. In mathematics, Al-Kindi emphasized its fundamental role as the foundation of all sciences. He regarded the study of arithmetic, geometry, astronomy, and music as essential disciplines for understanding both the natural world and metaphysical principles. One of his most innovative achievements was in cryptography. In his treatise *Risāla fī Istikhrāj al-Kutub al-Mu'ammāh* (*Manuscript on the Extraction of Encrypted Messages*), he introduced the method of frequency analysis for the first time in recorded history. He observed that in Arabic, certain letters appear more frequently than others (e.g., the letter alif (ا) occurs more often than ẓāʾ (ظ)). By analyzing these frequencies, he could break ciphers and decode encrypted messages, thus laying the groundwork for modern cryptanalysis.

In arithmetic, *Al-Kindi* attempted to formalize relationships between numbers. In his work *Kitāb fī al-Adad al-Muḍāʿaf* (*Book on the Doubling of Numbers*), he expressed 2^n for $n = 0, 1, 2, 3, \ldots$. This early treatment of exponential growth reso-nates with ideas later used in computer science and digital logic. He also worked extensively on proportional reasoning, building upon and extending ideas from Euclid. For instance, in geometric proportions, he used relationships such as $a/b = c/d$. This type of proportional thinking was applied not only in pure mathematics but also in optics and acoustics, especially in the mathematical analysis of musical harmony.

In mathematical optics, Al-Kindi was among the first to combine geometry with physical theories of light. He proposed a corpuscular theory of light propagation in straight lines and analyzed the laws of reflection and refraction using geometric tools. For example, he described the law of reflection $\theta_i = \theta_r$ (θ_i is the angle of incidence and θ_r is the angle of reflection).

Al-Kindi also developed a primitive logarithmic system to quantify the potency of medicines in his treatise De Gradibus (On Degrees). He proposed a numerical scale to describe drug strength and therapeutic effect, anticipating concepts used in modern pharmacology. Through his dedication to systematization, interdisciplinary thinking, and mathematical abstraction, Al-Kindi was truly the first philosopher-mathematician of the Islamic Golden Age. By bridging Greek science with Arabic and Iranian scholarship, he laid the groundwork for the flourishing of mathematics, logic, and science in the centuries that followed and helped preserve and transmit ancient knowledge to Europe, where it would later influence the Renaissance.

ii. Thabit ibn Qurra (826–901)

Thābit ibn Qurra, a Syrian philosopher, mathematician, astronomer, and physician of the Abbasid Caliphate, played a crucial role in transmitting and developing ancient Greek knowledge within the Islamic world. Born into the Sabian community in Harran, he was fluent in Syriac, Greek, and Arabic, which enabled him to translate and comment on the works of Greek scholars such as Archimedes, Euclid, and Ptolemy. Through his involvement with the House of Wisdom in Baghdad, under the patronage of the Banū Mūsā brothers and Caliph Al-Muʿtaḍid, he helped preserve and disseminate classical texts, forming a vital bridge between Greek and Islamic intellectual traditions. In addition to his contributions to astronomy, medicine, and music, Thābit is particularly known for his advancements in mathematics and his philosophical inquiries into the concept of infinity.

In mathematics, Thābit made remarkable contributions in number theory, algebra, geometry, and geometrical analysis. He was among the first to study amicable numbers, referring to the pairs of integers where each number is equal to the sum of the proper divisors of the other. He proposed a general method for generating such numbers, based on a relationship involving three specific prime numbers. Setting $p = 3 \cdot 2^n - 1$, $q = 3 \cdot 2^{n-1} - 1$, and $r = 9 \cdot 2^{2n-1} - 1$, if all three are prime, then $A = 2^n \cdot p \cdot q$ and $B = 2^n \cdot r$ form an amicable pair. For example, when $n = 2$, this yields $A = 220$ and $B = 284$, a well-known amicable pair. This formula was a significant advancement beyond earlier methods based merely on enumeration.

Thābit also contributed to algebra and the generalization of geometric means. He solved quadratic and cubic equations using geometric constructions, anticipating modern algebraic approaches. For instance, he examined equations such as $x^3 = a \cdot b^2$, which he solved through proportional mean constructions. His work demonstrated a deep understanding of the relationships between quantities and marked a transition toward more abstract algebraic thinking.

In geometric analysis, Thābit extended Archimedes' work by studying areas enclosed by conic sections, particularly parabolas. He developed techniques for calculating such areas, making him a forerunner of integral calculus. His ability to combine geometry, proportion, and early infinitesimal reasoning illustrates the depth of his mathematical thought and his originality in solving complex problems. His work left a lasting impact on the history of mathematics and philosophy, influencing both his contemporaries and later European scholars through Latin translations in the 12th century. His intellectual legacy is honored by the lunar crater *Thebit* and the enduring recognition of his contributions to science and mathematics.

iii. Al-Battani (858–929)

Al-Battani, born around 858 in Harran, made a lasting impact on the history of science as an influential astronomer and mathematician of the Islamic world. Trained by his father, a maker of astronomical instruments, he refined his knowledge in Raqqa and Baghdad before producing his seminal work, *Kitāb az-Zīj al-Sabi*. This 57-chapter treatise corrected Ptolemy's calculations on planetary motions, introduced precise solar and lunar tables, and accurately measured the length of the year. His innovative approach, combining trigonometry with meticulous observations, enabled him to calculate the precession of the equinoxes and the tilt of Earth's axis. His astronomical contributions were later translated into Latin and influenced major figures such as Copernicus, Kepler, and Galileo. In mathematics, he played a foundational role in the development of modern trigonometry. Unlike Ptolemy, who used chords, Al-Battani adopted the use of sines and tangents as the primary tools in trigonometric calculations that are now central in modern mathematics. He was among the first to tabulate values of the sine function and to define tangent and cotangent geometrically in terms of right triangles and circles. His shift from geometric to algebraic and functional representations marked a significant turning point in the history of trigonometry.

Al-Battani established and used trigonometric identities that are still taught today. One such identity he developed is the formula for the sine of the sum of two angles, written as Equation (2.15):

$$\sin(a+b) = \sin(a)\cos(b) + \cos(a)\sin(b) \qquad (2.15)$$

He also applied these formulas to solve astronomical problems such as calculating the height of celestial bodies or the time of their rising and setting. For example, to compute the altitude h of a celestial body, he would use the spherical law of sines (Equation 2.3). Moreover, Al-Battani was the first to derive the relation:

$$\tan(x) = \frac{\sin(x)}{\cos(x)} \qquad (2.16)$$

This formula, though obvious today, helped standardize the relationships between trigonometric functions and was used to create more accurate astronomical tables, replacing Ptolemy's less precise chord-based methods. He also provided values of the sine function with high precision (e.g., $\sin(30°) = 0.5$ or $\sin(60°) = 0.866$). These calculations were made using a sexagesimal (base-60) numeral system and marked a leap forward in computational trigonometry.

Even without direct contact with Indian astronomers like Āryabhata, Al-Battani managed to enrich and refine trigonometric techniques, bridging and systematizing knowledge from Greek, Babylonian, and Islamic sources. His work was later translated into Latin under the name Albategnius and served as a primary reference for European astronomers and mathematicians during the Renaissance. Through his mathematical rigor and observational precision, Al-Battani not only transformed astronomy but also laid a robust foundation for analytic trigonometry, making him a key figure in the history of mathematics. His name endures today, commemorated by the lunar crater Albategnius, and his formulas remain embedded in mathematical and scientific education across the world.

iv. Ibn Yunus (950–1009)

Ibn Yunus (950–1009), a distinguished Egyptian astronomer and mathematician, was renowned for his meticulous and groundbreaking work. Regarded as one of the greatest Muslim astronomers after Al-Battani and Abu Wafa Buzjani (940–998), he enjoyed the patronage of the Fatimid caliphs, who entrusted him with an observatory on Mount Mokattam near Cairo. His most significant contribution, al-Zij al-Kabir al-Hakimi, compiled exceptionally accurate astronomical tables that remained valuable for centuries, particularly for calculations such as the secular acceleration of the Moon. By systematically documenting celestial phenomena, including eclipses and planetary conjunctions, he laid the groundwork for modern observational astronomy. His legacy endures, with the lunar crater Ibn Yunus named in his honor.

In mathematics, Ibn Yunus made pioneering contributions to trigonometry, particularly spherical trigonometry, the same as Birūni as shown by Equation (2.3). This identity allows astronomers to determine unknown values of sides or angles when observing stars, predicting eclipses, or calculating prayer times and directions. One of Ibn Yunus's key mathematical innovations was his method of transforming multiplication into addition using trigonometric identities that significantly simplified calculations before the invention of logarithms (as expressed by Al-Battani and shown in Equation 2.15). For example, he employed identities such as:

$$\cos(A + B) = \cos A \cos B - \sin A \sin B$$
$$\sin(A + B) = \sin A \cos B + \cos A \sin B$$

(2.18)

These identities enabled him to perform complex astronomical computations more efficiently, using geometric and trigonometric transformations instead of direct numerical multiplications. His work anticipated the later development of logarithms by several centuries. He also created detailed trigonometric tables, including values of sine and cosine functions with high precision. Though many of his original tables have not survived, historical records confirm that he calculated sine values for every minute of arc. These tables were essential for determining the positions and altitudes of celestial bodies and were used to solve problems in both astronomy and geography.

Importantly, *Ibn Yunus* did not separate theory from practice. He combined precise mathematical reasoning with systematic observational data, applying spherical trigonometry directly to real phenomena like lunar and solar eclipses. This integration of mathematics and observation represents an early form of mathematical modeling in science. Although he did not formulate a logarithmic system, his transformation techniques laid the conceptual groundwork for logarithmic thinking, which would later revolutionize mathematics and astronomy in Europe. His influence, transmitted through Islamic and eventually Latin sources, helped shape the mathematical framework for astronomical calculations during the Renaissance. Ibn Yunus was also known for blending scientific rigor with poetic expression and philosophical curiosity, embodying the spirit of the polymath. His work reflects a harmonious blend of precise measurement, innovative thinking, and humanistic inspiration. His contributions remain foundational, not only in Islamic science but in the broader history of mathematics and astronomy.

v. Ibn al-Haytham (965–1040)

Ibn al-Haytham, known in the West as Alhazen, was one of the most influential figures of medieval science, with remarkable contributions to optics, mathematics, and the philosophy of science. Born in Basra around 965, he spent most of his life in Egypt, where he wrote the majority of his works. He is considered a pioneer of the scientific method, emphasizing the importance of experimentation and critical doubt, as demonstrated in his Book of Optics. Beyond studying the propagation of light and the laws of reflection and refraction, he introduced an interdisciplinary approach that combined physics, physiology, and psychology to understand vision. His innovative use of the camera obscura and his research on spherical lenses laid the foundations for modern optics. In philosophy, Ibn al-Haytham stressed the critical examination of established ideas, a perspective that influenced European science through Latin translations of his works.

In mathematics, he demonstrated exceptional skill, particularly in geometry and number theory, expanding upon the works of Greek mathematicians such as Euclid and Archimedes, as well as Arab scholars like Thābit ibn Qurra. One of his most famous mathematical achievements was his work on calculating volumes and surface areas, especially the volume of a paraboloid of revolution, the solid formed by rotating a parabola around its axis. To find the volume of a paraboloid, he used a method similar to what we now recognize as an early form of integral calculus. If a parabola $y = ax^2$ is rotated around the x-axis from $x = 0$ to $x = r$, the resulting volume is given by Equation (2.19):

$$V = \pi \int_0^r \left(ax^2\right)^2 dx = \pi a^2 \int_0^r x^4 dx = \pi a^2 \cdot \frac{r^5}{5} \qquad (2.19)$$

Although he did not write this in modern notation, his geometric arguments essentially led to the same result using exhaustion methods. Another of his most celebrated contributions is Alhazen's problem, a complex geometric challenge that involves finding the point on a spherical mirror where light from a given source reflects to reach the observer's eye, obeying the law of reflection (angle of incidence = angle of reflection). The solution to this problem leads to solving a quartic equation (fourth-degree polynomial), making it one of the earliest known instances where higher-order algebraic equations were applied to optical geometry. In his attempts to prove Euclid's fifth postulate (the parallel postulate), he made important advances in non-Euclidean geometry. Although he did not succeed in proving the postulate, his deep inquiry into its foundations and logical consistency prefigured the later development of hyperbolic and elliptic geometries in the 19th century.

Ibn al-Haytham also studied conic sections, ellipses, parabolas, and hyperbolas, not just as abstract geometric figures, but as practical tools for solving optical and astronomical problems. For instance, he analyzed how light rays converge or diverge when reflected from curved mirrors, using the properties of conics to model these behaviors. Beyond pure mathematics, Ibn al-Haytham's true innovation was his use of mathematical language to express physical principles, especially in optics and astronomy. By formulating physical laws with geometric and algebraic tools, he helped formalize the relationship between mathematics and the natural sciences (a fundamental shift in scientific thinking that would become standard in modern physics). Through translations of his works into Latin, particularly in the 12th and 13th centuries, his mathematical ideas influenced prominent European thinkers like Roger Bacon, Kepler, and Descartes. His synthesis of logic, mathematics, and experimentation laid the groundwork for the Renaissance and the Scientific Revolution that followed.

An illustration of major mathematicians from Arabic-speaking countries is included in Figure 2.10.

Thābit   Al-Battani   Ibn Yunus

Al kindi   Ibn al-Haytham

FIGURE 2.10   Major mathematicians from Arabic-speaking countries.

2.2.3.3 The Impact of Algebraic Methods from the Islamic World on Medieval Europe

The algebraic methods developed by Iranian mathematicians and scholars from other regions of the Islamic world had a profound and lasting influence on medieval Europe, marking a decisive turning point in the evolution of European mathematics. Before the introduction of algebra in Europe, mathematics was largely dominated by the geometric approaches inherited from the Greeks, which focused primarily on solving problems through geometric constructions. However, with the arrival of Persian algebraic methods, Europe discovered a new way of thinking about mathematics, centered on the symbolic manipulation of numbers and equations.

Khwarizmi's book, *Kitab al-Jabr wa-l-Muqabala*, introduced Europeans not only to algebra but also to the decimal numeral system and the use of Iranian-Arabic numerals. These innovations radically simplified calculations, replacing more complex numerical systems such as Roman numerals. *Khwarizmi*'s algebra, with its systematic methodology for solving linear and quadratic equations, enabled a more generalized approach to mathematical problem-solving, making mathematics more accessible and applicable to a wide range of fields.

The introduction of Persian algebraic methods also had a significant impact on the teaching of mathematics in Europe. As medieval universities began to develop as centers of learning, algebra was integrated into their curricula. The works of Persian mathematicians, translated into Latin, were used as reference manuals for teaching mathematics. This widespread dissemination of new ideas gradually supplanted traditional geometric approaches, making algebra a central discipline in university education and paving the way for further mathematical and scientific developments.

Persian algebraic methods also stimulated the development of new branches of mathematics in Europe. By adopting algebraic techniques to solve problems that previously required complex geometric methods, European mathematicians began exploring more abstract concepts. This shift toward abstraction led to the emergence of new mathematical theories, such as symbolic algebra, which was later developed by figures like François Viète (1540–1603). Symbolic algebra allowed for a more general and flexible approach to solving equations, laying the foundation for modern mathematical advancements. Moreover, these methods influenced the way Europeans approached mathematical problems and their solutions. Algebra introduced a more analytical and less intuitive approach, focused on manipulating symbols and formulas rather than relying solely on geometric constructions. This approach enabled mathematicians to tackle more complex problems, particularly in fields such as astronomy, mechanics, and architecture. For example, algebraic techniques were crucial for the development of celestial mechanics and the understanding of planetary motion, areas where medieval Europe had lagged behind the scholars of the Islamic world.

The influence of Persian algebraic methods in Europe was not limited to pure mathematics; it also had significant practical implications. In commerce and finance, the use of algebra facilitated solving complex problems related to goods valuation, profit distribution, and interest calculations. These practical applications contributed to the transformation of economic practices in Europe, fostering the rise of commercial cities and banking institutions and playing a role in the emergence of capitalism.

Furthermore, algebra enabled advancements in physics and engineering. Algebraic methods were applied to the study of forces and motion, particularly in the development of concepts in statics and dynamics. European engineers used these techniques to design more complex and efficient machines, contributing to the technological revolution that marked the end of the Middle Ages and the beginning of the Renaissance. The works of Alhazen on optics, influenced by algebraic methods, were also fundamental to the development of optical science in Europe.

The impact of Persian algebraic methods on medieval Europe was amplified by the fact that they laid the groundwork for the Scientific Revolution of the Renaissance. The concepts and techniques introduced by Persian mathematicians were integrated into the works of Renaissance scholars such as Copernicus, Kepler, and Galileo. These scientists used algebra to formulate and solve complex problems in various fields, including astronomy, physics, and geography, marking the beginning of modern science.

To complement this historical journey and provide a synthetic view of the key contributions to mathematics from ancient to modern times, a timeline of major discoveries, their authors, and geographic origins is presented in Table 2.5.

TABLE 2.5
Timeline of Major Mathematical Discoveries

Discovery	Scientist	Approx. Date	Location
Sexagesimal system	Sumer	−2000	Mesopotamia
Practical geometry	Egyptians	−1800	Egypt
Multiplication table	Babylonians	−1600	Mesopotamia
Foundations of logic and syllogistic reasoning	Aristotle	−350	Greece
Formalization of deductive geometry and axioms	Euclid	−300	Greece
Binary system	Pingala	−200	India
Zero and decimal system	Brahmagupta	628	India
Symbolic algebra	Khwarizmi	820	Iran
Introduction of sine and cosine functions with trigonometric tables	Al-Battani	880	Syria
Spherical trigonometry and Earth's radius calculation	Biruni	1020	Iran
Jalali solar calendar (precise astronomical computation)	Omar Khayyam	1079	Iran
Tusi Couple (circular to linear motion transformation)	Nasir al-Din Tusi	1247	Iran
Decimal system in Europe	Fibonacci	1202	Italy
Boolean logic (mathematical logic)	George Boole	1854	United Kingdom
Set theory	Georg Cantor	1874	Germany
Turing machine (foundations of computation)	Alan Turing	1936	United Kingdom
Information theory	Claude Shannon	1948	United States
Sexagesimal system	Sumer	−2000	Mesopotamia

2.3 ANCIENT MEASURING DEVICES

2.3.1 THE FIRST MEASURING DEVICES AND CALCULATING MACHINES

2.3.1.1 The Differences and Common Points between a Measuring Device and a Calculating Machine

Measuring devices and calculating machines serve distinct yet complementary roles in information processing. Measuring devices capture quantitative data from the physical environment, while calculating machines process this data to extract meaningful insights or perform complex analyses. A measuring device provides direct numerical data based on observations of physical phenomena, such as temperature, pressure, or mass. Examples include thermometers, scales, and voltmeters. A calculating machine, such as a calculator, computer, or slide rule, manipulates numerical data through arithmetic, logical, or algorithmic operations to solve problems, analyze trends, or simulate processes. Measuring devices and calculating machines are closely interconnected. Measurements serve as the foundation upon which calculations are based. While measuring devices supply raw, precise data, calculating machines transform these inputs into structured information for decision-making, forecasting, and deeper analysis. For instance, temperature data collected by a sensor can be processed by a computer to model climate trends or regulate industrial processes.

The synergy between measuring and calculating devices is vital across scientific, industrial, and technical fields. In industrial engineering, sensors monitor production parameters, while computers analyze the data in real-time to optimize operations. In meteorology, weather instruments gather environmental data, which supercomputers process to predict atmospheric patterns. In research laboratories, devices like spectrophotometers collect biological data, which is then interpreted by computers to generate scientific insights.

Advances in technology have enhanced both measuring devices and calculating machines, making them more precise, faster, and capable of handling larger datasets. Modern smart devices often integrate both functions, simultaneously collecting and analyzing data. This integration has fueled innovations like the Internet of Things (IoT) and enabled real-time monitoring and control in complex systems. Together, measuring devices and calculating machines create a powerful system that combines precision with analytical strength. Their integration accelerates discovery, optimizes industrial processes, and supports informed decision-making across diverse domains, demonstrating their indispensable role in modern science and technology.

2.3.1.2 Origins of Early Calculating Machines: Practical Necessities

The invention of the first calculating machines was primarily driven by practical needs related to data management, commercial calculations, financial transactions, astronomy, and administration. As societies became more complex, with expanding trade, sophisticated tax systems, and scientific advancements requiring precise calculations, the necessity to automate and facilitate these computations grew increasingly urgent.

One of the earliest motivations for developing calculating machines was the need to manage commercial and financial transactions. In ancient civilizations such as Mesopotamia, Egypt, and China, merchants and administrators required accurate record-keeping, interest calculations on loans, tax distribution, and currency exchange. Arithmetic operations involving large numbers and fractions were often tedious and error-prone, especially when performed manually. This led to the invention of tools like the abacus, which simplified and accelerated basic arithmetic calculations while reducing the risk of human error. The need for automated calculations was further emphasized by the demands of astronomy, where precise calculations were essential for predicting celestial events such as eclipses, moon phases, and planetary movements. Ancient astronomers from Greco-Roman, Indian, and Chinese civilizations performed complex calculations to establish accurate calendars, which were crucial for agricultural, religious, and administrative activities. These needs led to the design of instruments like the astrolabe, which helped determine the positions of stars and planets. Later, more sophisticated devices, such as the *Antikythera* mechanism (100 BCE), were developed to mechanically model celestial movements, demonstrating early advancements in machines capable of performing complex astronomical calculations.

Expanding tax and administrative systems in ancient and medieval societies also played a key role in the development of early calculating machines. Governments and empires required efficient methods for tax collection, budget management, resource distribution, and accurate record-keeping. These tasks demanded fast and precise calculations, especially on a large scale. For example, the Roman Empire, with its vast territories and large population, needed effective systems to calculate and collect taxes. Such requirements likely stimulated the development of more efficient calculating tools capable of processing large volumes of data quickly.

During the Renaissance, the rise of international trade and finance, particularly in European trading cities such as Venice, Florence, and Antwerp, further increased the demand for calculating machines. Bankers, merchants, and money changers needed to quickly compute exchange rates, compound interest, and profit shares in complex business transactions. In this context, devices like the slide rule were developed, enabling faster and more accurate mathematical operations. These tools became essential for managing financial transactions and supporting the flourishing international trade.

With the advent of modern science in the 17th century, the demand for advanced calculations grew even further, leading to the invention of the first mechanical machines capable of automating arithmetic operations. Scholars like Blaise Pascal (1623–1662) and Leibniz designed machines that could perform addition, subtraction, multiplication, and division. The Pascaline, invented by Pascal in 1642, was one of the earliest mechanical calculators, created to assist his father, a tax collector, in performing arithmetic computations quickly and accurately. Leibniz's machine, on the other hand, was capable of executing more complex operations and represented a significant step toward the automation of calculations.

The first calculating machines were invented to address essential practical needs across various fields, including commerce, finance, astronomy, and administration. These machines helped simplify, accelerate, and secure arithmetic operations, meeting the growing demands of complex societies. The development of these devices marked the beginning of automated computation, a process that continued to evolve and improve over the centuries, ultimately leading to the emergence of modern computers.

2.3.1.3 The Impact of Early Calculating Machines on Scientific and Technical Progress

The first calculating machines had a profound impact on scientific and technical progress, making calculations faster, more precise, and more complex than ever before. Their invention marked the beginning of the automation of calculations, which not only transformed the way calculations were made but also expanded the possibilities for scientific and technical exploration.

One of the major influences of the first calculating machines was their ability to significantly reduce the time required to perform complex arithmetic operations. Before their invention, calculations, especially those involving large numbers or complicated equations, were extremely labor-intensive and prone to human error. Machines like Pascal's Pascaline allowed for mechanical addition and subtraction, thereby reducing the risk of errors and speeding up the process. This increased speed allowed scientists to focus more on the analysis and interpretation of results rather than the calculations themselves. These machines also paved the way for advancements in fields like physics, astronomy, and mathematics. For example, the ability to perform precise and rapid calculations was essential for astronomers seeking to model the movements of celestial bodies. The calculations required to predict eclipses, the orbits of planets, and astral conjunctions were greatly facilitated by calculating machines. By reducing errors in these calculations, the machines contributed to refining astronomical models, leading to a more accurate understanding of the cosmos.

In physics, calculating machines allowed for significant advancements in mechanics and engineering. For example, the ability to perform rapid calculations was crucial for engineers working on problems of statics and dynamics, where forces and moments needed to be calculated precisely to design stable and safe structures. Calculating machines also played a key role in the rise of thermodynamics and electromagnetism, where the complex equations governing these fields required fast and accurate numerical solutions. The influence of early calculating machines was also felt in advancements in mathematics, particularly in algebra and differential and integral calculus. Mathematicians, using these machines, were able to explore new methods for solving equations and analyzing infinite series with increased precision. This allowed for the development of new theories and techniques, such as numerical analysis, which relies heavily on the ability to perform repetitive and precise calculations.

Moreover, calculating machines played a vital role in the industrialization and automation of production processes. They enabled the management of complex financial calculations, such as those related to accounting, inventory management, and production planning, with unprecedented efficiency. This led to improvements in industrial organization, logistics, and project management, allowing for faster and more profitable production. The impact of these machines on the business world was profound, contributing to the rise of industrial capitalism in the 19th century.

The further development of calculating machines, such as Charles Babbage's analytical engine (1791–1871), paved the way for modern computing. Although Babbage's machine was never built during his lifetime, his concepts laid the groundwork for programmable computers, which revolutionized science and technology in the 20th century. Babbage's ideas, combined with Ada Lovelace's (1815–1852) work on programming, showed how calculating machines could be used not only for arithmetic operations but also to solve complex problems using algorithms.

Early calculating machines also had an educational impact by democratizing access to advanced calculation tools. They allowed students and scientists to familiarize themselves with advanced mathematical concepts without having to master complex manual techniques. This contributed to the expansion of scientific education and an increased interest in science and mathematics, thus paving the way for a new generation of researchers and engineers. A summary of the domains transformed by early calculating machines is presented in Table 2.6.

TABLE 2.6
Domains Transformed by Early Calculating Machines

Domain	Examples of Impact
Astronomy	Improved celestial models
Physics	Mechanics and thermodynamics
Finance	Accounting and financial transactions
Industrial engineering	Process automation and optimization
Mathematics	Advancements in algebra and calculus

2.3.2   Ancient Measuring Devices and Early Calculating Machines: Operation and Presentation

2.3.2.1   Very Ancient Measuring Devices

i. Gnomon (Ancient Egypt, 3500 BC)

The gnomon is the first instrument used in astronomy. It is a simple vertical stick planted on a horizontal plane (see Figure 2.11). It has been known since ancient times (Egyptians, Chaldeans, Greeks). The length of the shadow cast allows for measuring the height of the celestial body (Sun or Moon). The direction of the shadow indicates the azimuth* of the celestial body. The gnomon is the ancestor of the sundial. Used as early as 3500 BC in Ancient Egypt, the gnomon is one of the first time-measuring instruments. Composed of a simple stick or a vertical column planted in the ground, it allowed for tracking the apparent movement of the Sun by observing the shadow it cast. The length and direction of this shadow varied throughout the day, indicating the hours. Additionally, the seasonal variations in the shadow's trajectory enabled the Egyptians to identify key astronomical events, such as the solstices, which were essential for regulating their calendar and planning agricultural activities, especially in connection with the annual flooding of the Nile.

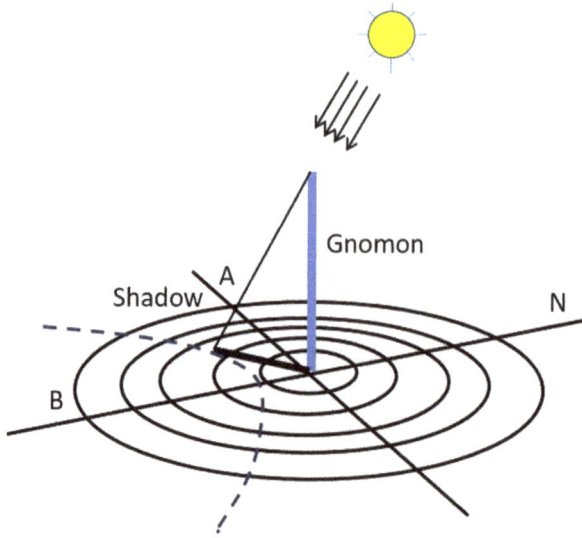

FIGURE 2.11   Diagram of the operating principle of a gnomon.

ii. Clepsydra (Egypt, 1500 BC)

The clepsydra, which appeared in Egypt around 1500 BC, is a water clock used to measure the passage of time in a regular manner. It operates through a perforated container, allowing water to flow at a constant rate. The level of water remaining in the container or accumulating in another was used as an indicator of elapsed time. Unlike the gnomon, which depended on sunlight, the clepsydra could function both day and night, providing a reliable measurement of time intervals. This innovative instrument was used in various fields, such as managing religious ceremonies, regulating public speeches, and synchronizing daily activities (Figure 2.12).

FIGURE 2.12 Egyptian water clepsydra decorated with a baboon (https://www.mariellebrie
.com/histoire-des-clepsydres-egyptiennes-a-eau/).

iii. Beam Balance (Ancient Egypt, 5000 BC)

The beam balance, used as early as 5000 BC in Ancient Egypt, is a simple yet effective device for measuring the mass of objects. It consists of a horizontal arm, supported at its center by a pivot, with two pans suspended at the ends. To determine the
mass of an object, it is placed on one pan while known weights are added to the other
until the arm is perfectly balanced. This principle of equilibrium between weights
remains fundamental in the operation of modern balances, illustrating the precision
and logic applied to mass measurement since antiquity.

iv. Quadrant (Ancient Greece, 300 BC)

The quadrant, used as early as 300 BC in Ancient Greece, is an angular measurement instrument designed to determine the height of a celestial object above the horizon. It consists of a quarter-circle, often graduated in degrees, and is equipped with
an alidade, a sighting device that allows precise aiming at the object to be observed.
By aligning the alidade with a celestial body and reading the angle indicated on the
quadrant's scale, Greek astronomers could measure vertical angles and thus calculate the position of celestial objects. This instrument played a fundamental role in
the astronomical studies of the time, enabling precise observations and significant
advancements in the understanding of the sky.

v. Astrolabe (Ancient Greece and Iran, 150 BC)

The astrolabe, invented around 150 BC in Ancient Greece, is a sophisticated instrument used to solve problems related to time and the position of stars. It consists of multiple engraved metal disks, stacked and rotatable. By adjusting these disks according to the observed positions of stars, the astrolabe allowed users to determine the time, measure latitude, and predict the movements of celestial bodies. This versatile and precise instrument played a crucial role in navigation and astronomy.

In Ancient Iran, the astrolabe was adopted and used for both astronomical and practical purposes long before its diffusion into the Islamic world. The ancient Persians adapted it to their needs, particularly in the fields of astronomy and time management. It was used to observe stars, determine the position of celestial bodies, and predict significant events. The astrolabe was also employed for calculations related to the seasons and the optimal timing for certain agricultural activities, essential for survival in Iran's arid regions. Thus, this instrument not only facilitated astronomical studies but also contributed to social organization and agricultural planning in Ancient Iran (Figure 2.13).

FIGURE 2.13 A Persian astrolabe, displayed at the Whipple Museum of the History of Science (Cambridge, UK).

vi. The Band-e Kaisar (Hydraulic Measurement System), (Iran, Sassanid Era)

The Band-e Kaisar, dating back to the Sassanid era (3rd to 7th century AD), illustrates the ingenuity of the hydraulic systems developed by the Persians to manage water resources. This dam, along with other similar structures, was equipped with sophisticated devices for measuring and controlling water flow. These systems included calibrated scales or openings, which allowed for precise evaluation of water volumes allocated for irrigation, domestic supply, or industrial use. They complemented the qanat network, underground irrigation channels, to ensure fair and efficient water distribution in often arid regions, demonstrating advanced technical expertise and a keen sense of natural resource management.

vii. Measurement Rules and Standards (Iran, Achaemenid Period)

Under the Achaemenid Empire, the Persians developed standardized measurement rules and benchmarks to ensure precision and uniformity in monumental construction projects. These instruments were used to measure the dimensions of stones and bricks employed in building their infrastructures, notably the palaces of Persepolis. These standards facilitated coordination among artisans and construction teams from various regions of the empire, ensuring consistent quality and architectural harmony. Moreover, these benchmarks reflected an advanced level of organization and played a crucial role in the execution of grand imperial projects.

viii. The Zoroastrian Calendar

The Zoroastrian calendar, introduced in Iran during the Achaemenid era and refined under the Sassanids, is a calendrical system based on precise astronomical observations. It is structured around a solar year divided into 12 months of 30 days each, supplemented by 5 intercalary days to align the civil year with the solar year. This calendar played a central role in religious life, marking major Zoroastrian festivals such as Nowruz (New Year) and Mehregan, while also regulating sacred rites and ceremonies. Additionally, it was essential for organizing agricultural cycles, synchronizing sowing, harvesting, and seasonal labor, as well as structuring the administrative and fiscal activities of the empire, ensuring efficient management of resources and territories.

2.3.2.2 Early Calculating Machines

i. Abacus (Mesopotamia, 2500 BC)

The abacus is a calculating tool consisting of a wooden or metal frame containing multiple rows of beads that slide along rods. Each row represents a power of 10, and the beads can be moved to represent numbers. Users manipulate the beads to perform basic arithmetic operations such as addition, subtraction, multiplication, and division. The abacus has been used for millennia across different cultures, notably in China, Greece, and Rome.

ii. Antikythera (Ancient Greece, 100 BC)

The Antikythera mechanism is a complex mechanical device, often considered one of the earliest analog computers. It was used to predict astronomical positions and eclipses on specific dates based on the Metonic cycle (a 19-year cycle). The mechanism consists of multiple bronze gears that, when turned, simulate the movement of celestial bodies. Its precision and complexity demonstrate the Ancient Greeks' advanced understanding of mathematics and astronomy.

iii. Pascaline (France, 1642)

Invented by Blaise Pascal, the Pascaline is one of the earliest mechanical calculating machines. It used a series of toothed wheels to perform addition and subtraction. Each wheel represented a digit (from 0 to 9), and by turning a wheel, the corresponding number was added or subtracted from the total. Carryovers were automatically managed as the calculation progressed from one wheel to the next. Though rudimentary compared to modern machines, the Pascaline laid the foundation for more advanced mechanical calculators (Figure 2.14).

FIGURE 2.14   A Pascaline, signed by Pascal in 1652, at the Musée des Arts et Métiers of the Conservatoire National des Arts et Métiers in Paris (https://fr.wikipedia.org/wiki/Pascaline).

iv. Slide Rule (England, Early 17th Century)

The slide rule is an analog instrument used for performing mathematical calculations, including multiplication, division, and trigonometric computations. It is based on logarithms and operates by aligning movable scales on a fixed rule. By sliding these scales relative to the fixed one, the user can read the result of the operation without performing complex manual calculations. The slide rule was a valuable tool for engineers and scientists until the advent of electronic calculators (Figure 2.15).

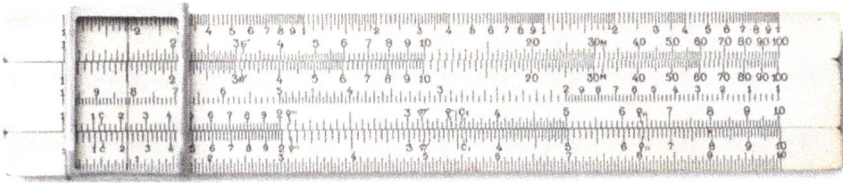

FIGURE 2.15   Photo of a slide rule.

These ancient measuring devices and calculating machines were fundamental tools in the development of science and technology, marking the first steps toward the modern measurement and calculation systems we use today. To consolidate the variety of tools and mechanisms discussed in this section, a typological classification of key astronomical instruments used across ancient civilizations is provided in Table 2.7. It includes their main functions and the cultures in which they were developed or widely adopted.

TABLE 2.7
Comprehensive Table of Ancient Astronomical Instruments

Instrument	Function	Civilizations of Use
Astrolabe	Measure the altitude of stars and planets; used for timekeeping and navigation	Ancient Greece, Iran, Arabic-speaking regions
Gnomon	Determines the solar time by casting a shadow	Babylonia, China, Greece
Clepsydra (water clock)	Measures time based on regulated water flow	Egypt, Greece, Iran, Arabic-speaking regions
Armillary sphere	Model of celestial spheres to demonstrate the motion of stars	Greece, China, Iran, Arabic-speaking regions
Quadrant	Measures angles in astronomy and navigation	Iran, Arabic-speaking regions, Europe
Sextant (early forms)	Determines the angle between celestial objects and the horizon	Europe (derived from Islamic instruments)
Nocturlabe	Determines the hour at night based on star positions	Iran, Arabic-speaking regions, Medieval Europe
Celestial planisphere	2D representation of the celestial sphere to locate constellations	Greece, Iran, Arabic-speaking regions
Celestial globe	Spherical model of the sky showing stars and constellations	Greece, Iran, Arabic-speaking regions, Renaissance Europe
Ballistic compass	Used to measure angles and distances in field applications	Iran, Arabic-speaking regions, Renaissance Europe
Geometron	Instrument for measuring complex geometric forms	Iran, Arabic-speaking regions, India
Jai yantra	Massive observational instrument for tracking celestial bodies	India (Jaipur, 18th century)
Mural quadrant	Wall-mounted device to measure the angular height of stars	Iran, Arabic-speaking regions, Central Asia

2.4 EUROPEAN RENAISSANCE AND THE EVOLUTION OF INTELLIGENCE

2.4.1 MATHEMATICAL REVOLUTION OF THE RENAISSANCE

The European Renaissance marked a period of intellectual and cultural revival, where mathematics played a central role in redefining the understanding of numbers and fundamental mathematical concepts. Among the key figures of this revolution were mathematicians such as Leonardo Fibonacci (1170–1250), Nicolaus Copernicus (1473–1543), and Gerolamo Cardano (1501–1576). Their works not only enriched the mathematical knowledge of the time but also laid the foundations for many modern mathematical concepts.

Leonardo Fibonacci (1170–1250), known for his famous work *Liber Abaci*, published in 1202, introduced the Indo-Irano-Arabic numeral system to Western Europe, which is now universally used. Before this introduction, Europe primarily relied on Roman numerals, a system impractical for complex calculations. The Indo-Irano-Arabic system, with its concept of zero and positional notation, greatly simplified and accelerated calculations. *Liber Abaci* also introduced the Fibonacci sequence, a series of numbers that revealed underlying mathematical relationships in nature and influenced fields such as number theory and biological modeling.

Nicolaus Copernicus (1473–1543), although primarily recognized for his heliocentric model in astronomy, based his work largely on mathematical advancements. Copernicus employed sophisticated geometric techniques to describe the movements of planets around the Sun. By breaking away from the Ptolemaic model, which relied on complicated epicycles, his simpler and more elegant mathematical approach not only revolutionized astronomy but also reinforced the idea that mathematics was the key to understanding the laws of the universe. This paradigm shift encouraged the use of mathematics to model physical phenomena, a fundamental principle in modern science.

Gerolamo Cardano (1501–1576), another great thinker of the Renaissance, made significant contributions to algebra. His work *Ars Magna*, published in 1545, is considered one of the first modern algebra books. In this work, *Cardano* presented solutions to cubic and quartic equations, which had remained unsolved for centuries. His method for solving these equations was a crucial step toward the development of modern algebra and introduced the concept of complex numbers, albeit in an informal manner. His acknowledgment of negative and imaginary roots, though not fully understood at the time, paved the way for their later acceptance in mathematics.

The introduction of logarithms by John Napier (1550–1617) and the works of his contemporaries were also influenced by Renaissance advancements. Although *Napier* came after Fibonacci, the intellectual environment of the Renaissance facilitated the diffusion and acceptance of new mathematical ideas. Logarithms transformed the way calculations were performed, simplifying complex multiplications and divisions into simple additions and subtractions. This innovation was essential to the development of trigonometry and astronomy.

The influence of these advancements extended far beyond the Renaissance. They laid the groundwork for the Scientific Revolution of the 17th century, where mathematicians like Descartes and Newton built upon the concepts developed by their predecessors. New algebraic, geometric, and arithmetic methods enabled progress in physics, engineering, and economics, demonstrating that mathematics could be applied to nearly all fields of knowledge. Moreover, the Renaissance saw a transition from the geometric approach inherited from the Greeks to a more algebraic and symbolic approach. This shift was facilitated by the standardization of mathematical symbols, such as the introduction of the plus (+) and minus (−) signs by mathematicians like Johannes Widmann (1460–1498). This evolution allowed for more abstract manipulations of equations and concepts, paving the way for modern symbolic algebra. Renaissance mathematics also influenced economics and finance, thanks to thinkers like Luca Pacioli, who codified the principles of double-entry bookkeeping. This advancement allowed for more rigorous financial management and laid the groundwork for the emergence of modern capitalism. The calculation techniques developed during this period were crucial for the rise of financial markets and international trade.

The mathematical progress of the Renaissance played a key role in education and the dissemination of knowledge. With the invention of the printing press, mathematical books became more accessible, allowing for the widespread distribution of new ideas. This created a culture of learning and research where mathematics was seen not only as an abstract field of knowledge but also as a practical tool for solving everyday problems. The works of mathematicians such as *Fibonacci*, *Copernicus*, and *Cardano* revolutionized the understanding of numbers and fundamental mathematical concepts by introducing new ideas, methods, and notations that transformed not only mathematics itself but also its applications to other domains of knowledge and human practice. These advancements not only marked a turning point in the history of mathematics but also prepared the way for the scientific and intellectual revolutions that followed.

2.4.1.1 The Impact of Renaissance Mathematical Advancements on European Sciences and Societies

The Renaissance was a key period in the history of mathematics, marked by the emergence and standardization of modern mathematical notation systems. This transformation played a crucial role in simplifying complex calculations, accelerating mathematical discoveries, and enabling the broader dissemination of knowledge. Previously, mathematics relied on verbal or geometric notation systems, which made calculations laborious and limited their use to a small circle of specialists. The Renaissance helped overcome these obstacles by introducing more abstract and symbolic notations, making mathematical manipulation easier and communication of ideas more effective.

One of the major contributions of the Renaissance was the adoption and spread of the Indo-Irano-Arabic numeral system, which included the use of zero. This system, promoted in Europe by *Fibonacci*, replaced Roman numerals, which were far less practical for arithmetic calculations. Thanks to its positional notation, the Indo-Irano-Arabic system simplified basic operations such as addition, subtraction, multiplication, and division, making mathematics more accessible and applicable to practical fields such as commerce, finance, and engineering. The Renaissance also saw the introduction of standardized mathematical symbols to represent operations and relationships between numbers. For instance, the plus (+) and minus (−) signs, which we use today, were introduced by Widmann in 1489. These symbols greatly simplified the expression of equations and mathematical relationships, making calculations faster and less prone to transcription or interpretation errors. This standardization also enabled clearer communication between mathematicians, facilitating intellectual exchanges and the dissemination of new ideas.

Algebra, which was previously described mainly in words, also benefited from the introduction of symbolic notation. Mathematicians like François Viète (1540–1603) and Gerolamo Cardano (1501–1576) played a crucial role in this transition. Viète, for example, introduced the use of letters to represent variables and coefficients, paving the way for modern symbolic algebra. This method allowed for the generalization of mathematical problems and systematic solutions of complex equations, significantly contributing to mathematical advancements.

Another significant development in mathematical notation during the Renaissance was the introduction of logarithms by John Napier (1550–1617) in the early 17th century. Logarithms revolutionized mathematical methods by simplifying multiplication and division into addition and subtraction. Logarithmic notation facilitated astronomical calculations, navigation, and other fields requiring complex mathematical operations, thus accelerating scientific discoveries. The Renaissance also enabled the widespread dissemination of mathematical methods, thanks to the invention of the printing press by Johannes Gutenberg in the mid-15th century. Mathematical books, once rare and expensive, became more accessible, allowing a larger number of people to learn and apply the new mathematical notations and techniques. This wider dissemination created a larger community of mathematicians and intellectuals capable of contributing to the advancement of knowledge, thereby accelerating progress in this field.

The new notations also played a crucial role in the development of analytic geometry, a discipline founded by René Descartes (1596–1650) in the early 17th century. By introducing a coordinate system to represent curves and geometric figures through algebraic equations, Descartes united algebra and geometry, opening new perspectives for solving complex geometric problems. This innovation laid the groundwork for differential and integral calculus, which would later revolutionize mathematics and the sciences. The adoption of new mathematical notations also had a significant impact on mathematics education. Concepts that were once difficult to explain in purely verbal or geometric terms could now be taught more directly and intuitively using symbols and equations. This contributed to the creation of more structured textbooks and courses, allowing students to develop a deeper and more systematic understanding of mathematics. The Renaissance also saw the emergence of new types of mathematical texts, such as manuals and computational tables, which contributed to the dissemination of these new notations. These works, often written in vernacular languages rather than Latin, made mathematics more accessible to a broader audience, including merchants, engineers, and sailors, who needed mathematical skills for their professional activities.

Mathematical progress during the Renaissance played a crucial role in the development of navigation, astronomy, and engineering, profoundly transforming European societies. One of the areas where these advances had an immediate and significant impact was navigation. The Renaissance saw the introduction of more precise mathematical methods for cartography and determining latitude and longitude, facilitating maritime explorations. Mathematical innovations, such as the use of logarithms to simplify distance and position calculations, allowed navigators to plan and conduct transoceanic voyages with unprecedented accuracy, paving the way for the Age of Exploration.

In astronomy, mathematical advancements enabled a more precise understanding of the movements of celestial bodies. Nicolaus Copernicus (1473–1543), with his heliocentric model, revolutionized the perception of the cosmos by placing the Sun at the center of the known universe instead of the Earth. This model, based on rigorous mathematical calculations, corrected the errors of the Ptolemaic system and laid the foundation for modern astronomy. Mathematics made it possible to model planetary orbits with greater accuracy, leading to more reliable astronomical predictions. This new vision of the universe not only challenged the religious and philosophical beliefs of the time but also encouraged a more scientific and empirical approach to studying the natural world. Engineering also greatly benefited from the mathematical advances of the Renaissance. The application of geometric and algebraic principles allowed for the design of more complex and robust structures, such as cathedrals, bridges, and fortifications. Engineers like Filippo Brunelleschi (1377–1446) used advanced mathematics to solve complex technical problems, such as the construction of the dome of Florence Cathedral, which remains an engineering and architectural masterpiece. These innovations not only transformed architecture but also led to developments in mechanics, hydraulics, and other engineering disciplines. The transformation of European societies through mathematical advancements was most evident in commercial and colonial expansion. New navigation techniques enabled Europeans to discover and conquer new lands, establishing lucrative trade routes and colonies in distant regions. This led to unprecedented economic expansion, enriching European nations and shifting power dynamics across the continent. Applied mathematics in navigation played a crucial role in establishing European dominance over global trade and geographical exploration.

Mathematical advancements in astronomy further sparked an intellectual revolution in Europe. The Copernican model, supported by rigorous mathematical calculations, acted as a catalyst for the Scientific Revolution, inspiring figures such as Johannes Kepler (1571–1630) and Galileo Galilei (1564–1642) to further explore the laws of nature. Kepler, for instance, used mathematics to formulate his laws of planetary motion, which were crucial for modern understandings of gravitation. This shift toward a mathematical interpretation of the cosmos changed how Europeans perceived their place in the universe, promoting a more scientific perspective and moving away from religious dogma.

Engineering, strengthened by mathematics, had a direct impact on European infrastructure development. Advanced construction techniques allowed for the building of larger, better-planned cities, with stronger defensive systems and more sophisticated transportation networks. This encouraged urbanization, accelerated trade and cultural exchanges, and contributed to the rise of modern nation-states. Improved infrastructure also stimulated economic growth and enabled more efficient resource management, reinforcing the power of monarchies and centralized governments.

Mathematical progress also enhanced education and knowledge dissemination, particularly in scientific disciplines. European universities began integrating more mathematics into their curricula, training a new generation of scholars who applied these concepts in navigation, astronomy, and engineering. This shift contributed to the emergence of a scientific culture in Europe, where reason and experimentation gradually replaced traditional explanations based on authority and tradition. The societal impact was not limited to the intellectual and political elite. Applied mathematics in navigation, astronomy, and engineering also had practical effects on everyday European life. Improved agricultural techniques, using geometric principles for land distribution, increased productivity, and helped feed a growing population. Likewise, advancements in hydraulic engineering improved urban water supply, contributing to better public health and further urbanization.

Renaissance mathematical advancements contributed to a major shift in European mentality, promoting a more rational and scientific approach to the world. The success of applying mathematics to practical problems strengthened confidence in human capacity to understand and master nature. This encouraged a culture of innovation and exploration, which not only transformed Renaissance societies but also laid the foundation for the scientific and technological advancements of the coming centuries. By redefining the role of mathematics in understanding and shaping the world, the Renaissance inaugurated a new era of progress and discovery, whose influence continues to shape modern society. A summary of Renaissance mathematical notations and their importance is presented in Table 2.8.

TABLE 2.8
Renaissance Mathematical Notations and Their Importance

Innovation	Contributor	Impact
Indo-Irano-Arabic numerals	Fibonacci	Simplified arithmetic
Plus (+) and Minus (−)	Widmann	Standardized operations
Symbolic algebra	Viète, Cardano	Generalized problem-solving
Logarithms	Napier	Accelerated calculations

2.4.2 The Precursors of Automation

The precursors of automation refer to the innovations, inventions, concepts, or practices that preceded and laid the groundwork for the development of modern automated systems. These precursors include the earliest machines and mechanisms that enabled the automation of specific tasks, the theoretical ideas that led to the understanding and advancement of automated processes, as well as the industrial and scientific practices that drove societies to seek ways to improve efficiency, precision, and productivity through automation.

The first mechanical machines, such as water mills, windmills, and early weaving machines designed by inventors like Leonardo da Vinci, played a significant role in automating certain human tasks, particularly in agriculture and textile production. Since Antiquity and the Middle Ages, inventors have developed mechanical automata capable of performing repetitive movements or tasks, including automatic clocks and humanoid automata. The development of control theory, feedback loops, and automatic control systems was crucial for automation. An early example of such a mechanism is James Watt's centrifugal governor for steam engines, which automatically adjusted the machine's speed. The Industrial Revolution introduced machines and processes that automated mass production, such as Richard Arkwright's spinning machine and Joseph-Marie Jacquard's loom, which used punched cards to automate complex weaving patterns.

2.4.3 THE FIRST CALCULATING MACHINES

Devices such as Pascal's machine (1623–1662) and later Babbage's analytical engine (1791–1871) laid the foundation for modern computers by automating arithmetic calculations. These precursors all contributed to the evolution of the automated systems we know today, enabling the delegation of repetitive or complex tasks to machines, increasing efficiency, reducing human errors, and paving the way for the era of industrial and digital automation.

2.4.3.1 Limitations of Early Mechanical Calculating Machines

Early mechanical calculating machines, although revolutionary for their time, had several limitations that restricted their efficiency and scope. One of the main limitations was their mechanical complexity. Calculating machines such as Pascal's Pascaline or Babbage's analytical engine were composed of numerous gears, levers, and other mechanical components, making their construction extremely complex and costly. This complexity not only increased the risk of mechanical failures but also required frequent and specialized maintenance, limiting their reliability and durability. Another significant limitation was the restricted range of operations they could perform. Early calculating machines were generally designed for simple arithmetic tasks, such as addition and subtraction. Even more advanced machines, such as those envisioned by Babbage, struggled to handle more complex calculations or be programmed for different tasks without hardware modifications. Additionally, these machines were often slow and required constant human intervention to operate, limiting their ability to process large amounts of data quickly or efficiently.

These mechanical and functional limitations hindered the widespread adoption of early calculating machines and delayed their general use until the advent of electronic technologies in the 20th century.

2.4.3.2 The Influence of Pascal's Machine on Future Calculating Inventions

Pascal's machine had a significant influence on future inventions in the field of computation by establishing a mechanical calculation model that inspired many later inventors. The Pascaline was one of the first machines capable of performing arithmetic operations, particularly addition and subtraction, in a semi-automatic manner. Its design, based on interconnected toothed wheels to represent and manipulate numbers, demonstrated that mathematical processes, previously performed only by humans, could be mechanized, paving the way for the idea that calculations could be automated by machines. This innovation directly influenced other inventors, such as *Leibniz*, who improved Pascaline's concept to develop a machine capable of multiplication and division, marking a significant advancement in the complexity of calculations that machines could perform. Additionally, the Pascaline laid the foundation for the development of future mechanical calculating devices, including Thomas de Colmar's calculating machines in the 19th century, which were widely used in commerce and industry.

By introducing the idea that arithmetic operations could be entrusted to machines, the Pascaline not only demonstrated the feasibility of automated calculations but also inspired a long tradition of innovation, ultimately leading to the development of the first electronic computers.

2.4.3.3 Leibniz's Objectives with His Mechanical Calculator

Leibniz (1646–1716), in designing his mechanical calculator, aimed to address several issues related to the limitations of existing calculating machines and to enhance the efficiency of mathematical processes. First, he sought to overcome the restrictions of machines like Pascal's Pascaline, which could only perform addition and subtraction. Leibniz understood that to truly revolutionize computation, a machine needed to handle more complex operations, such as multiplication and division, which were essential for the scientific and commercial needs of his time. His machine, known as the Stepped Reckoner, featured an innovative stepped-drum mechanism, allowing for the mechanical execution of multiplication and division, providing a practical solution for automating tedious arithmetic tasks.

Additionally, he aimed to make calculations faster and more reliable, reducing the human errors common in long manual computations. He envisioned his calculator as a tool that could free scientists and merchants from repetitive tasks, enabling them to focus on more analytical aspects of their work. By attempting to create a machine capable of performing calculations without human intervention at every step, Leibniz laid the foundation for the idea that machines could not only assist but potentially replace humans in certain mathematical functions, foreshadowing the development of modern calculators and computers.

2.4.4 AUTOMATA

2.4.4.1 Automata and Human Ingenuity

An automaton is a machine or mechanical device designed to imitate or automatically reproduce a series of actions, often without direct human intervention, once activated. Automata can be relatively simple, such as a spring-driven mechanism that moves a figurine, or highly complex, involving gears, levers, and other components to perform sophisticated movements or operations. Historically, automata have been used for various purposes, including entertainment, scientific experimentation, demonstration of technical skills, and even religious or symbolic functions. They can take the form of humans, animals, or other entities, and their movements range from simple gestures to more complex tasks, such as writing, playing music, or performing repetitive labor.

Today, the term *automaton* can also refer to modern automated systems, including industrial robots or software programs that execute tasks autonomously. However, these modern automata are typically more advanced and often controlled by computer systems rather than purely mechanical mechanisms.

2.4.4.2   Differences between Islamic and European Automata

Islamic automata differed from those developed in Europe in terms of design, function, and cultural context. In the medieval Islamic world, automata were often created not only as entertainment devices but also as tools to demonstrate advanced scientific and technical principles. Figures such as Al-Jazari (1136–1206), a 12th-century engineer and inventor, designed sophisticated automata that combined hydraulic and mechanical mechanisms. These machines, including musical fountains, automatic clocks, and beverage-serving devices, were often integrated into luxurious settings such as palaces and gardens, showcasing the ingenuity and technical expertise of their creators.

In contrast, European automata developed during the Middle Ages and the Renaissance often had different purposes. They were frequently used for religious demonstrations or as symbols of power and technical mastery, particularly in church clocks and mechanical figures. While European automata shared with their Islamic counterparts a fascination with movement and the illusion of life, they were often simpler in their mechanisms compared to Islamic creations, which had reached a particularly high level of technical complexity. Another notable difference lies in the cultural and intellectual context in which these automata were developed. In the Islamic world, interest in engineering and mechanics was closely linked to a broader tradition of science and technology, often inspired by Greek, Indian, and Persian texts translated into Arabic. Automata were part of a larger quest to understand mechanical principles and their practical applications, integrated within a scientific and technical curiosity-driven approach. In Europe, however, automata were sometimes perceived as curiosities or luxury objects, reflecting an approach more focused on spectacle and symbolism rather than scientific investigation. While Islamic and European automata shared similarities as mechanical devices, they differed significantly in design, function, and cultural context. Islamic automata were more scientific and technically advanced, whereas European automata were often geared toward symbolism and entertainment.

2.4.4.3   The Impact of Automata on the Perception
of the Mechanization of Thought

Automata played a crucial role in shaping the perception of the mechanization of thought, introducing the idea that certain functions previously considered exclusively human could be simulated by machines. From the earliest automata capable of reproducing complex movements and actions, the notion that human thought itself could be imitated by mechanisms began to take shape. These devices, by mimicking aspects of human behavior such as writing, music, or even conversation, led philosophers and scientists to question the boundaries between machine and mind.

A notable example is the automata created by inventors such as Jacques de Vaucanson (1709–1782) in the 18th century, particularly his famous "Digesting

Duck," which simulated biological actions like eating and digestion. Although these actions were purely mechanical, they raised profound questions about the nature of thought and life. *If a machine could imitate complex biological processes, did this suggest that thought itself could be broken down into mechanical processes?* These reflections fueled philosophical debates on materialism and the soul, foreshadowing modern conceptions of AI. Moreover, automata also influenced the development of early theories of mechanical intelligence. Philosophers like René Descartes used the concept of automata to formulate hypotheses about the human body as a machine, where bodily functions could be understood as mechanical processes governed by physical laws. This mechanistic view of the body was gradually extended to the mind, contributing to the question of whether machines could one day *'think.'*

Thus, automata not only shaped the collective imagination surrounding the mechanization of thought but also laid the foundation for philosophical reflections that would later influence modern conceptions of cognition and AI.

2.4.4.4 Main Applications of Automata in Both Cultures

The primary applications of automata in Islamic and European cultures varied depending on their social, religious, and technological contexts, yet they shared common objectives such as wonder, displays of power, and scientific advancement. In the medieval Islamic world, automata were often integrated into prestigious environments such as palaces and royal gardens, where they showcased technical ingenuity and mastery of mechanical sciences. For example, Al-Jazari, a 13th-century engineer, designed fountains, clocks, and entertainment automata that blended art and science to create impressive spectacles, often intended for the royal court. These devices were not merely for entertainment but also served as demonstrations of mechanical and hydraulic principles, illustrating the technological advancements of Islamic civilization.

In Europe, automata also had diverse applications, ranging from displays of wealth and power to religious and scientific purposes. Astronomical clocks and their associated automata, installed in cathedrals and public squares, served to awe the public while conveying religious or symbolic messages. These machines often depicted biblical scenes or allegorical figures, illustrating the passage of time and the relationship between humanity, nature, and the divine. Beyond spectacle, some European automata were designed for scientific study and experimentation. The growing interest in mechanics and physics during the Renaissance led to the development of more complex automata, which were used to explore the fundamental principles of movement and natural forces. In both cultures, automata served both practical and symbolic purposes, functioning as entertainment devices, displays of power, and instruments for scientific advancement. While in the Islamic world, automata were closely tied to engineering and courtly artistry, in Europe, they often carried religious and allegorical significance, while also being used to explore new frontiers in science and mechanics. These devices played a key role in spreading technical knowledge and shaped how each culture perceived and manipulated the relationship between humans, machines, and the natural world.

3 The Age of Enlightenment and Development of Thinking Machines

3.1 EVOLUTION OF MATHEMATICS DURING THE AGE OF ENLIGHTENMENT

The Age of Enlightenment, often referred to as the Century of Lights, was a major intellectual and cultural turning point in Europe, spanning roughly from the early 18th century until the French Revolution. This movement promoted values such as reason, liberty, equality, and fraternity, marking a significant break from the preceding centuries, which were dominated by religious dogmatism and absolute monarchical authority. Enlightenment thinkers, such as Voltaire (1694–1778), Rousseau (1712–1778), Montesquieu (1689–1755), Immanuel Kant (1724–1804), and many others, criticized existing political and religious systems and proposed new ideas that profoundly influenced Western thought.

One of the most significant contributions of this era lies in how rational thought was applied to understanding and reforming society. The Enlightenment encouraged a worldview grounded in empiricism and the scientific method, where observation, experimentation, and logical reasoning became the primary tools for uncovering truth. This approach led to spectacular advances in the natural sciences, mathematics, and philosophy, paving the way for the Industrial Revolution and the modern era. Regarding the mechanization of thought, the Enlightenment saw the emergence of the idea that human thought processes could be analyzed, modeled, and potentially replicated by machines. This concept stemmed in part from the development of formal logic, spearheaded by thinkers like Leibniz, who dreamed of creating a universal mathematics or a calculating language that could resolve all human disputes by reducing them to logical computations. This dream of mechanizing thought continued with the work of Boole in the 19th century, who formalized logic into a mathematical system, Boolean algebra, crucial for the later development of logic circuits used in computers.

Charles Babbage, meanwhile, stands as an iconic figure of this period for his attempts to create a machine capable of automating complex calculation processes. His Analytical Engine, designed in the mid-19th century, was a true innovation, often regarded as the first concept of a programmable computer. Although he was unable to complete its construction, Babbage laid the foundations for modern computing by

DOI: 10.1201/9781003613633-3

envisioning a machine capable of executing any sequence of arithmetic operations. Ada Lovelace (1815–1852) was a visionary in anticipating the capabilities of these machines far beyond mere calculation. She understood that Babbage's machines could manipulate symbols according to rules, thus laying the groundwork for what we now call programming. Lovelace is often cited as the first programmer in history, and her ideas profoundly influenced how we conceive of the interaction between machines and human thought. Presumably, the Age of Enlightenment was a period of deep reflection on the nature of thought, reason, and knowledge, giving rise to the radical idea that these processes could be systematically understood and even automated. This perspective not only laid the foundation for the Industrial Revolution but also for the computer revolution that would transform the world in the 20th century, leading to the emergence of AI as we know it today.

The evolution of mathematics from the Middle Ages through the Enlightenment and up to the birth of AI reflects a progressive and revolutionary development of concepts, methods, and applications. In what follows, a detailed explanation in several stages is given.

3.1.1 THE MIDDLE AGES: TRANSMISSION AND REVIVAL OF KNOWLEDGE

After the fall of the Roman Empire in the 5th century, Europe entered a period marked by a slowdown in scientific and technical progress, known as the Middle Ages. This era, often mistakenly labeled as the Dark Ages, nonetheless witnessed the preservation and enrichment of ancient knowledge in the Islamic world. While Western Europe focused primarily on spiritual and theological matters, sciences and mathematics continued to thrive in cultural centers such as Baghdad, Damascus, and Cordoba. These places became crossroads where Greek, Indian, and Persian knowledge intertwined, giving rise to numerous innovations.

One of the greatest contributors of this period was *Khwarizmi,* who played a key role in the development of algebra, particularly in solving quadratic equations (as explained thoroughly in the previous section). His method for solving this equation relied on a geometric and algebraic process, thus laying the foundations for modern algebra. This approach was revolutionary, introducing concepts still in use today. His work, *Kitab al-Mukhtasar fi Hisab al-Jabr wal-Muqabala* (*The Compendious Book on Calculation by Completion and Balancing*), represents the first systematization of this discipline and introduces methods for solving linear and quadratic equations. Furthermore, *Khwarizmi* was instrumental in introducing the Indo-Irano-Arabic numeral system to Europe, a far more efficient system for complex calculations than Roman numerals. This system, along with the concept of zero, revolutionized the way mathematics was taught and practiced in the West.

The Islamic world did not limit itself to generating new ideas; it also excelled in preserving and transmitting ancient knowledge. Foundational texts by Greek mathematicians such as Euclid (c. 300 BCE), Archimedes (c. 287–212 BCE), and Ptolemy (c. 100–c. 170 CE) were translated into Arabic by scholars like Hunayn ibn Ishaq (808–873) and Thabit ibn Qurra (826–901). These translations not only preserved these works but also enriched them with commentary and improvements. Later, these works were transmitted to Europe through Muslim Spain and Sicily, where scholars like Gerard of Cremona (1114–1187) translated them from Greek, Persian, or Arabic into Latin, facilitating their spread in the Christian world.

From the 12th century onward, the first European universities, notably those in Paris, Bologna, and Oxford, played a decisive role in reintroducing mathematics into academic circles. Influenced by scholars from Greece and the Islamic world, these institutions began incorporating Euclid's geometry into their curricula, marking a turning point in how mathematics was perceived and taught. These universities also laid the groundwork for the emergence of a more structured and systematic approach to mathematical knowledge. Geometry held a central place in mathematical education during this period, thanks to Euclid's Elements, regarded as an essential reference. The properties of geometric figures and their rigorous proofs captivated European scholars, who saw in these texts a model of logical and structured thinking. This influence extended beyond schools and universities into practical fields such as architecture and engineering. At the same time, commercial arithmetic experienced significant growth, driven by the expansion of international trade in the Middle Ages. European merchants, faced with calculation challenges related to exchange rates, weights of goods, and loan interest, quickly adopted the Indo-Irano-Arabic numerals and computational methods introduced by Khwarizmi. These innovations made mathematical operations faster and more reliable, thereby facilitating the growth of trade.

This growing interest in mathematics was accompanied by a revival in the creation of practical and educational manuals. Works like *Fibonacci*'s *Liber Abaci*, written in the 13th century, played a key role in popularizing Indo-Irano-Arabic numerals and algebraic techniques in Europe. Though aimed at a limited audience of merchant elites and university scholars, these books helped embed mathematics into European culture. The Middle Ages, therefore, was not a period of complete obscurantism, but rather a time of transition during which knowledge was preserved, enriched, and gradually reintroduced into Europe. Cultural exchanges between the Islamic world and the Christian West enabled the transmission of a rich and diverse mathematical heritage. Although innovations remained limited compared to the revolutions of later eras, the foundations laid during this period were essential for future developments.

3.1.2 THE RENAISSANCE: A PERIOD OF RENEWAL

The Renaissance, spanning from the 14th to the 16th century, marks a period of profound transformation in the history of mathematics, characterized by a renewed interest in the exact sciences. This movement is closely tied to humanism, a philosophy that places man and his capabilities at the center of intellectual pursuits and encourages the rediscovery of original Greek texts. Unlike the Middle Ages, where these texts were often transmitted by Iranian or Arabic translators, the Renaissance saw scholars return to the Latin and Greek sources, reestablishing a direct connection with antiquity. This quest for ancient knowledge was accompanied by a renewed enthusiasm for the study of mathematics. Among the major contributions of this era is the evolution of algebra, driven by mathematicians such as Girolamo Cardano (1501–1576) and Niccolò Tartaglia (1499–1557). In the 16th century, these two scholars revolutionized the field by developing methods to solve cubic and quartic equations that had confounded the brightest minds for centuries. Cardano's work, documented in his seminal book Ars Magna, became an essential reference and laid the groundwork for modern algebra. These advances enabled mathematicians to tackle increasingly complex equations, paving the way for a greater formalization of mathematics. In algebra, François Viète (1540–1603) also played a fundamental role by introducing a symbolic language to express mathematical relationships. His notations, which used letters to represent variables and parameters, marked a major break from the verbal and geometric approaches employed previously. This new tool offered unprecedented clarity and efficiency, simplifying the manipulation of equations and enabling the generalization of mathematical results. Viète is often regarded as one of the founders of symbolic algebra, a language that would become universal in the centuries that followed. These major contributions to algebra and symbolic notation are summarized in Table 3.1, which highlights the principal mathematical innovations of the Renaissance and their lasting impact on the evolution of scientific thought.

TABLE 3.1
Major Mathematical Innovations of the Renaissance

Innovation	Mathematician	Main Impact
Solving cubic equations	Tartaglia, Cardano	Advancement of algebra
Symbolic notation	François Viète	Formalization of mathematical language
Logarithms	John Napier	Simplification of calculations
Perspective in art	Piero della Francesca	Application of geometry to art
Indo-Iranian-Arabic numeration	Fibonacci	More efficient calculations in Europe

The Renaissance was not merely a period of theoretical reflection; it was also marked by the practical application of mathematics, particularly in the fields of perspective and applied geometry. Renaissance artists such as Leonardo da Vinci (1452–1519) and Albrecht Dürer (1471–1528) took a deep interest in representing space and objects realistically. This pursuit led to advancements in the understanding of linear perspective, a technique grounded in rigorous geometric principles. The works of Piero della Francesca (1415–1492) demonstrate how mathematics could enrich art by providing tools to depict depth and proportion with unprecedented precision. This interaction between art and mathematics illustrates how the Renaissance broke down barriers between disciplines, fostering an interdisciplinary approach to knowledge. Applied geometry, spurred by the needs of art and architecture, also found uses in other practical fields such as cartography and engineering. Marine charts, for example, benefited from progress in trigonometry and geometric projection, facilitating exploratory voyages and contributing to the expansion of international trade.

The impact of mathematics during the Renaissance extended beyond the arts and practical applications; it also became an essential tool for the natural sciences. Nicolaus Copernicus (1473–1543), in his work De revolutionibus orbium coelestium, employed mathematics to develop his heliocentric model of the universe, challenging the prevailing geocentric views since antiquity. By placing mathematics at the heart of astronomy, Copernicus paved the way for scientists like Johannes Kepler (1571–1630) and Galileo Galilei (1564–1642), who would refine these ideas with precise mathematical laws. Johannes Kepler relied on mathematics to formulate his famous laws of planetary motion. These laws, which describe the elliptical orbits of planets around the Sun, marked a decisive step in applying mathematics to understanding the cosmos. Kepler demonstrated that mathematics was not merely a language for describing the world but also a tool for uncovering the fundamental laws governing the universe. This perspective transformed how scholars conceived the relationship between nature and mathematics.

The Renaissance also marked a turning point in the social perception of mathematics. Long viewed as an abstract discipline reserved for an intellectual elite, mathematics gradually gained recognition as a practical and useful field of knowledge. Architects, engineers, and merchants increasingly adopted mathematical tools to solve real-world problems, reinforcing their relevance in daily life. This democratization of mathematics was facilitated by the publication of educational manuals, such as those by Luca Pacioli (1447–1517), which made mathematical concepts accessible to a broader audience. The invention of the printing press in the 15th century played a crucial role in the dissemination of mathematical knowledge. By making books more accessible and affordable, it enabled the rapid spread of new ideas. The works of mathematicians like Girolamo Cardano (1501–1576), François Viète, and Nicolaus Copernicus (1473–1543) reached a wider audience, fostering intellectual dialogue across Europe. This circulation of ideas also encouraged healthy competition among scholars, accelerating the pace of discoveries.

To summarize, the Renaissance was a period of renewal and transformation for mathematics. Inspired by humanism and the rediscovery of ancient knowledge, it witnessed major advances in algebra, geometry, and their practical applications. Mathematics became a central tool for the natural sciences, art, and technology, laying the groundwork for a scientific revolution that would peak in the 17th century. This era testifies to the power of mathematics as a universal language for understanding and transforming the world. Figure 3.1 presents the emblematic figures of this period.

Léonard de Vinci   Nicolas Copernic   Girolamo Cardano
(1452-1519)   (1473-1543)   (1501-1576)

François Viète   Johannes Kepler
(1540-1603)   (1571-1630)

FIGURE 3.1   The emblematic figures of the Renaissance period.

3.1.3 Mathematics as a Universal Language

3.1.3.1 Philosophical Context

The Enlightenment, spanning the 17th and 18th centuries, is characterized by an intellectual and cultural renewal that places reason at the core of human concerns. Thinkers of this era rejected explanations rooted in religious dogma, superstition, and unchanging traditions, favoring instead a systematic pursuit of truth through observation, experimentation, and logical deduction. This movement, deeply influenced by the scientific revolution of the preceding century, views knowledge as a tool for emancipation and progress. The philosophy of the Enlightenment promotes the idea that humanity can master its destiny by understanding and systematizing the laws of nature. In this context, mathematics emerged as a central discipline, perceived as the universal language capable of unveiling the underlying mechanisms of the universe. The Enlightenment embraced the scientific advances of the 17th century, such as René Descartes' analytic geometry or the differential and integral calculus developed by Newton and Leibniz, not only as practical tools but also as evidence of the power of human reason. These mathematical innovations demonstrated that natural phenomena, once attributed to supernatural forces, could be described by precise and rational laws.

One of the fundamental aspects of Enlightenment philosophy is the concept of systematizing knowledge. Inspired by figures like Francis Bacon (1561–1626) and René Descartes, the philosophers and scientists of this period adopted a methodical approach, seeking to organize knowledge into a coherent whole. Mathematics, with its logical and rigorous structure, became a model for other disciplines. Its ability to yield universally valid results, independent of cultural or historical contexts, made it a preferred tool for systematizing the natural sciences. The emphasis on experimentation, also central to this era, transformed how mathematics was perceived and applied. Unlike earlier periods when mathematics was often regarded as a purely speculative discipline, the Enlightenment highlighted its practical utility. Advances in fields such as mechanics, astronomy, and engineering relied on a combination of precise experiments and sophisticated mathematical models. This approach reflected the Enlightenment's belief in a convergence between theory and practice, between abstraction and application.

Moreover, the dissemination of mathematical ideas to a broader audience was a notable phenomenon of this period. Thinkers like Émilie du Châtelet (1706–1749) and Voltaire worked to make the complex concepts developed by Newton and Leibniz accessible to the general public. Their goal was not only to popularize science but also to demonstrate how rational principles could be applied to all aspects of human life, from politics to morality. This popularization helped solidify the notion that mathematics embodied the rationalist ideal of the Enlightenment. The systematization and dissemination of mathematical knowledge were also symbolized by landmark projects such as the Encyclopédie by Diderot and Alembert. This monumental work, intended to compile and transmit the entirety of human knowledge, gave significant prominence to mathematics and its practical applications. It reflected the

Enlightenment's ambition to democratize knowledge and make the tools of reason available to all.

3.1.3.2 The Mathematical Revolution of the 17th Century

The mathematical revolution of the 17th century was marked by major advances that redefined mathematics as a pivotal discipline in understanding the natural world. Among the most significant contributions are the invention of analytic geometry by René Descartes and the independent development of differential and integral calculus by Newton and Leibniz. These innovations transformed mathematics into a universal language and provided essential tools for physics and the natural sciences. They embody the birth of modern mathematics, with an impact that endures across all branches of science and technology. René Descartes, in his work 'La Géométrie' (1637), introduced analytic geometry, a revolutionary method that linked the concepts of algebra with those of geometry. Through this approach, it became possible to represent geometric curves with algebraic equations and, conversely, to visualize algebraic equations graphically. This connection enabled a deeper analysis of the properties of curves and geometric figures.

Analytic geometry extended beyond purely theoretical applications. It became a central tool for solving practical problems in fields such as astronomy, mechanics, and optics. By combining geometry and algebra, Descartes paved the way for a broader mathematization of physical phenomena, an approach later exploited by scientists like Newton and Huygens. This tool also gave rise to the Cartesian coordinate system, which allows a point in space to be located using a simple pair or triplet of values still used today across all scientific and engineering disciplines. In parallel, Isaac Newton and Leibniz, working independently of each other, developed differential and integral calculus during the second half of the 17th century. These two revolutionary mathematical tools enabled the analysis of continuous change and dynamic phenomena with unprecedented precision. Newton presented his work in the context of mechanics, particularly in his masterpiece *Philosophiæ Naturalis Principia Mathematica* (1687), where he introduced the foundational concepts of derivation and integration to explain the laws of motion and universal gravitation. *Leibniz*, on the other hand, developed an elegant and systematic notation for differential and integral calculus. His notation, still in use today, facilitates the understanding and application of these concepts across numerous scientific fields. Although disputes over the paternity of these discoveries marked their history, the contributions of Newton and Leibniz complement each other and lay the foundations for modern calculus. Differential calculus allows for the measurement of instantaneous changes, such as the velocity or acceleration of a moving object, by determining the slope of a tangent to a given curve. Integration, conversely, enables the calculation of aggregate quantities, such as the area under a curve or the volume of a solid. Together, these tools provide a refined understanding of physical and natural phenomena, such as the trajectories of planets, the flow of fluids, or the propagation of waves.

These mathematical advances were not limited to theoretical implications; they also revolutionized practical applications. Classical mechanics relies on the principles of calculus to model and predict the motion of objects. In astronomy, they enable the calculation of celestial orbits with remarkable precision, as demonstrated by Newton's work on gravitation. In engineering, these methods find applications in bridge construction, machine optimization, and the analysis of structural forces.

3.1.3.3 Increasing Formalization

The 17th century marks a crucial stage in the evolution of mathematics with an increasing formalization that transforms the discipline into a more abstract and rigorous science. This period, influenced by the rise of the scientific method and a growing interest in the systematization of knowledge, witnesses the emergence of new branches of mathematics, such as probability and statistics, alongside a deepening of conceptual foundations. This evolution not only refines mathematical tools but also broadens their scope across diverse fields like physics, finance, and the social sciences. One of the key features of this growing formalization is the effort to establish precise definitions, clear axioms, and rigorous proofs. This movement, inspired by figures like Euclid, seeks to eliminate ambiguities and ground mathematics in solid, coherent foundations. Descartes, for example, introduces systematic notations in algebra, while Newton and Leibniz build rigorous frameworks for differential and integral calculus. These efforts reflect an ambitious vision: to make mathematics a model of rational thought applicable to all sciences. This era sees the birth of probability theory through the work of Blaise Pascal (1623–1662) and Pierre de Fermat (1607–1665). Their collaboration, sparked by questions about games of chance, leads to fundamental concepts such as mathematical expectation and probability distributions. Pascal, in his Letters to Fermat, explores ways to fairly divide stakes between two players when a game is interrupted. These ideas, initially confined to gambling, lay the groundwork for a discipline that will profoundly influence fields as varied as statistics, statistical physics, and risk management. The development of probability also paves the way for more abstract reflections on uncertainty and predictability. Questions about the behavior of random phenomena, such as population fluctuations or financial market movements, find answers in this new branch of mathematics. These ideas are later enriched by the work of Jakob Bernoulli (1655–1705) and Abraham de Moivre (1667–1754), who formalize concepts like the law of large numbers and normal distributions.

Formalization does not stop at probability theory. Mathematics progressively becomes a universal framework for modeling complex phenomena, thanks to increased rigor and the emergence of standardized notations. These innovations facilitate the communication of ideas and accelerate their dissemination among scientists. The mathematical symbolism popularized by figures like Leibniz allows complex relationships to be expressed concisely and systematically for modeling and computation. In parallel, statistics emerges as a distinct discipline, initially driven by practical needs such as the analysis of demographic and economic data. John Graunt (1620–1674) and William Petty (1623–1687), for instance, used statistical methods to analyze mortality rates and understand population dynamics. These early efforts mark the beginning of a revolution that will transform data collection and interpretation across fields ranging from biology to economics.

By the 18th century, statistics takes on a more theoretical dimension with the work of Pierre-Simon Laplace (1749–1827), who develops tools for analyzing data and predicting future events. Laplace introduces the concept of conditional probability and applies statistics to diverse problems, notably in astronomy. His famous *Philosophical Essay on Probabilities* demonstrates how mathematics can rationalize uncertainty and guide decision-making. The growing formalization of mathematics also has a profound impact on philosophy and scientific methodology. Mathematics becomes a model for other disciplines, inspiring systematic and rigorous approaches in fields like physics, chemistry, and even the humanities. For example, *Newton*'s mechanics, grounded in precise mathematical principles, serves as a benchmark for other scientific branches seeking to establish universal laws.

This trend toward formalization sets the stage for future developments, particularly in logic and algorithmics, which will play a central role in the birth of computer science and AI. The rigor and abstraction of 17th-century mathematics thus form the foundations of an intellectual revolution that extends far beyond its initial scope. The increasing formalization of mathematics in the 17th century marks an essential step in its transformation into a universal and abstract science. The emergence of branches like probability and statistics reflects both the need to address practical problems and a quest for a deeper understanding of random phenomena. This evolution, driven by brilliant minds such as Blaise Pascal, Pierre de Fermat (1607–1665), and Pierre-Simon Laplace (1749–1827), lays the groundwork for subsequent advances in mathematics and numerous other fields of knowledge.

3.1.3.4   Practical Applications

The Enlightenment, with its emphasis on rationality and the practical application of science, saw mathematics play a central role in solving real-world problems related to engineering, navigation, and finance. This period was marked by a profound interplay between mathematical discoveries and their applications in everyday life, laying the foundations for disciplines and tools still in use today. In engineering, mathematical advances, particularly in differential and integral calculus, enabled the modeling of complex structures and the optimization of their design. Newton and Leibniz, through the development of infinitesimal calculus, provided engineers with tools to analyze forces, motion, and deformations. These concepts were applied in fields such as bridge construction, machine design, and even architecture, where an understanding of mechanical stresses allowed for bolder and more efficient constructions. In navigation, mathematics greatly facilitated the resolution of practical challenges. Methods of triangulation and the calculation of geographic coordinates, rooted in geometry and trigonometry, enabled navigators to determine their position with greater accuracy. The invention of the marine chronometer by John Harrison (1693–1776), combined with logarithmic tables and time equations, made it possible to determine longitude at sea. These advancements revolutionized transoceanic voyages and played a key role in the expansion of European colonial empires. In finance, the development of probability and statistics allowed for more precise modeling of risks and returns. The work of Pascal and Fermat on games of chance was quickly adapted to assess financial risks, particularly in insurance and investments. This era also saw the first attempts to formalize the foundations of economic theory using mathematical tools, setting the stage for future developments in quantitative economics. The impact of mathematics on physics, particularly Newton's laws of classical mechanics, cannot be overstated. Newton's *Philosophiæ Naturalis Principia Mathematica*, published in 1687, brilliantly demonstrates how mathematics can be used to express the fundamental laws of nature. The laws of motion and universal gravitation have been formulated in his work, which remained at the heart of physics until the 20th century. Expressed in mathematical language, these laws provide a unified framework for understanding and predicting the movements of terrestrial and celestial bodies.

The applications of Newton's laws were not confined to theoretical physics. They underpinned numerous practical advancements. For instance, in artillery, the equations of motion enabled precise calculations of projectile trajectories, enhancing military performance. Similarly, civil and mechanical engineers relied on these laws to design machines and structures capable of withstanding the forces they encountered. In astronomy, mathematics derived from classical mechanics allowed for highly accurate predictions of the movements of planets, comets, and eclipses. These advancements, achieved by figures like Johannes Kepler and later Pierre-Simon Laplace, bolstered confidence in mathematics as a tool for deciphering the laws of the universe. Maritime navigation and astronomical calendars directly benefited from these developments. Beyond these specific applications, the Enlightenment also witnessed the emergence of a systematic approach to solving complex problems. Engineers and scientists of the time began modeling natural phenomena and human systems with mathematical equations, establishing a direct link between theory and practice. This methodology laid the groundwork for modern applied sciences, where mathematics plays a critical role in prediction, optimization, and control. The ideas developed during this period also paved the way for industrialization. Mathematical tools used in engineering and mechanics were integrated into the design and production of machines during the Industrial Revolution. This not only improved the efficiency of industrial processes but also enabled greater automation, marking the initial steps toward the mechanization of thought.

Given the above-mentioned explanations, the mathematics of the Enlightenment was not limited to theoretical abstractions. Their power lay in their ability to address concrete problems in engineering, navigation, and finance, while also establishing universal laws such as those of Newton. These practical applications reinforced mathematics's central role in science and technology, decisively contributing to the cultural, economic, and industrial transformations of the era.

3.1.3.5   Philosophy of the Enlightenment and Mathematics

The philosophy of the Enlightenment, steeped in a rationalist ideal, profoundly influenced the role and perception of mathematics. This period saw a concerted effort to make mathematical concepts accessible to a broader audience while celebrating mathematics as a central pillar of reason and human progress. Two prominent figures of this movement, Émilie du Châtelet and Voltaire (1694–1778), perfectly illustrate the convergence between Enlightenment philosophy and mathematics. Émilie du Châtelet, a physicist and philosopher, played a key role in disseminating the mathematical and scientific ideas of the Enlightenment. Her translation and commentary on *Newton*'s *Philosophiæ Naturalis Principia Mathematica*, combined with her own analyses, helped popularize complex concepts such as universal gravitation and infinitesimal calculus. Through her pedagogical approach, she made these ideas accessible not only to scientists but also to an educated public, convincing them of the importance of mathematics in understanding the laws of nature. Voltaire, her companion and collaborator, also contributed to the popularization of mathematics. Though not a mathematician himself, he recognized their essential role in building rational knowledge. In his writings, Voltaire often praised mathematics as the universal language of reason, capable of illuminating minds and combating superstition. His influence as a writer and philosopher helped situate mathematics within a broader cultural framework, presenting it as a tool for intellectual liberation.

The success of mathematics during the Enlightenment both reflected and reinforced the rationalist ideal of the era. In a context where reason was upheld as the supreme guide for organizing society and understanding the world, mathematics embodied the purity and certainty of logical thought. They were seen as a model for other disciplines, from philosophy to politics, and as an antidote to arbitrariness and irrationality. This perception was bolstered by the major achievements of mathematics in solving both practical and theoretical problems. Advances in astronomy, mechanics, navigation, and finance demonstrated their effectiveness in decoding the laws of the universe and improving the human condition. These tangible successes reinforced the idea that reason, guided by mathematics, could positively transform the world.

Beyond their scientific applications, mathematics also played a symbolic role. They represented an ideal of universality, capable of transcending cultural and linguistic boundaries. The Enlightenment, driven by a quest for universal truth, saw mathematics as a common language to unite enlightened minds across Europe and beyond. The teaching of mathematics also expanded during this period, spurred by the rise of academies and universities. Pedagogical works, often inspired by the contributions of figures like Newton and Leibniz, that emphasized rigor and clarity associated with the Enlightenment spirit. These texts aimed to train citizens capable of logical reasoning, aligning with the educational ideals of the time. The Enlightenment philosophy also viewed mathematics as a tool for structuring thought and critically evaluating ideas. Philosophers of the era, such as Jean le Rond d'Alembert (1717–1783), stressed the importance of the mathematical method as a model for all forms of reasoning. This methodological paradigm influenced disciplines like sociology, economics, and even ethics. Philosophical debates about the nature of mathematics themselves reflected this rationalist ideal. The Enlightenment questioned the foundations of mathematics: *Were they a creation of the human mind or a discovery of universal laws?* These discussions, led by figures like *Kant* and *Leibniz*, reinforced the notion that mathematics lay at the heart of the Enlightenment's pursuit of truth.

However, the philosophy of the Enlightenment and mathematics nurtured a symbiotic relationship. Mathematics, popularized by figures like Émilie du Châtelet and Voltaire, embodied the rational and universal ideal of the era. Their success, both practically and symbolically, illustrated the power of enlightened reason and laid the groundwork for a worldview in which logic and science played a central role in improving the human condition. Figure 3.2 highlights some of the mathematicians who had the greatest impact during the Enlightenment period.

René Descartes
(1596-1650)

Blaise Pascal
(1623-1662)

Isaac Newton
(1643-1727)

Gottfried Wilhelm Leibniz
(1646-1716)

Émilie du Châtelet
(1706-1749)

Leonhard Euler
(1707-1783)

Joseph Louis de Lagrange
(1749-1827)

Pierre-Simon de Laplace
(1749-1827)

George Boole
(1815-1864)

FIGURE 3.2   The most influential mathematicians of the Enlightenment period.

3.1.4   FROM THE ENLIGHTENMENT TO THE BIRTH OF AI

3.1.4.1   19th Century: Abstraction and Unification

The 19th century represents a pivotal period in the history of mathematics, characterized by a significant shift toward abstraction and the unification of its various branches. This century witnessed the emergence of mathematical concepts that not only redefined the foundations of the science but also laid the groundwork for modern mathematics. Leading figures such as Carl Friedrich Gauss (1777–1855), Bernhard Riemann (1826–1866), Évariste Galois (1811–1832), Niels Henrik Abel (1802–1829), and Georg Cantor (1845–1918) were instrumental in these transformative developments.

One of the most significant breakthroughs was the emergence of non-Euclidean geometry, a radical departure from the Euclidean geometry that had dominated for centuries. Carl Friedrich Gauss (1777–1855) was among the first to explore the possibilities of non-Euclidean geometry, though his work remained unpublished during his lifetime. The core idea of non-Euclidean geometry is that Euclid's postulates, particularly the parallel postulate, are not necessarily true in all geometric contexts. Gauss speculated about a spherical geometry where, for instance, parallel lines would eventually intersect. It was Bernhard Riemann, however, who fully developed this concept, creating Riemannian geometry, which is based on curved surfaces and enables the treatment of n-dimensional spaces. This non-Euclidean approach not only revolutionized geometry but also paved the way for decisive advances in physics, notably in Albert Einstein's theory of general relativity, where spacetime is modeled as a curved manifold using the principles of Riemannian geometry.

Concurrently, a revolution unfolded in algebra through the work of Évariste Galois and Niels Henrik Abel. Galois laid the foundations of group theory, a concept that elucidates the symmetries and structures of polynomial equations. Through this theory, *Galois* demonstrated that equations of degree higher than four could not be solved by radicals, and thus, it opened new avenues in algebraic equations. His work also had a profound influence on physics, particularly in particle theories and symmetries in quantum mechanics. The Norwegian mathematician Niels Henrik Abel, meanwhile, proved that fifth-degree equations could not be solved by an algebraic formula, marking the end of centuries-long attempts to find a general solution. These discoveries signaled a transition from classical algebra to a more abstract and theoretical form, establishing the foundations of modern mathematics. The theory of complex numbers, also developed during the 19th century, played a central role in this abstraction. Although they had been used to solve equations since the 16th century, complex numbers were systematically integrated into algebra and analysis, becoming a fundamental tool in mathematics. Gauss notably introduced the geometric representation of complex numbers, placing them on the complex plane, which enhanced their application in understanding polynomial equations.

Another major advance of the 19th century was the birth of set theory, a revolution that would define the structure of mathematics from the early 20th century onward. Initiated by Georg Cantor, this theory redefined infinity and sets by demonstrating that some infinities are larger than others. Cantor introduced the concepts of cardinality and ordinality, tools for comparing the sizes of infinite sets, and showed the existence of countable and uncountable infinities. Though controversial at the time, these findings deepened the understanding of sets and became foundational to 20th-century mathematics.

The unification of mathematics in the 19th century was not limited to these fundamental discoveries. This period also saw the consolidation of relationships between different mathematical branches. Algebra, geometry, and analysis, previously studied in isolation, began to interact more fluidly. For example, algebraic geometry, which bridges algebraic and geometric ideas, emerged from the work of mathematicians like Felix Klein (1849–1925) and David Hilbert (1862–1943). These interconnections fostered a unification of mathematical concepts and paved the way for more general and integrated theories. Beyond abstraction, this unification also impacted the rigor of mathematical proofs. The 19th century marked a turning point in the formalization of mathematics, shifting from intuitive approaches to more rigorous and systematic methods. The notions of formalism and precision in mathematical demonstration gained strength, setting the stage for the systematization of axioms in the 20th century. Cantor's work on set theory exemplifies this rigor. By precisely defining sets and their relationships, Cantor expanded the understanding of mathematical structures and established a robust theoretical framework for the continued evolution of mathematics. The idea that mathematics is a precise and universal language became fully ingrained in the mindset of mathematicians of this era.

The developments in abstract algebra, complex numbers, non-Euclidean geometry, and set theory fundamentally altered the conception of mathematics. These new ideas introduced a more general and unified approach, greatly facilitating the emergence of more complex and advanced theories in the 20th century, particularly in logic and computer science. Beyond pure theory, the practical applications of these advances were not long in coming. Concepts from non-Euclidean geometry found immediate applications in physics, notably in Einstein's general relativity. Likewise, algebraic theories influenced diverse fields such as chemistry, computer science, and cryptography. Set theory, meanwhile, became essential to mathematical logic and the foundation of formal sciences.

The 19th century, with its strides in abstraction and unification, marked the end of an era of predominantly practical mathematics and the birth of modern mathematics, whose principles undergird the formal logic and algorithms that drive contemporary AI. It is within this context that the mathematical foundations of AI began to take shape, preparing the ground for 20th-century developments in fields as varied as theoretical physics, biology, and, of course, computer science. The repercussions of these discoveries were manifold. The work of Gauss, Riemann, Galois, Abel, and Cantor did not remain confined to their time (Table 3.2). It profoundly influenced subsequent generations of mathematicians and continues to guide contemporary research. These advances laid the groundwork for mathematical logic, graph theory, and algorithms for the construction of AI as we know it today.

TABLE 3.2

Major Mathematicians of the 18th—19th Centuries and Their Contributions

Mathematician	Contribution	Impact
Carl Friedrich Gauss (1777–1855)	Developed ideas of non-Euclidean geometry, complex numbers representation	Foundations of curved spaces and complex analysis
Bernhard Riemann (1826–1866)	Riemannian geometry, curved n-dimensional spaces	Basis for *Einstein*'s general relativity
Évariste Galois (1811–1832)	Founded group theory, solved polynomial symmetries	Modern abstract algebra, quantum symmetry
Niels Henrik Abel (1802–1829)	Proved insolvability of quintic equations	Transition to modern algebraic theory
Georg Cantor (1845–1918)	Developed set theory, cardinalities of infinity	Basis of mathematical logic and formal mathematics

3.1.4.2   19th–20th Centuries: Formalization and Logical Revolution

At the turn of the 19th and 20th centuries, a major upheaval occurred in the world of mathematics with the formalization and logical revolution. This era marked the transition of mathematics from a discipline rooted in intuition to a rigorous science built entirely on axioms and logical systems. The formalization of mathematics was driven by figures such as David Hilbert, Giuseppe Peano (1858–1932), and George Boole, who played essential roles in the evolution of mathematical logic, paving the way for fields like computer science and AI.

David Hilbert, one of the greatest mathematicians of this period, undertook a vast project to systematize mathematical axioms. His program, formulated at the beginning of the 20th century, aimed to formalize all of mathematics based on a clear and rigorous set of axioms from which all mathematical theories could be derived. He believed it was possible to prove the consistency of these axioms, which became a key driver of the development of mathematics and logic in the 20th century. His program not only reinforced the importance of foundations but also influenced branches such as number theory and functional analysis. In parallel, Giuseppe Peano, an Italian mathematician, made a major contribution to the formalization of mathematics with the construction of the Peano axioms. These axioms, which define the properties of natural numbers, played a central role in formalizing mathematical structures. They demonstrated that the properties of numbers could be derived from elementary principles, creating a systematic framework for arithmetic and set theory. This work, combined with Hilbert's efforts, profoundly shaped the development of modern mathematical and logical theories.

The contributions of Hilbert and Peano paved the way for an understanding of mathematics as a coherent set of axioms. However, this program also faced criticism and challenges, notably from Kurt Gödel (1906–1978), who, in 1931, proved his incompleteness theorems. These theorems revealed the limitations of Hilbert's program, showing that it was impossible to formalize all mathematical truths within a finite set of axioms. This discovery altered the perception of logic and mathematics but also solidified the role of formal logic as a central framework for science. Simultaneously, George Boole established the foundation of mathematical logic with his ideas on symbolic logic. Through his work, he introduced the algebra of propositions, a formal system that allows logical statements to be manipulated as algebraic objects. This binary logic, also known as Boolean algebra, is based on binary values (true or false) and lies at the heart of modern computing. Boolean logic is essential for designing electronic circuits and computer processors, as well as for programming and algorithmics. The invention of this symbolic logic thus laid the theoretical groundwork for computer science. Boole's work also marked a significant transition between mathematics and computing. Formal logic enabled the representation of complex reasoning through symbols, which was crucial for the development of computers. The concept of manipulating logical truths as binary numbers opened the door to the design of the first electronic computers in the early 20th century. As such, Boolean algebra was not merely a mathematical tool; it also transformed the practical applications of mathematics, enabling major technological innovations. These developments could be summarized in Table 3.3, which outlines the key stages and figures in the historical formalization of reasoning from Leibniz to Turing.

TABLE 3.3

Stages of the Formalization of Thought

Period	Key Figure	Fundamental Concept
17th century	Gottfried Wilhelm Leibniz	Calculus Ratiocinator (universal formal logic)
19th century	George Boole	Boolean algebra and symbolic logic
Early 20th century	Bertrand Russell, Alfred North Whitehead	Formalization of mathematics in *Principia Mathematica*
1930s	Kurt Gödel	Incompleteness theorems (limits of formalization)
1930s–1940s	Alan Turing	Turing Machine and the concept of computability
1940s	John von Neumann	Computer architecture based on formal logic

The unification of mathematical and logical ideas during this period also set the stage for decisive advances in theoretical computer science in the 20th century. The formalization of axioms and the systematization of logic enabled thinkers like Alan Turing (1912–1954) to devise theoretical models of computation, particularly through the Turing Machine. In 1936, Turing introduced his theoretical computer model, which became a cornerstone of theoretical computer science and AI. The Turing Machine is an abstract model that formalizes the concepts of algorithms and computability, inspiring the development of the first programmable computers. Formal logic and mathematical axioms also influenced how computer scientists design modern computer architectures. Von Neumann (1903–1957) played a pivotal role in developing modern computing architectures. By devising the von Neumann architecture, which relies on storing programs in memory, he enabled the creation of more powerful and flexible computers capable of executing complex programs, thus contributing to the birth of computing as we know it today.

These theoretical developments had a direct impact on the emergence of AI in the 1950s. The Dartmouth Conference of 1956 is often regarded as the founding moment of AI as a scientific field. During this conference, researchers defined AI as a scientific domain aimed at simulating human intelligence through algorithms and mathematical models. The connection between mathematical logic and AI is direct, as understanding algorithms, logical structures, and formal systems is essential for AI development. Mathematics also played a crucial role in structuring ML, a key subfield of AI. Linear algebra and optimization are at the core of modern SL techniques, enabling machines to learn from data. Similarly, graph theory and probability are used in NNs, an ML technique inspired by the human brain's functioning. Linear algebra, in particular, is employed to manipulate large data matrices, which is critical in training AI models. Differential calculus is a fundamental tool in the training process of AI models, particularly through the method of backpropagation. This method, which relies on calculating derivatives to adjust the weights of NNs, minimizes errors and improves model accuracy over time. The theory of functions and derivatives, developed in the 19th century, has thus become a central pillar in designing modern AI algorithms. The emergence of AI in the 20th century would not have been possible without the logical revolution of the preceding centuries. The work of Hilbert, Peano, Boole, and others built a robust mathematical and logical infrastructure upon which modern computing and AI technologies rest. Thus, centuries of mathematical formalization culminated in the birth of AI, marking a turning point in the history of science and technology.

3.1.4.3 20th Century: The Link between Mathematics and Computer Science

In the 20th century, one of the most significant developments in the fields of mathematics and computer science was the establishment of a deep connection between these two disciplines, propelling science into a new era of understanding and innovation. This link, forged through the pioneering work of figures like Turing and von Neumann, laid the foundations for modern computing, leading to advances that altered the course of scientific and technological history. Mathematics, with its rigor and ability to formalize abstract concepts, proved essential in the creation of computers and the computational algorithms that enabled the rise of AI.

In 1936, Turing invented the Turing Machine, a theoretical model that played a critical role in defining the limits of what can be computed. Through this abstract model, He formalized the notions of algorithm and computability, introducing the idea that a computer program could be a sequence of instructions manipulating symbols according to defined rules. The Turing Machine consists of an infinite tape that serves as memory, a current state, and a read/write head that can move along the tape. This theoretical model became a fundamental tool for understanding computational processes, directly influencing the architecture of modern computers. The Turing Machine formalized the concept of computability, defining what a computer could achieve. This concept had profound implications for theoretical computer science, particularly in understanding algorithmic complexity. For instance, problems that cannot be solved by Turing Machines, such as undecidable problems, opened new areas of research in theoretical computer science and logic. He thus laid the groundwork for what would become the field of theoretical computer science, and his work remains a cornerstone for understanding the limits of computation. Turing's work also raised the question of simulating human intelligence with machines. Although he did not directly work on AI as a field, his concept of a universal machine inspired future generations to design systems capable of simulating human cognitive processes. He proposed the idea of an "imitation game," now known as the Turing Test, which remains a central benchmark for assessing whether a machine can simulate human intelligence.

Meanwhile, von Neumann made essential contributions to the design of modern computers by developing what is known as the von Neumann architecture. His architectural model introduced the idea that programs and data could be stored in the same memory, which significantly enhanced the flexibility and power of computers. In this architecture, program instructions are stored in memory and executed by the processor's control unit, enabling computers to perform a wide range of complex tasks by following programmed instructions. The von Neumann architecture also introduced key concepts such as storage units (random-access memory—RAM), computational units (processors), and instruction sequencing, which remain integral to the design of modern computers. These principles established the foundation for programmable computing, allowing the creation of versatile machines capable of performing diverse tasks depending on the software provided.

The work of Turing and von Neumann transformed how mathematics was applied to information sciences. While Turing paved the way for studying computability and the limits of machines, von Neumann formalized the internal structure of computers, making these ideas tangible in the form of physical machines. Together, these contributions enabled computer science to emerge as an independent discipline, grounded in robust mathematical principles.

This connection between mathematics and computer science also led to the emergence of AI in the 20th century. In 1956, the Dartmouth Conference marked the official birth of AI as a scientific field. During this event, researchers articulated the idea that human intelligence could be simulated by machines and that algorithms could mimic human cognitive functions. This vision sparked decades of research, in which mathematics, particularly logic, probability, and linear algebra, became essential tools for understanding and modeling intelligence. One of the most promising areas in AI has been ML, which relies on solid mathematical foundations, including optimization and linear algebra. ML algorithms, such as NNs, use mathematical techniques to analyze data, learn patterns, and make predictions or classifications. These methods have applications across numerous fields, from speech recognition and computer vision to medicine and industrial process automation.

Probability and graph theory are also critical mathematical tools in NNs. Probabilistic models allow for handling uncertainty in data and learning complex representations of information. Probability is used to estimate relationships between variables in a network, while graph theory helps model the connections between different entities in a system. These concepts are central to modern AI systems, particularly in DNN models, which have seen explosive growth in recent years. Differential calculus, especially in the context of supervised learning, has also been crucial in developing backpropagation methods for training NNs by adjusting the weights of connections between neurons. Calculating derivatives optimizes a model's cost function, minimizing the error between predicted and actual outputs. This method is used in advanced applications like image recognition and machine translation.

The synthesis of mathematics and computer science enabled the birth of AI as we know it today. The formal foundations laid by pioneers like Turing and von Neumann built the infrastructure for modern computing systems, which use algorithmic and mathematical methods to simulate human intelligence. These advances revolutionized not only computer science and scientific fields but also sectors like industry, healthcare, and education, where AI plays a central role. The major contributions of figures such as Turing, von Neumann, and others forged an inseparable link between mathematics and computer science (Figure 3.3). Turing formalized the notion of computability, while *von Neumann* structured the architecture of modern computers. These developments culminated in the birth of AI, a field now ubiquitous, supported by robust and powerful mathematical methods capable of simulating human intelligence and profoundly transforming our society.

Charles Babbage
(1791 – 1871)

Ada Lovelace
(1815 – 1852)

Alan Turing
(1912 – 1954)

John Von Neumann
(1903 – 1957)

Claude Shannon
(1916 – 2001)

FIGURE 3.3 The main scientists of the period preceding the birth of AI.

3.1.5 THE BIRTH OF AI

3.1.5.1 AI and Human Intelligence

The birth of AI as a scientific field dates back to the famous Dartmouth Conference of 1956, a decisive turning point in the history of science. Organized by John McCarthy (1927–2011), Marvin Minsky (1927–2016), Nathaniel Rochester (1919–2001), and Claude Shannon (1916–2001), this conference is widely regarded as the official starting point of AI as an academic discipline. During this event, researchers articulated the ambitious idea that human intelligence could be artificially replicated through algorithms and mathematical models, ushering in a new era of research.

The primary goal of the Dartmouth Conference was to establish AI as an autonomous and distinct scientific field capable of simulating human cognitive processes. Participants proposed that problem-solving, perception, reasoning, and learning could be modeled using machines. This groundbreaking concept marked a paradigm shift, aiming not only to understand mental processes but also to create machines capable of mimicking them. The idea of "replicating" human intelligence became a long-term ambition for AI research. At the time, computers were already capable of performing complex calculations, but they could not learn or autonomously simulate human intelligence. The objective set by the conference organizers was to expand the capabilities of machines, enabling them to perform tasks that typically require cognitive processes, such as reasoning, decision-making, or natural language understanding. AI was thus envisioned as a scientific field tasked with addressing the question: *How can machines simulate human faculties?*

One of the initial ideas proposed at the conference was the use of algorithms and mathematical models to replicate human cognitive abilities. Researchers suggested that, just as humans use rules to solve problems or make decisions, machines could be programmed with logical rules and knowledge representation systems to simulate these mental processes. This approach formed the basis for the development of early AI systems, which focused primarily on specific tasks such as playing checkers or solving mathematical problems. Another significant aspect of the Dartmouth Conference was the recognition of the critical role of learning in AI development. Researchers quickly realized that to create intelligent machines, they needed to endow them with the ability to learn from experience and adapt to new situations. This insight spurred research into ML models, where machines could improve their performance over time by adjusting their algorithms based on processed data. This laid the groundwork for supervised and unsupervised learning (UL), fundamental techniques used in modern AI.

The Dartmouth Conference also emphasized the development of symbolic systems, which used formal representations to organize and manipulate knowledge. These systems were rooted in logic and set theory, inheriting the mathematical foundations of AI research. Machines were expected to process symbols, manipulate them, and draw logical conclusions, much like humans use abstract concepts and ideas to solve problems. This symbolic approach dominated AI research in its early decades, though it was later supplanted by data-driven and learning-based methods.

The conference also influenced the creation of new algorithmic approaches, particularly in areas such as pattern recognition, automated planning, and solving complex problems. These approaches relied on sophisticated mathematical models, often inspired by human cognitive processes. The notion that machines could *think* and *reason* enabled researchers to propose models and algorithms to simulate these processes, giving rise to systems that could address problems using heuristics and search strategies.

Despite the ambitious goals outlined at the Dartmouth Conference, early AI efforts encountered numerous obstacles, largely due to the technological limitations of the era. Computers were still slow and underpowered, making it challenging to implement complex AI models. Nevertheless, the conference marked a significant milestone by uniting a group of researchers around this innovative idea and fostering an interdisciplinary dialogue among mathematics, logic, psychology, and computer science. It paved the way for extensive research in the decades that followed. The concept of AI proposed at Dartmouth was also shaped by philosophical and cognitive influences. Participants drew on the work of figures like Turing and von Neumann, whose theories of computation and machines informed the design of early AI models. The conference thus bridged mathematical logic, computational theory, and cognitive science, creating fertile ground for the development of new ideas and approaches in AI.

This Conference acted as a catalyst for the establishment of numerous AI research institutions and laboratories. Following the event, researchers embarked on ambitious projects to demonstrate that AI could indeed be achieved by machines. Funding for AI increased, and several academic institutions emerged, such as the Stanford AI Laboratory and the Massachusetts Institute of Technology (MIT), which became leading research centers in the field. These labs advanced AI not only by theorizing it but also by putting it into practice. This Conference marked a historic turning point by defining AI as an autonomous scientific field aimed at replicating human cognitive processes through mathematical and algorithmic models. This event laid the foundation for future AI research, highlighting the potential of such technology while raising questions about its limits and capabilities. It also sparked a multidisciplinary dialogue that continues to drive advancements in the field to this day.

3.1.5.2   AI and Mathematics

Linear Algebra and Optimization for ML: Linear algebra and optimization are fundamental tools for the operation of ML. In particular, these concepts are central to the processes that enable models to learn from data, whether for regression, classification, or even DNNs (Figure 3.4).

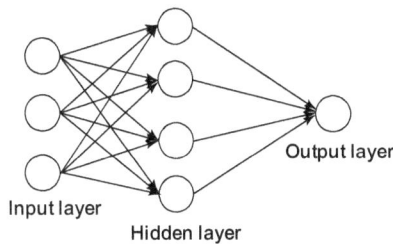

FIGURE 3.4   A schematic of the artificial neural network.

In this context, linear algebra provides a framework for representing and manipulating data through matrices and vectors, while optimization techniques are used to fine-tune model parameters by minimizing a cost function. A closer look at these concepts reveals that linear algebra plays a key role in ML by structuring data, encoding model weights, and supporting the operations performed by learning algorithms. It enables the representation of relationships between inputs and outputs through matrix and vector formulations, streamlining the process of making predictions. Typically, input data is organized in matrix form; for instance, in linear regression, the inputs can be arranged into a matrix X, where each row represents an individual data point and each column corresponds to a specific feature (Equation 3.1).

$$X = \begin{bmatrix} x_{1,1} & x_{1,2} & \cdots & x_{1,n} \\ x_{2,1} & x_{2,2} & \cdots & x_{2,n} \\ \vdots & \vdots & \ddots & \vdots \\ x_{m,1} & x_{m,2} & \cdots & x_{m,n} \end{bmatrix} \qquad (3.1)$$

where m is the number of examples and n is the number of features.

The goal is to predict an output vector y, representing the target values associated with each example (Equation 3.2):

$$y = \begin{bmatrix} y_1 \\ y_2 \\ \vdots \\ y_m \end{bmatrix} \qquad (3.2)$$

In a linear model, the predictions can be expressed as a matrix multiplication between the input matrix X and a weight vector θ, which can be expressed by Equation (3.3):

$$\hat{y} = X\theta \qquad (3.3)$$

where y is the vector of predictions. The weights θ represent the model's parameters, which must be adjusted during the learning process.

The goal of optimization in ML is to find the optimal values of the model's parameters θ that minimize a cost function (or loss function) $J(\theta)$. A common cost function in linear regression problems is the mean squared error (MSE), which measures the difference between the predictions $\hat{y}$ and the true values y using Equation (3.4):

$$J(\theta) = \frac{1}{2m} \sum_{i=1}^{m} (\hat{y}_i - y_i)^2 \qquad (3.4)$$

where m is the number of training examples.

Optimization involves adjusting the weights θ to minimize this cost function. A common method for doing so is gradient descent, which updates the weights in the direction opposite to the gradient of the cost function with respect to the parameters θ. The gradient is calculated using Equation (3.5):

$$\frac{\partial J(\theta)}{\partial \theta_j} = \frac{1}{m} \sum_{i=1}^{m} (\hat{y}_i - y_i) x_{ij} \qquad (3.5)$$

where x_{ij} is the value of the jth feature for the ith example.

The weight update is performed according to Equation (3.6):

$$\theta_j = \theta_j - \alpha \frac{\partial J(\theta)}{\partial \theta_j} \qquad (3.6)$$

where α is the learning rate, a parameter that controls the step size during the weight updates.

A common variant of gradient descent is stochastic gradient descent (SGD), where weight updates are performed iteratively after each example, rather than considering the entire dataset at once (Equation 3.7):

$$\theta_j = \theta_j - \alpha\left(\hat{y}_i - y_i\right)x_{ij} \tag{3.7}$$

This reduces computational costs and speeds up the learning process, although the updates may be noisier. In the case of NNs, models are generally more complex and involve successive layers of neurons, each with its own weights and biases. Optimizing these models requires techniques like backpropagation to adjust the weights at each layer based on the final error. The backpropagation algorithm uses the chain rule to calculate the gradients of the weights across all layers and update the network's parameters. Thus, linear algebra and optimization are essential tools for ML. Linear algebra enables the representation and manipulation of data as well as model predictions, while optimization allows for the minimization of cost functions to adjust model parameters. These two concepts are at the core of building and training modern AI models, particularly in areas such as linear regression, NNs, and other ML algorithms.

Graph Theory and Probability for NNs: Graph theory and probability play a central role in the design and understanding of NNs. These mathematical tools enable the modeling of complex relationships between neurons, the optimization of connections, and the integration of uncertainty into models. In what follows, a detailed exploration of these concepts is presented.

An NN can be seen as a directed graph $G = (V, E)$, where V is the set of nodes (the neurons or units) and E is the set of directed edges (the weighted connections between neurons). Each neuron u in V represents a computational unit, and an edge (u, v) in E represents a connection, often associated with a weight w_{uv}. The weights are adjusted during training to improve the model's performance—information propagation. The propagation of information in a neural network is analogous to the passage of a signal in a graph. For example, in a given layer, the output of a neuron v is calculated as a function of the weighted inputs from its neighbors u connected by edges (u, v) as shown in Equation (3.8):

$$z_v = \sum_{u \in N(v)} w_{uv} a_u + b_v \tag{3.8}$$

where z_v is the weighted sum of inputs for neuron v, w_{uv} is the weight of the connection between u and v, a_u is the activation of u, $N(v)$ is the set of predecessor neurons u connected to v, and b_v is the bias associated with neuron v. The activation a_v is then obtained by applying a nonlinear function σ (e.g., a ReLU or sigmoid function).

Graphs in Advanced Architectures: Some advanced neural network architectures, such as Convolutional Neural Networks (CNNs) or Graph Neural Networks (GNNs), directly exploit graph properties to capture local or nonlocal dependencies in the data. For instance, in GNNs, information is aggregated based on the graph's structure, making it possible to process data in graph form (such as social networks or molecules).

Probabilities in NNs: Probabilistic modeling. NNs often use probabilistic concepts to model uncertainty and make informed decisions. For example, in a classification problem, a model generates probabilities $P(y|x)$, where y is the predicted class for an input x. In a classification output layer, the probability distribution is often obtained via a SoftMax function (Equation 3.9):

$$P(y = k \mid x) = \frac{\exp(z_k)}{\sum_{j=1}^{C} \exp(z_j)} \tag{3.9}$$

where z_k is the raw score (logit) for class k, and C is the total number of classes.

Probabilities also come into play in *Bayesian* networks and regularization techniques. For instance, *Bayesian* networks aim to explicitly model uncertainty by treating weights as random variables with a prior distribution $P(w)$. Training then involves maximizing the posterior probability $P(w|D)$ using Equation (3.10):

$$P(W \mid D) \propto P(D \mid W) P(W) \tag{3.10}$$

where $P(D|w)$ is the likelihood of the data D, and $P(w)$ is the prior distribution over the weights.

A practical application of probabilities in NNs is dropout, a regularization technique that randomly deactivates certain neurons during training. This can be seen as an approximate estimation of an ensemble of models, as shown in Equation (3.11):

$$a_v^{(t)} = f(x) = \begin{cases} 0, & \text{with probability of } p \\ a_v, & \text{with probability of } 1 - p \end{cases} \tag{3.11}$$

where p is the dropout rate.

Combined graph theory and probabilities in advanced models like *Bayesian* GNNs, graph and probability concepts are applied to model structural dependencies and uncertainty. For example, edge weights can be probabilistic distributions, allowing uncertainty to be directly incorporated into the calculations using Equation (3.12):

$$w_{uv} \sim N(\mu, \sigma^2) \tag{3.12}$$

Differential Calculus for Training Models (Backpropagation): Differential calculus is at the heart of training NN models. The goal is to minimize a cost function L (or loss function), which measures the difference between the model's predictions and the true target values, by adjusting the network's weights w and biases b. The backpropagation method relies on calculating the partial derivatives of L with respect to the parameters to update them using the gradient descent algorithm. In a NN, for an input x, the activations $a\ (l)$ of the neurons in layer l are computed successively from the activations of the previous layer $a\ (l-1)$:

$$z^{(1)} = W^{(1)}a^{(l-1)} + b^{(1)} \tag{3.13}$$

$$a^{(1)} = \sigma(z^{(1)}) \tag{3.14}$$

where $W^{(l)}$ is the weight matrix of layer l, $b^{(l)}$ is the bias vector, σ is the activation function (e.g., ReLU or sigmoid), and $z^{(l)}$ is the pre-activation vector.

The cost function measures the difference between the prediction $\hat{y}$ and the true value y. For example, for a classification problem with C classes, cross-entropy is often used by Equation (3.15):

$$L(\hat{y}, y) = -\sum_{k=1}^{C} y_k \log(\hat{y}_k) \tag{3.15}$$

where y_k is the true probability for class k (often 0 or 1), and $\hat{y}_k$ the predicted probabilities for class k are considered.

Backpropagation involves calculating the gradients of the cost function L with respect to the parameters $W^{(l)}$ and $b^{(l)}$ of each layer, using the chain rule. For the output layer L, the gradient of L with respect to the pre-activations $z^{(L)}$ is given by Equation (3.16):

$$\delta^{(L)} = \frac{\partial L}{\partial z^{(L)}} = \frac{\partial L}{\partial a^{(L)}} \odot \sigma'\left(z^{(L)}\right) \tag{3.16}$$

where $\delta\ (L)$, the error of layer L, with element-wise multiplication and $\sigma'\ (z^{(L)})$ as the derivative of the activation function.

For an intermediate layer l, the error $\delta^{(l)}$ is computed from the error of the next layer $\delta\ (l+1)$, as shown in Equation (3.17):

$$\delta^{(L)} = \left(W^{(l+1)T}\delta^{l+1}\right) \odot \sigma'\left(z^{(l)}\right) \tag{3.17}$$

where $W^{(l+1)T}$ is the transpose of the weight matrix of layer $l + 1$.

The gradients of the parameters $W^{(l)}$ and $b^{(l)}$ for a layer l are given by:

$$\frac{\partial L}{\partial W^{(l)}} = \delta^{(l)}a^{(l-1)T}$$

$$\frac{\partial L}{\partial b^{(l)}} = \delta^{(l)} \tag{3.18}$$

indicate how $W^{(l)}$ and $b^{(l)}$ should be adjusted to reduce the loss.

The weights and biases are updated using gradient descent, as given by Equation (3.19):

$$W^{(l)} \leftarrow W^{(l)} - \eta \frac{\partial L}{\partial W^{(l)}}$$

$$b^{(l)} \leftarrow b^{(l)} - \eta \frac{\partial L}{\partial b^{(l)}} \tag{3.19}$$

where η is the learning rate, a hyperparameter controlling the size of the adjustments.

Differential calculus, through the chain rule, enables efficient gradient propagation in a neural network during backpropagation. These gradients are essential for adjusting the parameters and minimizing the cost function, forming the foundation of training AI models.

3.1.6 SYNTHESIS

From the Medieval Period to the dawn of modernity, mathematics evolved dramatically, shifting from a practical craft tied to tasks like land measurement, trade, and stargazing to a sophisticated, abstract field with universal scope. Pioneers such as Khwarizmi played a key role, establishing algebra as a structured system that laid the foundation for this change. The translation of Ancient Greek and the works of Iranian and Arabic scholars into European languages further spread this knowledge, gradually lifting it beyond its everyday uses into a wider theoretical domain. Though the mathematical methods of this time seem basic today, they already hinted at a broader, more universal perspective. The Renaissance sparked an explosive growth in mathematics, driven by the advent of the printing press and a growing fascination with the natural world. Innovators like Descartes and Fermat bridged geometry and algebra through analytical geometry, using equations to map out space in a groundbreaking way. This period also gave rise to calculus, thanks to Newton and Leibniz, whose discoveries equipped humanity to analyze intricate physical events. No longer limited to solving immediate challenges, these breakthroughs aimed to uncover the universe's core principles, setting the stage for deeper abstraction.

During the Enlightenment, mathematics matured into a precise, universal language of logic. Thinkers like Kant and Denis Diderot (1713–1784) hailed it as the epitome of certainty, a beacon for science and human reasoning. Laplace's work on celestial mechanics showcased this belief, using mathematics to distill natural phenomena into elegant equations. At the same time, early advances in probability opened doors to grasping randomness that would later prove vital for AI. The 19th century brought a wave of formalization, with luminaries like Gauss, Riemann, and Galois reshaping geometry, algebra, and group theory. Their ideas pushed abstraction further, moving beyond the physical world to probe idealized constructs. Cantor's set theory redefined infinity and the bedrock of mathematics, sparking intense debates about logic and axioms. This momentum carried into the 20th century with Hilbert's quest to anchor mathematics in unshakable rigor.

In the 20th century, mathematics and logic intertwined more tightly through the efforts of Boole, Frege, and Peano, who birthed symbolic logic and formal systems. Originally sparked by philosophical curiosity, these advances unexpectedly fueled computational theory, setting the stage for computer science. In 1936, Turing harnessed these ideas to propose the Turing Machine. Von Neumann built on this by crafting the blueprint for today's computers, integrating processing, memory, and step-by-step commands. This leap turned abstract theories into practical tools, propelling a technological upheaval. Meanwhile, probability, now firmly rooted, joined forces with linear algebra and analysis to address data-handling challenges, hinting at the ML algorithms to come.

The story of mathematics, from its humble beginnings to its modern peak, reveals a steady climb toward abstraction, precision, and universality. These steps not only illuminated the world but also forged instruments to reshape it. AI, a product of this legacy, marks the latest chapter in humanity's drive to push beyond the boundaries of understanding and invention.

3.2   MECHANIZATION OF THOUGHT PROCESSES

The mechanization of logic refers to the process by which operations of reasoning, once considered uniquely human, were formalized and eventually executed by machines. This idea emerged notably in the 19th century, with the development of symbolic logic, marking a decisive turn in the history of mathematics, computing, and AI. Until the 18th century, logic remained largely qualitative and verbal, rooted in philosophical argumentation. It was only when thinkers began formalizing the principles of reasoning into symbols and mathematical expressions that logic became subject to mechanical treatment. This transformation laid the foundation for automating reasoning and simulating aspects of human thought.

One of the earliest contributors to this idea was Gottfried Wilhelm Leibniz, who, in the 17th century, envisioned a universal formal system, the Calculus Ratiocinator, capable of expressing all truths in logic and mathematics. Though theoretical at the time, his vision prefigured symbolic logic and influenced later formalizations. In the 19th century, George Boole built on this legacy by introducing Boolean algebra, a mathematical system in which logical propositions are expressed through binary variables, true or false, 1 or 0. This approach allowed logical expressions to be manipulated using algebraic rules, opening the way for physical implementation through electrical circuits and paving the road to computational logic.

These developments profoundly reshaped how intelligence and reasoning were understood. Logic, once intangible and reserved for human minds, became a manipulable structure, formalized into rules and executable by machines. This conceptual shift was instrumental in the birth of computing and AI.

Charles Babbage, inspired by these formal frameworks, designed the Analytical Engine, a theoretical machine capable of manipulating symbols and executing a sequence of operations defined by a program. Though never fully built during his lifetime, the Analytical Engine was the first design for a general-purpose programmable computer. It introduced foundational ideas such as modular architecture (with components analogous to a CPU, memory, and control unit), programmability via punched cards, and even loops and conditional operations that still underpin modern computing.

Babbage's collaborator, Ada Lovelace, went even further. She recognized that such a machine could perform not only numerical but also symbolic tasks. In her famous 1843 notes, she proposed the first algorithm intended for machine execution, a procedure to compute Bernoulli numbers. She also anticipated that machines might be used to compose music or process abstract information, thereby extending the concept of computing beyond arithmetic. Lovelace introduced the essential notion of loops and emphasized that while machines could follow instructions, they lacked true creativity, a view that continues to shape debates on AI.

Today, Boolean algebra remains central to the design of logical systems. It allows engineers to structure and simplify logical expressions for implementation in digital circuits. The basic operations, AND, OR, and NOT, are carried out by logic gates, the physical building blocks of processors, memory units, and control devices. By applying Boolean laws such as commutativity, associativity, and distributivity, engineers can reduce the number of gates required to perform a function, resulting in more compact, faster, and energy-efficient circuits. This principle is critical in microprocessor design, where hardware optimization is paramount.

Moreover, Boolean algebra's impact extends far beyond processors. It plays a foundational role in communication networks, automated control systems, and cryptography, where logical operations ensure information integrity and security. From industrial automation to digital security, the ability to represent and manipulate logic systematically has become indispensable.

The mechanization of logic thus transformed reasoning into a formal system suitable for implementation in machines. This was a key condition for the emergence of AI. By making logic computable, it became possible to simulate decision-making, problem-solving, and other cognitive processes that were once the sole domain of human intelligence. From Babbage's engine to Lovelace's algorithms and Boole's algebra, this shift marks one of the most profound intellectual revolutions of modern times, one that continues to shape the development of intelligent systems today.

3.2.1 THE IMPACT OF THE ENLIGHTENMENT ON THE MECHANIZATION OF LOGIC

The scientific revolution of the Enlightenment played a crucial role in enabling the mechanization of logic by transforming the way knowledge and reason were conceived. This intellectual movement emphasized the value of reason, empiricism, and the scientific method as foundations for understanding the world. Enlightenment thinkers challenged established dogmas and embraced the idea that even abstract processes, such as logical reasoning, could be analyzed, formalized, and eventually automated.

A central consequence of this shift was the emergence of logic as a mathematical discipline. Previously confined to philosophical debate, logic began to be seen as a system of computation. Influenced by this context, *Leibniz* proposed a universal formal system, the Calculus Ratiocinator, in which reasoning could be expressed through symbols and rules, much like arithmetic. This radical idea suggested that cognitive operations could one day be executed by machines. In the 19th century, George Boole extended this vision by creating Boolean algebra, a symbolic system where logical propositions could be represented with binary variables and manipulated using algebraic rules. Boole's work demonstrated that logic could not only be mathematically formalized but also implemented through mechanical or electrical devices, laying the foundation for computational logic. This rationalist impulse also encouraged technological innovation. Advances in mathematics, physics, and engineering enabled the design of the first machines capable of manipulating symbolic instructions. Babbage's Analytical Engine, inspired by these ideals, was conceived as a programmable machine capable of executing algorithms, an early embodiment of mechanized thought.

The Enlightenment thus provided the conceptual and technical conditions for logic to evolve from philosophical speculation into a machine-executable discipline. By asserting that reasoning could be structured mathematically, it set the stage for modern computing and AI and redefined the relationship between human thought and technology.

3.2.2 SYMBOLIC LOGIC

3.2.2.1 George Boole's Symbolic Logic

George Boole's symbolic logic, developed in the mid-19th century, marks a crucial milestone in the evolution of logic as a mathematical discipline. Before Boole, logic was primarily a branch of philosophy, used to analyze and structure arguments within a verbal and qualitative framework. Boole revolutionized this approach by introducing a method to express logical propositions as symbols and manipulate them using algebraic rules, thereby creating what is now known as Boolean algebra.

One of the strengths of Boolean algebra lies in its ability to simplify complex logical expressions. By applying the properties and laws of Boolean algebra, such as the distributive law, the identity law, or De Morgan's laws, it is possible to transform and reduce logical expressions, making them easier to apply in practical contexts. For instance, a complex expression representing a decision-making condition in a computer system can be simplified to improve execution efficiency, thereby saving time and resources. Boole did not merely develop a formal method for manipulating logical propositions; he also opened the door to their application in mechanical and electronic systems. Boolean algebra found direct application in the design of logical circuits, which form the core of modern computers. Every logical circuit in a computer processor operates based on the principles of Boolean algebra, where electrical signals (representing 0s and 1s) are combined to perform fundamental logical operations. Logic gates, such as *AND*, *OR*, and *NOT* gates, are physical implementations of Boolean operations.

Thus, George Boole's symbolic logic and Boolean algebra not only formalized logical reasoning into a precise mathematical framework but also laid the groundwork for modern computing. By enabling the representation of abstract logical processes in a mathematical form that could be automated, Boole paved the way for the creation of machines capable of "thinking" logically, and for the development of computers and AI. Boolean algebra remains at the heart of computational logic today, serving as a fundamental language for information processing in the digital world.

I. The Use of Boolean Algebra in Modern Logical Systems

Boolean algebra is an essential component of modern logical systems, serving as the mathematical foundation for the design and operation of digital circuits that make up computers and many other electronic devices. This branch of symbolic logic, developed by George Boole in the 19th century, enables the representation and manipulation of logical variables that take binary values, typically 0 and 1, corresponding to the states "false" and "true," respectively. These simple yet powerful logical operations are used to design the logic circuits that execute the fundamental operations of digital systems.

In modern logical systems, Boolean algebra is directly applied to the design of integrated circuits, particularly in processors, memory units, and control devices. Logic gates, the building blocks of these circuits, implement the basic *Boolean* operations such as *AND*, *OR*, and *NOT*. For instance, an *AND* gate produces an output signal of 1 only if all its input signals are 1, mirroring the corresponding Boolean operation. Similarly, an *OR* gate produces an output of 1 if at least one of its inputs is 1, while a *NOT* gate simply inverts the state of its input. These gates are combined in various ways to perform more complex logical functions, such as binary addition, multiplexers, or memory registers.

Boolean algebra is also used to simplify the logical expressions that define the behavior of these circuits. When designing complex circuits, optimizing the use of hardware resources, such as circuit area and power consumption, is critical. By applying Boolean algebra laws, such as De Morgan's laws or distributive identities, engineers can reduce the number of logic gates required to implement a specific function, improving efficiency and lowering production costs. For example, a complex Boolean expression can be simplified to minimize the number of gates needed, resulting in more compact and faster circuits. Furthermore, it is utilized in control systems and programmable logic controllers that manage numerous industrial processes. In these systems, binary signals (representing states like "on" or "off") are combined to create logical conditions that trigger specific actions. For instance, in an automated production line, sensors may provide input signals that are processed by logic circuits, determining when to activate or deactivate certain machines based on observed conditions. Boolean algebra is fundamental in the field of software development, particularly in the conditional logic used in algorithms and computer programs. Conditional statements, such as "if," "then," and "else," rely on Boolean expressions to determine a program's execution flow. Logical operations are used to compare values and make decisions, which is essential for the operation of operating systems, software applications, and databases.

II. The Obstacles Boole Faced in Developing His Logical System

To develop his logical system, George Boole had to overcome several obstacles, both intellectual and practical, that shaped his journey. One of the first challenges was the need to rethink logic, a discipline that was largely qualitative and philosophical at the time, in quantitative and mathematical terms. Until then, logic had been dominated by Aristotelian methods, centered on syllogisms and the verbal analysis of arguments. Boole thus had to devise a new approach that transcended this tradition and allowed logic to be treated formally and symbolically, a revolutionary concept for his era.

Another major obstacle for Boole was the absence of a preexisting mathematical framework for formalizing logical operations. Unlike other branches of mathematics, such as algebra or calculus, logic had not yet been translated into a universal symbolic language that would allow it to be manipulated like a mathematical equation. Boole had to invent his own system of notation and rules to express logical operations in algebraic terms. This innovation required not only considerable creativity but also rigor to ensure that his system was consistent, complete, and applicable to a wide range of logical problems. Boole also had to convince his contemporaries of the validity and utility of his approach. At a time when applied mathematics focused primarily on physical and geometric problems, the idea of using algebraic techniques to address abstract logical issues could seem esoteric and irrelevant. He had to demonstrate that his algebra of logic could not only systematize logical reasoning but also apply to practical problems, laying the groundwork for what would later become computing.

Moreover, Boole had to work in relative intellectual isolation. Although he corresponded with other mathematicians and logicians of his time, he lacked a direct mentor or a robust academic support network in this emerging field. He thus developed his ideas largely on his own, relying on his intuition and ability to connect disparate concepts. This initial lack of recognition delayed the acceptance of his ideas, which would only be fully appreciated decades after his death when they were integrated into formal logic and used in the design of early computers. Boole also had to overcome the technological limitations of his era. Mathematical tools and computational resources were rudimentary, and the notion of machines capable of executing logical operations remained purely theoretical. Boole worked without the benefit of modern computing tools, making it all the more remarkable that he formulated a logical system that became a cornerstone of computer science. Boole faced significant conceptual, academic, and technological challenges to develop his logical system. His ability to transform logic into a formal mathematical discipline— despite initial skepticism and intellectual isolation—not only opened new horizons for mathematics but also laid the foundation for the modern digital era.

III. The Impact of Boolean Algebra on Computer Information Processing

Boolean algebra fundamentally transformed the way computers process information by providing a simple yet powerful mathematical framework for representing and manipulating data in binary form. Before the advent of Boolean algebra, information processing by machines was limited to relatively straightforward arithmetic calculations. The introduction of Boolean algebra enabled the formalization of logical operations, such as conditional decisions and comparisons, greatly expanding the capabilities of computers. The core of this transformation lies in the use of binary values, 0 and 1, to represent all forms of information processed by a computer, whether numbers, letters, colors, or sounds. Boolean algebra allows logical operations to be performed on these individual bits, combining or comparing their states according to precise rules. For example, operations like *AND*, *OR*, and *NOT* (fundamental concepts of Boolean algebra) are used to build logic circuits capable of making decisions based on the states of multiple binary inputs.

These logic circuits, constructed from logic gates (which implement Boolean operations), are the building blocks of all modern processors. A processor executes instructions by performing Boolean operations on sets of bits, enabling it to handle conditional instructions, manipulate data, and perform complex arithmetic operations. Thanks to Boolean algebra, computers can make comparisons, choose between different actions, and execute loops and conditions for the functioning of computer programs. Boolean algebra has also made it possible to optimize information processing by simplifying logic circuits. By applying *Boolean* laws such as commutativity, associativity, and distributivity, engineers can minimize the number of logic gates required to perform a given function, resulting in more compact, faster, and energy-efficient circuits. This ability to simplify is critical in the design of modern microprocessors, where efficiency and speed are paramount.

Furthermore, Boolean algebra paved the way for the design of memory and data storage systems. Boolean operations are used to organize and access data in memory efficiently, enabling rapid read, write, and modification operations on information stored in binary form. Sorting, searching, and data compression algorithms also rely on Boolean principles. Beyond computers, the impact of Boolean algebra extends to the design of digital systems in general, including communication networks, automated control systems, and even cryptography, where logical operations are essential for ensuring the security and integrity of information. Boolean algebra revolutionized how computers process information by providing a mathematical language to express and manipulate binary data logically and efficiently. This framework not only expanded the capabilities of computers beyond simple numerical calculations but also enabled the design of complex computing systems capable of performing diverse tasks with precision and speed.

These foundational concepts and their lasting impact on modern computation and artificial intelligence are summarized in Table 3.4.

TABLE 3.4
Symbolic Logic and Its Heritage

Concept	Inventor (Dates)	Modern Application
Symbolic logic	George Boole (1815–1864)	Logic circuits, computing, AI
Computer program	Ada Lovelace (1815–1852)	Algorithms, programming
Algorithm	Khwarizmi (c. 780–850)/Alan Turing (1912–1954)	Foundation of computing systems and AI
Computability	Alan Turing (1912–1954)	Defining the limits of automated processing
Formal proof	Gottlob Frege (1848–1925)/David Hilbert (1862–1943)/Kurt Gödel (1906–1978)	Mathematical logic, program verification

3.2.2.2   Charles Babbage and the Analytical Engine

Charles Babbage's Analytical Engine (Figure 3.5) stands apart from previous mechanical calculators due to its revolutionary design, making it the first true concept of a programmable computer, even though it was never fully built during his lifetime. Earlier mechanical calculators, such as Blaise Pascal's Pascaline or *Leibniz*'s calculating machine, were essentially devices dedicated to automating specific arithmetic operations like addition, subtraction, multiplication, and division. These machines were built to perform well-defined mathematical tasks but lacked the flexibility and capacity to execute complex sequences of instructions. In contrast, Babbage's Analytical Engine represented a major conceptual leap by introducing the idea of a machine capable of following a program, a predefined series of instructions, to perform a variety of tasks. Unlike mechanical calculators, which were limited to fixed operations, the Analytical Engine was designed to be versatile. *Babbage* envisioned a machine equipped with several innovative components, including an "arithmetic unit" (equivalent to a modern CPU), a "memory" to store numbers and intermediate results, and a "control unit" capable of reading instructions and executing them sequentially.

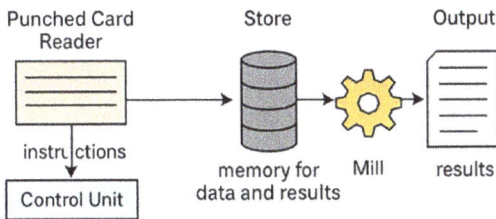

FIGURE 3.5   Architecture (left) and physical model (right) of *Babbage*'s Analytical Engine (https://edu-html.ac-versailles.fr/lyc-rabelais-meudon/EricThomasPaulMachines/La_Machine_analytique.html).

A key feature of the Analytical Engine was its use of punched cards to store instructions and data, an idea inspired by Jacquard looms. These punched cards allowed users to program the machine to perform complex operations, such as calculating mathematical functions or solving differential equations, without requiring human intervention at every step of the computation. This ability to be programmed and reprogrammed for different tasks radically distinguished the Analytical Engine from the rigid mechanical calculators that preceded it.

Moreover, the Analytical Engine incorporated advanced concepts such as loops and conditional branching, essential elements in modern computers that enable a machine to repeat operations or make decisions based on previous results. These concepts allowed Babbage's machine to perform far more sophisticated computations than those possible with earlier mechanical devices. For example, it could evaluate a complex expression, store the result in memory, and use that result in subsequent calculations. Although it was never completed, Babbage's Analytical Engine introduced the idea of a clear separation between hardware (the physical components) and instructions (the software), a principle that lies at the heart of all modern computers. While previous mechanical calculators were essentially monolithic devices, the Analytical Engine proposed a modular architecture in which different parts of the machine played specific roles in the computation process. This foreshadowed the von Neumann architecture and other computing models used today. Babbage's Analytical Engine differs from earlier mechanical calculators through its advanced design as a programmable machine capable of performing a variety of operations based on a set of predefined instructions. It introduced foundational concepts such as programming, memory, and conditional processing, laying the groundwork for modern computing. While mechanical calculators were limited to specific, repetitive tasks, the Analytical Engine was designed as a general-purpose tool capable of autonomously tackling complex mathematical problems, marking a significant milestone in the history of computing technology.

I. The Analytical Engine: Precursor to Modern Computers

Charles Babbage's Analytical Engine is often regarded as the precursor to modern computers due to its visionary concept, which incorporates several essential elements that define contemporary computing. Although it was never built during Babbage's lifetime, the Analytical Engine represented a major conceptual advancement, laying the theoretical groundwork for the computers we use today.

First and foremost, the Analytical Engine was designed to be programmable, fundamentally distinguishing it from earlier mechanical calculators. Babbage envisioned a system in which instructions could be encoded on punched cards, inspired by the Jacquard loom, to direct the machine's operations. This ability to execute a complex program and be reprogrammed for different tasks lies at the heart of the modern definition of a computer. Unlike the mechanical devices of its time, which were built for specific tasks, the Analytical Engine was intended to be a universal machine, capable of solving a wide variety of problems by following a set of programmable instructions.

Another critical aspect that positions the Analytical Engine as a precursor to modern computers is its design as a modular system with distinct components, each serving a specific function. Babbage planned an "arithmetic unit" to perform calculations, a "memory" to store intermediate results, and a "control unit" to manage operations based on instructions. This division of responsibilities among different components mirrors the architecture of modern computers, where the processor, memory, and control devices interact to execute programs. This modular architecture not only provides significant flexibility in the design and use of machines but also establishes a theoretical framework for the development of computing. The Analytical Engine also introduced advanced concepts such as loops and conditional branching, which are essential for complex automated computation processes. Babbage designed the machine to repeat certain operations (loops) and make decisions based on previous results (conditional branching), a fundamental requirement for executing sophisticated algorithms. These mechanisms enable a computer to perform tasks far more complex than simple sequential calculations, adapting its behavior based on the data it processes—a principle that underpins modern computer programming.

Moreover, the Analytical Engine foreshadowed the separation between hardware and software. Babbage designed a machine whose behavior could be entirely altered by changing the program (via punched cards) without needing to physically modify the machine itself. This concept of reprogramming is central to modern computers, where the same hardware can run a wide variety of software, forming the basis of the versatility of today's computing systems. Although the Analytical Engine was never built on a large scale due to the technological limitations of its era, its theoretical design had a lasting influence on the development of computing. Decades later, Babbage's ideas inspired the first electronic computers, such as the Electronic Numerical Integrator and Computer (ENIAC), and continue to form the foundation of computer science. The significance of the Analytical Engine lies not only in its technical innovations but also in how it captured and articulated the fundamental principles of computation, transforming the vision of what a machine could achieve.

II. Babbage's Ambitions for His Machine in Society

Charles Babbage's ambitions for the use of his Analytical Engine in society were vast and visionary, reflecting his deep desire to revolutionize not only the field of mathematics but also the way knowledge and information were processed on a large scale. Babbage did not see his machine merely as a tool for performing calculations more quickly; rather, he envisioned it as a device capable of catalyzing advancements across numerous scientific, industrial, and administrative domains. One of Babbage's primary ambitions was to automate the complex calculations required in science and engineering. In his era, producing accurate calculations (e.g., in astronomy or infrastructure engineering) demanded considerable human effort and was prone to errors. Babbage sought to create a machine that would eliminate these errors by performing calculations automatically and reliably while speeding up the process. He imagined that the Analytical Engine could generate complex mathematical tables with unparalleled precision, thereby contributing to significant progress in fields such as navigation, astronomy, and economics. He also harbored ambitions to apply his machine to the automation of administrative and bureaucratic tasks. He foresaw the Analytical Engine being used to manage and analyze vast amounts of data that was extremely labor-intensive and error-prone. For instance, he envisioned it being employed for censuses, processing economic statistics, or managing public finances. By automating these tasks, he hoped not only to increase the efficiency of governments and businesses but also to reduce costs and human errors, potentially having a profound impact on the administration of modern societies. Another facet of his ambition was to democratize access to scientific and technical knowledge. He believed the Analytical Engine could play a key role in education by enabling students and researchers to conduct complex mathematical experiments without spending hours on manual calculations. This would allow scientists to devote more time to analyzing and interpreting results rather than manipulating numbers, thereby accelerating research and innovation.

Babbage also saw revolutionary potential in how his machine could transform the production and dissemination of knowledge. He envisioned the Analytical Engine automatically printing the results of calculations, which he believed would enable the production of scientific and technical documents with unmatched accuracy. This ability to generate reliable, standardized information could have played a crucial role in establishing common standards and methodologies in science and industry. Babbage held a broader ambition of rationalizing and enhancing societal efficiency through the use of his machine. He believed that automating intellectual processes, much like physical ones, could free individuals from routine and repetitive tasks, allowing them to focus on more creative and productive endeavors. In this sense, Babbage saw the Analytical Engine not only as a technical tool but also as an instrument of social progress, capable of transforming society by optimizing the use of human and intellectual resources. His ambitions for the Analytical Engine's role in society extended far beyond mere computation. He envisioned a future in which machines would play a central role in science, industry, administration, and even education, automating complex tasks and freeing human minds for more creative and innovative work. His vision foreshadowed many aspects of the modern computing era, where computers have become indispensable tools in nearly every facet of daily life and technological advancement.

3.2.3 ALGORITHM

3.2.3.1 The Origins of Modern Algorithms

Ada Lovelace's notes (1815–1852) had a profound influence on the design of the earliest algorithms, marking a decisive turning point in the history of computing. Known for her collaboration with Charles Babbage on the Analytical Engine, Ada Lovelace is often regarded as the world's first programmer. Her notes, written in 1843, went far beyond merely describing the mechanical workings of the machine; they explored its potential to perform not only numerical operations but also conceptual ones, thus paving the way for computer programming. One of Lovelace's most significant contributions lies in her realization that Babbage's Analytical Engine could be programmed to execute a sequence of instructions, rather than just performing basic arithmetic calculations. In her notes, she provided a detailed description of an algorithm to calculate Bernoulli numbers, widely considered the first computer program ever devised. This algorithm, written as a sequence of instructions, demonstrated how the machine could be used to solve complex problems automatically by following a predefined set of rules. The idea of programming a machine to perform specific tasks through sequential instructions is at the core of what we now call an algorithm. Figure 3.6 illustrates the step-by-step logic of the first machine algorithm, written by Ada Lovelace to compute Bernoulli numbers using sequential instructions and loops.

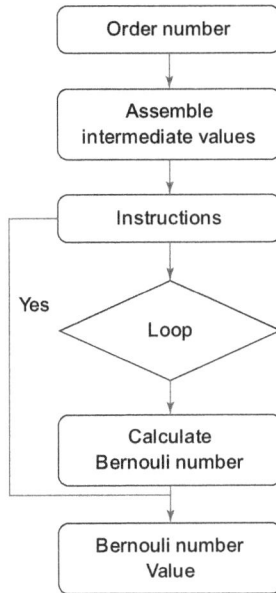

FIGURE 3.6   First machine algorithm by *Ada Lovelace.*

Lovelace also introduced the fundamental concept of the "loop" in her notes, an idea that remains essential in modern programming. She illustrated how certain operations could be repeated a specific number of times, simplifying the construction of algorithms for complex calculations. This ability to systematically structure repetitive processes is a key element of the efficiency of modern algorithms and has enabled the design of programs capable of handling far more sophisticated tasks than could have been imagined at the time. Moreover, Ada Lovelace was the first to grasp that algorithms could be applied beyond pure mathematics. She speculated that the Analytical Engine could, in principle, manipulate not only numbers but also general symbols, opening up the possibility of using algorithms for tasks such as composing music or creating artwork. This expanded vision of the machine's potential anticipated the modern idea that computers could be used for an almost infinite range of applications, from solving logical problems to generating artistic content. Lovelace also emphasized the importance of documentation and analysis in algorithm development. In her notes, she not only described how algorithms should be constructed but also analyzed their implications, the machine's limitations, and the types of problems it could address. This rigorous and systematic approach to algorithm development laid the groundwork for modern programming practices, where design, analysis, and documentation are critical steps in creating effective and reliable software.

Ada Lovelace's notes profoundly influenced the design of early algorithms by introducing foundational concepts such as sequential programming, loops, and the application of algorithms to non-numerical domains. Her work not only demonstrated the potential of Babbage's Analytical Engine but also established the theoretical foundations of modern computing. She showed that machines could be programmed to perform complex tasks autonomously, which remains at the heart of computing and algorithm design today. Her legacy endures in every computer program, where the principles she articulated continue to guide developers and engineers in creating innovative solutions.

3.2.3.2 A Revolutionary Vision of Algorithms and Computing

Ada Lovelace is regarded as a visionary in the field of computing due to her unique ability to perceive the potential of Charles Babbage's Analytical Engine far beyond what her contemporaries could imagine. At a time when machines were primarily seen as tools for performing arithmetic calculations, she foresaw that such devices could one day execute far more complex tasks, spanning diverse domains like music, art, and science. Her deep understanding of the underlying principles of the Analytical Engine and her imagination in applying them to novel ideas laid the groundwork for what we now call computing.

Lovelace recognized that the Analytical Engine was not merely an enhanced calculator but a machine that could be programmed to follow a series of instructions, enabling it to solve problems autonomously. This notion of programmability was revolutionary, as it introduced the idea that machines could be manipulated to perform a wide variety of tasks simply by altering the program they followed. This aligns with the modern concept of software, where the same hardware can execute different functions depending on the program provided. This vision transformed how future generations would conceive of the possibilities offered by computers. Another aspect of Lovelace's vision lies in her understanding that algorithms could be applied to fields beyond pure mathematics. In her famous notes, she speculated that the Analytical Engine could, in principle, be used to compose music, create artwork, or even generate complex ideas by following a set of instructions. This anticipation of machines manipulating symbols other than numbers paved the way for applications that would only be realized decades later (such as computer-generated music, digital graphics, and AI). Lovelace thus foreshadowed a world where machines interact creatively with human intelligence, contributing to the evolution of the arts and sciences. She also demonstrated an advanced understanding of the nature of algorithms and their importance in software development. She designed the first algorithm intended for machine execution, showing how a sequence of instructions could be used to calculate Bernoulli numbers. By documenting not only the procedure but also analyzing its operation and considering its limitations, Lovelace introduced practices that are central to software development today, where the analysis and optimization of algorithms are essential to creating efficient programs.

Beyond her technical contributions, Ada Lovelace is also celebrated for her ability to think abstractly and integrate concepts from various fields to envision future applications of technology. She understood that computing was not just about machines but also about logic, creativity, and innovation. Her vision encompassed a world where machines and humans collaborate to push the boundaries of what is possible, which remains central to discussions about AI and interactive systems.

3.2.3.3 Creativity and the Limits of AI

Ada Lovelace developed remarkably advanced ideas about creativity and what we might today call AI, long before these concepts were formally defined. In her notes on Charles Babbage's Analytical Engine, Lovelace speculated about the future capabilities of machines, envisioning applications that went far beyond mere calculation. Her reflections laid the initial groundwork for a philosophical and technical discussion about the nature of human creativity in relation to machine capabilities, which remains at the heart of debates about AI today.

Lovelace understood that the Analytical Engine could be programmed to execute a sequence of instructions to manipulate numbers and other symbols. However, she also emphasized that the machine could only accomplish what it had been programmed to do. It is in this observation that one of her central ideas about creativity emerges: she believed that machines, while immensely powerful in processing information, lacked initiative and true creativity. According to her, machines could follow instructions to produce complex results, but they could not "create" or "innovate" independently. This distinction between the automatic execution of tasks and genuine human creativity is known as the Lovelace paradox.

Nevertheless, Lovelace left the door open to deeper reflections on the potential of machines to mimic certain aspects of human creativity. For example, she suggested that the Analytical Engine could be used to compose music by following predefined rules and instructions. While this did not constitute creativity in the human sense, where intuition and inspiration play a central role, it nonetheless demonstrated that machines could be programmed to generate outcomes in domains traditionally associated with creativity, such as art or music. This idea foreshadowed modern developments in creative AI, where algorithms are used to generate music, artwork, or text, sometimes with surprisingly sophisticated results. However, Lovelace was clear that these capabilities reflected the creativity of the programmer, not the machine itself. For her, machines merely executed the ideas and instructions of the humans who designed and programmed them. In other words, machines were powerful tools that could extend human capabilities, but they were incapable of true creativity, which remained an intrinsically human faculty. This perspective long dominated thinking about the capacity of machines to replicate creative behavior and continues to influence debates about the limits of AI today. She also anticipated some of the ethical and philosophical questions that accompany the development of AI. By highlighting the limitations of machines in independent creation, she drew attention to the dangers of conflating the complexity of an algorithm with genuine understanding or consciousness. This distinction remains relevant in discussions about strong (or general) AI versus weak (or specific) AI, where the ability of machines to "think" autonomously is a subject of intense debate. Ada Lovelace saw machines as possessing computational and automation power capable of transforming many fields, including those related to creativity. However, she maintained that true creativity was an exclusively human quality, inaccessible to machines, which, in her view, merely followed instructions provided by humans. This fundamental distinction, which she anticipated long before the emergence of truly intelligent machines, continues to shape our understanding of what it means to create and innovate in a world increasingly influenced by AI.

3.3   THE PHILOSOPHICAL BASIS OF AI

3.3.1   THE EVOLUTION OF IDEAS ON CONSCIOUSNESS AND AI

The philosophical foundations of intelligence are rooted in millennia-old reflections on the nature of thought, consciousness, and knowledge. Since antiquity, philosophers have grappled with what constitutes human intelligence, seeking to understand not only how we think but also what it truly means to be "intelligent." These reflections have evolved over time, shaped by advancements in science, logic, and, more recently, the development of AI.

At the heart of the philosophical foundations of intelligence lies the question of the nature of the mind. Philosophers like Plato and Aristotle attempted to define intelligence in terms of cognitive capacities, such as reason and abstract understanding. Plato, for instance, viewed intelligence as a faculty tied to the knowledge of forms or ideas transcending the physical world. Aristotle, on the other hand, introduced the notion of the soul as the vital principle that endows living beings with the ability to think, distinguishing different forms of intelligence based on the capacities of humans and other creatures. With the advent of rationalism in the 17th century, thinkers like René Descartes shifted philosophical inquiry toward a more introspective approach, focusing on consciousness and thought as fundamental proofs of existence. Descartes, with his famous "Cogito, ergo sum" (*I think, therefore I am*), emphasized thought as the essence of intelligence, suggesting that the human mind, capable of conscious reflection, was fundamentally distinct from the material body. This Cartesian dualism opened the door to debates about the nature of intelligence and the relationship between mind and matter, profoundly influencing later conceptions of thought and consciousness.

Materialism, in contrast to Descartes' dualism, proposed that intelligence and thought could be fully explained by physical processes. Thomas Hobbes, for example, argued that all human thoughts and actions could be reduced to mechanical movements in the brain. This materialist view of intelligence laid the groundwork for the idea that thought could be simulated or replicated by machines for the development of AI. The introduction of formal logic and mathematics into the philosophy of intelligence, particularly through the works of Leibniz and later George Boole, enabled the formalization of certain aspects of reasoning. Leibniz dreamed of a "calculus ratiocinator," a universal system of calculation that could, in theory, solve all logical problems. This idea gave rise to the notion that intelligence could be broken down into a series of formal rules, manipulable by logical systems or machines, thus laying the foundations for modern computing.

In the 20th century, the philosophical foundations of intelligence were enriched by discussions about AI and the possibilities of thinking machines. As mentioned, Alan Turing, with his famous Turing Test, proposed a criterion for determining whether a machine could be considered intelligent: *if a machine could successfully imitate human behavior to the point where an observer could not distinguish between human and machine, then it could be deemed intelligent.* This test raised crucial questions about the nature of intelligence and the feasibility of artificially replicating it. At the same time, philosophical discussions about intelligence also turned to the issue of consciousness. John Searle, with his "Chinese Room" argument, critiqued the notion that the mere manipulation of symbols, as performed by machines, could equate to true intelligence or understanding. Searle argued that even if a machine could simulate intelligent behavior, it could not genuinely comprehend what it was doing, thus questioning whether machines could ever possess intelligence comparable to that of humans. Intelligence is also explored through the lens of ethics and moral responsibility. The ability of machines to make autonomous decisions raises questions about accountability and the morality of actions undertaken by AI. *If a machine makes an erroneous decision, who bears responsibility?* The philosophical foundations of intelligence must therefore consider not only what intelligence is but also how it should be framed within a moral and ethical context. Reflection on the philosophical foundations of intelligence continues to evolve today, as advances in neuroscience, AI, and robotics open new perspectives. Questions about the possibility of conscious AI or the limits of simulating human intelligence remain unresolved, fueling a dynamic debate among philosophers, scientists, and engineers. The nature of intelligence, its definition, and its potential remain complex topics, where philosophical contributions play an essential role in understanding the implications of this human capacity. Thus, the philosophical foundations of intelligence constitute a rich and multidimensional field, integrating perspectives on the nature of thought, consciousness, reasoning, and ethics. The debates surrounding these concepts are not merely theoretical but have practical implications for how we develop and interact with AI technologies, underscoring the importance of continuing to explore these questions in a world where the distinction between human and machine is increasingly blurred.

The Enlightenment, an intellectual movement of the 18th century, profoundly transformed the way human intelligence is understood and studied. At the core of this movement was the belief that reason and experience are the foundations of knowledge, leading to a reevaluation of human intellectual capacities. Enlightenment philosophers such as John Locke, David Hume, and Immanuel Kant emphasized the importance of empiricism and rationality, asserting that the human mind is not a passive receptacle of innate knowledge but an active tool that acquires and organizes knowledge through experience and reflection.

This new conception of intelligence spurred the emergence of psychology and the philosophy of mind as distinct disciplines dedicated to the systematic study of cognitive processes. The Enlightenment also fostered the idea that human intelligence could be enhanced through education and the rigorous application of the scientific method. This approach led to a valuing of public education and the dissemination of knowledge, seen as essential for the progress of humanity. Furthermore, the emphasis on rationality gave rise to the notion of thought as a mechanical process that could be modeled and, potentially, artificially reproduced. Thinkers like René Descartes laid the groundwork for this idea with their dualism, distinguishing the mind from the body, while later figures such as George Boole and Charles Babbage contributed to the development of the first systems of symbolic logic and computation, precursors to modern computers. Thus, the Enlightenment not only reshaped the understanding of human intelligence by grounding it in rational and empirical principles but also laid the foundations for the concept of AI, envisioning thought as a systematic process that could be analyzed, measured, and ultimately replicated.

3.3.2 The Relationship between the Mind and the Machine

3.3.2.1 The Mind and the Machine

I. Philosophical Implications of Reproducing Human Intelligence in Machines

The attempt to replicate human intelligence in machines raises profound and complex philosophical implications. Firstly, it challenges the very nature of intelligence and consciousness. If human intelligence can be simulated or reproduced by machines, it suggests that intelligence is not inherently tied to human biology but could be an emergent property of sufficiently complex systems, whether biological or artificial. This idea leads to a debate between materialism and dualism: *Is the human mind simply a physical process, or does an immaterial dimension exist, as dualists argue, that would be impossible to recreate in a machine?*. Moreover, the possibility of creating intelligent machines raises the question of artificial consciousness. If a machine could not only mimic human intelligence but also develop a form of consciousness, it would pose crucial ethical and moral questions. *Would it have rights or responsibilities? Should it be treated as a fully moral entity?* These questions touch on the very definition of what it means to be a "being" endowed with consciousness and autonomy. Additionally, replicating human intelligence in machines questions the uniqueness of the human experience. *If machines can think, learn, and perhaps even feel, what fundamentally distinguishes humans from machines?* This inquiry touches on existential questions about identity, freedom, and the meaning of human existence. In seeking to recreate our intelligence, we are forced to reflect on what constitutes the essence of our humanity and how technology might transform that essence.

These attempts also raise questions about the future of humanity. If machines can surpass human intelligence, it could lead to a disruption of social, economic, and political structures. Intelligent machines might alter our understanding of work, creativity, and even governance. It thus becomes critical to consider the implications of these technologies on society and the future of the human species, not only in terms of technical potential but also in terms of values and ethics. The debate over the mind and the machine, particularly through the works of René Descartes and Thomas Hobbes, is central to modern philosophy, especially in the context of materialism. Descartes, often considered the father of dualism, proposes a view of the mind as distinct from the physical body. In his major work, Meditations on First Philosophy (1641), Descartes asserts that the mind (or soul) is an immaterial substance, endowed with thought and consciousness, separate from the material body. This distinction rests on the idea that the body, like all matter, is subject to the laws of physics and can be analyzed mechanically, whereas the mind, being immaterial, escapes such mechanical reduction.

For Descartes, machines, no matter how sophisticated, can never truly possess consciousness or authentic thought. They might simulate intelligent behavior, but they lack the essence of human thought: the ability to doubt, conceive ideas, and be aware of their own existence. It is within this framework that Descartes celebrates his famous cogito, *I think, therefore I am*, asserting that thought is inseparable from conscious existence. According to him, while machines might mimic certain bodily functions, they can never possess a mind. In contrast, Thomas Hobbes, a contemporary of Descartes, offers a resolutely materialist view of the mind. In Leviathan (1651), Hobbes argues that everything that exists is material in nature, including mental processes. For Hobbes, thoughts, emotions, and human will are the products of mechanical movements in the brain. He thus reduces thought and consciousness to physical phenomena, asserting that, like any other part of the body, the mind can be studied scientifically and potentially reproduced mechanically. Hobbes goes further by suggesting that machines, if sufficiently complex, could in principle replicate the functions of the human mind. This materialist view of thought challenges the distinction Descartes draws between mind and matter, laying the groundwork for later mechanistic conceptions of thought, where the mind is seen as a kind of biological machine, subject to the same laws as any other material system. Hobbes' materialism raises significant philosophical questions, particularly regarding the nature of consciousness and personal identity. If thought is merely a mechanical process, it implies that the mind could, in theory, be replicated in a machine, paving the way for contemporary debates about AI and the possibility of creating conscious machines. By reducing thought to material movements, Hobbes offers a conception of the mind that aligns more closely with what some philosophers and scientists would later envision with the emergence of cybernetics and cognitive science. Thus, the perspectives of Descartes and Hobbes provide two contrasting views on the relationship between mind and machine. On one hand, Descartes maintains an insurmountable barrier between the immaterial mind and the material world of machines; on the other, Hobbes erases this distinction, viewing the mind as a material product that can be understood, analyzed, and potentially recreated in a machine. These debates have not only shaped modern philosophy but continue to influence contemporary discussions about AI, consciousness, and the nature of the mind.

II. The Distinction between Mind and Machine According to Descartes

René Descartes distinguishes the mind from the machine by relying on a dualistic conception of reality, in which he contrasts the thought (*res cogitans*) with that of physical extension (*res extensa*). For Descartes, the mind is an immaterial substance, characterized by thought, consciousness, and the capacity for reasoning. Unlike matter, the mind is not subject to the physical laws of nature, such as those of mechanics, which grants it autonomy and a unique quality that machines, being purely material, cannot possess. Descartes asserts that machines, no matter how sophisticated, can only simulate human actions without genuine understanding or consciousness. For example, a machine might be designed to mimic intelligent behaviors, such as speaking or responding to stimuli, but it would do so without awareness, merely following preprogrammed mechanisms. This distinction rests on the idea that the human mind is capable of introspective reflection and abstract understanding that seems impossible to replicate in a purely material machine. Another central aspect of this distinction is the capacity for language and abstract reasoning. Descartes argues that humans can generate and comprehend an infinite variety of new propositions across diverse contexts, thanks to their minds. Machines, on the other hand, can only operate within the limits of their programming and cannot autonomously produce new concepts or ideas. For Descartes, this ability to transcend programmatic rules is a distinctive mark of the mind, clearly highlighting the fundamental difference between human intelligence and the mechanics of machines.

III. The Influence of Hobbes's Mechanistic Vision on Conceptions of Intelligence

Thomas Hobbes's mechanistic vision, which regards thought and intelligence as entirely material processes, profoundly influenced subsequent conceptions of intelligence, particularly by paving the way for a scientific and empirical approach to the mind. By reducing mental operations to mechanical movements in the brain, Hobbes laid the groundwork for a conception of intelligence that could be studied, analyzed, and potentially replicated through mechanical or technological means. This perspective made it possible to view intelligence not as a mystical or immaterial quality, but as a phenomenon that could, in principle, be explained by the laws of physics and chemistry.

This mechanistic vision directly influenced the development of cognitive science and AI, where the mind is often modeled as an information processing system handling symbols according to logical rules, akin to a machine. Hobbes's ideas also fostered the notion that intelligence could be simulated in machines, opening the door to concepts such as automata and, later, programmable computers. The model of the mind as a machine inspired early work in AI, where researchers sought to create systems capable of simulating human cognitive processes such as reasoning, problem-solving, and learning. Moreover, Hobbes's mechanistic vision contributed to the conception of the mind as a "black box" whose internal processes could be broken down and studied in terms of functional components. This approach also influenced information theory and computing, where intelligence is frequently seen as the processing of information, comparable to a machine that receives, processes, and produces data. His mechanistic vision had a lasting impact on how intelligence is understood and studied, transforming it into an object of scientific inquiry accessible through mechanical and empirical analysis. This perspective not only guided early attempts to model the mind but continues to influence contemporary research in AI, neuroscience, and cognitive science.

IV. The Impact of Materialism on Early Concepts of AI

Materialism, by asserting that all realities, including mental processes, can be reduced to material interactions, has played a crucial role in shaping the early concepts of AI. This perspective made it possible to consider intelligence not as an intrinsically human and immaterial quality but as a phenomenon that can be simulated and reproduced by physical systems, such as machines. In other words, if thought results from material processes, then, in theory, these processes can be modeled and even replicated by mechanical or electronic devices.

This idea directly influenced the pioneers of AI, who sought to create machines capable of simulating aspects of human intelligence, such as logic, problem-solving, and decision-making. Materialism encouraged researchers to believe that cognitive operations could be broken down into a series of logical and mechanical processes, which could be programmed into computers. For example, the work of Claude Shannon on information theory and Alan Turing on his machine is deeply rooted in a materialist view of intelligence, where thought is seen as a form of information processing that can be executed by a machine.

Materialism also shaped the design of ANN, which is inspired by the material functioning of the human brain. AI researchers, influenced by materialism, attempted to replicate the structures and neural processes of the brain in the form of computational models. This approach, based on the idea that human intelligence emerges from complex interactions between physical neurons, led to the development of ML and DL, which are now at the core of modern AI. Materialism also led to a pragmatic approach to AI, where the focus is on the ability of machines to perform specific tasks rather than on replicating human consciousness or subjectivity. This orientation toward practical and tangible solutions (such as pattern recognition algorithms, optimization systems, and intelligent agents) reflects a materialist vision that prioritizes measurable and quantifiable results, reinforcing the idea that intelligence can be codified and executed by machines. It has shaped the early concepts of AI by legitimizing the idea that intelligence could be understood, modeled, and reproduced in purely material terms. This vision made it possible to transform abstract concepts of thought into functional models that laid the foundation for AI as we know it today.

3.3.2.2   The Emergence of Concepts of Consciousness and AI

The emergence of concepts such as consciousness and AI is closely linked to advances in philosophy, psychology, and cognitive sciences, which have gradually shifted the boundaries between humans and machines. At the heart of this evolution lies the fundamental question of whether a machine can not only perform intelligent tasks but also be aware of its actions, decisions, and existence. Historically, consciousness has been perceived as a unique human trait, tied to subjective experience and the ability for self-reflection. Modern philosophy, with thinkers like *René Descartes*, firmly established the idea that consciousness is an immaterial property, inextricably linked to the soul or human mind, and therefore unattainable by material entities such as machines. However, with the rise of materialism and scientific advancements, this view has been increasingly challenged. Progress in neuroscience has shown that consciousness could be linked to complex neural processes, fueling the idea that these processes could, in theory, be reproduced or simulated in sufficiently sophisticated machines. It is within this context that AI emerged as a serious scientific field, aiming not only to create systems capable of performing intellectual tasks but also to explore the possibility of conscious machines.

Early concepts of AI, influenced by pioneers like Alan Turing, primarily focused on simulating human intelligence. In his 1950 essay Computing Machinery and Intelligence, he introduced the famous Turing Test, which suggests that a machine could be considered intelligent if it could successfully convince a human that it, too, was human. While this test serves as a measure of intelligence, it implicitly raises questions about machine consciousness: *if a machine can imitate human thought indistinguishably, is it aware of its own actions?*' Over time, the development of AI has expanded to include debates on the nature of artificial consciousness. Discussions have intensified around concepts such as "strong AI," which posits that if a machine can perfectly imitate human intelligence, it could also possess some form of consciousness, and "weak AI," which views machines as highly efficient tools but fundamentally devoid of consciousness. The question of whether a machine can be conscious also raises profound ethical and philosophical considerations, such as the rights of artificial entities and the moral responsibilities of their creators.

Today, while we are still far from creating truly conscious machines, these debates continue to shape AI development. Research focuses not only on enhancing machine cognitive abilities but also on understanding the underlying mechanisms of consciousness, with the hope that one day we might be able to build systems that possess a form of consciousness or at least simulate its functional aspects. The emergence of consciousness and AI concepts represents a fascinating intersection of science, philosophy, and ethics, raising questions about the very nature of intelligence and consciousness and the limits of what machines can achieve. These debates are not merely theoretical but have practical implications for how we design and interact with future technologies.

3.3.3 Philosophical Debates Surrounding the First Thinking Machines

The design of the first thinking machines, particularly with the advent of computers and the earliest AI programs, sparked a series of philosophical debates that continue to resonate today. These debates revolve around fundamental questions concerning the nature of intelligence, consciousness, identity, and the ethical implications of creating machines capable of simulating aspects of human thought.

3.3.3.1   The Distinction between Strong and Weak Intelligence

One of the most central debates is the distinction between strong and weak AI. Strong AI posits that if a machine can perfectly imitate human cognitive processes, it could also develop a form of genuine consciousness or intelligence. In other words, a machine could, in theory, not only simulate thought but truly think. In contrast, weak AI argues that machines can simulate intelligent behavior without ever possessing real consciousness or understanding. This distinction raises the question of whether consciousness is an emergent property of complex systems or if it is inherently tied to biological matter. The Turing Test is another focal point of philosophical debates. This test aims to determine whether a machine can be considered "intelligent" by assessing its ability to imitate a human indistinguishably. However, the test has sparked criticism and discussions about what it truly means for a machine to be "intelligent."

With the development of machines capable of increasingly sophisticated cognitive processing, the question of artificial consciousness has become a major philosophical debate. Discussions focus on whether a machine could one day be conscious, experience emotions, or have subjective experiences. This debate raises questions about the very nature of consciousness: *is it purely the result of physical processes, or does it require an immaterial quality that machines could never possess?*

The idea of creating thinking machines has also given rise to ethical concerns. If a machine were to become capable of consciousness, *what would its moral status be? Would it have rights similar to those of human beings? And what responsibilities would its creators have?* These questions touch on the potential mistreatment of artificial conscious entities, as well as the possible dangers such entities could pose to humanity. The emergence of thinking machines has also stimulated debates about human identity and what fundamentally distinguishes us from machines. *If intelligence, creativity, and even emotion can be simulated by machines, what remains uniquely human?* These discussions explore the boundaries of humanity, challenging our conception of what constitutes a person and how this definition might evolve as technology advances.

The philosophical debates surrounding the first thinking machines address profound questions about the nature of intelligence, consciousness, and ethics. These discussions, far from being purely academic, influence how we approach the development and integration of AI technologies in society and continue to shape our understanding of what it means to be intelligent and conscious in a world where machines play an increasingly significant role.

3.3.3.2   Evolution of Consciousness Concepts with Advances in AI

The concepts of consciousness have evolved significantly with advances in AI, shifting from a largely philosophical and abstract notion to a multidisciplinary research subject involving philosophy, neuroscience, psychology, and computer science. This evolution reflects both technological progress in AI and growing questions about what it truly means to be conscious.

With the advent of AI, particularly ANNs and DL, the idea that consciousness could be an emergent phenomenon has become more plausible for some researchers. This concept suggests that consciousness is not necessarily tied to biology but could emerge in any sufficiently complex system capable of advanced and autonomous information processing. AI advancements have thus encouraged the exploration of consciousness as an emergent property, comparable to phenomena like life or intelligence, which appear at a certain level of organizational complexity. As AI capabilities have advanced, particularly with systems capable of simulating intelligent behaviors, the question of whether these systems could simulate a form of consciousness has gained importance. Sophisticated programs such as conversational agents (chatbots) and voice and image recognition systems have demonstrated an increasing ability to imitate complex human responses. However, this has also highlighted the distinction between simulating consciousness and truly possessing it. Researchers have thus explored the possibility of creating AI that, rather than merely simulating, could genuinely have conscious experiences. AI advancements have also stimulated the development of tests and criteria to evaluate artificial consciousness. Inspired by the Turing Test, these new tests aim to determine whether a machine can not only appear intelligent but also exhibit signs of subjective consciousness, such as the ability to feel, perceive, or engage in introspection. However, the challenge lies in the fact that consciousness is inherently subjective and internal, making its measurement in machines particularly complex and controversial. With the growing power of AI, concepts of consciousness have taken on significant ethical dimensions. If an AI were to become conscious, it would raise questions about its rights and how it should be treated. Discussions on the rights of conscious AI have intensified, questioning the responsibilities of its creators and the moral implications of interacting with potentially conscious entities. This includes debates on dignity, respect, and protection for AI, although these questions remain theoretical for now.

As AI continues to advance, particularly with approaches like Artificial General Intelligence (AGI), which aims to create systems capable of performing any intellectual task a human can, the concepts of consciousness are being pushed to their limits. Researchers are not only exploring how to simulate or recreate consciousness but also how an artificial consciousness might differ from human consciousness. This exploration raises questions about alternative forms of consciousness that could be non-biological, multiple, or qualitatively different from human experience.

3.3.3.3   Influence of Enlightenment Ideas on AI

The Enlightenment's ideas about the mind played a crucial role in shaping how we think about AI today. The Enlightenment, an intellectual movement of the 18th century, emphasized rationality, science, and empiricism, challenging traditional conceptions of the mind and human thought. These new perspectives laid the foundation for a systematic and scientific approach to intelligence, which greatly influenced later reflections on the possibility of creating thinking machines. It promoted the idea that the human mind is fundamentally rational, capable of understanding the world through logic and reason. This vision led to the notion that thought could be broken down into logical processes that could be analyzed and potentially replicated.

Philosophers such as John Locke and David Hume proposed that the mind is a "blank slate" (tabula rasa), shaped by experience and perception. This idea paved the way for the notion that intelligence could be simulated through mechanical or algorithmic processes. This mechanistic view of the mind, influenced by Enlightenment thought, is directly linked to the modern idea that human intelligence could be reproduced in machines through algorithms and logical systems.

The Enlightenment also advanced the idea that reason is a universal faculty, common to all human beings and potentially accessible to any form of intelligence capable of logic and calculation. This universality of reason encouraged the belief that human thought is neither unique nor inimitable but can be understood, codified, and applied to non-human entities such as machines. This concept contributed to the emergence of AI, where computational systems are designed to imitate or replicate these same rational abilities. Enlightenment thinkers emphasized the importance of explicability and the scientific method in understanding the mind. They sought to develop explicit models of thought that could be systematically studied and applied. This pursuit of clarity and method influenced the early developments of AI, where the creation of thinking machines was envisioned as an extension of formal logic and scientific methodology. The idea that human thought could be broken down into formal rules, as explored by George Boole with Boolean logic, is a direct inheritance of this Enlightenment vision.

The Enlightenment led to a deeper reflection on the very nature of intelligence, beyond mere cognitive abilities. This reflection pushed philosophers to question not only how intelligence functions but also what it is, opening discussions on the possibility of non-human intelligences. This perspective contributed to the conceptualization of AI not only as an imitation of the human mind but as a new form of intelligence that could, in principle, surpass or complement human intelligence. The Enlightenment's ideas about the mind have profoundly influenced thinking about AI by promoting a rationalist and mechanistic view of thought, encouraging the universality of reason, insisting on explicability and method, and fostering a reflection on the nature of intelligence itself. These intellectual contributions laid the groundwork for modern AI, making it conceivable that intelligence, far from being an unfathomable mystery, could be understood, modeled, and replicated in artificial systems.

4 From Calculator to Computer

4.1 THE EVOLUTION OF COMPUTATIONAL TOOLS

Chapter 3 examined the philosophical and symbolic foundations of mechanized reasoning. In this chapter, we turn to how those abstract principles gradually evolved into tangible devices and computational architectures.

The development of calculators into electronic brains is a process that dates back centuries, beginning with simple mechanical devices. Early calculators, such as the abacus, were created to assist in performing basic arithmetic operations. These tools, though rudimentary, marked the beginning of automated calculations. In the 1600s, inventors like Blaise Pascal designed machines capable of performing addition and subtraction using toothed wheels. These innovations, though significant, were still limited to very specific and simple operations.

In the 19th century, Charles Babbage introduced a revolutionary concept with his Analytical Engine, a theoretical calculator capable of executing any arithmetic operation, making the machine programmable. Although never completed, this machine laid the foundation for modern computers. It incorporated essential concepts such as memory and programmable instructions, marking a key step toward more versatile and automated calculators. The 20th century saw the emergence of electromechanical calculators, a significant advancement over purely mechanical devices. These new machines used relays and switches to perform more complex operations, such as multiplication and division. A notable example is the Zuse Z3, developed in 1941 by Konrad Zuse, which is considered the world's first programmable digital computer. It used relays to perform calculations automatically, laying the groundwork for the invention of the first electronic computers. The 1940s marked the transition from electromechanical calculators to electronic computers. Mechanical relays were replaced by vacuum tubes, which were much faster and more efficient. The ENIAC, completed in 1945, became one of the first fully electronic computers. It used thousands of vacuum tubes and could perform complex calculations at an unprecedented speed for its time, ushering in a new era of modern computing.

The invention of transistors in 1947 was another major breakthrough. These electronic components, smaller and more reliable than vacuum tubes, allowed computers to shrink in size while increasing their performance. During the 1950s and 1960s, transistors gradually replaced vacuum tubes in most computers, significantly reducing the size of machines while improving their reliability and speed. With the advent of integrated circuits in the 1960s, multiple transistors could be grouped onto a single chip. This innovation revolutionized the computing industry by making computers

DOI: 10.1201/9781003613633-4

smaller, more powerful, and cheaper to produce. The introduction of microprocessors in the 1970s marked another turning point. These compact components further miniaturized central processing units, leading to the creation of the first personal computers accessible to the general public.

Over the decades, advances in microelectronics have allowed computers to become increasingly powerful. Today, they can process billions of operations per second. Modern supercomputers, which combine thousands of processors working in parallel, are used to solve complex scientific problems. Multicore processors and Graphics Processing Units (GPUs) have also enabled computers to handle multiple tasks simultaneously at incredibly fast speeds, making them more versatile than ever. The future of computing appears to focus on two major revolutions: AI and quantum computing. AI is now solving problems such as voice recognition and ML, while quantum computing, still in its early stages, promises to radically change information processing. By leveraging the principles of quantum mechanics, these computers could solve problems that classical computers cannot even conceive, marking a new frontier in the evolution from calculators to electronic brains.

4.1.1 HISTORICAL NEEDS FOR CALCULATION: FROM ANTIQUITY TO THE MODERN ERA

Since the dawn of civilization, the need for computation has arisen from the necessity to solve practical problems in various contexts such as trade, agriculture, and resource management. In antiquity, societies such as those of Mesopotamia, Egypt, and Persia developed advanced numerical systems to track economic exchanges, measure land, and predict agricultural cycles. These civilizations used rudimentary tools like counting sticks or knotted ropes to perform calculations, and their innovations laid the foundations of geometry and arithmetic.

Among the earliest major inventions, the abacus stands out as an iconic tool. Used by the Chinese, Greeks, Romans, and in certain parts of Persia, this instrument allowed for arithmetic operations to be performed more quickly and reliably than with mental calculations. The abacus translated abstract concepts into physical actions, thus laying the groundwork for the automation of calculations. This tool remained in use for centuries, evolving across cultures while meeting the growing need for precision in trade and taxation.

During the Middle Ages, scholars like Khwarizmi revolutionized mathematics. He laid the foundations of algebra in his famous work, Al-Kitab al-Mukhtasar fi Hisab al-Jabr wal-Muqabala, introducing fundamental concepts and systematizing algorithms, a term derived from his name. His contributions extended beyond mathematics, as he also made advancements in geography and astronomy. This era saw the emergence of other great Iranian thinkers, such as Omar Khayyām, who refined cubic equations and developed a remarkably precise calendar, and Nasir al-Din Tusi, who contributed to trigonometry and astronomy.

During the Renaissance, as Europe rediscovered the knowledge of the ancient and medieval worlds, the works of Persian scholars, often translated into Latin, played a crucial role. The growing demands of navigators, astronomers, and engineers led to an explosion of innovations. The first logarithmic tables, developed by John Napier, were directly influenced by these earlier works. These innovations were accompanied by the invention of mechanical devices such as the slide rule, which became one of the first portable tools for scientific calculations. The 17th century marked another milestone with European scholars like Blaise Pascal and Leibniz, who developed mechanical machines to automate calculations. However, these advances were part of a historical continuum whose roots extended deeply into the work of Islamic, particularly Persian, scholars. The 19th century saw the emergence of more sophisticated machines to meet increasingly complex needs. Charles Babbage, with his Analytical Engine, and Ada Lovelace, a pioneer in programming, laid the foundations of modern computing. These advances, though revolutionary, were built upon centuries of mathematical contributions, including those of Iranian scholars who had refined the algebraic and geometric tools necessary for these developments.

The historical progression of computational tools, from rudimentary manual devices to early mechanical innovations, is summarized in Table 4.1 to provide a clear overview of their evolution across civilizations and their respective functionalities.

TABLE 4.1
Evolution of Calculation Tools through the Ages

Period	Main Tool	Civilization	Main Function	Key Advantage
Antiquity	Abacus	Mesopotamia, China, Iran	Simple calculations	Portability, speed
17th century	Pascaline	France	Addition, subtraction	Mechanization of calculation
17th century	Leibniz Wheel	Germany	Multiplication, division	Functional extension
19th century	Analytical Engine	United Kingdom	Programming	Computer concept
20th century	ENIAC, UNIVAC	USA	Electronic computation	Speed, storage

4.1.2 THE ROLE OF MATHEMATICS IN SCIENCE AND ENGINEERING

Since their inception, mathematics has served as a universal language for understanding, modeling, and transforming the natural world. Their role in science is essential, as they allow for the quantitative description of phenomena, the establishment of relationships between variables, and the prediction of the evolution of complex systems. Major scientific discoveries, whether it be Newton's law of universal gravitation or Einstein's general theory of relativity, rely on rigorous mathematical formulations that synthesize the fundamental laws of nature. These mathematical tools not only aid in interpreting the world but are also at the heart of technological innovations.

In engineering, mathematics provides methods for designing and optimizing systems. Linear algebra, for example, plays a key role in structural analysis, signal processing, and simulating mechanical behaviors. Engineers use differential equations to model dynamic phenomena such as fluid motion, mechanical oscillations, or electrical circuits. Recent technological advancements, such as modern airplanes, earthquake-resistant skyscrapers, or smartphones, would not have been possible without a deep understanding of mathematics. Classical mechanics, established in the 17th century, represents one of the first great syntheses of mathematics and engineering. Through the works of figures like Galileo and Newton, mathematics became a tool to describe motion and predict the interaction of forces. These ideas directly inspired the design of industrial machines and infrastructure, marking the beginning of the modern engineering era. Later, mathematics accompanied the industrial revolutions, helping to model and control increasingly complex systems, such as steam engines, electrical grids, and nuclear power plants.

In the 20th century, with the advent of electronics and computing, the role of mathematics further expanded. Mathematical algorithms enabled the creation of digital systems capable of processing data at unimaginable speeds. Advances in number theory and algebra directly led to the development of cryptography, which is essential for the security of modern communications. In science, mathematics has also been used to model phenomena that escape direct observation. For instance, in quantum physics, Schrödinger's equations and Heisenberg's matrices describe the behavior of subatomic particles, paving the way for innovations such as lasers or semiconductors. In biology, mathematical models help understand complex processes such as population evolution, disease spread, or ecosystem dynamics. This ability of mathematics to transcend disciplinary boundaries makes it an indispensable tool for scientific research.

Mathematics is also the foundation of simulation techniques, which are essential in engineering and other fields. Numerical simulations allow for testing virtual prototypes before their construction, thus reducing costs and risks. For example, in the aerospace industry, engineers use mathematical models to analyze stress on wings or to optimize fuel consumption. In urban planning, mathematical models predict traffic flow and improve infrastructure. Today, mathematics continues to play a central role in the emergence of new disciplines. In AI, for example, ANNs rely on concepts from linear algebra, probability theory, and analysis. Advances in ML and big data processing would not be possible without the solid mathematical foundations that underlie these technologies. From voice recognition to autonomous vehicles, mathematics is the silent engine behind the most spectacular technological advances of our time.

4.2   THE FIRST CALCULATING MACHINES

4.2.1   THE ABACUS: A MILLENNIAL TOOL

The abacus, one of the oldest calculating tools, illustrates humanity's quest to structure and manipulate numbers. Its first appearance dates back to Mesopotamia around

5,000 years ago, where it was used to perform basic arithmetic operations such as addition, subtraction, and sometimes multiplication and division. This rudimentary instrument evolved through various civilizations, adapting to the economic, scientific, and educational needs of each era, while remaining an essential calculating tool for millennia.

One of the most primitive versions of the abacus consisted of a tablet covered in sand or ash, on which marks were made to represent numbers. The Babylonians used small stones to manipulate values in their sexagesimal system. Later, the Greeks and Romans adopted an improved version, with grooves or columns for placing tokens to perform calculations. This model already laid the groundwork for positional arithmetic, a fundamental concept in the history of mathematics.

In Ancient Iran, similar counting techniques were employed. Archaeological and textual evidence suggests that the Achaemenid and later the Sassanid administrations used counting boards or grooved tablets, functioning much like the Greco-Roman abacus, for fiscal and administrative purposes. These instruments likely involved movable tokens or pebbles manipulated along designated rows to perform basic arithmetic. Though no wooden abacus frame has been preserved, the conceptual use of line-based or sand-based abaci is consistent with regional practices of the ancient Near East. The abacus operates based on the positional representation of numbers. Each column or row represents a power of the base used (usually 10), and the movable markers symbolize the values associated with each position. For example, to add two numbers, you simply move the markers in the appropriate columns and manage the carry-over when a column exceeds its capacity. This mechanism, while simple, allows for quick and precise calculations, even with relatively large numbers.

The Chinese abacus, known as *suanpan* (算 盘), introduced around the 13th century, represents a significant advancement. It consists of a wooden frame containing vertical rods, with beads placed on either side of a central bar. The upper beads represent multiples of five, while the lower beads represent units. With this structure, the *suanpan* not only allows addition and subtraction but also multiplication, division, and even square root calculations with remarkable efficiency. In medieval Europe, the abacus was an essential tool for merchants and bankers, allowing them to manage their accounts with precision. However, its use began to decline with the introduction of Iranian-Arabic numerals and written methods for performing calculations. Nevertheless, in some regions, especially in Asia, the abacus continued to be actively used, not only as a calculating tool but also as a teaching aid.

Beyond its functional role, the abacus holds symbolic importance as the precursor to modern computing technologies. It foreshadows the principle of automation, which is central to later mechanical and electronic devices. Modern calculators and computers are based on similar concepts of number representation and positional manipulation, though these are now carried out electronically. Today, the abacus is still used in some schools to develop mental arithmetic skills in children. It also remains a symbol of human simplicity and ingenuity in solving complex problems. Its users, capable of performing fast and accurate calculations, illustrate the efficiency of a tool that has endured through the ages while maintaining its relevance.

4.2.2 BLAISE PASCAL'S PASCALINE: A MECHANICAL PRECURSOR

As mentioned briefly in previous sections, the Pascaline is often considered one of the first mechanical calculating machines. This invention was born out of the need to assist his father, a tax collector, with the complex task of calculating tax revenues. Pascal, at only 19 years old, designed a device capable of performing addition and subtraction semi-automatically, thus reducing the mental burden of repetitive calculations.

Its operation relies on an ingenious system of gears and cogwheels. Each wheel corresponds to a digit in a number, and its movement drives the other wheels through an automatic carry mechanism. For example, when the units wheel completes a full revolution (reaching 10), it triggers the movement of the tens wheel by one notch, and so on for the hundreds, thousands, etc. This principle, known as "automatic carry," is one of the fundamental elements of modern mechanical calculators. The machine itself is presented in the form of a rectangular box containing several numbered windows, each corresponding to a decimal position. The user enters digits by turning dials or using sliders. Once the values are input, the results of the operations directly appear in the windows, thus avoiding manual calculation errors. Although limited to addition and subtraction, the Pascaline also allowed for repeated multiplication and division through successive iterations. This invention represented a major technological leap at a time when calculations were only performed using handwritten methods or rudimentary tools like the abacus. However, its complex manufacturing process and high cost made it difficult for the general public to access. Fewer than 20 units were built, and they were primarily intended for demonstrations or specific uses in administration. The Pascaline is also emblematic of Blaise Pascal's visionary genius, who saw in this invention much more than just a practical tool. It embodied the potential for the mechanization of intellectual processes, an idea that foreshadowed the evolution of calculating machines into modern computers. By streamlining and automating certain steps of calculation, Pascal paved the way for a new era where machines could accomplish tasks once reserved for the human mind. Despite its limitations, the Pascaline remains a significant achievement in the history of calculating technologies. It influenced other inventors, notably Leibniz, who refined the concept with a machine capable of performing all arithmetic operations. Furthermore, it represents a key step in the development of mechanical systems that would eventually lead to the first programmable machines.

4.2.3 LEIBNIZ'S CONTRIBUTIONS: THE LEIBNIZ WHEEL AND THE FOUNDATIONS OF BINARY CALCULATION

Leibniz is one of the greatest mathematicians and philosophers of his time. His contributions span many fields, but his work in calculation mechanics and mathematical logic is particularly remarkable. The Leibniz Wheel (Figure 4.1), a mechanical device, and his development of binary calculation are two major advances that laid the foundations for modern computing systems.

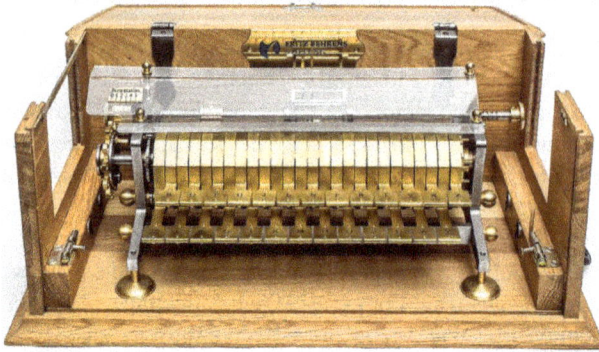

FIGURE 4.1   Leibniz's Arithmetic Machine.

The Leibniz Wheel, invented in 1673, is a major innovation in the history of cal-culating machines. It was a device designed to perform complex arithmetic opera-tions such as multiplication, division, and even square root extraction, in addition to addition and subtraction. Using a gear system, the wheel allowed a number to be multiplied by successively adding values, a process based on the mechanical repeti-tion of additions. This mechanism relies on a cylindrical toothed wheel whose posi-tion could be adjusted to represent different numerical values. Its operation is based on an ingenious principle: the wheel has nine teeth, corresponding to the digits from 0 to 9, and its movement is controlled by a crank. By turning the crank, the user advances the teeth of the wheel, with each position corresponding to a multiple of the input number. For example, to multiply 123 by 4, the machine would add 123 succes-sively four times, without requiring manual intervention to adjust intermediate val-ues. Although still limited, this automation represented a considerable technological advancement at the time.

However, Leibniz's ambitions were not limited to the mechanization of arithmetic calculations. His true vision was based on formalizing mathematical logic, paving the way for mechanized thinking. Leibniz is famous for introducing the binary num-bering system, based solely on two symbols: 0 and 1. Inspired by philosophy and the fundamental structures of logic, he viewed binary as a universal representation of numbers and concepts. He believed that every mathematical or logical problem could be broken down into a series of simple binary decisions. Leibniz's binary sys-tem is based on the idea that each position in a binary sequence represents a power of 2. For example, the decimal number 5 can be represented in binary as 101 ($1 \times 2^2 + 0 \times 2^1 + 1 \times 2^0$). This simplified representation, combined with its compatibility with fundamental logical operations (AND, OR, NOT), made binary an essential pillar of modern computing. Although the binary system was not immediately adopted in his time, it was rediscovered and applied in the 20th century, particularly with the advent of electronic computers. He saw in binary a deep connection between mathematics, philosophy, and theology. For him, 1 represented existence and 0 represented nothingness, a fundamental duality reflecting the universal order. This perspective transcended mathematics and highlighted the potential of his system to unify human knowledge into a single logical language.

His contributions, though advanced for his time, were not without challenges. The Leibniz Wheel, for instance, required highly skilled artisans to be manufactured precisely, limiting its widespread use. Additionally, the lack of practical systems to implement binary in mechanical technologies slowed its adoption. It was only with advancements in electronics, particularly through figures like Claude Shannon, that Leibniz's ideas flourished. While both Pascal and Leibniz made decisive contributions to the development of mechanical calculators, their inventions differed significantly in scope, mechanism, and functionality. A comparative summary between Pascal's Pascaline and Leibniz's stepped reckoner is presented in Table 4.2, highlighting their key technical differences and historical contributions to early mechanical computation.

TABLE 4.2

Comparison between *Pascaline* and *Leibniz's* Wheel

Criteria	*Pascaline* (1642)	*Leibniz's* Wheel (1673)
Operations	Addition, subtraction	All four arithmetic operations
Mechanism	Gear wheels and carry mechanism	Stepped drum with variable teeth
Capacity	Limited to small integers	Extended multi-digit manipulation
Intended use	Administrative calculations	Scientific and mathematical use
Limitations	Limited scalability, hand-crafted	Mechanical complexity and fragility

To summarize the key developments in manual and mechanical computation prior to the emergence of fully mechanical machines, Table 4.3 presents a historical overview of the most influential tools, their inventors, functions, and lasting impact on the evolution of intelligent computing systems. The evolution of mechanical calculators in the 17th and 18th centuries paved the way for a deeper conceptualization of programmable machines. Among the pioneers who took this leap was *Ada Lovelace*, whose vision extended far beyond mere calculation.

TABLE 4.3
Key Milestones in Manual and Mechanical Computation Tools

Period	Device	Origin	Main Function	Impact
3rd millennium BCE—7th century CE	Accounting tablets and positional counting tools	Ancient Iran (Elamites to Sassanids), influenced by Mesopotamia	Arithmetic operations for inventory, taxation, land division, and ration calculation	Supported the development of imperial management, taxation, and record-keeping across successive Persian empires
Prehistory	Counting tokens, bones	Mesopotamia and early human societies	Basic counting	First symbolic representations of quantity
Antiquity	Abacus	Mesopotamia, Egypt, Greece, China	Addition, subtraction	Facilitated rapid and visual calculation
8th–11th c.	Astrolabe	Al-Fazārī (Kufa, Abbasid Caliphate), Omar Khayyām (Iran), based on Greek and Alexandrian sources	Astronomical measurements and calendar computation	Introduced in the Islamic world by Al-Fazārī; used by Khayyām to create the highly accurate Jalālī calendar
13th c.	Spherical armillary instruments	Nasir al-Din Tusi (Iran)	Modeling planetary motion and celestial coordinates	Enabled precise computation at Maragha Observatory; precursor to mechanical astronomical models
1642	Pascaline	Blaise Pascal (France)	Addition, subtraction	First mechanical calculator
1673	Leibniz Wheel	Gottfried Wilhelm Leibniz	Multiplication, division	Introduced binary concepts and stepped-drum mechanism
1837	Analytical Engine	Charles Babbage (United Kingdom)	Programmable calculation	Conceptual precursor to modern computers
1941	Z3	Konrad Zuse (Germany)	Automatic binary computation	First programmable electromechanical computer
1945	ENIAC	Mauchly and Eckert (United States)	High-speed arithmetic	Beginning of the electronic digital computing era

4.3 ADA LOVELACE: THE FIRST PROGRAMMER AND HER VISION OF VERSATILE MACHINES

Ada Lovelace, often called the first programmer in history, is an iconic figure in the evolution of calculating tools and modern computing. The daughter of poet Lord Byron and Anne Isabella Milbanke, she grew up in an environment conducive to intellectual rigor. Her mother, a mathematics enthusiast, encouraged her from a young age to develop her skills in science and logic, preparing her to become a pioneer in a field then dominated by men. Her most famous contribution is related to her work with Charles Babbage on the Analytical Engine. This historical diagram of this machine is presented in Figure 4.2. The simplified diagram of this machine illustrates the main components of Babbage's Analytical Engine, including the arithmetic unit, memory, equalizing disks, and two distinct punched card readers: one for operations and another for variables and numbers (Figure 4.3).

Although this machine was never fully constructed, Ada quickly understood its revolutionary potential. Unlike Babbage, who primarily saw his invention as a calculating tool, Ada realized that the Analytical Engine could go far beyond simple arithmetic operations. She envisioned the possibility for a machine to manipulate symbols and data in a general way, thus paving the way for a vision of computers as versatile devices.

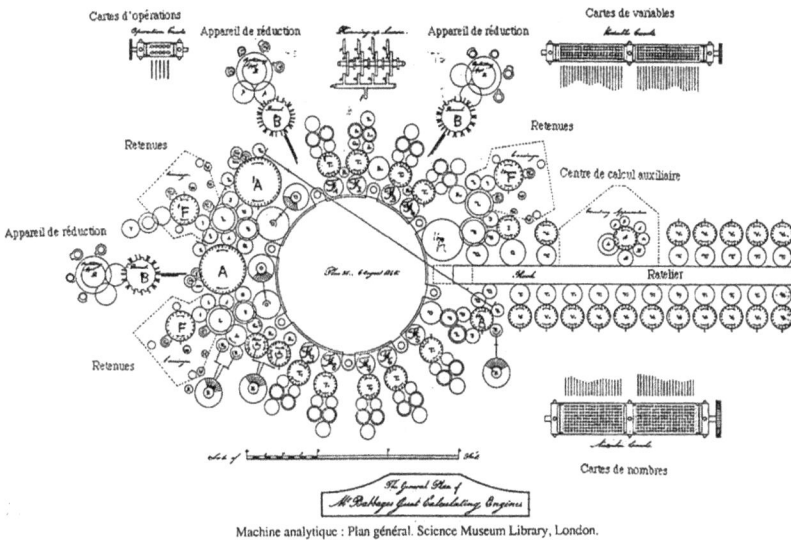

Machine analytique : Plan général. Science Museum Library, London.

FIGURE 4.2 Charles Babbage: Diagram of the Analytical Engine (1840), with the organizational components of the machine added (https://journals.openedition.org/dht/1526).

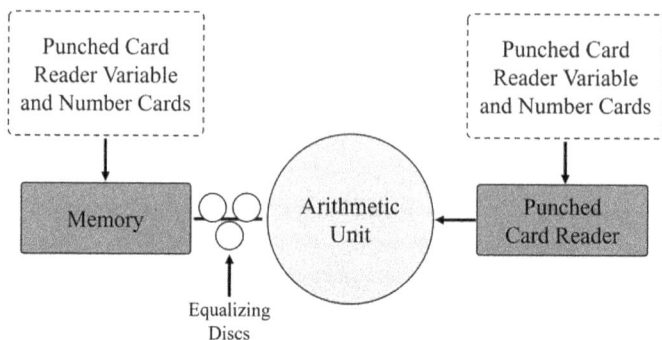

FIGURE 4.3   The main components of Babbage's Analytical Engine.

Ada Lovelace's role in this project is particularly remarkable for her work on the explanatory notes accompanying a translation she made of a scientific article on the Analytical Engine. Her notes, often longer than the original text, include reflections on the machine's capabilities and contain what is today considered the first-ever computer program. This program consisted of an algorithm to calculate a sequence of *Bernoulli* numbers using the Analytical Engine. This work demonstrated not only her mathematical skills but also her unique understanding of how machines worked. She was also fascinated by the ability of machines to transcend numerical calculation to manipulate other types of information, such as text and music. In her notes, she discussed the possibility that the Analytical Engine could compose melodies if programmed with the rules of musical harmony. This prophetic vision, long before the advent of modern computers, illustrates her ability to conceive innovative applications for technologies still in development. *Lovelace* also understood the limitations of machines, asserting that they could only perform the tasks for which they were explicitly programmed. This often-quoted observation makes a clear distinction between the mechanics of automated calculations and the capability of true AI. This reflection, known as the "Lovelace Paradox," remains relevant in modern debates about the nature of AI.

Her work, though largely unrecognized during her lifetime, had a lasting impact. In the 1950s, when the first electronic computers began to emerge, *Ada Lovelace's* contributions were rediscovered and celebrated. Today, the ADA programming language, used in critical systems such as aerospace, is named in her honor, acknowledging her role as a pioneer. In addition to her scientific achievements, she also represents a figure who challenged gender stereotypes in scientific and technological fields. By defying the norms of her time, she paved the way for many women in STEM (science, technology, engineering, and mathematics), showing that curiosity and intelligence transcend social barriers.

4.4   THE ELECTRIC AND ELECTRONIC REVOLUTION

4.4.1   THE EMERGENCE OF ELECTROMECHANICAL CALCULATORS

The emergence of electromechanical calculators in the 20th century marked a crucial step in the evolution of calculating tools. These machines, which combined traditional mechanical components with electrical devices like relays, represented a significant advancement over purely mechanical devices of the past. They introduced increased capabilities in terms of speed, reliability, and versatility, paving the way for modern computers.

The development of electromechanical calculators was driven by growing needs for complex calculations, particularly in the fields of scientific research, engineering, and finance. Figures such as Konrad Zuse in Germany and Howard Aiken in the United States played a central role in this technological revolution. Konrad Zuse, with his Z3 machine, is often credited with creating the first programmable and functional calculator. It is used to perform arithmetic operations and logical calculations, laying the groundwork for modern computer systems. Electromechanical calculators used a fundamental principle: electromagnetic relays acted as switches to manipulate data. These relays, though bulky and relatively slow compared to later electronic components, enabled automatic and programmable calculations. For example, this machine could read instructions from punched tape, introducing a level of programmability that clearly distinguished it from earlier mechanical machines.

In parallel, in the United States, the Mark I project, led by Howard Aiken at Harvard University, led to the construction of another remarkable electromechanical calculator. This project was completed in 1944, measured over 15 meters in length, and used thousands of relays and switches to perform complex calculations. It was capable of performing operations like multiplication and division on multiple digits with unprecedented precision for the time. Although slow by modern standards, the Mark I played a key role in scientific and military calculations during World War II. However, these machines were far from perfect. The relays, while innovative, had limitations in terms of speed and reliability. Their switching time was relatively long, and they were prone to mechanical failures. These limitations prompted researchers to explore alternatives, ultimately leading to the abandonment of electromechanical calculators in favor of electronic computers using vacuum tubes.

The impact of electromechanical calculators extends beyond their practical use. They represent a major transition in the design of calculating machines, integrating concepts such as automatic programming and temporary data storage for the first time. These ideas were carried over and perfected in electronic computers, marking a decisive turning point in the history of computing. Electromechanical calculators represent an essential transitional step between traditional mechanical machines and modern computers. Although their era was brief, their influence is undeniable, as they demonstrated the feasibility of programmable machines capable of solving complex problems automatically.

4.4.2   The First Electronic Machines: From ENIAC to UNIVAC

The first electronic machines represent a major breakthrough in the history of computing, marking the transition from electromechanical calculators to modern computers. Among these innovations, the ENIAC, completed in 1945, is often considered the first fully electronic computer. Designed by John Presper Eckert and John Mauchly at the University of Pennsylvania, the ENIAC was intended to perform complex ballistic calculations for the U.S. military during World War II. With

its 17,468 vacuum tubes, the ENIAC could perform 5,000 additions or 357 multiplications per second, a revolutionary speed for the time. Although the ENIAC
(Figure 4.4) was powerful, it was also a massive and power-hungry device. Weighing
nearly 30 tons and occupying 167 square meters, it required significant electrical
power and constant maintenance. Its operation was also cumbersome: it had to be
manually reprogrammed for each new task, which could take several days. Despite
these limitations, the ENIAC demonstrated the potential of electronic machines to
solve complex problems quickly and reliably. One of the main innovations of the
ENIAC was the use of vacuum tubes, which replaced the mechanical relays used in
earlier calculators. Vacuum tubes allowed much faster switching, making calculations instantaneous by the standards of the time. However, their fragility and limited
lifespan posed significant logistical challenges, influencing research for more robust
components, such as transistors, in the following decades.

FIGURE 4.4   The ENIAC: Historic photograph of the first fully electronic general-purpose
computer, developed by Eckert and Mauchly at the University of Pennsylvania (https://fr
.wikipedia.org/wiki/ENIAC).

Inspired by the success of the ENIAC, Eckert and Mauchly continued their
research to design a more advanced and accessible computer. This led to the creation
of the Electronic Discrete Variable Automatic Computer (EDVAC), which introduced the concept of a program stored in memory for the first time. This fundamental change, proposed by von Neumann, marked a break from previous architectures
by allowing machines to store their instructions and execute them sequentially or
conditionally. The von Neumann architecture remains at the core of modern computer design today. The UNIVersal Automatic Computer (UNIVAC), developed
in the 1950s, was the first commercially available computer in the United States,

marking the beginning of the computerization of businesses and government institutions. Unlike the ENIAC, the UNIVAC was designed to be versatile, capable of processing diverse types of data, such as weather forecasts or statistical analyses. Its ability to read magnetic tapes for data storage and retrieval illustrates another major innovation, laying the groundwork for modern file management systems.

The UNIVAC achieved notable success in 1952 when it was used to accurately predict the results of the U.S. presidential election, thereby reinforcing confidence in the reliability and usefulness of electronic computers. This event marked a turning point in the public perception of machines, transforming them from military or academic tools to practical instruments for solving everyday problems.

The rise of electronic computers during this period also reflects advancements in other fields, such as telecommunications and mathematical sciences. Claude Shannon's theories on information and coding directly influenced how data was processed and transmitted in these new machines. Furthermore, *Turing*'s work on universal machines provided a solid theoretical foundation for software development.

The first electronic machines, like ENIAC and UNIVAC, symbolize the transition to a new technological era. By overcoming the limitations of mechanical and electromechanical calculators, they introduced essential concepts that still define modern computing. Their impact goes far beyond their initial applications, shaping the foundations of our current digital society.

4.5 THE TRANSITION TO MODERN COMPUTERS

The evolution from mechanical calculators to fully programmable computers was not a sudden leap but the result of a series of incremental innovations across mathematics, logic, and engineering. This transition laid the foundations for modern computing, driven by theoretical advances and practical inventions. To better understand this technological shift, Table 4.4 provides a chronological summary of the key milestones that led to the emergence of the digital computer.

TABLE 4.4
Key Milestones in the Transition toward the Modern Computer

Year	Innovation or Event	Contribution
1837	Babbage's Analytical Engine	Conceptual foundation of the computer
1936	Turing Machine	Theoretical model of computability
1945	Von Neumann architecture	Logical structure of modern computers
1946	ENIAC	First general-purpose electronic computer
1951	UNIVAC I	First commercially available computer

4.5.1 VON NEUMANN ARCHITECTURE AND THE FUNDAMENTAL PRINCIPLES OF MODERN COMPUTERS

The von Neumann architecture, proposed in 1945 by mathematician and physicist von Neumann, is a key milestone in the history of computing. It laid the foundation for the design of modern computers by establishing a logical and unified structure for computing systems. This architecture is based on a simple but powerful model that continues to influence the construction of contemporary computers. At the heart of the *von Neumann* architecture is the idea of a system where both data and program instructions are stored in a shared memory. Unlike earlier systems, where instructions were hard-wired directly into the hardware, this model allowed computers to read and execute programs as needed, offering unparalleled flexibility. The concept of unified memory revolutionized programming by allowing instructions to be modified without physically rebuilding the machine. The model consists of several key components: a computation unit, a control unit, memory, and input/output devices (Figure 4.5).

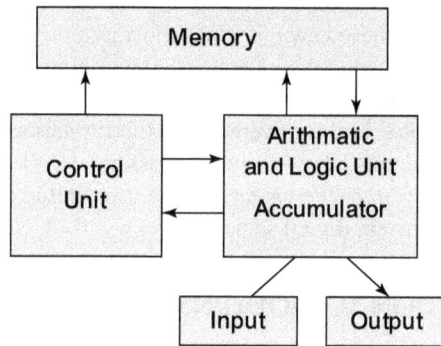

FIGURE 4.5   Simplified diagram of the von Neumann architecture.

The computation unit, also known as the arithmetic logic unit (ALU), is responsible for mathematical and logical operations. The control unit manages the flow of instructions and ensures their sequential execution. These two components are connected by a bus, a communication channel that transports data and commands between different parts of the system. The fundamental components of the von Neumann model are summarized in Table 4.5, which outlines the roles of each element in the operation of a modern computer.

TABLE 4.5
Core Components of the von Neumann Architecture

Component	Function
Control unit	Directs instruction execution
Memory	Stores data and program instructions
ALU (arithmetic logic unit)	Performs calculations and logic
Input/output devices	Interfaces with the external environment
Bus system	Transfers data among components

One of the most innovative aspects of this architecture is the use of an instruction register, which temporarily stores the instruction currently being executed. This allows the control unit to interpret and execute instructions sequentially or conditionally, enabling computers to handle complex and varied tasks. This logical sequence, known as the "instruction cycle," is at the core of the operation of modern computers. The introduction of von Neumann architecture also had a significant impact on memory management. By combining data and instructions in a single storage unit, it simplified hardware design and allowed major advancements in programming. However, this approach also introduced what is known as the "von Neumann bottleneck," a limitation related to the speed of data transfer between the processor and memory. This challenge remains relevant today and has led to innovations such as cache memory and parallel architectures.

Another key advantage of this model is its ability to execute stored programs. This paved the way for innovations such as high-level programming languages, which allow developers to create complex software without worrying about the underlying hardware details. Through this abstraction, computing expanded into many fields, from science to the arts to commercial applications. It was quickly adopted in early electronic computers, such as the EDVAC and UNIVAC, which demonstrated its feasibility and efficiency. Although alternatives, such as the Harvard architecture, emerged later to address some of its limitations, the von Neumann model remains a pillar of modern computing. The von Neumann architecture transformed computer design by introducing principles that remain at the heart of today's computer technology. Its simplicity, flexibility, and efficiency democratized computing and paved the way for innovations that continue to shape our digital world. This model, despite its challenges, remains an inspiration for engineers and researchers, illustrating the lasting impact of von Neumann's visionary ideas.

4.5.2 THE INTRODUCTION OF PROGRAMMING AND SYMBOLIC LANGUAGES

The introduction of programming and symbolic languages marked a crucial advancement in the evolution of computing. Before their beginning, machines required manual hardware adjustments to execute specific tasks, an approach that limited their efficiency and flexibility. The advent of programming languages allowed these limitations to be transcended by providing an interface between humans and machines, thus facilitating the creation, modification, and execution of programs.

The idea of programming dates back to the work of Charles Babbage and Ada Lovelace on the Analytical Engine in the 19th century. Although this machine was never completed, Lovelace understood the importance of describing instructions in a logical and sequential format. Her notes included algorithms for calculating mathematical series, foreshadowing modern programming languages. However, it was only in the 20th century, with advancements in electronics, that this vision became a reality.

The development of early electronic computers, such as ENIAC and EDVAC, required an efficient way to interact with these machines. Initially, programs were coded by directly modifying the wiring or inserting punch cards, a laborious and error-prone process. The introduction of memory systems and concepts like von

Neumann architecture paved the way for the use of stored programs, which could be stored, read, and modified directly in memory. One of the earliest symbolic languages was assembly language, which translated human-readable instructions (such as ADD or SUB) into binary machine language, understandable by the computer. This intermediate language simplified the programming process while remaining close to the hardware. However, it was still complex and required in-depth knowledge of the hardware architecture. The true revolution came with high-level programming languages, such as Fortran (1957) and COBOL (1959). Fortran, designed for scientific and technical applications, introduced control structures such as loops and conditions, making programs more readable and modifiable. COBOL, on the other hand, was aimed at business applications and distinguished itself with syntax close to English, making it easier for non-technical users to adopt. These languages marked a break from the past, allowing programmers to focus on the logic of applications rather than hardware details. To provide a clearer overview of this historical progression, Table 4.6 presents a summary of the main programming languages, their key characteristics, and their typical applications across different eras.

TABLE 4.6
Evolution of Programming Languages

Period	Language	Characteristics	Applications
1950s	Assembly	Low-level, hardware-specific	Machine control, early computers
1960s	Fortran	High-level, scientific focus	Numerical computation, engineering
1970s	C	Structured, general-purpose	Operating systems, embedded systems
1980s–1990s	C++, Java	Object-oriented, modular	Software development, user interfaces
2000s–today	Python, R, others	Readable, data-driven	AI, data science, automation

Programming also became more accessible with the introduction of compilers, software that automatically translated source code into machine instructions. This innovation significantly reduced errors and sped up the development process. Pioneers such as Grace Hopper, who played a key role in the creation of COBOL, understood the importance of automating and simplifying the link between humans and machines. The emergence of structured languages in the 1960s and 1970s, such as C and Pascal, introduced concepts such as functions, modules, and libraries, which encouraged logical and modular organization of programs. This facilitated collaborative work and allowed for the management of more complex software projects. These languages laid the groundwork for modern paradigms, notably object-oriented programming, which emerged with languages like Smalltalk and later Java and C++. Symbolic languages also played a central role in the development of AI.

Lisp, developed in the 1950s, was the first language dedicated to manipulating symbols and solving logical problems. Its list-based approach and recursive expressions made it an essential tool for AI research, influencing the development of other specialized languages. At the same time, the introduction of declarative languages like Prolog in the 1970s expanded the horizons of programming. Prolog, primarily used in AI and knowledge processing, allowed programmers to define logical relationships and let the computer solve problems by exploring those relationships. This approach contrasted with traditional imperative languages, where each step of the computation had to be explicitly defined.

Today, programming and symbolic languages continue to diversify to meet the growing needs of modern computing. Languages like Python, with their simple syntax and versatility, dominate the current landscape, making programming accessible to millions of developers worldwide. Moreover, specialized languages such as *R* for statistical analysis or Swift for mobile app development illustrate the adaptability and modularity of the concepts introduced in the programming era.

4.6 TURING'S THEORIES: TURING MACHINE AND COMPUTABILITY

The theoretical contributions of George Boole to symbolic logic, detailed in Chapter 3 (see the section "George Boole's Symbolic Logic"), provided the algebraic framework necessary for digital circuit design and logical reasoning. These foundations paved the way for Alan Turing, who would later establish the formal principles of computation.

Alan Turing stands as one of the most influential figures in the history of computing. His major contribution, the Turing machine, is a theoretical model that laid the groundwork for computability and modern computing. Introduced in 1936, it aimed to define the limits of computation and offered a systematic method to determine what a computer could achieve. The model consists of three key components: an infinite tape divided into cells, a read-write head, and a finite set of rules. The tape acts as memory, the head reads and writes symbols, and the rules dictate the machine's actions based on the current state and input symbol. Though theoretical, this model can simulate any algorithm or computer program, thus earning the title of a "universal computer." Turing originally designed it to address the Entscheidungsproblem (decision problem) posed by David Hilbert. He demonstrated that certain problems cannot be solved algorithmically, thereby establishing fundamental limits to computation and introducing the notion of undecidability.

A key concept linked to the Turing machine is the idea of a stored program. Unlike earlier methods requiring different hardware for each task, the Turing machine could run multiple programs by simply altering the instruction set. This insight directly influenced the von Neumann architecture, which underpins modern computers. Turing's exploration of the machine's potential also led to philosophical considerations about human cognition and AI. He proposed that if a machine could execute any algorithm, it could, in theory, replicate aspects of human intelligence. This idea culminated in the Turing Test introduced in his 1950 paper "Computing Machinery and Intelligence." The test evaluates whether a machine can convincingly imitate human behavior in a text-based conversation. If a human cannot distinguish the machine from another person, the machine is considered "intelligent." While widely referenced, the Turing Test has also sparked debate about the nature of intelligence and consciousness. Beyond philosophical implications, the Turing machine had a tangible influence on early computing technology. Turing's ideas contributed to the development of the Colossus during World War II, a machine used to decrypt German communications. This project demonstrated the real-world application of his theoretical framework and its effectiveness in solving complex tasks.

The concept of computability introduced by Turing is now central to various domains of computer science. It serves to analyze algorithmic limits, problem complexity, and data processing capabilities. Concepts such as polynomial time and NP-completeness stem from his vision of the universal machine. Turing's influence also extends to AI: whether in neural networks or heuristic methods, modern AI systems follow the principle that complex operations can be reduced to simpler steps, a notion rooted in his work. His ideas even found applications in fields like computational biology. In the 1950s, Turing published models of morphogenesis using mathematical equations to explain natural pattern formation. This interdisciplinary application exemplified his ability to bridge logic, mathematics, and computation.

4.7   FROM AUTOMATION TO INFORMATION PROCESSING

4.7.1   EARLY DATABASES AND AUTOMATED CALCULATIONS

The rise of databases and automated calculations represents a fundamental advancement in the history of computing. These technologies transformed how information was collected, stored, and analyzed, laying the foundation for modern information systems. Initially, these concepts emerged to address specific needs in commerce, science, and administration.

The first databases were essentially structured files, often stored on punched cards or magnetic tapes. Punched cards, introduced on a large scale by Herman Hollerith in the late 19th century, were primarily used for census and statistical processing. The idea of encoding information using holes and spaces allowed repetitive tasks to be automated and reduced human error. This approach was adopted across various sectors, from public administration to railroads. With the advent of electronic computers in the 1940s and 1950s, the concept of databases evolved. Early systems, such as sequential files, were designed to read and write data in a linear order. Although rudimentary, these systems facilitated the management of large volumes of data, especially in banking and scientific fields. For example, banks used databases to manage transactions and client balances.

The real revolution in databases came with the introduction of database management systems (DBMSs) in the 1960s. Systems like IBM's hierarchical model and the CODASYL network model (refers to Conference on Data Systems Languages) allowed data to be structured more flexibly. Relationships between records could be explicitly defined, making searches and updates easier. These innovations significantly accelerated administrative and scientific processes. Meanwhile, automated calculations progressed with the introduction of specialized software. Early automation programs were often written in machine language or assembly language, requiring significant technical expertise. However, the emergence of high-level programming languages like Fortran and COBOL simplified the development of automated systems. These languages enabled companies to develop specific applications for accounting, inventory management, and planning. Automation also had a major impact on science. Research laboratories adopted computers to perform complex simulations, analyze experimental data, and solve differential equations. For example, the Los Alamos computers were used to simulate nuclear reactions, playing a crucial role in the Manhattan Project. These tools opened new possibilities in fields like meteorology, particle physics, and biology.

Advances in databases and automated calculations were catalyzed by the development of the von Neumann architecture, which introduced the concept of stored programs. This innovation allowed computers to execute complex algorithms, integrating storage, processing, and data retrieval steps. This architecture made it possible to design interactive systems capable of responding in real time to user queries. Relational databases, introduced in the 1970s by Edgar F. Codd, marked another turning point. This model, based on relational algebra, allowed data to be manipulated using declarative languages like *SQL*. Unlike hierarchical and network models, the relational model offered greater flexibility in structuring and querying data, facilitating its adoption across many sectors.

With the evolution of storage technologies, databases have gained in capacity and efficiency. Hard drives, and later SSDs, replaced magnetic tapes, allowing fast random access to data. This transition not only improved database performance but also enabled the development of real-time information management systems, such as those used in stock exchanges and military applications.

In automated calculations, the introduction of ML opened new perspectives. Modern algorithms use massive databases to train models capable of recognizing complex patterns. These advances, based on developments from the 1960s and 1970s, are now foundational to technologies like voice recognition, computer vision, and recommendation systems.

4.7.2 FROM SPECIALIZED MACHINES TO VERSATILE SYSTEMS

The transition from specialized machines to versatile systems represents a turning point in the history of computing. In the early days, machines were designed to perform specific tasks, such as calculating astronomical tables or automating textile production. While these machines were groundbreaking for their time, their inflexibility highlighted the need for systems capable of adapting to multiple uses. Specialized machines like Joseph-Marie Jacquard's loom or Charles Babbage's Difference Engine provided early examples of automation. The Jacquard loom, introduced in 1804, used punched cards to control the weaving of intricate patterns. Although limited to textiles, it demonstrated the potential of programmable machines. Similarly, Babbage's Difference Engine was designed to calculate polynomial functions, showcasing the power of mechanical computation within a narrow scope.

As technological needs evolved, particularly during the Industrial Revolution, the demand for more flexible systems grew. Industries required machines that could handle diverse tasks without extensive reconfiguration. This need drove innovations that would lay the groundwork for modern computing. One of the key advancements in this transition was the development of programmable logic. Herman Hollerith's punched card system allowed data to be processed and stored efficiently. Though still specialized, Hollerith's system introduced the concept of using a standard input medium to direct machine operations, paving the way for greater adaptability.

The introduction of electronic components further accelerated the shift to versatility. Early computers, like the ENIAC, initially required manual rewiring to switch between tasks. However, the subsequent EDVAC incorporated *von Neumann*'s stored-program architecture. This breakthrough allowed instructions to be stored in memory alongside data, enabling computers to switch between tasks without hardware modifications. His architecture marked a paradigm shift. By separating hardware and software functionality, it enabled machines to execute a variety of programs. This flexibility was critical in transforming computers from single-purpose tools into general-purpose systems capable of performing diverse operations.

The evolution of programming languages also contributed significantly to this transformation. Early languages like assembly provided a way to write instructions that could be executed by different machines with minimal adaptation. The development of higher-level languages, such as Fortran and COBOL, further abstracted hardware complexities, enabling programmers to focus on problem-solving rather than machine-specific details. Another major milestone was the advent of time-sharing systems in the 1960s. These systems allowed multiple users to access a single computer simultaneously, each running their own programs. Time-sharing demonstrated the potential of versatile systems to serve a variety of users and applications, laying the foundation for modern multitasking operating systems.

The introduction of microprocessors in the 1970s further expanded the possibilities for versatile computing. These compact, powerful chips integrated the core components of a computer's CPU onto a single silicon chip. Microprocessors not only reduced the size and cost of computers but also made them accessible to a wider audience, driving the development of personal computers. With the proliferation of personal computers in the 1980s, the concept of versatility became a defining characteristic of computing systems. Machines like the IBM PC could run a wide range of software, from word processing and spreadsheets to games and educational programs. This adaptability made computers indispensable in both professional and personal contexts.

The rise of the Internet further amplified the importance of versatile systems. Computers connected to global networks need to perform diverse tasks, from browsing web pages and sending emails to running servers and hosting databases. This connectivity underscored the necessity of systems that could adapt to rapidly changing technological landscapes. In AI, the shift to versatile systems has been particularly impactful. Early AI systems were often designed for narrow tasks, such as playing chess or solving mathematical equations. Modern AI systems, however, leverage versatile computing architectures to perform a wide range of functions, from NLP to image recognition and predictive analytics. Cloud computing represents another leap in versatility. By abstracting physical hardware into virtualized environments, cloud platforms allow users to deploy and scale applications on demand. This flexibility has transformed industries, enabling businesses to innovate and adapt quickly to market needs without investing in dedicated infrastructure.

As we look to the future, the evolution from specialized machines to versatile systems continues to shape technological progress. Advances in quantum computing, for instance, promise to unlock new levels of adaptability by enabling systems to solve problems that were previously intractable. Similarly, edge computing brings versatile capabilities closer to end-users, enabling real-time processing for applications like autonomous vehicles and smart cities.

4.8 TOWARD AI

4.8.1 INFORMATION THEORY

The mechanization of reasoning, once a philosophical pursuit, evolved into a concrete process of information manipulation. Building on the conceptual groundwork presented in Chapter 3, we now examine the key milestones that enabled machines to encode, transmit, and compute information.

Information theory, developed by Claude Shannon in the 1940s, is a branch of mathematics and engineering that studies the quantification, storage, and communication of information (simplified diagram is shown in Figure 4.6). It focuses on how information is coded, transmitted, and processed, while also taking into account the errors that can occur during transmission. This theory forms the foundation for modern communication technologies such as the Internet, telecommunications, and even data encryption. Shannon proposed a way of measuring information, called entropy, which indicates the amount of uncertainty or "disorder" in a message. The more unpredictable a message is, the higher its entropy. For example, a repetitive message has low entropy because it contains little new information, whereas a completely random message has a high level of entropy. Information theory also introduces key concepts such as source coding (how to optimally code data for transmission) and channel coding (how to transmit it efficiently and without errors). *Shannon* also formulated the channel capacity theorem, which states that there is a maximum limit to the amount of information that can be transmitted through a channel in the presence of noise.

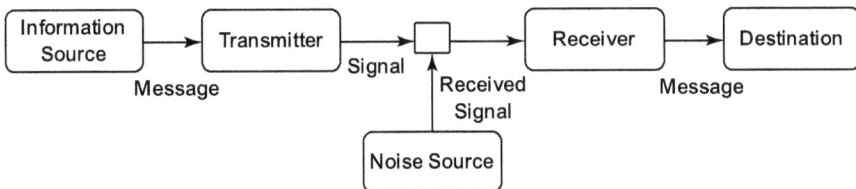

FIGURE 4.6 *Shannon*'s model of communication.

Computing emerged as a new scientific discipline in its own right due to a convergence of theoretical discoveries, practical needs, and technological advancements during the 20th century. Its origins trace back to the first mechanical calculations, but it was truly with the work of Turing and Claude Shannon that computing began to structure itself as a distinct field. Turing laid the foundation for algorithms and computational models. Meanwhile, Shannon developed information theory, which helped understand how to transmit, encode, and process data efficiently. These works established the mathematical and theoretical foundations for what would become modern computing.

The need for machines capable of fast calculations became especially urgent during World War II, particularly for decrypting codes and performing ballistic calculations. The first electronic computers, like the ENIAC, were developed to meet these needs, and their success demonstrated the practical potential of these machines to solve complex problems. After the war, computers rapidly evolved, thanks to advancements like transistors and integrated circuits, making the machines smaller, faster, and more powerful. This technological explosion made computers accessible to a broader range of scientific and industrial disciplines. As computers became more widespread, programming methods and data organization developed, giving rise to concepts like programming languages, operating systems, and data structures. Universities began creating departments and programs dedicated to computing, recognizing that it was not just a tool for mathematicians or engineers but a discipline in itself with its own theories, methodologies, and fields of research.

Today, computing is recognized as an autonomous science due to its impact on numerous fields, from biology to physics to social sciences. It continues to grow in importance with the advent of technologies like AI, data science, and quantum computing, which constantly push the boundaries of what computers can achieve. In short, computing has established itself as a scientific discipline through its central role in the development of information processing tools and its transformative impact on nearly every sector of society. The early practical applications of information theory in the development of AI played a crucial role in how machines process, store, and learn from data. Information theory, formulated by Claude Shannon, provided a mathematical framework to understand the transmission and transformation of information, concepts that became essential for the development of AI systems. One of the first applications was in data compression and transmission, where information theory helped optimize how machines received and processed information more efficiently, reducing errors and increasing the speed of signal transmission in early AI systems.

Another area where information theory had a direct impact on AI was in ML. Specifically, Shannon's concept of entropy helps assess uncertainty and the amount of information contained in data. This was used to guide learning algorithms, particularly in methods of probability estimation, classification, and decision-making. For example, decision trees, used in supervised learning, often rely on entropy to measure the effectiveness of a data split, optimizing the performance of algorithms. Minimizing entropy helps create more accurate and robust models.

Moreover, information theory influenced the development of NNs, particularly in how networks adjust the weights of connections between neurons. The goal of AI is to maximize useful information while minimizing errors, and concepts like cross-entropy are used to measure the difference between a network's predictions and actual results. This principle guides adjustments in NN models so they can learn more effectively. Information theory has also been applied in pattern recognition and computer vision, two key branches of AI. Here, the ability to reliably and efficiently extract meaningful information from vast amounts of raw data has enabled AI algorithms to better interpret images, sounds, and texts. These early practical applications of information theory have served as pillars for the development of more advanced AI technologies, fundamentally influencing how machines process and learn from information.

4.8.1.1 Simulated Intelligence

The development of the Turing machine introduced a revolutionary concept, as thoroughly described. This theoretical machine was not a physical device but rather a mathematical idea designed to define the limits of computation. It helped understand what a computing system could theoretically accomplish with simple rules, such as reading and writing symbols on an infinite tape. The Turing machine served as an abstract model for modern computers and laid the foundation for the notion of algorithms. The machine also brought a crucial advancement in the development of AI. Turing explored the idea that, if a machine could perform any human algorithmic task, it could potentially simulate human intelligence. This led Turing to design his famous Turing Test in the 1950s. The test aims to determine whether a machine can pass as a human in a text-based conversation, without the interlocutor being able to distinguish if they are interacting with a machine or a human. If a machine succeeds in this test, it could be considered "intelligent." This concept remains a landmark in AI research.

The idea of machine-simulated intelligence raised philosophical questions about the nature of thought, consciousness, and the distinction between human and AI. Turing's work paved the way for decades of AI research, influencing the design of the first programmable computers. His legacy is visible in modern AI systems, from voice assistants to NNs, which attempt to replicate specific aspects of human intelligence. It not only revolutionized theoretical computation but also laid the groundwork for discussions about AI. With his abstract model of computation and pioneering ideas, Alan Turing set the stage for contemporary advances in intelligence simulation, bringing machines closer to the human ability to think and learn. It is a theoretical model that illustrates the functioning of a universal calculator. It consists of three main components: an infinite tape divided into cells, a read/write head, and a set of rules defining the machine's actions. The tape can contain symbols, and the read/write head can move across the tape, read the symbol in the cell, write a new symbol, or modify the state of the machine according to predefined rules. These rules dictate how the machine reacts to each symbol read, allowing the machine to process information sequentially.

The operation of the machine is based on a key concept: it simulates an algorithm by executing instructions step by step. Each step of the computation process involves reading a symbol, making a decision based on that state, and then moving on to the next step. This simplicity is deceptive because, in theory, the Turing machine can execute any calculation that can be described by an algorithm, no matter how complex. It is often considered a "universal computer" capable of simulating any programmable computing system. This abstraction laid the foundation for modern computers.

This machine is crucial for AI because it defined the limits of what a machine could accomplish in terms of computation. By proving that a machine can simulate any algorithmic process, he suggested that AI systems could, in theory, simulate forms of human intelligence. This idea gave birth to the concept of AI, where machines attempt to replicate cognitive tasks such as problem-solving, decision-making, and even learning. The Turing Test, which evaluates a machine's ability to mimic human intelligence, directly stems from this reflection on the capabilities of machines to simulate intelligence.

In his 1950 essay "Computing Machinery and Intelligence," his main objective was to explore the fundamental question: Can machines think? Rather than trying to rigorously define the concept of "thinking," Turing proposed reformulating the question in a more concrete and testable way, introducing what would become the famous Turing Test. This test aims to determine whether a machine can imitate human behavior convincingly enough that, in a conversation, an interlocutor cannot distinguish whether they are interacting with a human or a machine. For him, if a machine passed this test, it could be considered "intelligent."

A central goal of Turing's was to refute the prevailing ideas of his time, which argued that machines could not simulate human cognitive processes. He challenged the belief that human thought was fundamentally different from anything a machine could accomplish. For him, intelligence was not tied to a human essence but to the ability to perform certain intellectual tasks. By introducing his Test, he sought to shift the debate away from metaphysical questions about the nature of thought and focus it on observable and measurable behaviors. He also anticipated some objections to the idea of a thinking machine, such as those based on creativity, emotions, or unpredictability. In his essay, he responded to these critiques by asserting that, if a machine could behave like a human in a wide range of situations, there would be no reason to deny its intelligence. His goal was therefore to challenge the rigid distinction between human abilities and machine capabilities, while laying the foundation for what would become a central field in the development of AI.

Ultimately, Turing sought to encourage his contemporaries to seriously consider the possibility that machines could, one day, simulate human intellectual processes. His essay was not only meant to establish theoretical concepts but also to provoke a paradigm shift in how we understand intelligence and its relationship with machines. It thus opened the door to decades of research into the possibility of creating intelligent machines.

The Test influenced the idea that AI can be measured not by its ability to reason like a human but by its ability to produce intelligent responses in various situations.

This pragmatic approach encouraged researchers to develop systems capable of mimicking certain aspects of human behavior, such as natural language understanding or problem-solving. This led to the development of virtual assistants, chatbot systems, and many other AI applications focused on human–machine interaction. Therefore, the test shaped part of AI's objectives, focusing on smooth communication and language processing. However, the Test has also sparked criticisms and debates about what it truly means for a machine to be "intelligent." Some researchers argued that the test focuses too much on the external simulation of human behavior without considering the machine's understanding or actual consciousness. This has encouraged the development of additional criteria to evaluate AI, such as a machine's ability to learn autonomously, solve complex problems, or simulate a deeper form of understanding than mere imitation.

Despite these criticisms, the Test remains a cornerstone in the history of AI. It laid the groundwork for a philosophical and scientific debate on the nature of AI and helped define the early goals of the field. By focusing on observable results and interactions, it promoted the design of AI systems that effectively meet human needs, paving the way for numerous innovations in information processing and human–machine interaction.

4.8.1.2   Cybernetics

The main concepts of cybernetics, according to Norbert Wiener, are based on the study of communication and control systems, both in living beings and in machines. In the 1940s, Wiener developed cybernetics as a new scientific discipline that explores how systems, whether biological or artificial, can regulate and self-correct their behavior through feedback processes. This central concept of feedback, fundamental to cybernetics, allows a system to adjust its actions based on information received about its past performance. Thus, machines, like living organisms, are capable of achieving goals by adapting their actions, granting them a form of "intelligent behavior." Another key concept of cybernetics, according to *Wiener*, is the idea that information, rather than matter or energy, is at the core of every regulatory system. He viewed information as a measure of order or organization within a system, which allows understanding of the interactions between its various parts. This approach led to the design of systems capable of communicating and processing information, marking the early steps toward automation and AI. Indeed, Wiener considered machines as information systems capable of imitating certain human abilities, such as decision-making and adaptation, based on information management. A third fundamental concept of cybernetics is the idea of open systems, in which exchanges with the environment are essential to maintaining stability or equilibrium. Cybernetic systems are capable of interacting with their environment by receiving signals and adjusting their behavior according to these signals. This model applies to both living organisms and mechanical systems, such as thermostats or speed regulators. *Wiener* demonstrated that these regulatory mechanisms were not limited to machines but could also explain certain aspects of human and animal behavior.

Cybernetics played a fundamental role in the early developments of robotics and AI by introducing key concepts that inspired the creation of autonomous machines capable of regulating and adapting their behavior. The central idea of feedback, developed by *Wiener*, was crucial for the development of robotic systems capable of reacting to their environment by adjusting their actions based on the information received. For example, early robots were equipped with sensors that allowed them to gather data about their environment and make decisions based on this information, thus imitating the regulatory processes that *Wiener* had observed in biological and mechanical systems.

In robotics, cybernetics enabled the emergence of automatic control systems, where machines could correct their errors in real time. An early example is autonomous robots capable of moving through an environment while avoiding obstacles using feedback mechanisms. This ability to adjust behavior based on external data was directly inspired by cybernetic ideas about adaptation and self-regulation. These principles allowed the development of increasingly sophisticated robotic systems capable of performing a variety of tasks and functioning autonomously in dynamic environments.

In AI, cybernetics also influenced the early attempts at modeling intelligent behavior. By focusing on the idea that machines, like living organisms, could process information and make decisions based on incoming data, AI researchers designed systems capable of imitating certain human cognitive processes. Early AI programs, such as the first ANNs, were designed to process information and adjust their responses based on past experience, a principle borrowed from cybernetics. This approach laid the groundwork for ML and the development of machines capable of acquiring new skills over time.

Cybernetics transformed the understanding of human–machine communication by introducing fundamental concepts about how information flows between biological and mechanical systems, particularly through the feedback process. *Wiener*, in developing cybernetics, showed that biological systems and machines could be viewed as systems capable of receiving, processing, and emitting information, thus establishing a common base for understanding communication between humans and machines. This enabled the design of interactive machines capable of responding to human commands in real time, such as the first automatic control systems and human–machine interfaces, where human actions trigger mechanical or digital responses based on feedback loops. It also brought a new perspective on information processing, considering the human as a system that communicates with machines through signals. This model allowed for understanding that human–machine communication is not simply about sending instructions from a human to a machine but also involves the machine returning information to enable the human to adjust their actions accordingly. This bidirectional dynamic of communication laid the foundation for the development of intuitive interfaces and interactive systems. For example, in the design of graphical interfaces, autopilot systems, or virtual assistants, the machine analyzes human commands and adapts its responses based on needs or changes in the environment.

Moreover, cybernetics introduced the idea that communication was based on not only explicit messages but also the interpretation of non-verbal signals and environmental contexts. This led to the development of more sophisticated systems capable of processing complex information such as speech recognition, gestures, or facial expressions, thus improving the fluidity of human–machine interaction. For example, modern AI systems, such as voice assistants or social robots, are heirs of this cybernetic approach, as they interpret vocal instructions, adjust their behavior based on the situation, and return appropriate responses in real time.

4.8.1.3   Shannon's Information Theory

Claude Shannon's information theory has profoundly influenced the way data is processed in AI systems. By defining information as a measure of uncertainty and developing concepts like entropy, Shannon provided a mathematical framework to understand and optimize the transmission, storage, and processing of data. This approach transformed AI systems, making them capable of efficiently processing large amounts of data while minimizing information loss. For example, in ML, entropy is used to measure uncertainty in data, helping algorithms select the most informative features and make more accurate decisions.

The theory of information also enabled the design of efficient data coding and compression mechanisms, which are essential in AI systems that handle vast data sets. These techniques make it possible to reduce redundancy in the data without compromising the quality or relevance of the processed information. This is particularly useful in areas such as speech recognition, computer vision, and NLP, where AI systems must process massive data streams in real time. By optimizing how information is encoded, information theory allowed AI systems to become more efficient and faster while preserving data richness. Another major impact of information theory on AI is the improvement of decision-making and learning. AI algorithms, such as NNs and decision trees, use principles derived from information theory to assess the quality of data and predictive models. For example, concepts like information gain are used to determine which data variables are most relevant for decision-making. This allows AI systems to learn more effectively from the available data by maximizing useful information and minimizing errors.

Claude Shannon's key contributions to modern communication and AI lie in his creation of information theory, a mathematical framework that revolutionized the way information is transmitted, stored, and processed. Shannon transformed the understanding of communication by introducing concepts such as entropy, which measures uncertainty or the amount of information contained in a message. This allowed for the optimization of communication systems, maximizing transmission efficiency while minimizing errors. This concept led to data compression, which is essential in transmitting information over modern networks like the Internet, and laid the foundation for modern telecommunications technologies. By defining information in quantifiable terms and proposing methods to assess the quality of transmission in channels disturbed by noise, Shannon enabled the design of robust communication systems. For example, his channel capacity theorem establishes the maximum amount of information that can be transmitted through a noisy channel, leading to the development of error correction techniques that improve transmission reliability. This theoretical framework has had direct implications on how telecommunications networks are built today, enabling the development of the Internet, mobile phones, and communication satellites. Thanks to Shannon, effective communication is now possible even in noisy environments, which is crucial in a hyperconnected world.

Shannon's work also had a significant impact on AI, particularly in the management of information and the optimization of decision-making algorithms. Concepts like reducing uncertainty and selecting the most relevant information are at the core of many ML systems. For example, entropy and information gain (two central concepts in Shannon's theory) are used in algorithms like decision trees to choose the best data features to analyze. These tools allow AI systems to process vast amounts of data, make more accurate decisions, and learn autonomously. Another essential contribution of Shannon to AI is the influence of his work on information coding in NNs and NLP systems. By processing information optimally, encoding and compressing it, modern algorithms can handle large volumes of data more quickly and efficiently, reducing complexity and the risk of errors. This approach is particularly evident in speech recognition systems, machine translation, and other AI applications where real-time data processing is critical.

His concepts have had a profound impact on the development of computers and networks by providing a mathematical framework for the transmission, processing, and storage of information. Shannon's information theory introduced a new and effective way of understanding how data is encoded and transmitted through computer systems and communication networks. One of his most important contributions was the concept of entropy, which measures the amount of uncertainty or information contained in a message. This concept led to the creation of data compression algorithms, essential for efficiently storing and transmitting information over computer networks and storage systems.

In computer science, he structured how information is encoded using binary systems. His approach showed that by using only 0s and 1s, any type of information (text, images, or sound) could be represented. This fundamental principle is the basis for digital processing in modern computers. Thanks to this approach, computers can process complex data quickly and reliably, with a lower probability of errors. Indeed, how data is encoded and decoded is crucial to ensure that information flows without distortion, even in environments affected by noise, a central issue that Shannon addressed with his concept of channel capacity. He also revolutionized communication networks, particularly with the development of algorithms that correct errors during data transmission through noisy channels. His work on error correction directly influenced the transmission protocols used in computer networks, such as the Internet, where information must be routed through complex and disturbed environments. Thanks to his coding and error correction techniques, modern networks can ensure efficient and reliable data transmission over long distances, even in the presence of interference or packet loss.

Another area where Shannon's concepts have been applied is computer security. Information coding and redundancy management have influenced the development of encryption and cryptography systems used in modern networks to protect sensitive information. Shannon's principles enabled the structuring of systems where information can be encoded to ensure that it remains understandable only to authorized recipients while resisting external attacks. These encryption systems are at the heart of online transactions, secure communications, and data privacy across networks.

4.8.2 TOWARD AI

The first steps toward modern AI date back several decades and involve a mix of theoretical, mathematical, and technological advancements. Among the key figures, Alan Turing stands out as one of the founding fathers of AI. In 1936, he proposed his machine, a mathematical model that formalized the concept of computation. Then, in 1950, he introduced the Turing Test in his paper Computing Machinery and Intelligence, aimed at assessing whether a machine could be considered intelligent. During this same period, Shannon established information theory in 1948, a crucial advancement for modern communications and data manipulation, essential for the development of AI. A landmark moment occurred in 1956 at the Dartmouth College conference, often considered the official birth of AI. This conference, organized by John McCarthy, Marvin Minsky, Nathaniel Rochester, and Claude Shannon, brought together researchers who explored the possibility of creating machines capable of "thinking." It was at this conference that the term AI was used for the first time by McCarthy. In the years that followed, significant advances were made in AI algorithms. The "Logic Theorist" program, created by Allen Newell and Herbert A. Simon, in 1955, is often considered the first AI program. It could prove mathematical theorems using symbolic logic. In 1957, Frank Rosenblatt developed the perceptron, a learning model inspired by biological neurons, marking one of the first attempts to model ANNs, paving the way for research in NNs.

The 1960s and 1970s were marked by great optimism regarding AI. Systems like ELIZA, an NLP program developed by *Joseph Weizenbaum*, and *Shakey*, the first mobile robot capable of reasoning about its actions, demonstrated that it was possible to create machines capable of interacting rudimentarily with their environment. It was also the time of the first expert systems, such as DENDRAL in 1965 and MYCIN in 1972, which showed that AI could be successfully applied to complex tasks, like analytical chemistry and medical diagnosis. These systems used a knowledge base and an inference engine to solve problems in specific domains.

However, the 1970s and 1980s saw a period of disillusionment with AI due to the limitations of the computers of the time and the lack of progress toward truly intelligent machines, often referred to as the "AI winter." Despite this, the field experienced a revival in the 1980s with ML. Research on NNs was revitalized by figures such as Geoffrey Hinton and Yann LeCun, who overcame some of the limitations of the perceptron by introducing techniques like backpropagation. At the same time, tools like Support Vector Machines (SVMs) and decision trees strengthened ML, laying the groundwork for modern AI. These early steps thus paved the way for contemporary advancements, where AI now relies on complex models and vast amounts of data, with applications spanning numerous fields, from image recognition to voice assistants.

The development of modern AI systems has been marked by several major technical challenges. One of the first obstacles was the computational power available at the time. In the early years of AI, computers were slow and underpowered, limiting the complexity of the algorithms that could be executed. The systems of that time could only process limited amounts of data, and programs like *Rosenblatt*'s perceptron, although innovative, were constrained by the available hardware. This hardware limitation slowed the progress of ML, especially for NNs, which require intensive calculations. Another major technical challenge was data management. For AI systems to learn and generalize from examples, they needed large amounts of well-structured data. However, in the early days of AI, collecting, storing, and managing large databases was difficult and expensive. Moreover, methods for organizing and processing this data efficiently were still under development. This lack of quality data limited the ability of systems to adapt to varied environments or tackle complex problems.

The design of learning algorithms also posed an important technical problem. Early algorithms lacked flexibility and robustness in the face of unforeseen situations or noisy data. For example, the perceptron, one of the first attempts to model NNs, could not solve nonlinear problems, leading to some pessimism regarding ML. It took several decades and advances such as backpropagation to overcome these algorithmic limitations and allow NNs to solve more complex problems. Understanding and modeling human reasoning represented a considerable technical challenge. Early AI researchers quickly realized that modeling human cognitive processes, such as reasoning or problem-solving, was extremely complex. Expert systems from the 1970s, which attempted to replicate the knowledge of human experts in specific fields, required a vast base of manually defined rules, making their extension to new areas difficult and costly. The inability of these systems to generalize from these rules showed the limitations of traditional symbolic approaches. Thus, the technical challenges in the development of early AI systems involved computational power, data management, the design of robust algorithms, and the modeling of human reasoning. It took several decades of research and progress in these areas to bring about the modern AI systems we know today, capable of processing massive amounts of data and learning autonomously.

The first AI programs were designed to simulate specific aspects of human intelligence, focusing mainly on capabilities such as logic, problem-solving, and language manipulation. One of the first notable examples is the Logic Theorist program. This program was intended to reproduce the human ability to solve logical problems by proving mathematical theorems. It used symbolic logic to mimic human reasoning in proving theorems, a task considered a form of abstract thinking. The goal was to show that machines could, through logical rules, reproduce cognitive processes like deduction and solving complex problems. Another example is the ELIZA program, created by Joseph Weizenbaum in 1966, which aimed to simulate the human ability to hold a conversation. ELIZA used predefined scripts to interact with users, mimicking the behavior of a psychotherapist. Although ELIZA did not actually understand natural language, it was able to give the illusion of an intelligent conversation by analyzing the user's input and providing responses based on simple patterns. This program showed that even rudimentary mechanisms could evoke aspects of human intelligence, such as understanding and responding to language. The expert systems of the 1970s, like MYCIN, were designed to simulate human expertise in specific fields, such as medical diagnosis. MYCIN used a base of rules manually defined by human experts to analyze a patient's symptoms and suggest appropriate treatments. This type of program tries to capture the human intelligence aspect related to expertise and decision-making in complex and uncertain situations. These systems were based on formal knowledge and attempted to reproduce how a human expert would formulate a judgment from precise rules. In parallel, the development of NNs, notably through Frank Rosenblatt's perceptron in 1957, aimed to simulate how the human brain processes information. Inspired by biological neurons, the perceptron modeled simple connections between information processing units (the "neurons"), capable of "making decisions" based on weighted inputs. This model reflected an attempt to reproduce cognitive aspects related to pattern recognition, an essential capability in many human cognitive functions, such as visual perception.

Thus, the first AI programs were designed to simulate specific aspects of human intelligence, focusing on key skills such as logic, language, and decision-making. Although these attempts were rudimentary by modern standards, they laid the foundation for AI research by demonstrating that it was possible to approximate certain human cognitive abilities through algorithms and computer systems.

4.8.2.1 The Beginning of AI

After World War II, the first applications of AI in military and industrial fields focused on automating complex tasks, simulation, and processing large amounts of data to improve decision-making. These applications were still rudimentary but laid the foundation for the technological advancements that would follow. In the military domain, one of the first AI applications was simulating combat scenarios. The military sought to develop systems capable of modeling and predicting the behavior of troops and armaments in wartime situations. These systems were often based on rules and mathematical models, allowing strategists to test different strategies and improve operational planning. For example, in the 1950s and 1960s, the first computer simulations of battlefields used concepts derived from game theory, an applied mathematics branch that influenced the modeling of conflicts and strategic decisions. Another early military application of AI was cybernetics, the study of control systems, which influenced the development of automated systems for missile guidance and navigation. Programs using AI algorithms were employed to improve the accuracy of guided weapons, such as ballistic missiles. These automated control systems used real-time data to adjust missile trajectories based on external conditions, a process requiring rapid and complex analysis.

The first AI applications in industry focused on automating manufacturing processes and predictive maintenance. In the 1960s and 1970s, manufacturing industries began exploring the use of rule-based systems and AI algorithms to automate repetitive and complex tasks on assembly lines. Early expert systems, which mimicked human reasoning to make complex decisions, were used for production planning and quality control. These systems allowed factories to reduce human errors and increase efficiency by anticipating machine failures and optimizing manufacturing processes. One of the first major breakthroughs of AI in industry was the use of robots in manufacturing. The first industrial robots, like the Unimate robotic arm, designed in 1961, were used in the automotive industry for repetitive tasks such as welding and assembly. Although these robots were not truly intelligent, they paved the way for integrating more advanced technologies in factories. In the following decades, AI-based control systems allowed robots to make real-time autonomous decisions, such as adjusting their movements based on the environment. AI also began to be used for processing large amounts of data in fields like logistics and resource management. For example, companies began using algorithms to optimize their supply chains by predicting raw material needs and adjusting inventories based on demand. These systems could analyze historical data and make recommendations to improve efficiency, using optimization and modeling techniques.

The creation of the first AI algorithms, such as Frank Rosenblatt's perceptron in 1957, marked another key turning point. The perceptron, inspired by biological neurons, was a simple model of a neural network capable of learning from training data. Although limited in its ability to solve nonlinear problems, this work introduced the first ideas on ML, a fundamental component of modern AI. DNNs directly stem from the ideas developed around the perceptron and artificial neurons in the 1950s and 1960s. Expert systems, developed in the 1970s, also laid the foundation for applied AI systems. Programs like MYCIN and DENDRAL used rule-based systems to simulate human expert reasoning in specific fields, such as medicine or chemistry. They demonstrated that it was possible to reproduce complex decision-making using automated systems, foreshadowing the use of decision-making algorithms and rule-based systems found today in various domains such as finance, medicine, and resource management. Cybernetics and early work on control systems also left a lasting imprint. These works focused on how machines could interact with their environment and adjust their behavior accordingly, which forms the basis of modern adaptive intelligence systems. The ideas of feedback and regulation became crucial for robotics, where machines must make real-time decisions and adjust their actions based on the information they receive.

4.8.3 KEY INNOVATIONS: LOGIC THEORIST AND PERCEPTRON

The Logic Theorist, developed by Allen Newell and Herbert A. Simon, sought to solve specific problems related to proving theorems in mathematical logic, particularly those found in reference works on formal logic, such as Whitehead and Russell's *Principia Mathematica*. The main goal of the Logic Theorist was to automatically prove theorems using formal rules of logic, thereby simulating human deductive reasoning. The program addressed several specific aspects of logic and theorem proving. It aimed for automatic theorem proving, a task considered a test of a machine's ability to simulate aspects of human reasoning. It explored ways to derive a conclusion (the theorem) from given premises and axioms by following formal deduction rules. The program was also capable of manipulating symbols and logical formulas automatically. It used a heuristic-based approach to explore the search space of solutions, which represented an advance for systems capable of handling abstract concepts without direct human intervention.

The Logic Theorist did not simply search exhaustively for all possible solutions but aimed to select the most probable paths to a solution. *Newell* and *Simon* introduced the idea of heuristic search, where approximations and strategies were used to make the proof process more efficient, thereby reducing the computational time needed to find a solution. The program also tackled complex problems by decomposing them into simpler subproblems, a method widely used in human reasoning. This decomposition approach, which broke down a theorem into more manageable components, is still a technique employed in many modern AI systems. One of the major successes of the Logic Theorist was its ability to prove 38 out of the first 52 theorems in *Principia Mathematica*. For one of these theorems, it even proposed a more elegant proof than the one provided by the original authors of the text.

The perceptron, developed in 1957 by Frank Rosenblatt, influenced NN research significantly. The perceptron, inspired by biological neurons, was a simple model of an NN that could learn from training data. Though limited in its ability to solve nonlinear problems, it introduced the first ideas about ML as a key component of modern AI. The DNNs at the heart of contemporary AI are directly inspired by the ideas developed around the perceptron and artificial neurons in the 1950s and 1960s.

Early AI programs, though innovative, suffered from several limitations that hindered their ability to solve complex problems. One major limitation was the lack of computational power. Computers in the 1950s and 1960s were relatively slow and lacked the necessary computational power to run complex algorithms or process large amounts of data. This hardware limitation made it difficult to implement learning algorithms or simulate sophisticated cognitive processes. The solution to this was the exponential increase in computational power, mainly due to *Moore*'s Law, which helped overcome this limitation. As computers became faster and capable of storing and processing more data, AI algorithms could be executed more efficiently. Today, specialized processors such as Graphics Processing Units (GPUs) and Tensor Processing Units (TPUs) allow for the training of complex AI models on massive data volumes.

Another limitation was the use of simplistic or limited algorithms. Early algorithms, such as those used in the perceptron, were limited in their ability to solve nonlinear or complex problems. For example, a single-layer perceptron could not solve the XOR problem, which required a nonlinear separation of data. Additionally, rule-based systems, such as expert systems, were often rigid and incapable of adapting to new or unforeseen situations. This limitation was overcome by introducing multilayer NNs and the backpropagation algorithm in the 1980s. Multilayer NNs allowed the modeling of complex relationships by adding intermediate layers (hidden layers), enabling the network to learn nonlinear structures. Backpropagation, which adjusts weights across all layers based on the output error, solved the problem of learning in complex NNs. Furthermore, the dependence on rigid rules. Early AI programs, such as expert systems (e.g., MYCIN), operated using explicit rules defined by human experts. While these systems worked well in restricted domains, their rule-based approach limited their ability to generalize or adapt to new situations. This led to systems that were fragile and inflexible, unable to handle problems for which they hadn't been specifically programmed. The introduction of ML allowed AI systems to learn from data rather than rely solely on fixed rules. ML replaced the rigid approach with models capable of adapting to new situations by learning from examples and past experiences. Furthermore, the development of DL networks enabled AI models to learn more abstract data representations, making systems more versatile and adaptable. The inability to handle massive data was another major limitation. Early AI systems were limited in their ability to process large datasets, partly due to hardware constraints and partly because the algorithms themselves were not designed to efficiently handle large amounts of data. The solution to this was the development of new architectures for processing big data, such as distributed databases and learning algorithms for massive datasets, which allowed modern AI systems to handle large volumes of data. The rise of big data and the availability of large training datasets enabled the use of techniques like DL and SL at scale.

Perception and recognition issues also hindered early AI systems. Early AI systems, including the perceptron, had limited capabilities in solving pattern recognition problems, such as image or speech recognition. The models were incapable of properly understanding or interpreting complex data, such as images or sounds. The advent of CNNs and Recurrent Neural Networks (RNNs), combined with increased computational power and large databases, enabled AI systems to excel at visual and audio recognition tasks. CNNs, in particular, revolutionized image recognition by introducing specific layers capable of hierarchically extracting visual features.

The lack of general intelligence was a significant limitation. Early AI systems were highly specialized and could only solve specific problems for which they had been designed. They lacked what is now called AGI, the ability to understand and learn flexibly and broadly, much like a human does. While AGI has not yet been achieved, advances in areas like reinforcement learning (which allows AI to learn through trial and error in dynamic environments) and Transfer Learning (TL) models (which allow knowledge acquired in one domain to be applied to another) have made AI systems more flexible and capable of generalizing to more diverse tasks.

5 The Main Models of AI

5.1 GENERAL OVERVIEW OF AI APPROACHES

AI has evolved remarkably, from ancient mathematical concepts to today's ML and DL models. This journey, shaped by technological breakthroughs and methodological innovations, has redefined our interaction with intelligent systems, from early computational tools like the Antikythera mechanism and *Hero of Alexandria*'s automata to modern ANNs and DL frameworks. The theoretical foundations of AI emerged in the mid-20th century with pioneers like Alan Turing, whose Turing Test laid the groundwork for modern computing and AI. Subsequent decades introduced diverse approaches (expert systems, genetic algorithms, and Bayesian networks) each enriching the field. ML marked a pivotal shift, enabling machines to learn from data without explicit programming and unlocking applications like speech recognition, product recommendation, and fraud detection. DL, driven by CNNs and RNNs, propelled further advances in NLP and computer vision [3].

Yet, AI's progress faces significant hurdles. Ethical challenges, such as algorithm transparency, data privacy, and algorithmic bias, are increasingly urgent. Jobin et al. [4] mapped global AI ethics guidelines, highlighting shared concerns, while Mittelstadt [5] critiques the limits of ethical principles, urging stronger solutions. Technologically, the need for vast datasets, immense computational power, and manageable model complexity must be addressed for responsible AI adoption. Understanding AI's historical evolution, methodological roots, and future challenges is essential to discerning its potential and limits, ensuring its ethical integration into society.

5.1.1 CLASSIFICATION OF MODELS: SYMBOLIC, CONNECTIONIST, AND EVOLUTIONARY

AI can be understood through a variety of conceptual frameworks that reflect distinct visions of how to simulate intelligence. One of the most fundamental classifications distinguishes three main families of models: symbolic approaches, connectionist approaches, and evolutionary approaches. Each of these families is rooted in different theoretical assumptions, relies on specific mechanisms of learning or reasoning, and is suited to particular domains of application. This classification is conceptual, representing competing and often complementary paradigms in artificial cognition.

Symbolic models, often referred to as Good Old-Fashioned Artificial Intelligence (GOFAI), stem from the early efforts to model intelligence through logic and formal reasoning. These models represent knowledge using explicit symbols and manipulate these symbols using formal rules. Their strength lies in the capacity to perform complex deductive reasoning, to provide clear explanations for decisions, and to

DOI: 10.1201/9781003613633-5

incorporate human-encoded domain knowledge. Expert systems, inference engines, and first-order logic representations are classic examples of this paradigm. However, symbolic models have shown limitations in handling uncertainty, noise, and unstructured or dynamic environments, which has hindered their broader deployment. In contrast, connectionist models are inspired by the structure and functioning of the human brain, particularly NNs. Instead of manipulating symbolic representations, these systems process information through layers of interconnected artificial neurons that learn from data. Learning is central to these systems, either supervised, unsupervised, or reinforcement-based. DNNs, now at the core of image recognition, NLP, and machine translation systems, are the direct descendants of this tradition. Their strength lies in their ability to extract high-level representations from raw data without explicit human intervention.

Evolutionary approaches represent a third paradigm, distinct from both symbolic and connectionist models. They are inspired by biological evolution mechanisms such as natural selection, mutation, and crossover. Evolutionary Algorithms (EAs), including genetic algorithms, evolutionary strategies, ant colony systems, and Particle Swarm Optimization (PSO), aim to solve complex problems by exploring large solution spaces in a distributed and stochastic manner. These approaches are particularly well-suited to optimization tasks, strategic planning, and the design of intelligent systems in ill-defined or changing environments. What fundamentally differentiates these three approaches is their respective way of representing knowledge, learning, and reasoning. Symbolic approaches manipulate abstract entities defined by formal rules; connectionist models transform data flows into emergent representations through learned weights; evolutionary models evolve populations of potential solutions over time according to a fitness criterion. These differences directly affect their capabilities, limitations, and suitability for particular use cases.

Historically, symbolic AI dominated the early decades of AI research, particularly from the 1950s to the 1980s. It led to the creation of early systems capable of simulating human-like reasoning in domains such as medical diagnosis or financial planning. However, the challenge of exhaustively formalizing knowledge and the inability of symbolic systems to learn autonomously gradually led to a shift in interest toward connectionist models, especially as computational power and data availability increased. Though originally proposed in the mid-20th century, connectionist models saw a dramatic resurgence in the 2010s with the rise of DL. Through deep architectures such as convolutional and RNNs, these systems became capable of rivaling or even surpassing human performance in some perceptual tasks. This breakthrough also reignited interest in biologically inspired models more broadly, including evolutionary approaches, which began to be integrated with NNs to create more adaptive and robust systems.

While evolutionary models may have remained somewhat under the radar compared to DL, they play a fundamental role in scenarios where finding a solution involves exploring a vast space of possibilities such as in evolutionary robotics, intelligent design systems, or automatic program generation. They are also often incorporated into hybrid approaches, for example to optimize the parameters of NNs or to evolve new learning strategies. Each of these paradigms offers clear strengths but also faces significant limitations. Symbolic models excel in interpretability and formal reasoning; connectionist models in learning and pattern recognition; evolutionary models in adaptation and search. It is this complementarity that has motivated the recent rise of hybrid models, which aim to combine the strengths of these approaches to build more versatile and powerful AI systems. Thus, the tripartite classification into symbolic, connectionist, and evolutionary models provides a foundational lens for understanding the diversity of AI methods. It helps locate each approach in terms of its origins, internal mechanisms, purposes, and effectiveness across contexts. In the following sections of this chapter, we will go deeper into these paradigms, their evolution, typical applications, and the increasing intersections among them.

5.1.2 Logic-Based Systems and Rule-Based Reasoning

Among the earliest approaches to AI, logic-based systems and rule-based reasoning stand out for their rigorous reliance on formal logical structures. These systems aim to replicate human deductive reasoning by encoding knowledge in a structured format and applying well-defined inference mechanisms. Logic serves here not just as a mathematical tool, but as a language for representing and manipulating knowledge. From syllogisms to predicate calculus, these systems operate under strict principles of validity, ensuring conclusions follow unambiguously from premises. In logic-based systems, the knowledge base is typically structured around facts and rules, often expressed in propositional or first-order logic. The reasoning engine, often called an inference engine, applies rules of inference to derive conclusions or new facts. This mechanism enables the automation of tasks that require logical consistency, such as diagnosing faults, configuring systems, or interpreting legal regulations. These systems are deterministic by design, yielding predictable outputs when given a defined set of inputs. Rule-based systems are a pragmatic implementation of logic-based AI. They rely on if-then statements, where specific conditions trigger corresponding actions or conclusions. While they may lack the formal rigor of full logical systems, their simplicity and flexibility have made them extremely popular in domains requiring decision trees or procedural knowledge, such as business process automation or expert medical systems. A rule might state, for example, If temperature is above 100°C, then activate cooling system, encoding procedural knowledge in a directly interpretable form.

One of the main strengths of rule-based and logic-based AI is transparency. Each conclusion reached by the system can be traced back through a series of explicit logical steps or rule applications. This traceability makes these systems highly interpretable, allowing human experts to audit and verify decisions. Such clarity is particularly important in sensitive domains like healthcare, legal reasoning, and safety-critical engineering, where decisions must be explainable. However, the rigidity of logic-based reasoning can also be a significant drawback. These systems struggle in environments where uncertainty, ambiguity, or incomplete knowledge is prevalent. Unlike data-driven models, they require domain knowledge to be explicitly formalized by human experts, a process that is both time-consuming and limited by the expert's own understanding. Furthermore, maintaining consistency in large rule sets becomes increasingly difficult, often resulting in conflicts or redundancy.

To mitigate these limitations, logic-based systems have been extended through various enhancements. Fuzzy logic allows for degrees of truth rather than binary evaluations, enabling reasoning in uncertain or imprecise contexts. Nonmonotonic logic permits the withdrawal of inferences when new information contradicts previous assumptions, better reflecting human reasoning. Probabilistic logic introduces statistical uncertainty into logical frameworks, bridging the gap between symbolic reasoning and probabilistic modeling.

Another development in this field is the use of description logics, which underlie ontologies and semantic web technologies. These formal systems provide a balance between expressiveness and computational tractability, making them suitable for managing and querying large structured knowledge bases. They are particularly effective in applications involving taxonomies, classification hierarchies, and concept relationships, as seen in healthcare informatics or intelligent information retrieval.

Logic-based reasoning also plays a foundational role in planning systems, where a goal state is achieved through a sequence of logically valid actions. Classical planning frameworks use preconditions and effects defined in logic to simulate the consequences of actions over time. These systems are widely used in robotics, logistics, and automated scheduling, where goal-oriented behavior is essential. Despite their challenges, rule-based and logic-oriented approaches remain central to the evolution of AI. Their influence persists in hybrid systems where logic provides structure and coherence, while ML handles perception and adaptation. The current trend in XAI also renews interest in logic-based methods, given their natural affinity for transparency and accountability.

5.1.3   DATA-DRIVEN LEARNING APPROACHES

Data-driven learning approaches represent a pivotal shift in AI, moving away from hard-coded rules and explicit symbolic reasoning toward systems that improve their performance by learning from empirical data. Rather than specifying every decision logic in advance, data-driven models allow the system to infer structure, patterns, and correlations directly from examples. This approach aligns more closely with how humans acquire knowledge through experience, making it highly effective for perception tasks and complex real-world problem-solving. The core principle of data-driven AI is generalization. Given a sufficiently diverse and representative dataset, a learning algorithm can capture underlying statistical regularities and apply them to new, unseen instances. This capability makes such models especially powerful in domains characterized by high variability and ambiguity, such as NLP, speech recognition, and computer vision. The success of these models depends heavily on the quantity, quality, and diversity of the data they are exposed to during training.

These approaches are intrinsically empirical. Rather than relying on prior domain knowledge encoded by experts, data-driven systems construct models through iterative exposure to samples. In supervised learning, the system learns a mapping from inputs to outputs based on labeled examples. In UL, the system identifies hidden structures, such as clusters or latent variables, without external guidance. RL, while often treated separately, also follows a data-driven paradigm, where experience collected through interaction with an environment refines decision-making strategies. The statistical foundations of data-driven AI are crucial to its operation. Concepts from probability theory, information theory, and optimization underpin the mathematical models used for learning. For example, the likelihood function, loss minimization, and Bayesian inference are central tools for guiding the training process. These foundations allow models to balance fit and generalization, prevent overfitting, and make predictions under uncertainty. One of the defining features of data-driven models is their adaptability. As new data becomes available, the models can be retrained or updated, allowing them to remain relevant in changing environments. This is particularly important for applications in fraud detection, recommender systems, and predictive maintenance, where patterns evolve over time. Online learning and incremental training techniques further enable continuous adaptation without retraining from scratch.

Data-driven systems are often evaluated empirically rather than formally. Their success is measured by performance metrics derived from test data, such as accuracy, precision, recall, F1 score, and Area Under the Curve – Receiver Operating Characteristic (AUC-ROC). Benchmark datasets and standardized tasks are widely used to compare models and track progress in the field. However, this empirical emphasis also raises concerns about reproducibility, fairness, and the hidden biases present in training data. The rise of big data and the proliferation of sensors, logs, and digital interactions have created fertile ground for data-driven AI. From user behavior on social networks to medical imaging and autonomous vehicle telemetry, vast quantities of data are generated continuously. This abundance provides both opportunities and challenges: while it enables the training of powerful models, it also demands scalable infrastructures, data governance strategies, and ethical safeguards. Data preprocessing and feature engineering are essential steps in the data-driven pipeline. Raw data is rarely usable in its original form, and it must be cleaned, normalized, encoded, and sometimes transformed to extract meaningful representations. Although DL has reduced the reliance on manual feature engineering by automating representation learning, many tasks still benefit from domain-specific preprocessing and engineered features to enhance model performance.

The black-box nature of many data-driven models, particularly DL systems, has prompted increasing scrutiny. Unlike rule-based or logic-driven systems, which can explain their reasoning step by step, many learned models offer limited interpretability. This opacity poses problems in critical domains such as healthcare and law, where accountability and transparency are essential. As a result, XAI has emerged as a subfield focused on making data-driven decisions more understandable to humans.

Despite their power, data-driven approaches are not without limitations. They require large quantities of labeled data, which can be expensive or impractical to obtain. In some domains, labeled data may be scarce or nonexistent, necessitating alternative strategies such as Semi-Supervised Learning (SSL), TL, or data augmentation. Moreover, these models can inadvertently learn and reinforce biases present in the training data, leading to ethical and social concerns. Another challenge lies in generalization across domains. A model trained on one dataset may perform poorly when applied to a different but related task. This issue has motivated the development of domain adaptation techniques, which aim to bridge the gap between training and deployment conditions. Robustness and transferability remain active areas of research within the data-driven paradigm.

While symbolic approaches emphasize explicit knowledge and logical reasoning, data-driven models excel in handling noise, ambiguity, and high-dimensional data. Their success is particularly evident in tasks that are difficult to formalize but rich in perceptual or behavioral patterns. Yet, their reliance on patterns alone can sometimes lead to superficial understanding or make them vulnerable to adversarial inputs, which are subtle perturbations that dramatically alter model predictions. The growing availability of pretrained models and open datasets has democratized access to data-driven AI. Practitioners can now fine-tune existing models on small, task-specific datasets, reducing the barrier to entry for various applications. This shift has empowered industries, startups, and individual developers to incorporate AI into products and services without requiring deep technical expertise in model development. The future of data-driven AI lies not only in bigger models and more data but also in better data, diverse, and ethically sourced. Techniques like active learning, synthetic data generation, and collaborative data sharing are emerging to address the limitations of existing datasets. At the same time, federated learning is allowing models to learn from decentralized data sources without compromising privacy.

5.1.4 EMERGENCE OF HYBRID METHODS

The evolution of AI has progressively revealed the limitations of isolated paradigms, prompting a shift toward hybrid methods that aim to combine the strengths of multiple AI approaches. As real-world problems grow in complexity, no single methodology, whether symbolic, connectionist, or evolutionary, proves universally sufficient. Hybrid models have emerged in response to this challenge by integrating distinct forms of reasoning, learning, and representation within a unified framework. At the heart of hybrid AI is the ambition to achieve complementarity. Logic-based systems offer transparency and explainability but struggle with adaptability. In contrast, data-driven models thrive in learning from patterns but often act as black boxes. By blending symbolic reasoning with statistical learning, hybrid methods aspire to bridge the gap between interpretability and empirical performance, resulting in more robust and context-aware systems.

One of the earliest forms of hybridization appeared in expert systems augmented with ML components. Here, ML was used to populate knowledge bases or optimize rule selection, improving the responsiveness and coverage of symbolic engines. These systems retained human interpretability while adapting to novel or evolving data environments. More recently, the hybridization of DL and symbolic reasoning has attracted considerable attention. Neural-symbolic systems attempt to embed logical constraints within neural architectures, ensuring that learned models respect formal knowledge. Alternatively, symbolic modules can guide the architecture or training of NNs, acting as a form of high-level supervision or structure. This bidirectional flow of influence helps tame the unpredictability of connectionist models.

The RL paradigm also lends itself well to hybridization. Agents may rely on symbolic planning to define high-level goals while using DL to navigate complex, continuous environments. This combination allows for both long-term reasoning and reactive decision-making. For example, a robotic assistant might plan tasks logically while using visual perception systems to adjust actions in real time. Hybrid models are also increasingly employed in natural language understanding. Symbolic parsers can be used to analyze sentence structure, while neural embeddings capture the contextual subtleties of meaning. In machine translation, hybrid systems have combined rule-based grammatical models with NNs to improve syntactic fidelity and fluency. Such combinations reflect the multi-layered nature of language itself. An emerging direction in hybrid AI is the integration of EAs with learning systems. Evolutionary strategies can optimize hyperparameters, neural architectures, or even entire policies in RL. These methods allow models to search vast solution spaces that would be intractable through gradient descent alone. This evolutionary learning can be embedded into training loops, yielding more exploratory and resilient systems.

Hybrid architectures are also instrumental in building systems that require both structured reasoning and unstructured perception. For instance, in autonomous driving, decision logic must operate over symbolic representations like traffic rules or route planning, while sensor inputs such as camera or lidar data require DL to interpret. The fusion of these modalities ensures both adherence to constraints and adaptability to unpredictable scenarios. One key benefit of hybrid systems is their potential for enhanced explainability. By externalizing part of the reasoning process into symbolic components, they allow users and auditors to trace decisions back to understandable rules or models. This is particularly important in applications requiring compliance, transparency, and user trust such as finance, medicine, or law. Despite their promise, hybrid models present nontrivial integration challenges. Combining components built on different mathematical and computational principles requires careful interface design and modular abstraction. Ensuring coherent communication between neural and symbolic modules, managing error propagation, and resolving conflicting outputs are all areas of active research and engineering concern. The emergence of hybrid systems also has implications for AI development workflows. These architectures often require interdisciplinary teams, where domain experts, data scientists, logicians, and engineers collaborate to define components and their interactions. This multidisciplinary nature aligns with the real-world complexity that AI systems increasingly seek to address. From a theoretical perspective, hybrid methods challenge long-standing dichotomies in AI such as reasoning versus learning, logic versus probability, or structure versus emergence. By embracing these tensions rather than avoiding them, hybrid AI offers a more nuanced and layered model of intelligence, closer to the richness of human cognition. On the engineering side, new platforms and frameworks are being developed to support hybrid AI workflows. Tools that support declarative knowledge, symbolic programming, and ML pipelines are being integrated, enabling experimentation with combinations that were previously difficult to manage. Libraries for neural-symbolic integration, differentiable logic, and neuroevolutionary are gaining traction.

Hybrid AI is not a final destination but a dynamic field of convergence. As new models emerge, such as Transformers capable of learning programmatic reasoning, or knowledge graphs fused with embeddings, the boundaries between symbolic, connectionist, and evolutionary techniques become increasingly blurred. Hybridization becomes a process rather than a fixed architecture.

5.2 SYMBOLIC MODELS (LOGICAL AND DEDUCTIVE)

As introduced in the section "Classification of models: symbolic, connectionist, evolutionary," symbolic AI models are based on formal logic and structured representations. In this section, we explore in greater depth the main symbolic paradigms and their practical applications.

5.2.1 EXPERT SYSTEMS AND KNOWLEDGE REPRESENTATION

Expert systems are a foundational component of symbolic AI, developed with the goal of encapsulating specialized human knowledge into computer programs that can solve complex problems within defined domains. Rather than attempting to emulate human cognition broadly, expert systems are highly focused, simulating the decision-making ability of human specialists through rule-based reasoning, structured knowledge, and logical inference mechanisms. The architecture of an expert system typically includes three key components: the knowledge base, the inference engine, and the user interface. The knowledge base stores the domain-specific information, structured as facts and rules. Figure 5.1 illustrates the typical architecture of an expert system and the interaction between its components. These rules are crafted from the insights and experiences of human experts, often in the form of conditional statements or logical relations. Capturing this tacit knowledge requires close collaboration between domain specialists and knowledge engineers. Knowledge in expert systems is usually represented through formal structures such as production rules, semantic nets, frames, or ontologies.

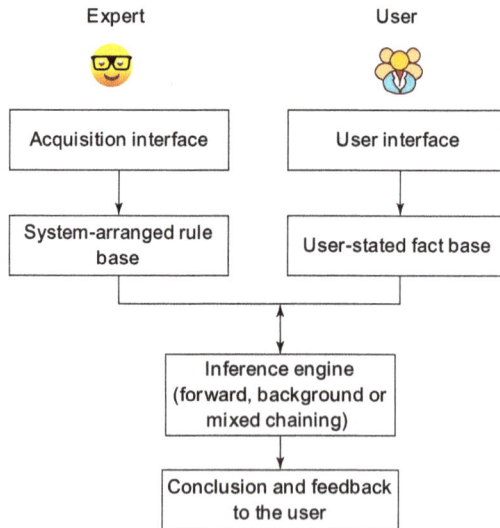

FIGURE 5.1 Architecture of a typical expert system.

Production rules, consisting of if-then clauses, are particularly popular due to their simplicity and logical clarity. Frames extend this idea by associating properties and behaviors with classes of objects, while ontologies provide more hierarchical and relational frameworks suited for large-scale and dynamic systems.

The inference engine is responsible for interpreting and applying the rules contained in the knowledge base. It analyzes user input, searches through the rules to find matches, and chains together logical steps to arrive at conclusions. Forward chaining and backward chaining are two widely used reasoning strategies. Forward chaining begins with known facts and proceeds toward conclusions, while backward chaining works from hypotheses toward supporting facts. What distinguishes expert systems from conventional software is their reasoning capability and their ability to offer explanations. When a conclusion is reached, the system can often provide a detailed trace of the reasoning path it followed. This explainability is critical in areas where transparency is legally or ethically required, such as medical diagnosis, legal advisory systems, and financial decision support.

Expert systems have historically thrived in environments where the domain is well-defined, the knowledge can be explicitly formalized, and the rules of inference remain relatively stable. They have been successfully deployed in diverse fields such as geology (for mineral exploration), chemistry (for molecular analysis), and engineering (for troubleshooting and design assistance). These systems serve both as problem-solving tools and as repositories of expert knowledge. One of the challenges in building expert systems lies in the acquisition and formalization of knowledge. Experts may have deep intuitive understanding that is difficult to articulate in logical terms. Furthermore, inconsistencies or ambiguities in expert knowledge can result in contradictory rules or gaps in reasoning. The process of knowledge engineering is thus iterative, involving validation, refinement, and testing to ensure accuracy and coherence. Scalability is another issue. As the knowledge base grows, the complexity of reasoning increases, often leading to performance bottlenecks and maintenance difficulties. Adding new knowledge without disrupting existing rule chains can be nontrivial. Some systems have attempted to address this through modular knowledge organization or by incorporating learning components to assist in rule refinement and evolution. Modern advancements in AI have led to renewed interest in integrating expert systems with other models. For instance, ML can be used to infer rules from data, which are then validated and embedded within symbolic frameworks. Conversely, symbolic systems can impose logical constraints or prior knowledge onto learning algorithms, providing structure in situations where data is sparse or noisy.

Another area of development involves probabilistic reasoning within expert systems. Traditional deterministic rules are often ill-suited to uncertain or incomplete information. Probabilistic expert systems extend classical models by associating confidence values or belief measures with rules and conclusions. This allows for more flexible and realistic modeling, particularly in fields like diagnostics or risk assessment. Knowledge representation itself has evolved, moving from static rule sets to more dynamic and semantic approaches. Ontologies and knowledge graphs are now widely used to model complex relationships between entities and to support reasoning over diverse and interconnected information sources. These tools enhance both the expressiveness and the interoperability of expert systems. Despite competition from data-centric AI paradigms, expert systems continue to offer unmatched advantages in interpretability and precision within well-defined domains. Their explicit reasoning processes, clear structure, and adaptability to regulation-heavy environments make them particularly suitable for enterprise and institutional applications where accountability is paramount.

5.2.2 FORMAL LOGIC AND INFERENCE ENGINES

Formal logic constitutes the mathematical backbone of symbolic AI, enabling machines to reason with precision and consistency. Unlike heuristic or data-driven methods, formal logic provides a rigorous, rule-governed framework for representing knowledge and deducing new information. It serves as the theoretical foundation for many AI systems that rely on structured reasoning, particularly those requiring explainability and verifiability. At the core of logic-based AI lies the use of propositional and predicate logic. Propositional logic operates with statements that are either true or false, allowing systems to manipulate combinations of truth values. Predicate logic extends this by introducing quantifiers, variables, and predicates, enabling a richer and more expressive representation of facts and relations. For example, a statement like *All humans are mortal* can be formalized using universal quantification, while *Socrates is human* becomes a specific instance that leads to a deductive conclusion.

Inference engines are designed to operate over such logical formalisms. These engines apply rules of deduction such as modus ponens, resolution, or unification to derive conclusions from a knowledge base. Inference can be deductive (from general rules to specific facts), inductive (from examples to general rules), or abductive (inferring the most likely explanation). Deductive reasoning is the most commonly used in logic-based AI, ensuring that all conclusions are logically entailed by the premises. One prominent example of a formal logic system in AI is Prolog, a logic programming language based on first-order predicate logic and resolution-based theorem proving. Prolog allows users to define facts and rules, and then pose queries to determine whether certain statements can be derived. A classic use case is in NLP or solving logic puzzles, such as planning a route or diagnosing a system failure. For instance, rules like parent(X, Y) :- mother(X, Y). or ancestor(X, Y) :- parent(X, Y). enable recursive reasoning.

Another major application of formal logic is in automated theorem proving. These systems attempt to demonstrate the validity of logical statements by constructing formal proofs. One well-known example is the resolution theorem prover developed for first-order logic. Automated theorem provers have been used in mathematics to verify complex conjectures and in software engineering to check the correctness of code and protocols, as seen in tools like Coq, HOL, and Isabelle. Formal logic also underpins planning systems in AI. In classical planning, the world is modeled using logical predicates and actions are defined by preconditions and effects. Stanford Research Institute Problem Solver (STRIPS) is a formalism that represents actions in terms of logical transitions. A planning algorithm searches for a sequence of actions that transform an initial state into a goal state. For example, a robot tasked with setting a table might use logic to determine the necessary steps: locate the plate, pick it up, and place it on the table, provided that all preconditions are satisfied.

Constraint satisfaction problems (CSPs) are another important domain where formal logic plays a central role. In CSPs, variables are assigned values from specific domains, and constraints define the permissible combinations of these values. Solvers apply logical inference to reduce the search space and identify valid assignments. Classical examples of CSPs include scheduling, map coloring, and resource allocation. Systems like MiniZinc and Choco provide platforms for formulating and solving such problems through formal logical constraints. Moreover, inference in logic-based systems can be extended using nonclassical logics. For example, modal logic introduces concepts like necessity and possibility, making it useful for reasoning about knowledge, belief, and time. Temporal logic is applied in the verification of systems that evolve over time, such as embedded or concurrent systems. Deontic logic, which models norms, obligations, and permissions, is particularly relevant in legal AI and ethical reasoning systems. Despite their strengths, formal logic systems are often computationally intensive. The more expressive the logic, the more difficult it becomes to ensure tractability. First-order logic is undecidable in general, meaning that no algorithm can determine the truth of all possible formulas. To address this, many AI systems restrict the expressiveness of the logic (e.g., using Horn clauses) or adopt approximation strategies to balance reasoning power and efficiency. Formal logic also supports knowledge validation and verification. When knowledge is encoded in a logical system, it can be checked for consistency, redundancy, and completeness. This capability is essential in mission-critical applications like aerospace, medical devices, or nuclear safety systems, where unintended consequences of faulty reasoning must be avoided at all costs. Modern research in symbolic AI continues to build upon formal logic by integrating it with learning techniques. For example, neuro-symbolic systems use logical constraints to guide the training of NNs, ensuring that the learned models adhere to predefined rules. Differentiable logic programs enable gradient-based optimization while preserving symbolic structure. Such combinations seek to combine the strengths of logical rigor with the adaptability of learning.

In the context of the Semantic Web, formal logic powers ontologies and reasoning engines that help interpret and connect vast amounts of structured data. Description logic, a decidable fragment of first-order logic, underpins standards like Web Ontology Language (OWL) and is used by reasoning tools such as Pellet and HermiT. These systems are employed in domains like biomedical informatics, e-commerce, and enterprise knowledge management.

5.2.3 ARGUMENTATION-BASED REASONING

Argumentation-Based Reasoning (ARG) is a symbolic approach in AI that seeks to model and simulate the process of constructing, evaluating, and resolving arguments. Unlike purely deductive or rule-based systems, ARG incorporates mechanisms to manage conflict, inconsistency, and nonmonotonic reasoning, all of which are essential characteristics of natural human discourse. The field emerged prominently in the late 1980s and early 1990s as a response to the need for more flexible and human-centric models of reasoning. At its core, argumentation involves building justifiable positions from a knowledge base and managing potential contradictions through structured debate. An argument is typically a pair $\langle S, c \rangle$ where S is a set of premises and c is a conclusion derived from S. What makes ARG powerful is that multiple such arguments may conflict, and the system must provide mechanisms to evaluate which arguments are acceptable. The roots of formal argumentation can be traced to the work of *Dung* (1995), who introduced the Abstract Argumentation Framework (AAF), a formalism that represents arguments as abstract entities and defines a binary relation of attack between them. This model separates the logical structure of arguments from the dialectical processes that govern their interaction.

Formally, an Abstract Argumentation Framework is defined as a tuple $\langle A, R \rangle$, where A is a set of arguments and $R \subseteq A \times A$ is the attack relation. For instance, if $(a_1, a_2) \in R$, then argument a_1 attacks argument a_2. The central task is to compute extensions, which are evaluated under different semantics such as grounded, preferred, stable, and complete semantics. These semantics differ in how they handle defense against attacks. For example, the grounded extension represents the minimal (least committed) set of acceptable arguments, whereas a preferred extension is maximal (most committed). A fundamental property in argumentation frameworks is conflict-freeness: a set of arguments S is conflict-free if there are no arguments $a, b \in S$ such that a attacks b. Building on this, notions such as admissibility and acceptability are defined. A conflict-free set S is admissible if every argument in S is defended against all its attackers by arguments within S. To illustrate, consider the following three arguments:

- a_1: "The car is not starting, therefore the battery is dead."
- a_2: "The lights turn on, so the battery is not dead."
- a_3: "A battery can have enough charge for lights but not for starting the engine."

Here, a_2 attacks a_1, and a_3 defends a_1 against a_2. Under grounded semantics, both a_3 and a_1 might be accepted, while a_2 is excluded due to insufficient defense. The richness of ARG stems from its ability to model nonmonotonic reasoning. In classical logic, adding new premises cannot invalidate previous conclusions. In argumentation, however, new arguments can attack and defeat earlier ones, altering the outcome. This dynamic capacity closely mimics human deliberation and legal reasoning. A key aspect in ARG is the notion of defeat, which can be based on strict attack or on preferences. In value-based argumentation frameworks (VAFs), introduced by

Bench-Capon (2003), arguments are associated with values, and defeat depends on value preferences. This allows systems to prioritize arguments according to context or stakeholder views.

Another important extension is structured argumentation, where arguments are built from premises using explicit inference rules. One widely used framework is ASPIC+, which allows combining strict (deductive) and defeasible (default) rules. This reflects how humans reason from both facts and typical cases. In ASPIC+, arguments are represented as derivation trees. For instance, from premises p and rule $p \Rightarrow q$ (defeasible), one can derive argument A: $[p \Rightarrow q]$. If another argument B uses r and rule $r \Rightarrow \neg q$, B attacks A on its conclusion. Conflict resolution is then based on comparing argument strength or rule priorities. Table 5.1 summarizes differences between key ARG frameworks.

TABLE 5.1
The Differences between ARG Frameworks

Framework	Arguments	Attacks	Extensions	Example Use Case
Dung AAF	Abstract	Binary	Grounded, preferred	Dialogue systems
VAF	With values	Value-sensitive	Value-based extensions	Ethical decision-making
ASPIC+	Structured	Rule-based	Justified arguments	Legal reasoning, AI, and law

Argumentation systems have been applied to various domains. In law, they are used to model legal reasoning and case analysis. Tools like ARGUE! and PROLEXS enable simulation of legal disputes, where each side builds arguments from statutes and precedents. The system identifies winning strategies and potential counterarguments. In Multi-Agent Systems (MASs), ARG allows agents to negotiate, persuade, or coordinate. Agents may have conflicting goals or beliefs, and argumentation provides a protocol for resolving these conflicts. For instance, in automated negotiation, agents propose plans and defend them with reasons, adjusting strategies dynamically. Healthcare is another area of ARG application. In clinical decision support systems, conflicting recommendations (e.g., drug interactions vs. guidelines) can be modeled as arguments. The system helps clinicians understand the rationale behind decisions, making transparent the trade-offs and supporting shared decision-making. In the field of ethics and AI alignment, argumentation models are being explored to help systems reason about moral dilemmas. When actions conflict with different ethical principles, argumentation enables comparison and justification. For example, in autonomous vehicles, arguments for passenger safety may conflict with pedestrian protection, requiring contextual prioritization. The logical foundation of ARG can be enhanced by modal and deontic logics, allowing reasoning about obligation, permission, and belief. These logics support richer argument structures in domains where time, uncertainty, or norms are essential.

Argumentation is also key in XAI. Rather than just outputting decisions, ARG systems can provide chains of reasoning and counterfactual scenarios: *If this symptom had not been present, the diagnosis would have changed.* This transparency is vital in sensitive domains such as finance, medicine, or law. Recent developments include probabilistic argumentation, where arguments are assigned probabilities based on confidence or data reliability. This allows soft reasoning where not all premises are certain. Systems like PrASP integrate probabilistic reasoning with argumentation frameworks. From a computational perspective, ARG poses complexity challenges. Computing extensions under different semantics is computationally demanding typically NP-hard or worse. Therefore, approximate algorithms and heuristics are often used in real-time systems. In education, ARG is used to teach critical thinking and logic. Systems like ARGUETutor engage students in structured debates, helping them construct and evaluate arguments interactively. This pedagogical use of ARG shows its potential for shaping human and artificial reasoning alike. In recent years, argument mining has emerged as a subfield of NLP, focusing on automatically detecting and extracting arguments from texts, such as political speeches, reviews, or legal documents. This bridges symbolic reasoning and data-driven learning.

Tools and platforms such as Arg2P, TOAST, and Carneades provide implementations of various ARG models. They are used in academic research, legal tech, and even policy-making, where arguments for and against legislation can be weighed systematically. As AI grows more interactive and socially embedded, the capacity to argue, justify, and respond becomes essential. Argumentation provides a formal yet intuitive bridge between logic, language, and human reasoning. It turns symbolic AI from a static knowledge processor into a dynamic participant in dialogue.

5.2.4   LIMITATIONS OF SYMBOLIC APPROACHES

Despite their foundational role in the development of AI, symbolic models face several significant limitations that restrict their scalability, adaptability, and general applicability to real-world problems. These limitations, often exposed through both theoretical analysis and empirical constraints, have led to a gradual decline in purely symbolic systems since the late 1980s, giving rise to alternative paradigms like connectionist and statistical approaches.

One major issue with symbolic models is their reliance on manually crafted knowledge bases. This so-called "knowledge acquisition bottleneck" was identified as early as the 1980s during the expert system boom. Constructing and maintaining large rule sets or ontologies demands considerable time from domain experts and knowledge engineers, which is both costly and error-prone. Symbolic AI also suffers from brittleness. These systems perform well only within tightly bounded domains. When encountering scenarios outside their original programming, they often fail entirely. A rule-based troubleshooting assistant for printers, for example, cannot help when faced with a new printer model unless its rules are updated. This brittleness is exacerbated by the closed-world assumption prevalent in symbolic systems. In this assumption, what is not known is considered false. This is unrealistic in most dynamic or open-ended environments, such as web services or real-time robotics, where information is often incomplete. Another key limitation lies in nonmonotonic reasoning. Classical symbolic logic is monotonic: adding new facts cannot invalidate previous conclusions. However, real-world reasoning is often nonmonotonic; new information can change our beliefs. Extensions like default logic and circumscription were proposed in the 1980s, but they increase the complexity of reasoning and are rarely used in practical systems.

Symbolic approaches are also weak in handling uncertainty. Traditional logic does not accommodate probabilistic reasoning, which is essential in domains like medical diagnosis or autonomous driving. Fuzzy logic and probabilistic logic were introduced to address this, but they lack the efficiency and versatility of probabilistic graphical models like Bayesian networks. A related concern is the difficulty of handling ambiguity and imprecision, especially in natural language. Symbolic grammars and rule-based NLP systems were dominant until the early 1990s but performed poorly in large-scale or ambiguous language tasks, ultimately being displaced by statistical and neural models. Symbolic models often require predefined features and explicit structure, making them ill-suited to perceptual tasks like image classification or speech recognition. These domains rely heavily on high-dimensional, continuous data that symbolic models struggle to represent efficiently.

Another practical constraint is computational complexity. Many reasoning tasks in first-order logic are undecidable or require exponential time. For example, even simple planning tasks using STRIPS-like representations may become intractable with increasing problem size, limiting their use in real-time systems. In inference, chaining rules in large systems can lead to combinatorial explosions. Forward- and backward-chaining engines must consider numerous permutations of rule activation, especially when rule dependencies or conflicts arise. This limits scalability. The lack of learning is perhaps the most critical limitation of symbolic AI. These systems cannot learn from data or experience unless explicitly reprogrammed. This contrasts sharply with ML systems that can improve automatically as new data becomes available.

Symbolic models also lack the ability to process sub symbolic information such as continuous, unstructured, or latent patterns that emerge from data. Concepts like image textures, accents in speech, or emotional tone are difficult to represent in symbolic terms but naturally captured in connectionist systems. Moreover, symbolic systems have limited mechanisms for generalization. A symbolic system that recognizes a cat in one context cannot generalize to different breeds or image conditions without explicit new rules. This is in stark contrast to DL models that abstract representations over vast training datasets. Symbolic models are also challenged in modeling time and change. The "frame problem" in classical AI highlighted the difficulty of representing what remains unchanged after an action. Solutions like situation calculus or temporal logics exist, but they are cumbersome and rarely deployed in large-scale systems. The symbolic approach does not naturally support incremental adaptation. Any change to rules or structure may require global consistency checks, whereas statistical models can be updated incrementally using stochastic gradient methods or reinforcement signals. To highlight these differences, Table 5.2 contrasts symbolic and connectionist approaches.

TABLE 5.2
A Comparison through Symbolic and Connectionist Approaches

Feature	Symbolic AI	Connectionist AI
Learning	Manual only	Automatic from data
Uncertainty handling	Limited	Probabilistic
Scalability	Poor with large KBs	Scales with data and compute
Noise robustness	Low	High
Interpretability	High	Often low
Generalization	Weak	Strong

Symbolic AI is also difficult to integrate with sensory data. In robotics, perception modules (vision, lidar, audio) produce data streams ill-suited to rule-based processing. Hence, symbolic planners are often combined with data-driven perception systems in modern hybrid architectures. Even in domains like legal reasoning, where logic seems a natural fit, symbolic AI struggles. Law involves ambiguity, competing interpretations, and evolving norms. Rule-based systems can encode statutes but cannot fully capture interpretive nuance or moral reasoning without massive context modeling. Another limitation is the inflexibility of symbolic representations. Adding a new concept or relationship often requires reworking existing rule sets, leading to a cascading need for maintenance. Ontologies can partially address this but are still manually curated. Symbolic systems are often nonrobust under adversarial conditions. If input deviates slightly from expectations (e.g., unexpected terminology), symbolic parsers or inference engines can break, whereas neural models might still yield a plausible output. In terms of development effort, symbolic systems require significant up-front investment. Unlike data-driven systems that can be bootstrapped with labeled datasets, symbolic systems demand extensive expert collaboration, formalization, and testing before deployment. While symbolic AI excels in explainability, this comes at the expense of adaptability. The internal logic can be audited, but the system cannot respond to feedback or self-correct without intervention. This static nature makes symbolic models less viable in fast-changing environments.

In multi-agent environments, symbolic agents are limited in their ability to negotiate or adapt. While connectionist agents can learn behaviors, strategies, and communication protocols, symbolic agents remain constrained by fixed action sets and predefined rule sets. Moreover, symbolic systems lack the capacity for emergent behavior, which is a key characteristic of many modern AI systems. Neural models, for example, can spontaneously develop internal structures such as word embeddings or feature hierarchies that capture complex dependencies without being explicitly programmed. Symbolic systems also struggle with emotional and social modeling. Human communication often involves nuance, tone, and empathy, aspects that are difficult to represent with rigid symbolic logic but are more accessible through data-driven models and affective computing. Furthermore, symbolic models do not naturally support multimodal learning, where diverse inputs like vision, text, and sound are integrated. In contrast, neural models can fuse these modalities within shared embeddings, enabling tasks such as image captioning or video question answering, which symbolic systems cannot handle effectively.

5.3   MACHINE LEARNING MODELS

5.3.1   DEFINITION, PRINCIPLES, AND ARCHITECTURE OF ML SYSTEMS

ML is a subfield of AI concerned with the development of algorithms that allow computers to learn from data and improve their performance on a task without being explicitly programmed for each new situation. The core idea is to create systems that generalize from examples rather than memorize fixed procedures or rules. The origins of ML date back to the mid-20th century, notably with Arthur Samuel's checkers-playing program in the 1950s, which is considered one of the earliest demonstrations of learning in machines. However, the modern theoretical foundations were formalized in the 1980s and 1990s, with concepts such as the Probably Approximately Correct (PAC) framework and the development of statistical learning theory by Vapnik and Chervonenkis.

A standard definition of ML, as stated by Tom M. Mitchell (1997), is: "A computer program is said to learn from experience E with respect to some class of tasks T and performance measure P if its performance at tasks in T, as measured by P, improves with experience E." This formalism highlights the core components of any ML system: data (E), task (T), and evaluation (P). ML systems typically follow a pipeline structure, beginning with data acquisition and preprocessing, followed by model selection, training, evaluation, and deployment. The architecture of such systems depends on the problem domain but often includes components for input transformation, feature extraction, and prediction output, sometimes wrapped in an end-to-end framework.

There are several principal learning paradigms in ML: SL, UL, and RL. SL involves labeled datasets; UL works with unstructured data to find patterns; and RL uses a reward mechanism to learn optimal actions in dynamic environments. One of the fundamental concepts in ML is the hypothesis space, denoted $\mathcal{H}$, which contains all functions or models a learning algorithm might choose from. During training, the algorithm searches this space to find the hypothesis $h \in \mathcal{H}$ that best approximates the target function $f: X \rightarrow Y$, given the data. To measure model performance, ML uses a loss function $\ell\,(y, \hat{y})$ that quantifies the error between the true label y and the prediction $\hat{y}$. The learning objective is to minimize the expected loss (risk) over the data distribution, usually approximated by empirical risk as shown by Equation (5.1):

$$R_{\mathrm{emp}}\left(h\right) = \frac{1}{n}\sum_{i=1}^{n}l\left(y_i, h\left(x_i\right)\right)$$
(5.1)

The learning process typically involves optimizing the parameters θ of the model to minimize this risk, often via algorithms such as gradient descent or its variants (e.g., SGD, Adam). Model complexity plays a crucial role in learning. Simple models may underfit the data, failing to capture relevant patterns, while overly complex models may overfit, capturing noise instead of the underlying structure. The bias-variance trade-off is a central theoretical insight that guides this balance. Regularization techniques help prevent overfitting by penalizing model complexity. For example, L2 regularization adds a penalty term to the loss function using Equation (5.2):

$$\mathcal{L}(\theta) = R_{emp}(h_\theta) + \lambda \parallel \theta \parallel^2 \qquad (5.2)$$

where λ controls the trade-off between fitting the data and keeping the model parameters small.

In terms of architecture, ML systems may be simple (e.g., linear regression models) or highly complex (e.g., DNNs). Regardless of complexity, most systems include mechanisms for input processing, feature representation, learning (training), validation, and prediction. A typical ML architecture includes:

- Data pipeline: Acquisition → Cleaning → Transformation
- Model core: Learning algorithm + loss function
- Optimization loop: Gradient computation and parameter update
- Validation: Performance assessment using held-out data
- Deployment: Application in real-world environments

Feature engineering has historically played a key role in ML. Selecting and transforming input variables into a suitable representation is often critical to performance. However, the advent of DL has enabled automatic feature extraction from raw inputs. The training-validation-test split is a standard protocol to assess model generalization. Data is divided into subsets to train the model, tune hyperparameters, and evaluate final performance. Metrics vary by task: classification uses accuracy, precision, recall; regression uses MSE or MAE; and ranking uses NDCG or MAP. The choice of algorithm depends on data characteristics, problem formulation, and computational constraints. Classical models include decision trees, SVMs, k-nearest neighbors (k-NN), and ensemble methods like random forests or boosting. Some ML systems employ probabilistic models, such as Naive Bayes or Gaussian Mixture Models (GMMs). These systems not only make predictions but also quantify uncertainty, which is valuable in critical applications like medical diagnosis. Table 5.3 summarizes key model types in classical ML.

TABLE 5.3
Different Types of Key Model in Classical ML

Algorithm	Type	Use Case	Key Feature
Linear regression	Regression	House price prediction	Interpretability
Logistic regression	Classification	Fraud detection	Probabilistic output
Decision tree	Both	Customer segmentation	Rule-based, fast
SVM	Classification	Image recognition	High-margin separation
k-NN	Both	Recommendation systems	Instance-based
Random forest	Both	Credit scoring	Ensemble of trees
Gradient boosting	Both	Forecasting, competitions	Highly accurate, less interpretable

Cross-validation techniques such as k-fold cross-validation enhance robustness in performance estimation. These approaches involve training and testing on multiple data splits, thereby reducing variance in performance metrics. Modern ML architectures often include hyperparameter optimization routines. These are higher-level parameters (e.g., number of trees in a forest, learning rate in SGD) that are not learned from data but significantly affect model performance. Techniques include grid search, random search, and Bayesian optimization. The deployment of ML models introduces new concerns: inference speed, model size, update frequency, and integration into existing systems. Production environments may require batch inference, streaming inputs, or edge computing. Interpretability remains a major issue in ML. Simpler models like decision trees offer transparency but may lack accuracy. Complex models often require explainability tools such as SHapley Additive exPlanations (SHAP) or Local Interpretable Model-agnostic Explanations (LIME).

Ethical concerns such as algorithmic bias, privacy, and fairness are central to modern ML. Models trained on biased data can reproduce and even amplify existing social inequities, prompting the development of tools for fairness-aware learning and privacy-preserving techniques like differential privacy and federated learning. Scalability poses another major challenge, as large datasets and complex models demand distributed computing frameworks such as Hadoop, Spark MLlib, or TensorFlow Extended (TFX), while cloud platforms like AWS SageMaker and Google Vertex AI enable ML at scale. In production environments, continuous monitoring and retraining are essential to maintain model reliability, as model drift can significantly degrade performance over time. Despite its many successes, ML is not a universal solution; it often struggles in low-data settings, unstructured environments, or domains where expert knowledge is critical. In such cases, hybrid approaches that integrate logic or domain-specific rules tend to yield better outcomes.

5.3.2 SUPERVISED LEARNING: CLASSIFICATION AND REGRESSION

SL is one of the most widely used paradigms in ML. It refers to the process in which a model learns to map inputs to outputs based on a labeled dataset. Each training instance includes both the input features and the desired output (also known as the ground truth), allowing the model to generalize from known examples to make predictions on unseen data. Historically, the concept of SL emerged alongside statistical methods like linear regression, which were formalized in the 19th century. However, its broader adoption in AI and computer science occurred from the 1960s onward, with pattern recognition systems and perceptrons paving the way. Today, SL powers many of the AI applications we interact with daily, including spam filters, facial recognition, and speech-to-text systems. SL tasks are typically divided into two categories: classification and regression. Classification involves assigning inputs to discrete categories (e.g., spam vs. not spam), whereas regression predicts continuous outputs (e.g., predicting housing prices or temperature).

A SL model can be represented as a function $f: X \rightarrow Y$, where X denotes the input space and Y the output space. For classification, Y is a finite set of labels; for regression, $Y \subseteq R$ or R^n. The learning process consists of finding a function $\hat{f}$ that approximates f based on the training data $\left\{\left(x_i, y_i\right)\right\}_{i=1}^{n}$. In classification, one of the simplest yet most effective algorithms is logistic regression. Despite its name, logistic regression is a classification algorithm that models the probability of a binary outcome using the logistic (sigmoid) function, as expressed in Equation (5.3):

$$P\left(y = 1 | x\right) = \frac{1}{1 + e^{-\left(w^T x + b\right)}} \tag{5.3}$$

The model is trained by minimizing the binary cross-entropy loss, which penalizes incorrect predictions more heavily the more confident they are. For multi-class classification problems, extensions such as softmax regression are used, which compute probabilities over all classes using Equation (5.4):

$$P\left(y = k | x\right) = \frac{e^{w_k^T x}}{\sum_{j=1}^{K} e^{w_j^T x}} \tag{5.4}$$

Classification models are evaluated using metrics like accuracy, precision, recall, F1 score, and ROC-AUC, depending on whether the focus is on overall correctness or handling class imbalance and misclassification costs. In regression tasks, a common objective is to minimize the MSE (as presented in the section "The Birth of AI" of Chapter 3). Another popular metric is the MAE, which is more robust to outliers than MSE. Many supervised models fall under the category of parametric models, such as linear regression, SVMs, and NNs. These models assume a functional form for f and learn its parameters from data. Nonparametric methods like k-NN make predictions based on proximity in feature space without assuming any underlying model. For classification, the predicted label is typically the majority vote among the k-nearest labeled examples. Decision trees and ensemble methods such as random forests and gradient-boosted trees are powerful SL techniques. They operate by recursively partitioning the input space and aggregating predictions across multiple decision paths or trees.

Training supervised models requires splitting the dataset into training, validation, and test sets. Cross-validation, especially k-fold cross-validation, is used to ensure robust estimates of model performance and to avoid overfitting. Feature selection and feature engineering are critical steps in SL pipelines. Irrelevant or redundant features can degrade performance, while properly engineered features can significantly improve results, especially when data is limited. SL also faces the challenge of class imbalance, where some labels are significantly underrepresented. Techniques such as oversampling (e.g., SMOTE), undersampling, or cost-sensitive learning can mitigate this issue. In high-dimensional spaces, especially in genomics or text classification, regularization techniques like L1 (Lasso) and L2 (Ridge) are used to prevent overfitting and improve generalization.

DL models, particularly CNNs for images and Transformers for text, have achieved state-of-the-art results in supervised tasks. These models require large labeled datasets and significant computational resources. An example of large-scale

SL is ImageNet, a dataset with over 14 million labeled images. It enabled the training of Deep Convolutional Neural Networks (DCNNs) like AlexNet (2012), VGGNet (2014), and ResNet (2015), revolutionizing computer vision. TL is often used in SL to reduce the data and computational requirements. Pretrained models are fine-tuned on task-specific data, achieving high performance with fewer examples.

In some domains, acquiring labeled data is expensive or impractical. Active learning is a strategy where the model selectively queries for labels on the most informative examples, thereby reducing annotation costs. SSL bridges supervised and unsupervised paradigms by using a small amount of labeled data and a large quantity of unlabeled data. It is especially useful in fields like bioinformatics or speech recognition. SL is also widely used in healthcare, from disease diagnosis using medical images to predicting patient outcomes based on historical records. Ensuring interpretability and fairness is critical in such applications. Another major application is in finance, where supervised models are used for credit scoring, fraud detection, and algorithmic trading. Here, models must be accurate and auditable due to regulatory constraints. In NLP, SL powers tasks like sentiment analysis, spam detection, and machine translation. Annotated corpora such as the Penn Treebank and GLUE benchmark are commonly used. In industrial settings, predictive maintenance leverages supervised models trained on sensor data to anticipate equipment failures and schedule interventions, improving reliability and reducing costs. Time series forecasting is a special form of regression where the target variable depends on time. Supervised models must incorporate temporal features, often using lag variables, trend decomposition, or recurrent neural architectures.

While powerful, SL is not always ideal. Its performance heavily depends on the availability and quality of labeled data. Label noise, annotation bias, or shifts in data distribution can all degrade performance. Modern frameworks such as Scikit-learn, TensorFlow, and PyTorch have streamlined the implementation of SL models, offering modular components for data processing, model training, and evaluation.

5.3.3 Unsupervised Learning: Clustering and Dimensionality Reduction

UL is a branch of ML that deals with uncovering hidden patterns in data without the use of labeled outputs. Unlike SL, where models are trained using input-output pairs, UL operates on datasets consisting solely of input features, aiming to discover structure, groupings, or compressed representations. Historically, the development of UL can be traced back to the mid-20th century, with early methods like Principal Component Analysis (PCA) introduced by Karl Pearson in 1901. However, computational versions of PCA and clustering algorithms such as k-means began to be widely used in the 1960s and 1970s as computing resources became more accessible. The two most prominent tasks in UL are clustering and dimensionality reduction. Clustering involves grouping data points based on similarity, while dimensionality reduction aims to represent high-dimensional data in fewer dimensions without significant loss of information. Clustering algorithms attempt to partition data points $(x_1, x_2,..., x_n)$ into k groups (clusters) such that intra-cluster similarity is maximized and inter-cluster similarity is minimized. The most widely known clustering method is k-means clustering, proposed by Stuart Lloyd in 1957.

In k-means, the algorithm initializes k centroids randomly, assigns each data point to the nearest centroid, and then updates the centroids based on the mean of the assigned points. This process repeats until convergence, typically minimizing the Within-Cluster Sum of Squares (WCSS) that is presented by Equation (5.5):

$$\text{WCSS} = \sum_{i=1}^{k} \sum_{x \varepsilon C_i} \| x - \mu_i \|^2 \qquad (5.5)$$

Despite its simplicity and efficiency, k-means has limitations: it assumes spherical clusters, requires the number of clusters k to be known in advance, and is sensitive to initialization. Hierarchical clustering is another major approach. It creates a tree-like structure (dendrogram) by iteratively merging (agglomerative) or splitting (divisive) clusters. Agglomerative hierarchical clustering begins with each data point as a singleton cluster and merges the closest pair based on a linkage criterion, such as single, complete, or average linkage.

A major strength of hierarchical clustering is that it does not require the number of clusters to be specified upfront. The resulting dendrogram can be cut at various levels to produce different clustering. Density-based clustering, such as Density-Based Spatial Clustering of Applications with Noise (DBSCAN). It is robust to outliers and can identify clusters of arbitrary shapes. Other clustering methods include GMMs, which use a probabilistic approach by modeling the data as a mixture of multiple Gaussian distributions. Each data point has a probability of belonging to each cluster, and the model parameters are estimated using the Expectation-Maximization (EM) algorithm. A comparison through key clustering algorithms is presented in Table 5.4.

TABLE 5.4
Comparison of Key Clustering Algorithms

Algorithm	Assumptions	Strengths	Limitations
k-means	Spherical clusters	Fast, simple	Sensitive to k, poor with nonglobular clusters
Hierarchical	Tree structure	No need for k, interpretable	Computationally expensive
DBSCAN	Density regions	Detects outliers, irregular shapes	Struggles with varying densities
GMM	Gaussian distributions	Probabilistic, soft assignment	Sensitive to initialization

Clustering performance can be evaluated using internal metrics like Silhouette Score and Davies-Bouldin Index, or external metrics like Adjusted Rand Index (ARI) and Normalized Mutual Information (NMI) when ground truth labels are available.

Beyond clustering, dimensionality reduction is another critical task in UL, especially for high-dimensional data such as images, text, or gene expressions. These methods aim to project data into a lower-dimensional space while preserving meaningful structure.

PCA is the most classical technique. It finds directions (principal components) in the feature space that capture the maximum variance. PCA projects data into the space spanned by the top k eigenvectors of the covariance matrix. Mathematically, given centered data matrix $X \in R^{n \times d}$, PCA finds the orthonormal matrix $W \in R^{d \times k}$ such that the projection $Z = XW$ retains maximal variance using Equation (5.6):

$$\underset{w}{\text{maximize}} \, \text{Tr}\left(W^T X^T XW\right) \text{subject to} \, W^T W = I \tag{5.6}$$

While PCA is linear, many datasets lie on nonlinear manifolds. To address this, kernel PCA, Isomap, t-distributed Stochastic Neighbor Embedding (t-SNE), and Uniform Manifold Approximation and Projection (UMAP) have been developed to preserve nonlinear structures. t-SNE, proposed by *Laurens van der Maaten* and *Geoffrey Hinton* in 2008, is particularly popular for visualizing high-dimensional data. It maps high-dimensional distances into low-dimensional space while preserving local similarities. However, it is computationally intensive and sensitive to hyperparameters like perplexity. UMAP, introduced in 2018, is a newer technique that provides faster computation and better global structure preservation than t-SNE, making it a preferred choice in bioinformatics and NLP for visualization tasks. Dimensionality reduction is also used for preprocessing, reducing computational cost and mitigating the curse of dimensionality, which can degrade model performance in high-dimensional spaces due to sparse data distributions. UL also finds applications in anomaly detection, where models identify data points that do not conform to the general pattern. Isolation Forests, One-Class SVM, and autoencoders are common tools in this domain.

In document clustering, algorithms like Latent Dirichlet Allocation (LDA), proposed in 2003, uncover latent topics within a corpus. LDA models documents as mixtures of topics and topics as distributions over words. Autoencoders, NNs trained to reconstruct input data, are widely used for nonlinear dimensionality reduction. By compressing input into a latent space and reconstructing it, autoencoders learn compact representations useful for denoising, compression, or anomaly detection. Self-Organizing Maps (SOMs), introduced by *Teuvo Kohonen* in the 1980s, are neural networks used for dimensionality reduction and visualization. SOMs preserve the topological properties of input space in a lower-dimensional representation. UL is especially valuable in exploratory data analysis, where no prior labels are available. It allows researchers to identify natural groupings, trends, and relationships before applying supervised methods. In genomics, unsupervised techniques are used to cluster genes with similar expression profiles, which may indicate shared biological functions. In e-commerce, customer segmentation via clustering helps target marketing strategies. A key challenge in UL is evaluation. Without ground truth labels, validating model performance becomes subjective or reliant on indirect criteria, such as cluster compactness or reconstruction error. Recent advancements integrate UL with deep architectures, such as deep clustering, which jointly learns feature representations and cluster assignments. These models scale better and provide more meaningful groupings on complex data.

In NLP, UL underpins word embeddings like *Word2Vec* (2013) and *GloVe* (2014), which learn vector representations of words by analyzing word co-occurrence statistics without any labels. Another unsupervised paradigm is contrastive learning, where the model learns to distinguish between similar and dissimilar pairs of inputs. This has led to breakthroughs in self-supervised representation learning, exemplified by methods like SimCLR and MoCo. As AI systems become more data-hungry, UL offers a scalable alternative where labels are expensive or unavailable. It supports pretraining, pattern discovery, and structure extraction across diverse domains.

5.3.4 REINFORCEMENT LEARNING: AGENTS, ENVIRONMENTS, AND REWARDS

RL is a distinct paradigm within ML that focuses on learning optimal behavior through interaction with an environment. Unlike SL and UL, RL does not require labeled data; instead, it relies on rewards and penalties to guide learning. The agent must discover the sequence of actions that maximizes cumulative reward over time, a process reminiscent of trial-and-error learning in biological systems. The mathematical formalism behind RL is rooted in Markov Decision Processes (MDPs), introduced in the 1950s by Bellman. An MDP is defined by a tuple (S, A, P, R, γ), where S is the set of states, A the set of actions, P the state transition probabilities, R the reward function, and $\gamma \in [0,1]$ the discount factor. The objective is to learn a policy $\pi : S \to A$ that maximizes the expected return. The return, or cumulative reward, is often formalized based on Equation (5.7):

$$G_t = \sum_{k=0}^{\infty} \gamma^k R_{t+k+1} \tag{5.7}$$

where γ determines the importance of future rewards: a smaller γ prioritizes immediate gains, while a value closer to 1 emphasizes long-term outcomes.

This formulation allows RL agents to balance exploitation and exploration as the two central challenges in sequential decision-making. At the heart of RL is the value function, which estimates how good it is to be in a given state (or to take a given action from a state). The state-value function is defined based on Equation (5.8):

$$V^{\pi}(s) = \mathbb{E}_{\pi} \langle G_t | S_t = s \rangle \tag{5.8}$$

and the action-value function as shown in Equation (5.9):

$$Q^{\pi}(s,a) = \mathbb{E}_{\pi} \langle G_t | S_t = s, A_t = a \rangle \tag{5.9}$$

These functions can be learned directly via Dynamic Programming, Monte Carlo methods, or Temporal Difference Learning (TDL). TD methods, such as TD(0), and bootstrap value estimates are foundational to modern RL algorithms.

One of the most influential RL algorithms is Q-learning, introduced by *Watkins* in 1989. It is an off-policy TD control method that updates the action-value function based on Equation (5.10):

$$Q(s,a) \leftarrow Q(s,a) + \alpha \left(R + \gamma \max Q(s',a') - Q(s,a) \right) \qquad (5.10)$$

where α is the learning rate. Q-learning has the advantage of converging to the optimal policy under certain assumptions, even when the policy being followed is exploratory.

In contrast, State–Action–Reward–State–Action (SARSA) is an on-policy algorithm that updates using the action actually taken by the agent. This subtle difference affects the learning behavior in environments with stochastic or risky transitions. The architecture of a RL system consists of an agent, an environment, and the interaction loop. At each time step, the agent observes the current state, selects an action, receives a reward, and transitions to a new state. This feedback loop continues until a terminal state is reached or indefinitely in continuous tasks. Applications of RL have expanded dramatically in recent years. In games, DeepMind's AlphaGo and AlphaZero used reinforcement learning to defeat world champions in Go and chess. These agents combined DNNs with RL through Deep Q-Networks (DQNs) and policy gradient methods, demonstrating superhuman performance.

Policy gradient methods, such as REINFORCE and Actor-Critic algorithms, directly optimize the policy function. The REINFORCE update rule is shown in Equation (5.11):

$$\theta \leftarrow \theta + \alpha \nabla_\theta \log \pi_\theta (a|s) G_t \qquad (5.11)$$

where π_θ is a parameterized policy.

These methods are especially effective in high-dimensional or continuous action spaces, where value-based methods become inefficient.

Actor-Critic architectures combine the benefits of value-based and policy-based methods. The actor selects actions according to a learned policy, while the critic evaluates them using a value function. This dual structure enables stable and scalable learning in complex environments. Another crucial development in RL is the incorporation of function approximation, particularly via DNNs. Deep Reinforcement Learning (DRL) methods like DQN, DDPG, and PPO can handle large state spaces (e.g., images, sensor readings) where tabular methods are infeasible. A comparison through the several keys for RL algorithms is presented in Table 5.5.

TABLE 5.5
Comparison of RL Algorithms

Algorithm	Type	Model-Free	Policy-Based	Use Case
Q-learning	Off-policy	Yes	No	Discrete control tasks
SARSA	On-policy	Yes	No	Risk-sensitive agents
REINFORCE	On-policy	Yes	Yes	Continuous control
DQN	Off-policy	Yes	No	Atari games

Exploration is a fundamental aspect of RL. Common strategies include epsilon-greedy policies (where a random action is chosen with probability ϵ) and Boltzmann exploration (actions chosen based on a softmax of Q-values). Balancing exploration and exploitation is critical, especially in sparse-reward settings. In robotics, RL enables autonomous agents to learn motor skills such as walking, grasping, and balancing. Simulated environments, like OpenAI Gym or MuJoCo, allow safe and efficient training before deploying models in physical robots. In operations research, RL is applied to optimize supply chains, inventory management, and traffic control. Here, the environment is partially observable and stochastic, making RL a suitable approach where traditional optimization methods struggle. Multi-Agent Reinforcement Learning (MARL) extends RL to environments with multiple interacting agents. MARL introduces challenges such as nonstationarity and partial observability but also models realistic social and economic systems. Despite its power, RL is data-hungry and computationally intensive. Sample efficiency is a major concern, especially in real-world applications where data collection is costly or slow. Solutions include model-based RL, imitation learning, and reward shaping. Reward design is another critical challenge. Sparse, delayed, or misleading rewards can hinder learning or lead to unintended behavior. Reward shaping, curriculum learning, and human-in-the-loop RL are strategies to address these issues. Safety and ethical concerns are increasingly relevant in RL. Agents trained to optimize rewards without constraints may exhibit unsafe or manipulative behaviors. Research on safe RL and constrained MDPs aims to impose risk-sensitive or ethical constraints on agent behavior. Reinforcement learning provides a powerful framework for autonomous decision-making in dynamic environments. Its foundation in formal decision theory, combined with modern advances in DL and function approximation, positions it at the frontier of intelligent systems. However, its success depends on careful design, abundant data, and robust evaluation strategies.

5.3.5 SELF-SUPERVISED LEARNING: BRIDGING SUPERVISION AND AUTONOMY

Self-supervised learning (SSL_self) has emerged in recent years as a powerful ML model that aims to bridge the gap between supervised and UL. The central idea is to create pseudo-labels or supervision signals from raw, unlabeled data, enabling models to learn meaningful representations without requiring manual annotation. This technique reduces dependence on labeled datasets and fosters autonomy in learning processes. The concept of SSL dates back to early research in representation learning, but it gained major traction in the 2010s, especially with the rise of DL and the need to scale learning algorithms beyond the constraints of human-labeled datasets. In particular, the success of pretraining strategies in NLP, such as Word2Vec (2013) and BERT (2018), highlighted the power of learning from unlabeled corpora through carefully designed predictive tasks. SSL_self operates by defining pretext tasks, which serve as learning objectives derived directly from data. These tasks are not the final goal but act as a means to extract useful features. Once a model is pretrained on a pretext task, it can be fine-tuned or transferred to downstream tasks using fewer labeled examples, thereby improving efficiency and performance.

A classic example of a pretext task is context prediction in text. Given a sequence of words, the model is asked to predict a missing word (masked language modeling, as in BERT) or the next word (as in GPT). The input provides its own supervision, and the resulting model learns syntactic and semantic structures useful for many NLP tasks. In the vision domain, SSL_self has leveraged tasks such as image colorization, jigsaw puzzle solving, rotation prediction, and contrastive learning. For instance, in rotation prediction, the model is trained to identify the angle of rotation applied to an image (e.g., 0°, 90°, 180°, 270°). Although the task itself is simple, it encourages the model to learn spatial and object-level features. One of the most influential breakthroughs in SSL came through contrastive learning, especially in computer vision. Methods such as SimCLR (2020), MoCo (2020), and BYOL (2020) demonstrated that representations could be learned by maximizing the agreement between differently augmented views of the same input while contrasting them with other instances. This framework can be formalized using a contrastive loss function using Equation (5.12):

$$\mathcal{L}_{\text{contrastive}} = -\log \frac{\exp\left(\text{sim}\left(z_i, z_j\right) / \mathcal{T}\right)}{\sum_{k=1}^{2N} 1_{(k \neq i)} \exp\left(\text{sim}\left(z_i, z_k\right) / \mathcal{T}\right)} \tag{5.12}$$

where sim denotes similarity (e.g., cosine), z_i and z_j are representations of positive pairs, τ is a temperature parameter, and N is the batch size.

A defining advantage of SSL is its ability to learn from abundant unlabeled data. In domains such as medical imaging, where annotation is costly, SSL enables pre-training on large unlabeled datasets and fine-tuning on small annotated sets, often outperforming fully supervised baselines. In speech processing, SSL has led to models like wav2vec (2019) and HuBERT (2021), where audio signals are used to predict future segments or masked frames. These models have significantly improved speech recognition, even outperforming traditional supervised models when fine-tuned with limited labeled data. In Table 5.6, a comparison is provided through different SSL models.

TABLE 5.6
Comparison of SSL Models across Modalities

Domain	SSL Method	Pretext Task	Year
NLP	BERT	Masked language modeling	2018
Vision	SimCLR	Contrastive instance learning	2020
Vision	BYOL	Bootstrap targets	2020
Speech	wav2vec	Future frame prediction	2019
DQN	Off-policy	Yes	Atari games

In multimodal SSL, models like Contrastive Language–Image Pretraining (CLIP) train on image-caption pairs to align representations across text and vision. This enables zero-shot classification, where the model can recognize unseen classes based on textual descriptions alone, showing strong generalization. Unlike SL, SSL minimizes human bias during labeling, potentially leading to fairer representations. However, the design of pretext tasks must be done carefully to ensure alignment between the pretext and downstream tasks. Poorly chosen tasks may result in representations that do not generalize. Recent research in noncontrastive SSL has shown that effective representations can be learned even without negative samples. For example, BYOL and SimSiam demonstrate that, under certain architectural conditions and regularizations, a model can avoid collapse (identical outputs) and learn discriminative features by matching representations from different augmentations. Mathematically, these methods minimize loss functions based on Equation (5.13):

$$\mathcal{L}_{\mathrm{BYOL}} = \left\| \mathrm{stopped}\left(z'\right) - z \right\|^2 \tag{5.13}$$

where z' and z are representations of two augmented views and the gradient is stopped on one branch to prevent collapse.

SSl_self is also linked to representation learning theory. SSL often seeks to discover latent factors of variation within the data, implicitly learning a manifold structure. Such representations are beneficial for downstream generalization, robustness, and transferability. In robotics, SSL facilitates perception modules that can learn affordances, grasping points, or trajectories without labeled supervision. By interacting with the environment and using proprioceptive feedback, robots can learn meaningful control representations that improve over time. The flexibility of SSL extends to domains such as chemoinformatics and genomics, where pretext tasks include predicting masked tokens in sequences of molecules (SMILES) or DNA, capturing biochemical or biological relationships useful for drug discovery or diagnostics. SSL has also influenced pretraining paradigms in large-scale models. Vision Transformers (ViTs), for instance, benefit from self-supervised pretraining on massive image datasets before being fine-tuned for classification, detection, or segmentation tasks. Another important contribution of SSL is its role in Few-Shot Learning (FSL). Representations learned via self-supervision often generalize well to new classes with only a few examples. This is especially useful in low-resource settings or in applications involving rare or emerging categories. The scalability of SSL makes it ideal for continual learning and federated learning setups, where labeled data is scarce, distributed, or private. SSL can be deployed locally to extract features before any supervised task is learned, preserving privacy while leveraging local data.

A major trend in SSL is its integration with Transformers. Models like DINO (2021) leverage self-distillation and SSL to train Vision Transformers without supervision, demonstrating emergent properties like semantic segmentation and part recognition. While SSL offers numerous benefits, challenges remain. Defining universally effective pretext tasks across domains is nontrivial. Moreover, computational demands during contrastive learning or large-scale pretraining are significant, requiring careful engineering. There is also active research on evaluating the quality of learned representations. Metrics such as linear probe accuracy, nearest neighbor classification, and clustering scores are used, but standardization remains an open issue. Understanding the inductive biases introduced by different pretext tasks is an ongoing theoretical effort. Ethical considerations in SSL mirror those of data-driven AI. Since SSL uses raw web-scale data, it may encode unwanted social biases or copyright content. Researchers are exploring filtering strategies and bias-aware training to address these risks. SSl_self represents a paradigm shift toward more autonomous, scalable, and efficient learning systems. By creatively leveraging structure within data, SSL has unlocked new capabilities across domains and set the stage for increasingly general and adaptable AI.

5.3.6 FEW-SHOT AND ZERO-SHOT LEARNING

FSL and Zero-Shot Learning (ZSL) are two advanced paradigms in ML that aim to address the limitations of traditional supervised learning, particularly its reliance on large quantities of labeled data. These approaches attempt to enable models to generalize to new tasks or classes with little to no training data for scenarios where labeled examples are scarce, expensive, or unavailable.

FSL refers to the ability of a model to learn a new task or recognize a new class using only a few labeled examples, often as few as one (one-shot learning) or five (five-shot learning). In contrast, ZSL requires the model to perform a task or recognize a class it has never seen during training, relying solely on high-level semantic descriptions or shared features between known and unknown classes.

The interest in few-shot and ZSL has grown significantly with the advent of DL, where large datasets and extensive training are typically required to achieve high performance. However, real-world applications such as medical diagnostics, rare language processing, or novel product classification often provide only limited labeled examples. These paradigms provide a pathway to scalability without exhaustive labeling. Mathematically, FSL is often framed as a meta-learning problem, where the goal is to learn how to learn. Given a distribution over tasks $p(\tau)$, the learner is trained over a set of tasks sampled from this distribution. Each task includes a small support set S and a query set Q. The model must adapt to S and generalize to Q with minimal data. One of the earliest and most influential models in FSL is the Matching Network, introduced by Vinyals in 2016. It uses attention and metric learning to compare the embedding of a query instance with those in the support set. The prediction is based on a weighted combination of the labels of the support set as Equation (5.14):

$$\hat{y} = \sum_{i=1}^{k} a\left(x, x_i\right) y_i \tag{5.14}$$

where $a(x, x_i)$ measures similarity, typically using cosine similarity, between the query x and support instances x_i.

Another prominent few-shot method is Prototypical Networks, proposed in 2017 by *Snell*. This approach computes a prototype (mean embedding) for each class in

the support set, and classifies queries based on distance to these prototypes according to Equation (5.15):

$$c_k = \frac{1}{|S_k|} \sum_{(x_i, y_i) \varepsilon S_k} f_\theta(x_i) \qquad (5.15)$$

where f_θ is a feature extractor and d is a distance metric such as Euclidean or cosine
distance.

FSL also benefits from optimization-based meta-learning algorithms such as
Model-Agnostic Meta-Learning (MAML), introduced by *Finn* in 2017. MAML
seeks to learn model parameters that can be quickly adapted to new tasks using a
few gradient steps. It does so by optimizing for performance after adaptation using
Equation (5.16):

$$\min_\theta \sum_{T_i \sim p(T)} \mathcal{L}_{T_i}\left(U\left(\theta, T_i\right)\right) \qquad (5.16)$$

where U denotes the adaptation process, such as one or more gradient updates.

ZSL, on the other hand, often relies on semantic embeddings or auxiliary information to enable generalization. One common approach is to use attributes or textual
descriptions of classes, and align the visual and semantic spaces. This is often done
through joint embedding techniques. For example, consider a model trained on animals like cats and dogs, with attributes like "has fur," "barks," "meows." To classify
a zebra (never seen during training) the model maps both images and class descriptions into a shared space and matches them via similarity.

A landmark in ZSL is the DeViSE model (*Frome*, 2013), which projects image
features and word embeddings (e.g., from Word2Vec) into a joint semantic space.
The classification is done by choosing the class whose embedding is closest to the
image representation.

Mathematically, the score of an image x and class y is given by Equation (5.17):

$$s(x, y) = f(x)^T g(y) \qquad (5.17)$$

where $f(x)$ is the image feature vector and $g(y)$ is the class embedding.

The model is trained to maximize the score for the correct class and minimize it
for others using a ranking loss.

In recent years, large-scale pretraining and TL have greatly improved zero-shot
performance. Transformer-based models like GPT-3 (2020) and CLIP (2021) demonstrate strong zero-shot capabilities by training on massive, diverse datasets. CLIP,
in particular, aligns vision and language modalities using contrastive learning and
enables tasks like zero-shot image classification. Prompting techniques also play a
key role in enabling Few-Shot Learning (FSL) and Zero-Shot Learning (ZSL) in
Large Language Models (LLMs). For example, GPT-3 can solve tasks by seeing just
a few examples embedded in the prompt (in-context learning), or even by understanding task instructions alone. Table 5.7 compares prominent approaches.

TABLE 5.7

Comparison of Prominent Approaches

Method	Year	Task	Principle
Matching networks	2016	Few-shot	Attention over support set
Prototypical networks	2017	Few-shot	Class prototypes in embedding
MAML	2017	Few-shot	Fast adaptation by meta-gradient
DeViSE	2013	Zero-shot	Joint visual-semantic embedding
CLIP	2021	Zero-shot	Image-text contrastive learning

5.4 DEEP LEARNING

5.4.1 NEURAL NETWORKS

NNs are one of the fundamental pillars of modern AI. Inspired by the way the human brain processes information, these models are composed of interconnected units called neurons, arranged in layers. Their ability to learn and capture complex relationships from data makes them particularly well-suited for tasks such as classification, regression, image recognition, automatic translation, and many more. A NN consists of multiple layers, each playing a distinct role in processing and transforming data. A general overview of this layered architecture, comprising input, hidden, and output layers is illustrated in Figure 3.4 (see the section "AI and Mathematics" of Chapter 3) and serves as a foundation for the discussions here. The first layer, known as the input layer, receives raw data in the form of vectors or matrices. Each neuron in this layer represents a feature of the input data, passing information forward to the next stage. Between the input and output lies one or more hidden layers, which are responsible for learning increasingly abstract representations of the data. The number of these layers and the number of neurons per layer depend on the complexity of the problem being solved. These hidden layers extract meaningful patterns, allowing the network to make sense of complex relationships. The output layer provides the final predictions or classifications based on the information processed by the hidden layers. The number of neurons in this layer depends on the specific task, whether it's binary classification, multi-class classification, or continuous value prediction.

5.4.1.1 How Neurons Work?

Each neuron in an NN receives multiple inputs, assigns a weight to each, sums them together, and then applies an activation function to produce an output. This process can be mathematically expressed by Equation (5.18):

$$y = f\left(\sum_{i=1}^{n} w_i x_i + b\right) \tag{5.18}$$

where y is the neuron's output, $x_1, x_2, \ldots, x_n$ are the input values, $w_1, w_2, \ldots, w_n$ are the associated weights, b is a bias term, and f is the activation function.

The activation function plays a crucial role by introducing nonlinearity into the model, allowing the neural network to learn complex relationships rather than just linear mappings. Common activation functions include the sigmoid function, which squashes outputs between 0 and 1; the Rectified Linear Unit (ReLU), which sets all negative values to zero while keeping positive values unchanged; and the tanh function, which maps inputs to a range between −1 and 1. During training, the network adjusts its weights and biases to minimize the error between its predictions and the actual target values. This adjustment process is what allows the network to learn from data over time.

5.4.1.2   Training a Neural Network

Training an NN involves optimizing its weights and biases to minimize a predefined loss function. The most commonly used method for this is gradient descent, an algorithm that iteratively updates the parameters in the direction that reduces the error. The loss function, often referred to as the cost function, quantifies the difference between the network's predictions and the true target values.

For regression problems, a common loss function is the MSE (as presented in the section "The Birth of AI" of Chapter 3). Gradient descent works by computing the gradient of the cost function with respect to the network's parameters and then updating the parameters in the opposite direction of this gradient. The update rule is given by Equation (5.19):

$$w_i \leftarrow w_i - \alpha \frac{\partial C}{\partial w_i} \tag{5.19}$$

where θ represents the network's parameters (weights and biases), α is the learning rate, and $\partial C / \partial \theta$ is the computed gradient.

The learning rate controls how big the updates are; setting it too high can lead to instability, while setting it too low can slow down the training process.

5.4.1.3   Backpropagation

Backpropagation is the fundamental algorithm that allows NNs to learn by systematically adjusting their weights to minimize prediction errors. It operates as an SL method, enabling the network to improve its performance through iterative refinement. The core idea behind backpropagation is to propagate the error from the output layer back through the network, allowing each neuron to update its weights in a way that reduces the overall discrepancy between predicted and actual outputs. The process begins with a forward pass, where the input data moves through the network, layer by layer, until it reaches the output layer. At this stage, the network generates predictions, which are then compared to the actual target values. This comparison is quantified using a loss function, which measures the difference between the predicted output and the true output. Common loss functions include the MSE for regression tasks and cross-entropy loss for classification problems. The goal of backpropagation is to minimize this loss by adjusting the network's weights and biases. Once the loss is calculated, the backward pass begins. The key mathematical tool used in this phase is the chain rule of differentiation, which allows the network to compute how changes in each weight affect the final loss. The error is first computed at the output layer, representing how far the network's predictions are from the correct values. This error is then propagated backward through the network, moving from the output layer toward the input layer. At each step, the network determines how much each neuron contributed to the overall error and adjusts its weights accordingly. This two-phase process, forward propagation followed by backward error propagation, is illustrated in Figure 5.2.

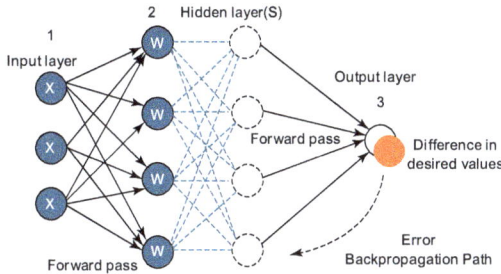

FIGURE 5.2 Forward and backward propagation in a deep neural network. The input moves forward through successive layers to produce an output (forward pass), and the error between the predicted and expected output is propagated back through the network to update weights (backpropagation).

By using gradient descent, the weights and biases are updated in a way that reduces the error. The learning rate plays a crucial role in this process, controlling the size of these updates. If the learning rate is too high, the network might fail to converge, jumping over optimal values. If it is too low, learning will be slow and inefficient.

This entire process is repeated for multiple training cycles, gradually refining the weights so that the network learns to map inputs to outputs with increasing accuracy. Over time, the adjustments become smaller, and the network reaches an optimal balance between learning from the training data and generalizing well to new, unseen data. Backpropagation has been a breakthrough in NN training, enabling DL models to handle complex problems such as image recognition, NLP, and autonomous decision-making. However, for deeper networks, it faces challenges like the vanishing gradient problem, where gradients become too small for effective learning. Solutions such as activation functions like ReLU, batch normalization, and advanced optimizers like Adam have been developed to address these issues and enhance training efficiency. Ultimately, backpropagation remains the foundation of DL, providing a systematic and efficient way for NNs to learn from data, adapt, and improve their predictions over time.

5.4.1.4   Types of Neural Networks

There are several types of NNs, each designed to handle specific types of data and problems. A Multi-Layer Perceptron (MLP) is the simplest form of an NN, consisting of multiple fully connected layers where each neuron in one layer is connected to all neurons in the next. These networks are commonly used for general classification and regression tasks. For image processing tasks, CNNs are widely used. Instead of fully connected layers, CNNs use convolutional layers that apply filters to small regions of an image, enabling the network to detect patterns such as edges, textures, and shapes. These networks are the foundation of modern computer vision applications. For sequential data such as time series and natural language, RNNs are preferred. Unlike standard feedforward networks, RNNs have connections that loop back, allowing them to retain information from previous inputs. This makes them ideal for applications like speech recognition, text generation, and machine translation. More advanced RNN variants, such as Long Short-Term Memory (LSTM) networks and Gated Recurrent Units (GRUs), address the problem of vanishing gradients, making them better suited for learning long-term dependencies in sequences. These networks are widely used in machine translation, chatbots, and predictive text systems.

5.4.1.5   Optimization and Overfitting

Optimization is a crucial aspect of training NNs, ensuring that they not only learn from the data but also generalize well to new inputs. However, one of the biggest challenges in this process is overfitting, where the model becomes too specialized in the training data, capturing noise and irrelevant patterns instead of extracting meaningful, generalizable features. When this happens, the network performs exceptionally well on training examples but struggles to make accurate predictions on unseen data. To combat overfitting, several regularization techniques are commonly used. One effective method is dropout, where a random fraction of neurons is temporarily deactivated during training. This prevents the model from relying too heavily on specific pathways and forces it to develop more robust and distributed representations of the data. Another widely used approach is L_1 and L_2 regularization, which introduce penalty terms in the loss function to discourage overly large weights. L_1 regularization encourages sparsity by pushing some weights toward zero, while L_2 regularization helps prevent excessive weight magnitudes, promoting a more stable and generalized model. By applying these techniques, NNs can maintain a balance between learning the details of the training data and ensuring their ability to generalize effectively to new, unseen inputs. Proper optimization not only improves performance but also enhances the model's ability to handle real-world variability, making it more reliable and adaptable in practical applications.

5.4.1.6   Applications of Neural Networks

NNs have transformed numerous industries and are now at the core of many cutting-edge applications. In image recognition, convolutional networks power facial recognition, medical imaging diagnostics, and self-driving car vision systems. In NLP, recurrent networks and Transformers are used for tasks like machine translation, text summarization, and chatbot interactions. Speech recognition technology, such as voice assistants, also relies heavily on DL models. In finance, neural networks are used for stock price prediction, fraud detection, and risk assessment. In the field of science and engineering, they contribute to drug discovery, weather forecasting, and material design. The versatility of NNs makes them an indispensable tool in AI, driving innovations that were once considered science fiction. NNs have revolutionized the way machines learn and process information, enabling breakthroughs in fields ranging from healthcare to autonomous systems. However, successfully training and deploying these models requires careful tuning of hyperparameters, proper handling of data, and rigorous evaluation to ensure that they are both accurate and reliable. As research continues to advance, NNs will only become more powerful, unlocking even more possibilities in AI.

5.4.2 DEEP ARCHITECTURES: CNNs, RNNs, AND TRANSFORMERS

DL architectures have undergone significant evolution over the past two decades, with a particular emphasis on specialized structures tailored to specific data types and tasks. While fully connected networks laid the groundwork for artificial NNs, their limitations in handling high-dimensional or sequential data soon became apparent. This led to the emergence of three groundbreaking architectures: CNNs, RNNs, and, more recently, Transformers. Each of these architectures introduced novel computational paradigms and structural innovations that reshaped the landscape of ML.

CNNs first gained widespread recognition in the late 1990s and early 2000s, particularly with the work of Yann LeCun and collaborators on the LeNet architecture for digit recognition. The defining feature of CNNs is their use of convolutional layers, which apply spatially local filters to detect features across an image. Instead of connecting every neuron to all inputs as in dense layers, CNNs exploit the spatial locality and translational invariance of image data. This architectural refinement significantly reduces the number of trainable parameters and allows the network to focus on hierarchical feature extraction. Mathematically, a 2D convolution operation for an image I and a kernel K is defined based on Equation (5.20):

$$S(i,j) = (I * K)(i,j) = \sum_m \sum_n I(i+m, j+n) K(m,n) \qquad (5.20)$$

This operation is repeated across the entire input, enabling the network to detect features like edges, corners, or textures at different spatial locations. CNNs typically include multiple convolutional layers followed by pooling layers, which down sample the spatial dimensions, and finally, fully connected layers for classification or regression. The rise of large-scale image datasets, particularly ImageNet, and the availability of GPUs accelerated the development of DCNNs in the early 2010s. AlexNet (2012), which won the ImageNet competition by a large margin, showcased the power of DCNNs trained with ReLU activations, dropout, and data augmentation. This success was followed by increasingly deeper architectures like VGGNet

(2014), GoogLeNet (2014), and ResNet (2015), the latter introducing residual connections to facilitate training of very deep networks.

Convolutional architectures have been extended to nonvisual data as well. For
example, 1D convolutions are used in time series analysis and audio processing,
while 3D convolutions are applied to volumetric data in medical imaging or video
sequences. CNNs are also integrated into hybrid architectures for multimodal learning, such as image captioning systems that combine visual features with language
models. While CNNs are inherently suited for spatial data, RNNs are designed for
sequential data processing. RNNs maintain a hidden state that evolves over time,
capturing dependencies between elements in a sequence. The generic RNN update
equation is indicated as Equation (5.21):

$$h_t = \tanh(W_{hh}h_{t-1} + W_{xh}x_t + b_h) \tag{5.21}$$

where x_t is the input at time step t and h_t is the hidden state.

This formulation allows RNNs to retain memory of previous inputs, making
them ideal for tasks such as speech recognition, language modeling, and time series
forecasting.

Despite their theoretical appeal, vanilla RNNs suffer from vanishing and exploding gradient problems, making it difficult to learn long-range dependencies. To
address this, the LSTM architecture was introduced by Hochreiter and Schmidhuber
in 1997. LSTMs include memory cells and gates (input, forget, and output) that regulate the flow of information, enabling stable training over longer sequences. Another
variant, the GRU, simplifies the architecture while maintaining similar performance.
RNNs have been widely used in NLP, powering tasks such as machine translation,
text generation, and sentiment analysis. Encoder–decoder architectures based on
RNNs became standard for sequence-to-sequence learning. However, as tasks grew
in complexity and dataset sizes expanded, the sequential nature of RNNs, where
computation at time t depends on $t-1$, became a computational bottleneck, limiting
parallelization and increasing training time.

The breakthrough that transformed sequential modeling came with the introduction of the Transformer architecture in 2017 by Vaswani in the paper *Attention is
All You Need*. Transformers abandon recurrence altogether and rely entirely on self-
attention mechanisms to capture dependencies across sequences. This allows them
to model long-range relationships directly and efficiently, with full parallelization
during training. The core mechanism of the Transformer is scaled dot-product attention. Given query Q, key K, and value V matrices, the attention output is computed
based on Equation (5.22):

$$\text{Attention}(Q, K, V) = \text{softmax}\left(\frac{QK^T}{\sqrt{d_k}}\right)v \tag{5.22}$$

where d_k is the dimensionality of the key vectors.

This formulation enables each token in a sequence to attend to all other tokens,
allowing rich context modeling. The Transformer includes multiple such attention

heads and a feedforward network within each layer, along with residual connections and layer normalization. The complete encoder–decoder architecture of the original Transformer model is illustrated in Figure 5.3.

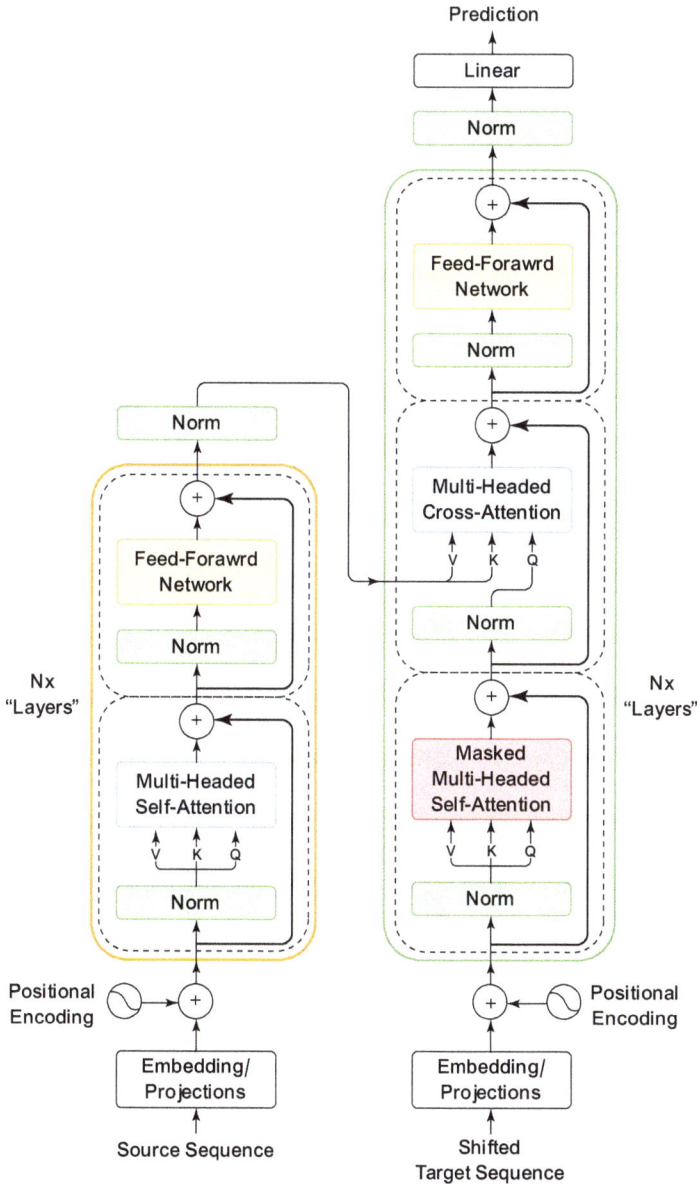

FIGURE 5.3 The original Transformer architecture (Adapted with permission from [6]).

Transformers quickly became the de facto standard in NLP, replacing RNN-based models across the board. BERT (2018), GPT-2 (2019), and GPT-3 (2020) demonstrated the power of pretraining on massive corpora followed by fine-tuning on specific tasks. These models achieved state-of-the-art results in question answering, summarization, translation, and dialogue generation. Beyond NLP, Transformers have been extended to vision and other domains. Vision Transformers (ViT), introduced in 2020, treat image patches as tokens and process them using standard Transformer layers. Despite lacking the inductive bias of CNNs, ViTs match or exceed CNN performance when trained on large datasets. Transformers have also been applied to protein folding (AlphaFold), image generation (DALL·E), and reinforcement learning (Decision Transformer). The shift from CNNs and RNNs to Transformers marks a unification of DL architectures around attention mechanisms. Transformers offer flexibility, scalability, and modularity, enabling large-scale pretraining and TL across diverse tasks and modalities. However, they are computationally intensive and require substantial data and hardware, raising concerns about accessibility and environmental impact.

Each of these architectures (CNNs, RNNs, and Transformers) has distinct strengths. CNNs excel at spatial structure, RNNs at temporal dynamics, and Transformers at global context modeling. Their integration into unified systems such as CNN backbones feeding into Transformers for image captioning, or hybrid RNN-Transformer models for speech processing highlights the increasing convergence in DL design. Despite their power, deep architectures face ongoing challenges. These include model interpretability, data efficiency, robustness to adversarial attacks, and scalability to edge devices. Techniques such as pruning, quantization, and knowledge distillation aim to reduce model size and computation, while advances in visualization and saliency methods attempt to make internal mechanisms more transparent.

5.4.3 REPRESENTATIONAL POWER AND HIERARCHICAL LEARNING

The representational power of DL models, particularly those based on ANNs, stems from their capacity to learn hierarchical abstractions from raw data. This notion that multiple layers of computation can progressively transform input representations into increasingly abstract features is a central tenet of modern DL and a key to its success in domains ranging from vision to language to bioinformatics. The concept was first articulated clearly in the 1980s but only gained practical traction with the advent of deep architectures in the 2000s and 2010s. At the heart of this hierarchical learning lies the multilayer composition of nonlinear functions. Let x denote an input, and let $f(x)$ represent the output of a NN. A deep model expresses $f(x)$ as a composition $f(x) = f_n(f_{n-1}(\ldots f_1(x)))$, where each f_i is a layer of transformations involving affine mappings followed by nonlinearities. This composition enables the network to model highly complex and nonlinear relationships in data.

Lower layers in such a network typically capture local, low-level features. In image processing, for example, early convolutional layers detect edges, textures, and corners. Mid-level layers begin to identify parts of objects or common shapes, and deeper layers encode entire objects or semantic concepts. This progression from specific to general is a form of representational abstraction that mimics the hierarchy observed in biological visual cortices. Formally, the ability of a network to approximate functions is governed by the Universal Approximation Theorem, which states that a feedforward network with a single hidden layer containing a sufficient number of neurons can approximate any continuous function on compact subsets of R^n (n-dimensional real space). However, while this result guarantees representational capacity, it does not address issues of efficiency, generalization, or trainability. Deeper networks can express certain functions exponentially more efficiently than shallow ones. For example, functions that require compositional computation such as parsing sentences, computing parity, or classifying textures benefit from depth because they involve nested or structured patterns that are difficult to flatten. Telgarsky (2016) showed that there exist functions computable by deep networks with a polynomial number of parameters that would require exponentially more parameters in shallow counterparts.

The hierarchical structure of DL also contributes to robustness and transferability. Learned representations in intermediate layers often generalize across tasks and domains, enabling TL. A CNN trained on ImageNet, for instance, can be adapted to classify medical images with few modifications. This is because the lower-layer features are generic, while task-specific information is captured in higher layers. Hierarchical representations are particularly valuable for structured data. In natural language, embedding layers transform words into dense vectors that encode syntactic and semantic similarity. Recurrent or Transformer-based architectures then model the compositional structure of sentences, capturing grammar, dependencies, and discourse relations. Such layering is essential for tasks like translation, summarization, and question answering. Autoencoders are another paradigm where hierarchical learning is evident. In a deep autoencoder, the encoder maps input data into a compressed latent space, and the decoder reconstructs the input. The latent space acts as a bottleneck that forces the network to learn abstract features. Stacked autoencoders, where multiple encoders are layered, further deepen the abstraction process and can uncover features useful for clustering, anomaly detection, or visualization.

The expressiveness of deep networks has also been studied from an information-theoretic standpoint. The Information Bottleneck Theory posits that deep networks learn to compress input data while preserving relevant information for the target task. Layers closer to the input retain more variability, while deeper layers distill this variability into compact, task-relevant codes. This suggests that representational power is not merely about capacity but also about selective abstraction. Despite their power, deep hierarchical models are prone to overfitting if not properly regularized. Techniques such as dropout, batch normalization, and weight decay help control the effective complexity of the model and encourage generalization. Dropout, for instance, randomly disables neurons during training, forcing the network to develop redundant pathways that enhance robustness. Another limitation lies in interpretability. While the hierarchical nature of features can be visualized and understood to some extent (e.g., via feature maps in CNNs or attention maps in Transformers) deeper layers often encode abstract patterns that are hard to relate directly to human concepts. This black-box nature is a challenge in safety-critical applications.

Training very deep networks also presents optimization difficulties. The vanishing and exploding gradient problems, particularly acute in networks with dozens of layers, can hinder learning. Solutions like ReLU activations, residual connections, and normalization layers have been instrumental in enabling the training of deeper architectures. Residual networks (ResNets), introduced in 2015, revolutionized hierarchical learning by enabling networks with hundreds or even thousands of layers. A residual block computes $y = f(x)+x$, allowing gradients to flow more easily during backpropagation. This innovation addressed the degradation problem, where deeper models paradoxically performed worse than shallower ones. Hierarchical learning also facilitates modularity and reuse. Features learned in one domain can often be repurposed in another, as seen in multitask learning and TL. Shared intermediate layers allow different tasks to benefit from common abstractions, improving data efficiency and generalization.

In UL and SSL_self, hierarchical representations emerge even without explicit labels. Models such as SimCLR or BERT learn layer-wise abstractions where lower layers encode general structure and upper layers refine this into task-specific representations. These hierarchies arise from the learning objective and the architecture itself, without the need for human-defined supervision. From a computational perspective, deep models require careful management of memory and time complexity. The deeper the model, the greater the number of parameters and the longer the training time. Techniques such as layer-wise pretraining (used in early deep belief networks) and gradient checkpointing mitigate these costs. Hierarchical features also underpin recent advances in generative modeling. In variational autoencoders and Generative Adversarial Networks (GANs), latent variables are organized hierarchically to capture high-level semantics and fine details. Hierarchical VAEs, for example, use multiple latent layers to model complex distributions with greater fidelity. In RL, hierarchical architectures enable multi-level control. High-level policies plan over abstract actions or goals, while low-level controllers execute detailed movements. This division of labor allows for more scalable and transferable behaviors across environments and tasks. The concept of compositionality, where complex concepts are built from simpler parts, is naturally captured by hierarchical learning. In language, for instance, words combine into phrases, which in turn form sentences. Hierarchical models mirror this structure, enabling syntactic parsing and semantic interpretation. Theoretical work has begun to explore the mathematical limits of hierarchical representation. Recent studies use topological data analysis and manifold learning to examine how layers deform data geometry. These insights reveal how deep networks disentangle data manifolds, flattening or stretching them to simplify decision boundaries.

Another frontier is the use of hierarchical attention mechanisms, particularly in Transformer models. In models like Longformer or BigBird, attention is structured hierarchically to scale to longer sequences. This layering preserves local detail while enabling global context integration, enhancing performance in document understanding and genomic analysis. Hierarchical learning is also at the core of curriculum learning, where models are trained on tasks of increasing complexity. This mirrors human pedagogy and facilitates stable convergence. By building on prior layers of knowledge, the model progressively masters more abstract and complex behaviors. Cross-modal learning benefits from hierarchical alignment between modalities. In CLIP, for example, visual and textual representations are aligned at multiple levels, allowing the model to generalize across domains. This alignment is only possible because each modality encodes a hierarchy of features that can be mapped onto each other. To ensure robustness, adversarial training has been applied to hierarchical models. Perturbations at different layers can help the model learn invariant representations that withstand noise and adversarial manipulation, a key requirement for deployment in safety-critical systems.

5.4.4 KEY APPLICATIONS: VISION, LANGUAGE, AND PATTERN RECOGNITION

DL's transformative impact on AI has been most visibly realized in its applications to computer vision, NLP, and pattern recognition. These domains, historically challenging due to their high dimensionality and variability, have become fertile ground for the deployment of deep architectures such as CNNs, RNNs, and Transformers. The surge in practical success dates to the early 2010s, notably after the landmark performance of AlexNet in the 2012 ImageNet competition, which demonstrated a dramatic leap in image classification accuracy.

In computer vision, CNNs have become the de facto standard for image-related tasks, owing to their ability to exploit spatial hierarchies in data. A typical CNN uses convolutional layers to extract local features, pooling layers to reduce spatial dimensions while retaining salient information, and fully connected layers for classification or regression tasks. This architecture allows for translational invariance and parameter sharing, which is crucial in tasks where patterns may appear in different locations. Applications of CNNs span across facial recognition, medical image analysis, object detection (e.g., YOLO, SSD), and autonomous vehicle perception systems. Image classification tasks have been revolutionized by deeper CNN architectures such as VGGNet (2014), ResNet (2015), and EfficientNet (2019), each improving on model accuracy and training efficiency. In object detection and segmentation, models like Mask R-CNN (2017) have introduced parallel branches to simultaneously detect object boundaries and classify instances, enabling real-time applications in healthcare diagnostics, industrial quality control, and smart surveillance. In the domain of language, RNNs were long the backbone of sequence modeling. However, their limited ability to handle long-term dependencies led to the rise of gated architectures such as LSTM and GRUs, first proposed in the 1990s but popularized in the 2010s. These models allowed for capturing context in sentence structures and temporal sequences, supporting tasks such as speech recognition, machine translation, and text generation.

The model shift in NLP occurred with the introduction of the Transformer architecture in 2017 by Vaswani. By discarding recurrence and using self-attention mechanisms, Transformers achieved parallelization during training and captured global dependencies more effectively. This model became the basis for *BERT* (2018), GPT (2018 onward), and numerous other LLMs. Today, tasks like question answering, summarization, and dialogue generation are dominated by Transformer-based systems, with open-ended generative capabilities and TL made possible via pretrain-ing–fine-tuning workflows.

Pattern recognition, broadly encompassing tasks in vision, audio, and time series analysis, has also benefited from DL's hierarchical feature extraction. In audio recognition, convolutional and recurrent models are used to classify sound events, recognize speech, and transcribe music. WaveNet, introduced by DeepMind in 2016, leveraged dilated convolutions to model raw audio waveforms, achieving realistic speech synthesis. Similarly, spectrogram-based inputs fed into CNNs or Convolutional Recurrent Neural Networks (CRNNs) yield strong results in audio tagging and music information retrieval. In biometric recognition, DL has enabled robust identification through iris patterns, fingerprints, voice signals, and gait. These applications demand high accuracy and low false acceptance rates, often requiring ensemble models and large-scale pretraining. The representational depth of NNs allows for extracting invariant features from noisy, high-variability input data, which is particularly valuable in security-sensitive domains. Medical imaging is another domain that exemplifies the practical value of DL. From the classification of chest X-rays to the segmentation of brain tumors in MRI scans, CNNs have been trained to assist radiologists with accuracy that sometimes rivals human performance. TL has been essential in overcoming the scarcity of labeled data.

In industrial applications, pattern recognition is used in predictive maintenance, anomaly detection, and process control. Time series data from sensors are modeled using LSTMs or 1D-CNNs to forecast machine failures or detect deviations from normal operations. These systems contribute significantly to reducing downtime and improving reliability in manufacturing and energy sectors. Vision-based quality inspection in manufacturing employs high-resolution cameras and DCNNs to iden-tify defects in products at speeds and accuracies unattainable by human inspectors. Such systems are increasingly integrated with robotics, enabling automated sort-ing, assembly, and inspection pipelines. In agriculture, vision systems powered by DL identify crop diseases, estimate yield, and guide precision farming equipment. Drones equipped with image recognition systems capture multispectral data, which is processed in real time to make agronomic decisions. These applications support sustainability and optimize resource utilization. In education and e-learning, NLP-based applications analyze student writing, offer automated feedback, and detect plagiarism. Speech recognition systems provide accessibility tools, while recom-mendation engines personalize learning content. These intelligent systems often rely on pretrained Transformer models and fine-grained pattern classifiers. In finance, DL is used for fraud detection, credit scoring, and algorithmic trading. CNNs and LSTMs analyze transactional patterns to detect anomalies, while attention-based models forecast market trends using historical and textual data from financial reports or news. These models often operate under real-time constraints and must be robust against adversarial manipulation. In environmental monitoring, satellite imagery processed through deep networks is used for land use classification, defor-estation tracking, and natural disaster prediction. Semantic segmentation models enable pixel-wise classification of terrain, aiding decision-making in urban planning and disaster response.

The scalability of DL models to large data volumes is a key enabler in these applications. Distributed training on cloud-based platforms and the use of model compression (e.g., pruning, quantization) have allowed deployment in edge devices, such as smartphones or embedded systems in autonomous vehicles. Autonomous systems such as drones, robots, and self-driving cars combine computer vision, sensor fusion, and RL to perceive their environment, make decisions, and take actions. DL models analyze LiDAR data, camera feeds, and radar signals to perform tasks like lane detection, object avoidance, and path planning. In social media platforms, content recommendation systems utilize deep embeddings and collaborative filtering techniques to suggest posts, videos, or ads based on user behavior. These models learn high-dimensional representations of both users and content, often using architectures like deep factorization machines or Transformers.

Gaming and entertainment have also embraced DL. Character animation, behavior simulation, and procedural content generation are driven by NNs trained on motion capture data or gameplay histories. DRL has been used to train agents that learn complex strategies in games like Dota 2 and StarCraft II.

The ability of DL to extract hierarchical representations is a common thread across these applications. Whether through spatial hierarchies in images, temporal hierarchies in sequences, or semantic hierarchies in text, the models learn abstract features that capture essential structure while discarding irrelevant variation. Nevertheless, challenges remain. DL systems require substantial labeled data, and many domains suffer from annotation scarcity. Moreover, ensuring model fairness, interpretability, and robustness under adversarial conditions is an ongoing concern. Regulatory frameworks in sectors like healthcare and finance further demand transparency in automated decision-making. Evaluation in applied DL goes beyond traditional metrics. In medical imaging, for example, precision-recall trade-offs may have life-critical implications, necessitating the use of ROC curves, sensitivity-specificity analysis, and expert validation. Similarly, in recommendation systems, metrics like NDCG or click-through rate are prioritized over raw accuracy. The real-world impact of DL across vision, language, and pattern recognition is vast and growing. These models have moved from research labs into products and services, transforming how machines perceive and interact with the world. As model architectures evolve and data availability expands, the integration of DL into complex, human-centric environments will continue to accelerate, reshaping industries and redefining the boundaries of AI.

5.4.5 LINKS WITH FEW-SHOT, SELF-SUPERVISED, AND REINFORCEMENT LEARNING

The convergence of DL with other paradigms such as FSL, SSL_self, and RL has given rise to a new generation of models that are more flexible, generalizable, and efficient. While each of these approaches was initially conceived in relative isolation, recent research has increasingly blurred the boundaries between them. The underlying motivation is to address some of the longstanding limitations of DL, particularly its dependence on large labeled datasets and its limited adaptability to novel or low-data situations. FSL, which became prominent around 2015 with works like

Matching Networks and later Prototypical Networks (2017), aims to enable neural architectures to generalize from only a handful of examples. These methods often rely on an embedding function f_θ learned via DL. This use of a learned metric space aligns well with deep representation learning and forms a natural link between DL and few-shot approaches. ZSL pushes this generalization even further by expecting models to classify or act upon entirely unseen classes. Typically, this is achieved by leveraging auxiliary information, such as class descriptions, attributes, or embeddings in a shared semantic space. One well-known early example is the DeViSE model (2013), which projected both images and class labels into a common vector space. More recently, models like CLIP (2021) have demonstrated the power of joint image-text training, using contrastive learning to learn transferable representations without explicit supervision.

SSL_self has emerged as a powerful enabler of both few-shot and zero-shot capabilities. By leveraging massive unlabeled datasets and pretext tasks, SSL allows networks to acquire rich, general-purpose representations that can be adapted to downstream tasks with minimal supervision. Contrastive learning objectives, masked prediction (e.g., BERT, MAE), and self-distillation techniques (e.g., BYOL, DINO) have all contributed to the robustness and versatility of DL backbones. A central idea connecting SSL and FSL is that of pretraining followed by fine-tuning or adaptation. When a model is pretrained via self-supervised methods, it learns a structured feature space that captures semantic relationships between inputs. This structure greatly facilitates the rapid learning of new tasks from few examples, as the model needs only to learn lightweight task-specific adaptations rather than building representations from scratch. In many ways, SSL is a bridge between the generalization capability of DL and the data efficiency demanded by few-shot scenarios. For example, the combination of MoCo (2020) for pretraining and Prototypical Networks for downstream adaptation has achieved strong results in few-shot image classification benchmarks like miniImageNet and tieredImageNet. These pipelines have also demonstrated robustness in real-world domains such as medical imaging, where labeled data is expensive.

Reinforcement learning also intersects with DL in critical ways. DRL, which emerged in full force with the success of DQNs in 2015, relies on deep architectures to approximate value functions or policies over high-dimensional state spaces. However, DRL traditionally requires large amounts of interaction data, often millions of steps, which poses practical challenges. Here, SSL_self has been proposed as a way to improve sample efficiency by learning representations of the state space that facilitate downstream value estimation or policy optimization. For example, Self-Predictive Representations (SPR) and contrastive RL methods like CURL exploit auxiliary losses to pretrain encoders in an RL pipeline. These methods introduce an additional objective to be able to calculate using Equation (5.23):

$$\mathcal{L}_{\text{SSL}} = \mathcal{L}_{\text{RL}} + \lambda \mathcal{L}_{\text{aux}} \tag{5.23}$$

where L_{RL} is the standard RL loss (e.g., Q-learning), and Laux is a self-supervised objective (e.g., contrastive loss). The regularization parameter λ balances learning from rewards and from structural properties of the input data.

Meta-reinforcement learning provides another point of convergence with FSL. In this paradigm, agents learn to adapt quickly to new tasks or environments after limited interaction. Algorithms such as MAML have been extended to RL settings, allowing agents to optimize for adaptability. The meta-objective is to minimize post-update loss after a small number of gradient steps on a new task using Equation (5.24):

$$\min_{\theta} \sum_{T_i \sim p(T)} \mathcal{L}_{T_i}\left(U_\theta\left(T_i\right)\right) \tag{5.24}$$

where $U_\theta\left(T_i\right)$ is the updated model after inner-loop adaptation to task T_i.

This aligns strongly with FSL goals and has led to new RL agents capable of rapid online adaptation.

Zero-shot RL, while less mature, is also emerging as a field of research. The idea is to train agents on a distribution of environments such that they can generalize to entirely novel configurations without retraining. This may involve using high-level goal descriptions, language instructions, or environment attributes to enable transfer. Models like Decision Transformer (2021), which formulate RL as a sequence modeling problem, offer promise in this direction by conditioning on desired outcomes rather than policies or value estimates. Multimodal pretraining, particularly using vision-language models like CLIP or Flamingo, further tightens the link between SSL and zero-shot generalization. These models learn aligned representations across modalities and are thus capable of zero-shot classification, image captioning, and instruction following all without task-specific fine-tuning. This cross-modal ability is deeply rooted in the representational power of deep architectures. Table 5.8 summarized key methods and their cross-paradigm capabilities.

TABLE 5.8
A Summary of Key Methods and Their Cross-Paradigm Capabilities

Method	Model(s) Involved	Contribution	Year
PrototypicalNet	Few-shot + DL	Metric-based adaptation	2017
MoCo	SSL + DL	Contrastive pretraining	2020
CURL	SSL + RL	Self-supervised encoder in RL	2020
CLIP	SSL + Zero-shot + Vision/ Text	Contrastive multimodal training	2021
MAML-RL	Few-shot + RL	Fast task adaptation	2017+
Decision Transformer	Zero-shot + RL + DL	Goal-conditioned sequence modeling	2021

The increased availability of large-scale pretraining data (e.g., web-scale text and image corpora) has allowed deep models to acquire abstract structures that enable few-shot or zero-shot behavior even without explicit design. This observation led to the emergence of foundation models like GPT, which display emergent generalization capacities that resemble zero-shot reasoning capabilities. In robotics and embodied AI, these integrations are increasingly operational. Agents that interact with real-world environments often have limited supervision and must adapt on the fly. Using SSL for perception, few-shot for skill acquisition, and RL for control, these systems demonstrate the practical synthesis of these learning strategies. However, combining these paradigms is not without challenges. Alignment between pretraining objectives (e.g., SSL) and downstream tasks (e.g., RL policies) is not always guaranteed. Furthermore, issues such as representation collapse, overfitting in few-shot adaptation, or reward sparsity in RL continue to limit performance and stability. Another practical consideration is computational cost. Training large self-supervised models, few-shot learners, and DRL agents all demand significant resources. Jointly optimizing across paradigms further increases complexity, requiring careful model design and training schedules. Despite these challenges, the synergy between deep architectures, FSL, self-supervised methods, and reinforcement learning is increasingly viewed as essential for building adaptive, general-purpose intelligence. These connections provide not only efficiency in learning but also flexibility in behavior and reasoning. Ultimately, the most promising frontier in AI lies not in the supremacy of any one model, but in their thoughtful integration. The fusion of SSL, RL, and FSL under the umbrella of DL enables machines to perceive, adapt, and act in complex and changing environments with minimal human supervision as an essential step toward truly autonomous AI.

5.5   OTHER CONNECTIONIST AND EVOLUTIONARY MODELS

5.5.1   EVOLUTIONARY ALGORITHMS

EAs constitute a family of optimization methods inspired by biological evolution and collective behavior observed in nature. These algorithms diverge fundamentally from gradient-based learning methods, as they do not require differentiable objective functions and can efficiently search large, complex, and multimodal spaces. The earliest roots of evolutionary computation can be traced back to the 1950s and 60s, when researchers like *Alan Turing*, *Alex Fraser*, and *Ingo Rechenberg* explored the idea of artificial evolution. However, the field crystallized with the formalization of genetic algorithms by *John Holland* in 1975 through his seminal book Adaptation in Natural and Artificial Systems. A Genetic Algorithm (GA) operates by simulating the Darwinian process of natural selection. A population of candidate solutions, represented typically as binary or real-valued strings (chromosomes), evolves through successive generations by undergoing selection, crossover (recombination), and mutation. The fitness of each individual is assessed using a predefined fitness function that quantifies its quality with respect to the problem at hand. Crossover enables the recombination of good traits, while mutation introduces variability to explore new regions of the search space. Over generations, fitter individuals are more likely to reproduce, leading to the emergence of high-performing solutions.

The GA cycle begins with an initial random population and proceeds iteratively as follows: evaluate the fitness of all individuals, select parents based on fitness (e.g., roulette-wheel, tournament selection), apply crossover and mutation to generate off-spring, and replace part or all of the population. Figure 5.4 illustrates the generic workflow of an evolutionary algorithm, including the initialization, evaluation, selection, crossover, mutation, and replacement stages, as well as the stopping criterion.

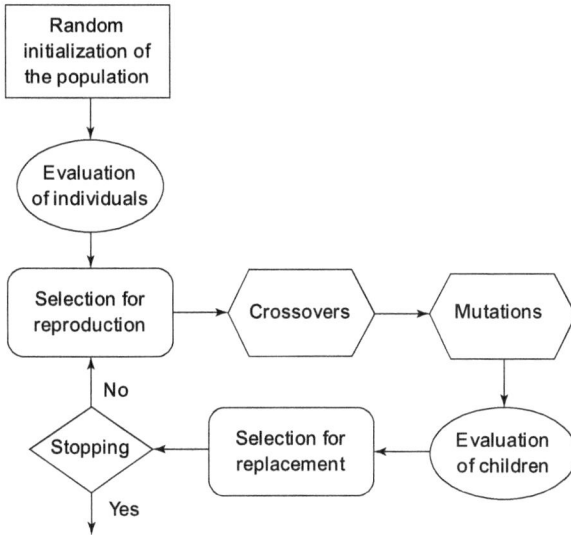

FIGURE 5.4   General structure of an evolutionary algorithm.

This simple yet powerful mechanism allows GAs to optimize highly nonlinear and poorly understood functions, making them suitable for design, scheduling, tuning, and combinatorial problems. Parallel to GAs, evolutionary strategies, pioneered by Rechenberg and Schwefel in the 1970s in Germany, focused more on continuous optimization problems. ES differs from GAs by using self-adaptive mechanisms to control mutation rates and search step sizes. In ES, individuals often carry strategy parameters that evolve alongside the solution vector. This allows the algorithm to fine-tune its exploration behavior autonomously and has led to applications in aerodynamic design, structural optimization, and robotics. In the 1990s, the scope of evolutionary computation expanded with the introduction of swarm intelligence models. Particle Swarm Optimization (PSO), developed by Kennedy and Eberhart in 1995, was inspired by the coordinated movement of bird flocks and fish schools. In PSO, each solution is a particle in the search space with a velocity vector. Particles adjust their positions based on their own experience and that of their neighbors, converging toward optimal regions through social interaction and personal memory. Mathematically, the velocity update rule in PSO is given by Equation (5.25):

$$v_i\left(t+1\right) = \omega v_i\left(t\right) + c_1 r_1\left(p_i - x_i\left(t\right)\right) + c_2 r_2\left(g - x_i\left(t\right)\right) \qquad (5.25)$$

where v_i is the velocity of particle i, x_i its position, p_i its best-known position, g the global best, ω the inertia weight, and r_1, r_2 are random scalars. The constants c_1 and c_2 control the balance between individual learning and social learning.

Ant Colony Optimization (ACO), introduced by Dorigo in 1992, draws inspiration from the foraging behavior of real ant colonies, where ants deposit pheromones on paths to communicate promising routes. ACO is particularly suited to discrete combinatorial problems like the Traveling Salesman Problem (TSP), vehicle routing, and network routing. In ACO, artificial ants probabilistically build solutions and reinforce successful paths by depositing more pheromones, creating a feedback loop that balances exploration and exploitation. The probabilistic transition rule in ACO typically shown as Equation (5.26):

$$P_{ij}^k\left(t\right) = \frac{\left(T_{ij}\left(t\right)\right)^\alpha \cdot \left(\eta_{ij}\right)^\beta}{\sum_{l \in N_i} \left(T_{ij}\left(t\right)\right)^\alpha \cdot \left(\eta_{ij}\right)^\beta} \qquad (5.26)$$

where τ_{ij} is the pheromone level on edge (i, j), η_{ij} is the heuristic value (e.g., inverse of distance), and α, β control the influence of pheromone and heuristic information, respectively.

5.5.2 METAHEURISTICS AND INTELLIGENT OPTIMIZATION

Metaheuristics are high-level problem-independent algorithmic frameworks designed to find near-optimal solutions for complex optimization problems. Unlike exact algorithms, which guarantee optimality but often at prohibitive computational costs, metaheuristics provide practical approaches to tackle intractable, nonconvex, discontinuous, and high-dimensional problems. The term "metaheuristic" gained popularity in the 1980s and 1990s with the proliferation of population-based and trajectory-based optimization techniques inspired by natural and physical processes. These methods are especially valuable in AI for model tuning, feature selection, hyperparameter optimization, and combinatorial planning. One of the earliest and most influential metaheuristics is Simulated Annealing, introduced by Kirkpatrick, Gelatt, and Vecchi in 1983. It is inspired by the physical process of annealing in metallurgy, where a material is slowly cooled to achieve a minimum energy state. SA explores the solution space by accepting not only better solutions but also, with a probability decreasing over time, worse ones—thus allowing it to escape local minima. The probability of accepting a worse solution ΔE at temperature T is governed by Equation (5.27):

$$P = \exp\left(-\frac{\Delta E}{T}\right) \qquad (5.27)$$

This stochastic acceptance criterion enables a global exploration early on and gradually shifts toward exploitation as the temperature decreases, typically following an exponential or logarithmic cooling schedule.

Another milestone in metaheuristics is the Tabu Search, proposed by Fred Glover in 1986. Unlike greedy approaches that may get trapped in cycles or local minima, Tabu Search maintains a memory structure (the "tabu list") that forbids or penalizes revisiting recently explored solutions. This memory-guided exploration promotes diversification and avoids short-term repetitions. The method has been highly successful in solving scheduling problems, traveling salesman variants, and integer programming cases. GAs and PSO, while already considered evolutionary methods, also fall under the metaheuristic umbrella due to their stochastic, iterative nature and general applicability. These algorithms excel in exploring large solution spaces without requiring gradient information and are especially effective in AI when tuning parameters of NNs, SVMs, or fuzzy systems. In the early 2000s, newer nature-inspired metaheuristics emerged. Harmony Search (HS), introduced by Geem, Kim, and Loganathan in 2001, mimics the improvisation process of musicians aiming to achieve harmony. Solutions correspond to musical harmonies, and the algorithm searches through pitch adjustment, memory consideration, and randomization. Despite its simplicity, HS has shown competitive performance in continuous optimization and engineering design problems. Another popular technique is the Firefly Algorithm (FA), developed by Xin-She Yang in 2008. Inspired by the flashing behavior of fireflies, this algorithm attracts solutions based on their brightness (objective function value), modulated by distance and a light absorption coefficient. It is particularly effective for multimodal function optimization and has been adapted for feature selection and clustering tasks in ML. Cuckoo Search (CS), introduced by Yang and Deb in 2009, draws inspiration from the brood parasitism of some cuckoo species. It uses Lévy flights—a form of random walk with heavy-tailed distributions—to ensure both local and global search. New candidate solutions (eggs) replace worse ones in nests with a fixed probability. CS has found applications in model selection, forecasting, and energy system optimization.

One of the key advantages of metaheuristics is their broad applicability. They are not tailored to specific problem structures and can often be implemented with minimal problem-specific modifications. This flexibility has made them central to intelligent optimization in AI, particularly in scenarios where objective functions are expensive to evaluate, noisy, or lack gradient information. However, the performance of metaheuristics is often sensitive to algorithmic parameters such as cooling schedules, population sizes, mutation rates, or memory lengths. Proper tuning, sometimes requiring meta-optimization (e.g., using one metaheuristic to tune another), becomes essential for achieving competitive results. Hybridization strategies combining, for example, PSO with local search, or integrating SA with NNs, help balance exploration and exploitation. In recent years, metaheuristics have been integrated into DL workflows, especially in neural architecture search and hyperparameter tuning. Methods like genetic programming or swarm intelligence are used to evolve network topologies or learning parameters. While computationally intensive, these approaches have achieved state-of-the-art results in image classification, language modeling, and reinforcement learning tasks. Theoretical analysis of meta-heuristics remains a challenge due to their stochastic and problem-dependent nature. However, convergence proofs and empirical benchmarks continue to expand understanding, especially regarding balance between diversification and intensification. Benchmarking platforms like CEC competitions provide standardized environments to test and compare metaheuristics.

5.5.3 CONTRIBUTIONS TO COMPLEX PROBLEM-SOLVING

The integration of connectionist and evolutionary models into the domain of complex problem-solving has marked a significant milestone in the development of AI since the 1980s. These models have proven particularly effective in addressing problems characterized by high dimensionality, combinatorial complexity, nonlinearity, and incomplete or noisy information. Their ability to navigate rugged search spaces, escape local optima, and exploit implicit structure makes them powerful tools in domains where traditional analytical methods or classical logic-based approaches often fall short. One of the earliest and most influential contributions in this context came from neuroevolution techniques, which aim to evolve the architecture and/or parameters of NNs using genetic algorithms or other evolutionary strategies. The NeuroEvolution of Augmenting Topologies (NEAT), introduced by *Kenneth Stanley* in 2002, provided a way to simultaneously evolve network weights and structure. NEAT dynamically grows the topology over generations, beginning with simple networks and gradually increasing complexity, which is especially advantageous for reinforcement learning tasks where the network's structure is not known a priori. NEAT and its variants have been used to solve problems in game playing, robot navigation, and function approximation. EAs have also been employed to solve NP-hard problems in scheduling, resource allocation, and logistics. For instance, Multi-Objective Evolutionary Algorithms (MOEAs), such as NSGA-II, allow for the simultaneous optimization of conflicting objectives, producing a Pareto front of nondominated solutions. These methods have been widely adopted in manufacturing systems, transportation planning, and even drug discovery, where trade-offs between efficiency, cost, and robustness must be managed simultaneously.

In symbolic regression and analytical model generation, Genetic Programming (GP), originally proposed by John Koza in 1992, enables the automatic discovery of mathematical expressions or algorithmic structures that explain data or perform tasks. GP has been applied to discover physical laws from raw data (e.g., *Schmidt & Lipson*, 2009), to automate the creation of financial models, and to evolve control systems in autonomous agents. The flexibility of the tree-based representation in GP allows it to explore a vast and expressive hypothesis space, albeit with computational cost. Swarm-based algorithms have also been applied successfully to complex pattern recognition tasks. PSO and ACO are often used to fine-tune NN hyperparameters, select optimal features in high-dimensional datasets, or perform clustering in unstructured data. For instance, hybrid PSO-ANN models have shown competitive performance in classification tasks in medical diagnostics, where the solution space is highly nonlinear and noisy. Similarly, ACO has been used in bioinformatics to identify motifs in DNA sequences and to optimize routes in network communication systems. In intelligent control systems, connectionist-evolutionary hybrids have enabled the real-time adaptation of controllers for dynamic systems. Examples include evolving fuzzy-neural controllers for robotics and unmanned aerial vehicles, where system dynamics are partially unknown or change over time. These adaptive models rely on feedback from the environment and evolutionary search to continuously refine control rules or network weights, making them suitable for deployment in unpredictable environments. The integration of these models into simulation-based problem solving has also opened new frontiers. In digital twins and simulation-based optimization, surrogate models built using NNs are coupled with evolutionary search to iteratively refine design configurations. This is particularly useful in engineering disciplines where running high-fidelity simulations (e.g., CFD or FEA) is computationally expensive. The surrogate models provide quick approximations while evolutionary strategies guide the exploration toward promising regions.

Connectionist and evolutionary approaches have also played a crucial role in MAS, where decentralized agents interact to solve distributed problems such as traffic control, disaster response, or resource distribution. Swarm intelligence principles, particularly from ant and bee colonies, inform collective behaviors like foraging, task allocation, and pathfinding. Evolutionary learning enables agents to adapt strategies over time, leading to emergent coordination without centralized control. One area that illustrates the potential of these models in complex problem-solving is game AI. From neuroevolutionary models for agent behavior in strategy games to genetic algorithms used to evolve winning strategies in board games, these models have been used not just for automation but also for the generation of novel and human-competitive behaviors. In procedural content generation, GP and EAs are used to create maps, levels, or puzzles in an adaptive and user-responsive manner. In the energy sector, hybrid evolutionary models have been used to optimize smart grid operations, energy consumption forecasting, and the configuration of renewable energy systems. These problems involve large-scale variables, temporal dynamics, and multiple stakeholders. Techniques like differential evolution and evolutionary multi-objective optimization have been integrated with ANN-based forecasting models to balance supply and demand with minimal carbon footprint. Similarly, in healthcare, evolutionary NNs have been employed for early disease detection, prognosis modeling, and personalized treatment planning. The complexity of biomedical data, heterogeneous, temporal, and often incomplete, necessitates flexible models that can generalize while remaining robust. The ability to optimize feature subsets, network architectures, and interpretability constraints simultaneously is one of the core strengths of these methods in such domains.

A further contribution is seen in the area of adversarial problem-solving and security. Evolutionary models have been used to generate adversarial inputs for robustness testing of DL systems, revealing vulnerabilities in classification boundaries. At the same time, co-evolutionary strategies have been explored where classifiers and adversaries evolve in tandem, promoting resilience and robustness.

5.6 TOWARD HYBRID AND DISTRIBUTED INTELLIGENCE

5.6.1 HYBRID APPROACHES: COMBINING LOGIC AND LEARNING

The convergence of logic-based reasoning and learning-based models has seen significant advancements in recent years, particularly between 2020 and 2024, marking a renewed interest in hybrid architectures capable of balancing formal expressiveness and statistical adaptability. While symbolic AI, grounded in logic and rules, provides structured reasoning and interpretability, it lacks robustness when exposed to noisy or unstructured data. On the other hand, neural models excel at generalizing from raw data but often fail to provide guarantees of consistency or explainability. The hybrid paradigm addresses this divide by integrating symbolic knowledge into differentiable models, thereby creating AI systems that are more adaptable, interpretable, and context-aware across a wide range of applications.

A key milestone in this evolution was the introduction of Logic Tensor Networks (LTNs), refined significantly between 2020 and 2022, which embed logical formulas within continuous vector spaces, allowing soft reasoning with learnable predicates. LTNs support reasoning under uncertainty while maintaining compatibility with classical first-order logic. Their differentiable nature permits integration with modern neural architectures, enabling end-to-end training of models that can infer, complete, or verify knowledge bases, especially useful in medical informatics and compliance-sensitive fields. Another prominent development is Neural Theorem Provers (NTPs), enhanced between 2021 and 2023, which blend symbolic backward-chaining proof search with trainable similarity functions. These models apply gradient descent to theorem proving by relaxing symbolic unification into continuous similarity scoring. NTPs have been shown to scale to large knowledge graphs and provide generalization beyond observed facts, addressing limitations in both classical provers and black-box models. More recently, DeepProbLog 2.0, released in 2023, has extended probabilistic logic programming to incorporate neural predicates and stochastic reasoning in a unified computational graph. It allows symbolic logic and DL modules to operate jointly, with applications ranging from robotics planning under uncertainty to AI safety systems. The key innovation lies in backpropagation-compatible semantics, making symbolic programs trainable by standard SGD, and thus compatible with existing DL frameworks.

Hybrid approaches are also increasingly employed in vision-language tasks, particularly in large-scale models trained on multimodal datasets. Between 2021 and 2024, models like FLAVA (2022), OWL-ViT (2023) and Kosmos-2 (2023) have demonstrated how symbolic grounding (e.g., object categories, scene graphs) can be integrated into Vision Transformers. These systems achieve superior performance in image captioning, visual question answering, and grounded language understanding by encoding symbolic structures into prompts or alignment layers, improving robustness and reducing hallucination. In program synthesis, hybrid models are gaining traction. Systems like CodeT5+ (2023) and OpenAI's Codex (2021–2022) incorporate programming language syntax and semantic rules into Transformer architectures, enabling the generation of syntactically correct and semantically meaningful code. These systems implicitly learn constraints from code corpora, but recent works—such as Neural-Symbolic Execution Networks (NeSy-X, 2024)—make these constraints explicit by incorporating logical type checking and execution verification into the generation pipeline. The symbolic regularization paradigm has also matured in recent years. Methods proposed in 2021–3 use logical constraints directly in the loss function, such as monotonicity, fairness, or causal consistency. For example, in clinical applications, hybrid models ensure that a predicted dosage does not decrease with increased severity of symptoms, encoding such rules as differentiable inequalities in the training objective. This improves trust and usability, particularly in high-stakes domains. Notably, language models are now being fine-tuned with symbolic feedback. Since 2022, the alignment of LLMs like ChatGPT or Claude with human preferences has incorporated structured knowledge distillation from symbolic rules or expert systems. Efforts like TruthfulQA with Logical Constraints (2023) inject logical consistency checks post-generation, reducing factual errors and improving reasoning in multi-hop question answering.

In robotics and embodied AI, hybrid agents increasingly combine symbolic task planners with learned policies. Between 2020 and 2024, frameworks like Learning Execution via Grounded Optimization (LEGO) and VIPER have enabled robots to decompose high-level symbolic goals (e.g., "pick and place") into low-level control commands using neural controllers trained via imitation learning. These approaches allow task generalization across environments, combining the flexibility of perception models with the precision of logic-based planners. A key application area for hybrid AI is scientific reasoning. Since 2021, systems like AI-Feynman 2.0 and Eureqa-PG have demonstrated that NNs trained on simulation data can identify symbolic equations consistent with known physical laws. These models use NNs to detect patterns, then apply symbolic regression or theorem proving to formulate interpretable hypotheses, assisting physicists and chemists in generating verifiable models from raw experimental data. In healthcare, hybrid architectures are helping bridge structured knowledge and unstructured records. Between 2022 and 2024, hybrid diagnostic models have integrated neural feature extractors with logical symptom-disease ontologies. For example, NNs classify medical imaging data, while symbolic systems verify diagnostic paths against clinical guidelines encoded in knowledge graphs like SNOMED CT or UMLS. This not only improves diagnostic accuracy but ensures alignment with medical standards. In education and intelligent tutoring systems, hybrid models are used to assess learner behavior and provide adaptive instruction. As of 2023, systems like EDU-BERT integrate rule-based content models with Transformer-based interaction analyzers. Symbolic rules represent curriculum structure and prerequisite logic, while neural models assess student engagement and infer knowledge gaps, enabling personalized feedback with interpretable justifications.

In explainable XAI, recent hybrid models combine counterfactual reasoning with deep classifiers. Since 2022, methods like Neural-Symbolic Counterfactual Explainers (NSCE) use symbolic logic to generate minimal changes required to alter a prediction, while neural models provide confidence scores and feature attribution. This pairing has improved transparency in financial risk scoring and credit assignment systems. In automated theorem proving, the integration of DL with symbolic systems has yielded breakthroughs. Tools like MiniF2F (2021) and GPT-f (2022) use large Transformers to propose proof sketches, which are then validated or completed by symbolic logic engines. This mixed approach has enabled systems to prove theorems from formalized mathematical corpora such as Metamath and Lean, achieving results previously considered out of reach. In causal inference, hybrid models encode causal graphs and intervention logic into deep learners. Frameworks like Neural Causal Models (2023) combine neural representation learning with symbolic do-calculus. These models can identify causal structure from observational data and simulate counterfactuals, facilitating applications in policy design, marketing, and epidemiology. Efforts in ethical AI and machine law also benefit from hybridization. Between 2021 and 2024, systems have been proposed that blend neural classifiers for perception or language interpretation with deontic logic rules specifying ethical constraints (e.g., "a robot shall not harm a human"). These systems are being explored in autonomous vehicles, military robotics, and judicial AI for compliance and explainability.

In MAS, hybrid AI enables agents to reason about rules, roles, and strategies while learning from interactions. Recent platforms such as NeSyMAS (2023) incorporate symbolic goal planning and logical protocol adherence into decentralized neural agents, allowing emergent cooperation in competitive or collaborative environments, including simulated economies and distributed robotics. In generative AI, hybrid symbolic-latent models are now used to enforce structure in outputs. Tools like GenSymNet (2023) integrate symbolic grammars or constraints during generation, ensuring that generated molecules, code, or design artifacts conform to physical or logical constraints, which is crucial in drug discovery and architecture.

5.6.2   MULTI-AGENT SYSTEMS: COLLECTIVE INTELLIGENCE AND AUTONOMY

5.6.2.1   Conceptual Foundations and Emergence of MAS

The emergence of MAS represents a significant shift in the conception of distributed intelligence, where a system's global behavior emerges from the local actions and interactions of autonomous components. Unlike centralized AI systems, where intelligence is typically encapsulated in a single decision-making entity, MAS is based on the coordination of multiple agents, each with its own knowledge, goals, and capabilities, working collaboratively or competitively to solve complex tasks. The theoretical underpinnings of MAS trace back to the 1980s and 1990s in the context of distributed problem-solving, robotics, and artificial life. These early foundations emphasized the notions of autonomy, social ability, reactivity, and proactiveness, characteristics that still define intelligent agents today. Each agent in a MAS operates based on its internal state, perceives its local environment, and interacts with other agents through defined protocols, often inspired by social or biological metaphors such as insect colonies, ecosystems, or markets.

The key motivation behind MAS lies in its scalability, robustness, and adaptability. Complex problems such as logistics optimization, smart grid management, or emergency response planning are inherently distributed by nature and benefit from decentralized approaches. MAS offer a natural framework for modeling such systems, where central control is impractical or undesirable. Moreover, the ability of MAS to function under partial information, asynchronous timing, and dynamic environments makes them suitable for real-time and mission-critical applications. The autonomy of agents allows for parallelism, fault tolerance, and resilience to changes in system configuration or agent failure. At the heart of any MAS is the notion of agency. An agent is typically defined as a computational entity capable of perceiving its environment through sensors, acting upon it through effectors, and pursuing goals based on its internal reasoning. Some agents are reactive, operating on a stimulus-response basis, while others are deliberative, planning actions based on models and beliefs. Hybrid agents combine these modalities. In a MAS, agents may be homogeneous, sharing similar functions and roles, or heterogeneous, with different capabilities and decision-making mechanisms. This diversity enables the system to handle multi-faceted problems through specialization and cooperation. MAS are often described through organizational metaphors: societies of agents form coalitions, teams, or institutions; agents negotiate, coordinate, compete, or cooperate; roles and protocols define interaction rules. These metaphors are not just illustrative but operational: Agent Communication Languages (ACLs) formalize interaction through performatives (e.g., request, inform, propose), while organizational models like Contract Net Protocol or organizational ontologies such as MOISE+ define task delegation and authority hierarchies. These elements allow the design of MAS that are not only functional but explainable and predictable in their collective behavior.

The development of MAS has benefited from interdisciplinary inputs, ranging from distributed systems and control theory to cognitive science and social psychology. Cognitive MAS, for instance, incorporate models of belief, desire, and intention (BDI), enabling agents to reason about their mental states and those of others. This is particularly valuable in strategic planning, negotiation, and collaborative problem solving, where understanding the goals and expectations of peers improves coordination. The BDI architecture, formalized by Rao and Georgeff in the 1990s, remains a cornerstone in agent modeling and has been implemented in various agent development platforms like JADEX or JACK.

5.6.2.2   Coordination and Communication

In MAS, coordination and communication are foundational for enabling decentralized agents to achieve coherent global behavior. These agents, often endowed with autonomy and local knowledge, must interact and synchronize their decisions to ensure system-level consistency and optimality. The challenge lies in managing heterogeneity, uncertainty, and distributed control across multiple agents with possibly conflicting goals and perceptions. This has led to the development of a rich set of coordination paradigms, ranging from explicit negotiation to implicit emergent strategies, depending on the application domain and agent architecture.

Coordination in MAS typically involves task allocation, resource sharing, conflict resolution, and decision synchronization. One of the earliest models to support such coordination is the Contract Net Protocol (*Smith*, 1980), where agents assume roles of managers or contractors and coordinate via a bidding process. This model, though simple, laid the groundwork for more sophisticated mechanisms involving dynamic coalition formation and decentralized planning. More advanced coordination schemes incorporate market-based mechanisms, consensus protocols, and swarm-inspired strategies, depending on the required trade-off between efficiency, robustness, and scalability. Agent communication is essential to coordination, enabling information exchange, negotiation, and alignment of intentions. Communication can be direct, via message-passing systems using ACLs like KQML or FIPA-ACL, or indirect, using stigmergy, where agents communicate by modifying the environment (as in ant colonies using pheromones). Direct communication allows precise intention exchange, while stigmergic approaches favor robustness and scalability in large-scale, loosely coupled systems. The choice of communication paradigm depends heavily on the domain: real-time robotic coordination favors low-latency messaging, while large-scale simulations may leverage shared memory spaces or broadcast protocols. Coordination strategies in MAS are often classified as centralized, decentralized, or distributed. Centralized coordination offers optimality and global consistency but lacks fault tolerance and scalability. In contrast, distributed coordination enhances robustness and autonomy but may suffer from slower convergence and inconsistency under partial observability. Decentralized approaches, where agents operate based on local information and coordination emerges from interactions, offer a practical balance. Algorithms such as distributed constraint satisfaction (DisCSP) and distributed planning illustrate this hybrid design, optimizing local objectives under global constraints.

Another critical aspect of agent coordination is organizational modeling. Agents can be structured into hierarchies, teams, or institutions, each with defined roles, norms, and authority structures. Organizational frameworks like MOISE+ and OperA model agent roles and responsibilities explicitly, facilitating coordination in large MAS. These models support norm enforcement, conflict mediation, and adaptation to role changes, allowing MAS to operate in dynamic environments such as emergency response systems or multi-robot missions. Agents coordinate not only through rules or contracts but also by modeling each other's beliefs and intentions—a concept known as mutual modeling or theory of mind. In Belief-Desire-Intention (BDI) architectures, agents reason about their own and others' goals to align behavior strategically. This is particularly relevant in competitive settings or cooperative teams were anticipating the behavior of other agents enhances performance. For example, in autonomous driving scenarios, agents must predict whether neighboring vehicles intend to change lanes or yield, and respond accordingly in real-time.

Coordination also relies heavily on synchronization mechanisms. In time-sensitive environments, ensuring that agents update their states consistently is vital. Protocols like Lamport timestamps or vector clocks ensure causal ordering in message delivery, while consensus algorithms like Paxos or Raft are used in safety-critical distributed systems to maintain agreement among agents. In simulation-based MAS, discrete-event synchronization ensures that agents perceive and act based on consistent world states. In learning-based MAS, coordination is often emergent rather than rule-driven. MARL techniques enable agents to learn cooperative or competitive policies through experience. Techniques like Centralized Training with Decentralized Execution (CTDE) or value decomposition networks (e.g., QMIX) allow agents to learn global strategies while acting locally. Communication-learning approaches, such as CommNet or TarMAC, further enhance coordination by optimizing communication policies alongside action policies. These advances are particularly useful in robotics, strategic games, and dynamic resource allocation problems. MAS coordination also entails semantic interoperability, especially when agents are developed independently. Shared ontologies and knowledge representation standards are essential to ensure consistent interpretation of messages and facts. This is particularly important in heterogeneous systems like healthcare or logistics, where agents might belong to different organizations or vendors. Using description logics and semantic web standards (e.g., OWL, RDF), agents can interpret context, disambiguate terminology, and align their internal models for cooperative reasoning.

5.6.2.3   Integrating Learning into MAS

Integrating learning capabilities into MAS represents a pivotal evolution in the design of autonomous, adaptive, and scalable AI systems. Originally, MAS were primarily rule-based and designed for reactive or deliberative decision-making within predefined environments. However, as the complexity of tasks and the dynamism of real-world applications increased, the need for agents to learn from experience, improve performance over time, and adapt to unforeseen changes became evident. This integration merges two foundational aspects of AI: the distributed intelligence inherent in MAS and the empirical adaptation capabilities of ML.

The early 2000s saw the first systematic efforts to incorporate learning within MAS architectures, particularly in domains like distributed robotics and adaptive networks. Initially, RL was the primary approach adopted, allowing agents to optimize actions based on reward signals gathered through environmental interaction. Techniques such as Q-learning were applied to decentralized contexts, but challenges quickly emerged, including nonstationarity due to concurrent learning agents, credit assignment problems, and convergence issues. These complexities led to the development of specialized MARL algorithms, such as Independent Q-learning, multi-agent deep deterministic policy gradient (MADDPG), and QMIX, which facilitate coordinated learning under partial observability and dynamic environments.

Beyond RL, supervised and UL techniques have been integrated into MAS to improve perception, prediction, and communication. For example, in surveillance networks or sensor grids, agents employ UL to detect anomalies or changes in patterns without prior labels. In team-based robotics, SL is used to train agents to recognize gestures, interpret commands, or classify terrain types from camera inputs. These capabilities allow MAS to move beyond static rule-following to dynamic behavior shaping driven by data and context. The integration of learning also affects the internal architecture of agents. Cognitive agents increasingly embed NNs or decision trees within their reasoning modules, creating hybrid systems where symbolic plans are modulated by learned insights. In some architectures, learning modules act as advisory systems, suggesting decisions which are then filtered by logical constraints. In others, learning fully overrides static behavior once confidence thresholds are met. This interplay requires careful design to ensure consistency, stability, and interpretability, particularly in safety-critical applications such as autonomous vehicles or industrial control. Learning within MAS can be categorized at multiple levels: individual agent learning, where each agent adapts independently based on local data; team-level learning, where shared experiences and outcomes guide group adaptation; and system-level learning, where emergent properties are optimized through collective feedback mechanisms. For example, swarm robotics often relies on implicit collective learning, where repeated agent interactions refine global behaviors without centralized coordination or explicit communication. Alternatively, in collaborative MAS such as multi-drone delivery, agents may share experiences via centralized memories or distributed blackboards to accelerate team learning.

One major challenge is enabling learning in open MAS, where agents may be designed by different developers or belong to competing organizations. In such settings, agents must not only learn tasks but also infer the strategies and intentions of others. Here, opponent modeling and meta-learning approaches become vital. Agents learn to predict the behaviors of others and adapt strategies accordingly, especially in competitive or adversarial scenarios. This is particularly relevant in economic simulations, security protocols, and strategic gaming, where success depends on anticipating the moves of potentially deceptive or evolving opponents. Recent research has also explored federated learning in MAS, where agents train models locally and share updates rather than raw data. This approach is well-suited to privacy-sensitive environments such as healthcare or edge computing, where decentralized data cannot be pooled. Federated MARL and federated SL frameworks have been proposed to align agent learning without compromising security, leveraging synchronization protocols and aggregation algorithms to maintain performance while preserving autonomy.

Another critical dimension is the role of communication in enabling effective learning. Agents must decide what, when, and how to communicate to facilitate coordination without overwhelming the system with noise. Communication-aware learning strategies, such as attention mechanisms, message compression, and information value estimation, help agents focus on sharing only the most salient and contextually useful information. In cooperative MAS, communication protocols themselves can be learned through interaction, leading to emergent languages or negotiation strategies adapted to the task at hand. In practical applications, the integration of learning into MAS has been transformative. In smart energy grids, agents representing households or substations use RL to optimize energy consumption and respond to dynamic pricing. In traffic systems, autonomous vehicles coordinate routes while learning from real-time congestion data. In disaster response, heterogeneous agents, including robots, drones, and software services, learn environmental models and adapt plans based on evolving sensor inputs. These examples underscore how learning not only enhances individual intelligence but elevates the collective performance of the MAS. Looking ahead, integrating lifelong learning and continual adaptation into MAS is an active research frontier. Agents must retain useful knowledge, avoid catastrophic forgetting, and update beliefs incrementally as new data becomes available. Techniques from continual learning, such as elastic weight consolidation or rehearsal buffers, are being adapted to distributed settings. As MAS become embedded in increasingly dynamic, uncertain, and multi-modal environments, their success will depend on their capacity to learn continuously, communicate meaningfully, and reason collectively.

5.6.2.4 Architectures, Communication, and Decision-Making

The architecture of a MAS determines how agents are structured internally and how they interact externally. Internally, agents may be modeled as finite-state machines, rule-based systems, logic-based reasoners, or neural architectures. Externally, MAS design involves defining topologies (e.g., centralized, distributed, peer-to-peer), communication protocols, and control flows. Communication is crucial for MAS operation and ranges from direct messaging (point-to-point or broadcast) to stigmergic interaction via the environment (e.g., digital pheromones in swarm intelligence). The design of MAS often hinges on achieving a balance between autonomy and coordination: agents must be sufficiently independent to make local decisions while sufficiently aware to align with collective goals. Coordination mechanisms in MAS can be categorized as cooperative, competitive, or mixed. In cooperative MAS, agents share information and pursue joint objectives. Coordination is achieved through protocols such as task allocation, consensus algorithms, or planning negotiation. In competitive MAS, agents act selfishly to maximize their own utility, often within game-theoretic frameworks. Mixed MAS model real-world scenarios where some agents cooperate while others compete, such as in economic markets or resource allocation games. Auctions, voting mechanisms, and coalition formation algorithms play key roles in such settings. Coordination may be explicit via negotiation and contracts or implicit via environmental cues or learning from observation.

Decision-making in MAS is inherently decentralized and can be local (based solely on an agent's perspective) or global (influenced by shared knowledge). Techniques such as distributed constraint satisfaction, distributed optimization, and distributed planning provide the theoretical tools for achieving coherence in MAS decisions. Agents may use heuristics, logic-based inference, probabilistic reasoning, or ML to evaluate options and select actions. RL has been extended to MARL, allowing agents to learn optimal policies in shared environments. Algorithms like MADDPG and QMIX represent recent advances in this domain, balancing individual learning with team objectives. Agent coordination is further facilitated by ontologies and shared knowledge bases, enabling semantic interoperability. Ontologies define shared vocabularies and conceptual frameworks that agents can use to interpret information consistently. Knowledge sharing may occur through blackboard architectures, tuple spaces, or decentralized data stores. Reputation systems and trust models are also employed to regulate agent behavior in open MAS, particularly when agents are designed by different parties or interact in competitive settings. These mechanisms support stability and robustness in large-scale MAS, especially in dynamic or partially observable environments.

From an implementation perspective, MAS frameworks such as Java Agent DEvelopment Framework (JADE), GAMA, and SPADE provide middleware for developing and deploying agent-based systems. These platforms support agent communication, life cycle management, behavior scripting, and integration with sensors and actuators. MAS simulation environments like NetLogo or MASON allow researchers to test coordination strategies and emergent behaviors in controlled settings. Increasingly, MAS are being embedded into cyber-physical systems, where agents interact with physical devices and real-time processes, such as in smart manufacturing or autonomous vehicle fleets.

5.6.2.5 Practical Applications and Advantages of MAS

The practical applications of MAS are numerous and expanding. In logistics and transportation, MAS are used for dynamic routing, fleet management, and supply chain coordination. Each vehicle or logistic node can act as an agent, negotiating paths or loads based on real-time data. In smart grids, agents manage energy consumption, storage, and distribution across households, substations, and power plants, optimizing load balancing and cost. In disaster response, MAS support distributed sensing, resource allocation, and coordinated action among rescue teams, robots, and command centers. These applications leverage the scalability, adaptability, and fault tolerance of MAS.

In financial systems, MAS model market dynamics and simulate trader behaviors. Agents with varying strategies and risk preferences engage in auctions, arbitrage, or speculation, producing emergent patterns that mirror real-world phenomena like bubbles or crashes. In health care, MAS coordinate patient monitoring, diagnostics, and treatment planning among heterogeneous devices and systems. Multi-agent simulations also support epidemiological modeling, capturing the spread of diseases across populations with agent-level granularity. The advantages of MAS over centralized systems include scalability (as new agents can be added with minimal reconfiguration), robustness (as the failure of one agent does not compromise the system), and flexibility (as agents can adapt to changing environments). MAS also facilitate modular development and reuse, enabling systems to evolve incrementally. Their distributed nature makes them ideal for applications where central coordination is infeasible or undesirable, such as planetary exploration or underwater robotics. Furthermore, MAS align with ethical and regulatory demands for decentralized AI, where decisions are traceable and locally accountable.

5.6.2.6 LLM-Based Autonomous Agents and Multi-Agent Collaborations

Recent developments in LLMs have brought a paradigm shift in how autonomous systems can reason, plan, and collaborate across complex environments. Unlike traditional MAS, where agent logic and behavior are hard-coded or rule-based, LLM-based autonomous agents leverage natural language as an interface for perception, communication, and decision-making. This shift enables a new form of flexible, context-aware, and language-mediated collaboration among agents. LLMs such as GPT, Claude, and Gemini can act as autonomous reasoning engines when coupled with tools like memory, code execution, web access, and file manipulation. In agent frameworks such as AutoGPT, BabyAGI, AgentVerse, and CrewAI, LLMs are orchestrated into roles such as researcher, planner, coder, or tester, each assigned with specific goals and allowed to interact through structured prompts or dialogue.

This approach mimics conventional multi-agent system architecture but integrates adaptive language understanding and emergent capabilities. Unlike symbolic agents or reactive systems, these agents operate through prompt-based instructions, allowing them to understand ambiguous goals, decompose tasks, and coordinate dynamically. Their autonomy stems from chain-of-thought reasoning, task planning, and recursive self-correction.

In LLM-based MAS, multiple language model agents operate either independently or cooperatively. For instance, in the ChatDev framework, a virtual software company is simulated where each agent, such as a CEO, CTO, or Developer, is a language model assigned a role and personality. Through natural dialogue, they iteratively develop software. In the AutoGen system, agents exchange structured messages, enabling back-and-forth reasoning, debugging, and consensus building. These agents simulate real-world multi-stakeholder collaboration where consensus, negotiation, and dynamic role-switching are essential. The underlying infrastructure may include memory modules, long-term knowledge bases, and custom reward or evaluation functions to steer decision-making. In engineering systems, LLM-based agents could assist in collaborative design reviews, where one agent evaluates mechanical tolerances while another handles material selection. They may also support automated simulation loops, in which agents analyze results from finite element analysis or computational fluid dynamics and iteratively update design files. Additionally, they can contribute to code generation and verification, writing, testing, and optimizing G-code or control scripts for manufacturing. This approach enhances decision support systems, reduces manual workload, and introduces a semantic layer of intelligence into traditional agent-based workflows.

Despite their promise, these systems raise important challenges. Reliability and hallucination control, coordination failures due to misaligned goals or ambiguous outputs, computational costs, and scalability issues are among the primary concerns. Moreover, evaluating such systems is complex, as traditional multi-agent success criteria may not fully capture emergent behaviors arising from language-based interaction. Ongoing research explores solutions such as role specification languages, message protocols, and behavior evaluation frameworks designed specifically for LLM-based MASs. The fusion of language models with MAS architecture introduces a powerful new paradigm in which agents communicate and act through language, enabling more human-like collaboration and problem-solving. As the tools and frameworks evolve, these systems are expected to become integral to the automation of complex workflows in engineering, manufacturing, and digital design domains.

5.6.2.7   Case Study: MAS for Centrifugal Pump Design and Analysis

One promising and innovative application of MAS lies in the design and optimization of turbomachines, particularly centrifugal pumps. These systems involve multidisciplinary, multiscale variables such as hydraulics, thermodynamics, structural mechanics, and materials which must be integrated coherently. Traditional design methods often require sequential iterations between isolated software modules and experts. MAS provides a way to model the design process as a distributed problem, where each aspect is handled by a dedicated agent, promoting parallelism and collaborative intelligence. In this context, each agent specializes in a function: one agent may optimize the blade geometry, another may evaluate flow dynamics via CFD simulations, a third may assess vibration or thermal stress, while others ensure manufacturing feasibility or cost constraints. These agents interact via communication protocols to propose, refine, and validate design alternatives. Coordination is orchestrated either through a central facilitator agent or via market-like mechanisms where design components are negotiated and evaluated dynamically. This distributed structure is illustrated in Figure 5.5, which presents the functional architecture of the multi-agent (four agents) system developed for centrifugal pump design. Each agent is assigned a specific role in the collaborative design chain, from data preprocessing to final optimization.

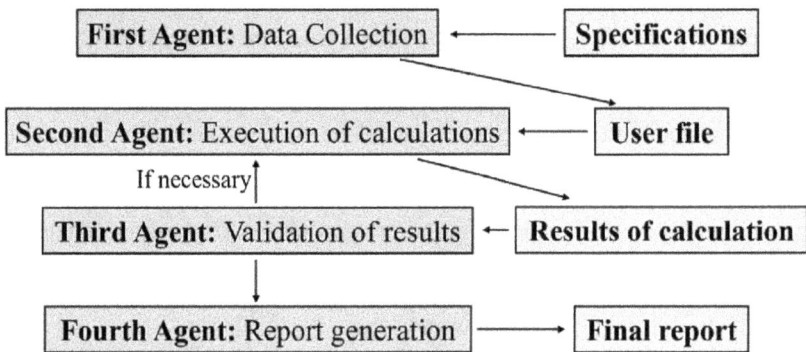

FIGURE 5.5 Schematic representation of functional architecture of a MAS applied to centrifugal pump design.

The MAS approach has been implemented in design chains where knowledge-based agents encapsulate expert rules and heuristics, while data-driven agents use ML models trained on simulation results or experimental data. For example, surrogate models based on NNs predict performance metrics (e.g., head, efficiency, NPSH) from geometry descriptors, allowing rapid exploration of the design space. These predictions are refined by agents running detailed simulations when necessary, balancing speed and precision. Schematically, the system is structured around interacting layers: perception (input data), reasoning (design rules and simulation feedback), coordination (agent negotiation and task distribution), and execution (design generation and evaluation). The result is a closed-loop intelligent system where agents continuously evaluate and improve the design until convergence is achieved. The diagrams illustrate interactions among knowledge bases, optimization loops, and collaborative decision-making paths, highlighting the system's modularity and scalability.

This MAS-based design framework allows turbomachinery manufacturers to reduce design cycles, explore a broader range of configurations, and ensure that trade-offs between performance, cost, and reliability are made transparently and efficiently. The effectiveness of this agent-based optimization process is clearly demonstrated in Table 5.9, which compares key pump design parameters before and after the MAS-based intervention. It highlights improvements in efficiency, energy consumption, and geometry. These results validate the MAS framework's ability to coordinate specialized agents effectively, yielding optimized designs with better performance and lower resource requirements. Moreover, it opens the way to collaborative design platforms where human experts and software agents co-create solutions in real time. As turbomachines become more complex and custom-tailored, such distributed intelligent systems will be essential to maintain competitiveness and innovation in the energy, aerospace, and fluid machinery industries.

TABLE 5.9
Comparison of Centrifugal Pump Parameters before and after MAS-Based Optimization

Parameter	Before MAS	After MAS
Impeller diameter (mm)	130	115
Number of blades	7	6
Hydraulic efficiency (%)	61	67
Available NPSH (m)	3.11	2.75
Power absorbed (kW)	3.05	2.78

6 Advanced Applications of AI and Ethical Challenges

6.1 DIGITAL TWINS

6.1.1 DIGITAL TWINS: DEFINITIONS AND FRAMEWORKS

6.1.1.1 Principles, Architecture, and Integration with AI

The concept of digital twins (DTs) has become a cornerstone in the development of intelligent systems across multiple domains. A DT is defined as a virtual representation of a physical object, process, or system, continually updated using real-time data and simulations to mirror the status, behavior, and performance of its physical counterpart. The origin of DTs can be traced back to NASA's Apollo program in the 1970s, where virtual models of spacecraft were used to simulate and resolve problems occurring in space. However, the term *digital twin* was formally introduced in 2002 by *Michael Grieves* during a presentation at the University of Michigan, and its popularity has since surged with the advancement of the IoT, cloud computing, and AI. Since 2015, its integration with AI and ML has made DTs an essential tool in predictive modeling, diagnostics, and decision-making.

A robust DT framework typically consists of three interconnected components: the physical system (e.g., a machine or human organ), the virtual model (a computational representation), and the communication layer that ensures real-time synchronization. The communication layer enables bi-directional data flow, creating a feedback loop between the real and virtual entities. The state of the physical system is continuously monitored and mirrored by its digital twin, and the difference between the actual and virtual states (synchronization error) is a key factor in assessing performance. Minimizing this error over time is a critical objective in DTs' design. Achieving this requires sophisticated data acquisition (from sensors), preprocessing, model calibration, and ML algorithms that refine predictions and recommendations. Modern implementations rely on edge computing to process sensor data closer to the source, reducing latency and increasing responsiveness.

The integration of AI, especially ML, has elevated the functionality of DTs from passive monitoring to active reasoning. Algorithms such as NNs, SVMs, and RL are now embedded within DT platforms to enhance their predictive and prescriptive capabilities. A DT of an aircraft engine, for instance, can predict potential failures by analyzing vibration and temperature data using LSTM networks. These networks forecast Remaining Useful Life (RUL) and schedule maintenance proactively. The performance of such AI models is evaluated using metrics like Root Mean Square

DOI: 10.1201/9781003613633-6

Error (RMSE) and the coefficient of determination (R2), ensuring that the twin mirrors the physical entity with high fidelity. A major strength of DTs lies in their ability to simulate "what-if" scenarios in real time, and the simulations are often governed by Partial Differential Equations (PDEs) representing physical processes.

6.1.1.2 Applications across Key Sectors

DTs are now extensively used in sectors such as manufacturing, energy, healthcare, transportation, urban planning, and agriculture. In advanced manufacturing, companies like Siemens and GE employ DTs to monitor and optimize factory operations, reduce downtime, and enhance product quality. Siemens introduced the Digital Enterprise Suite in 2020, integrating DTs into their automation systems. In the automotive sector, Tesla uses digital twins to simulate vehicle dynamics, test autonomous driving algorithms, and push over-the-air updates tailored to individual cars. In healthcare, Philips has developed DTs of human organs to model disease progression and personalize treatment. A DT of the heart, for instance, can simulate different pharmacological responses based on patient-specific data, enhancing diagnostic accuracy and therapeutic outcomes.

Urban-scale DTs contribute significantly to smart city development. Cities like Singapore and Helsinki use them to model traffic flows, energy consumption, waste management, and public health systems. These virtual cities allow planners to simulate infrastructure projects, optimize public service delivery, and test emergency response strategies. In the energy sector, wind farms use DTs to monitor turbine performance, predict component wear, and adjust blade angles to maximize energy capture. Offshore platforms simulate the effects of extreme weather, ensuring safety and reducing maintenance costs. In oil and gas, DTs monitor pipelines and drilling equipment to preempt failures. Agriculture is also transforming through DT technology. Smart farms integrate data from drones, soil sensors, and weather forecasts to simulate crop growth and irrigation needs. A DT of a vineyard might simulate how different pruning strategies affect grape yield and sugar content. These systems support decision-making for fertilization, pest control, and resource allocation, optimizing yields and sustainability.

Environmental modeling and climate technology are increasingly leveraging DTs to address large-scale ecological challenges. Digital replicas of natural systems such as watersheds, forests, or coastal ecosystems enable scientists to simulate climate change scenarios, assess biodiversity impacts, and forecast long-term environmental shifts. For instance, digital twins are used to model urban heat islands, track deforestation, and evaluate the effectiveness of carbon mitigation strategies. Climate-sensitive infrastructure, such as dams or flood barriers, can be tested under extreme weather conditions within virtual environments before real-world implementation. These applications support proactive policy-making, climate resilience planning, and adaptive environmental management.

Table 6.1 shows the application of digital twins in different sectors.

TABLE 6.1

Applications of Digital Twins across Sectors

Sector	Application Example
Healthcare	Patient-specific organ simulation for personalized treatment
Manufacturing	Factory operations monitoring and predictive maintenance
Smart cities	Traffic simulation and infrastructure planning
Energy	Wind turbine optimization and grid load balancing
Automotive	Autonomous vehicle testing and performance simulation
Agriculture	Precision irrigation and crop health forecasting

6.1.1.3   Technical Foundations and Current Challenges

The deployment of DTs at scale relies heavily on cloud and edge computing. Cloud platforms provide the computational scalability needed to process large volumes of sensor data, often using frameworks like Apache Spark or AWS IoT Greengrass. Edge computing, by contrast, ensures low latency by placing computing resources near the data source. The hybrid model combining both approaches is particularly effective for time-sensitive systems such as autonomous vehicles or robotic surgery. At the core of digital twin optimization lies the minimization of a cost function $J(\theta$), where θ represents system parameters. Solving $\theta^* = \arg\min_\theta J(\theta)$ via gradient descent or EAs enables real-time calibration for improved efficiency and resilience.

Despite their advantages, digital twins face several critical challenges. Data quality remains a foundational issue: erroneous, missing, or delayed sensor readings can lead to flawed predictions. Cybersecurity and privacy are also vital concerns, especially in applications involving personal health or critical infrastructure. Furthermore, the computational complexity of real-time simulation, especially in systems governed by non-linear dynamics or involving large-scale interactions, requires significant resources. In response, research has turned to XAI and federated digital twins (FDTs), where multiple DTs collaborate without directly exchanging sensitive data.

6.1.1.4   Trends and Prospects in Intelligent DT Systems

Human-in-the-loop interaction is becoming central to modern DT systems. Engineers, doctors, and operators increasingly interface with DTs through Augmented Reality (AR), dashboards, or voice control. These interfaces enable better oversight and real-time feedback in domains like aerospace, where predictive models identify structural fatigue and recommend interventions. Moreover, digital twins are beginning to integrate with generative AI tools. LLMs and GANs can enhance the ability of DTs to auto-generate simulation configurations, explore design alternatives, and interpret results more naturally. Urban planners are already experimenting with LLM-enhanced DTs to simulate public behavior and test policy outcomes before implementation. By 2030, the global market for digital twins is projected to exceed $100 billion. This growth is driven by the convergence of AI, edge computing, and the proliferation of sensor-rich environments. As these systems evolve, DTs will not only reflect real-world systems but also anticipate their future states, enabling more adaptive, autonomous, and intelligent decision-making across critical sectors.

6.1.2 COUPLING AI AND SIMULATION: ADAPTIVE AND PREDICTIVE SYSTEMS

The convergence of AI and simulation technologies marks a profound transformation in the design and operation of complex systems. While the architectural principles and integration mechanisms have already been outlined in the sections "Principles, Architecture, and Integration with AI" and "Integration with DTs and Engineering Workflows", this section focuses on their practical consequences in engineering and industry. AI models require data to learn and generalize, but real-world data collection can be expensive, dangerous, or impractical in sectors such as aerospace, healthcare, and energy. Simulation environments offer a controlled and repeatable setting for training, testing, and validating AI systems. DTs provide a compelling example of this synergy. These dynamic digital replicas combine sensor data, simulation models, and AI-based analytics to produce real-time insights and enable predictive control. For instance, a DT of a wind turbine can integrate environmental data (e.g., wind speed, temperature) with simulation results to anticipate failure modes or optimize energy output using machine learning algorithms. The simulation engine and AI model operate in tandem to continuously refine predictions and adapt the system's behavior to changing conditions.

Mathematically, let $x(t)$d enote the state vector of a physical system at time t, and let $\hat{x}(t)$ be the simulated estimate from the DT. The prediction error is given by $e(t) = x(t) - \hat{x}(t)p$, and adaptive algorithms aim to minimize this error using feedback control and online learning (Figure 6.1).

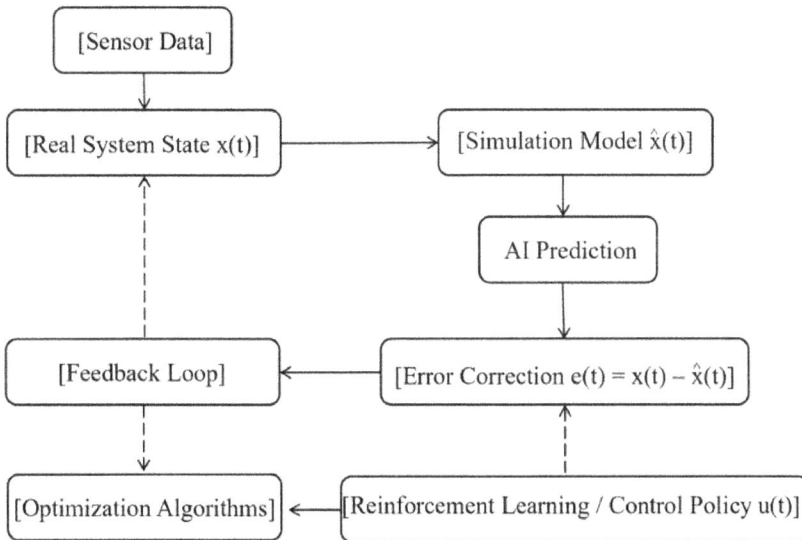

FIGURE 6.1 Real-time simulation loop showing AI-assisted prediction, system behavior simulation, and adaptive feedback for closed-loop optimization.

In practice, algorithms such as *Kalman* filters, RNNs, and Bayesian filters are used to update the DT state estimates in real time. RL agents within simulation environments learn optimal control strategies by maximizing reward signals defined over long time horizons. In manufacturing, predictive maintenance solutions rely on simulations to produce synthetic failure data, which is then used to train DL models for fault detection and prognosis. Semiconductor fabrication processes, for example, combine physics-based lithography simulations with AI to enhance product yield and reduce defects.

The use of simulation-driven AI is particularly valuable in energy systems, where smart grid DTs dynamically adjust power distribution based on real-time demand, weather forecasts, and grid conditions. The optimization of such systems can be represented by the objective function as shown in Equation (6.1):

$$J(u) = \int_0^T \left(P_d(t) - P_g(t, u) \right)^2 dt \tag{6.1}$$

where P_d is the demand and P_g is the generated power as a function of control input. This real-time coupling enables decentralized, predictive energy management and integration of renewables like wind and solar.

Simulation also enhances the safety and reliability of AI models by enabling extensive testing on rare or adversarial scenarios. In autonomous vehicles, platforms like CARLA simulate weather conditions, traffic variations, and edge cases to fine-tune perception and decision-making algorithms. Similarly, in healthcare and finance, simulations support stress testing of AI models before they are applied in high-stakes environments. The emergence of Simulation-as-a-Service (SaaS) platforms like Unity ML-Agents and NVIDIA Omniverse has democratized access to high-fidelity simulation environments. These tools support the creation of realistic and interactive virtual worlds, where AI models can be trained, evaluated, and deployed efficiently. In robotics, frameworks like Isaac Gym and Gazebo allow for rapid prototyping of control policies, which are then transferred to real-world applications using techniques such as sim-to-real transfer or domain randomization. These methods mitigate the domain gap between virtual training and physical deployment. Despite the promise of this integration, challenges remain: computational cost, fidelity of the models, and explainability of AI decisions trained on simulations. These issues are addressed by emerging hybrid methods that combine surrogate models, explainable AI (XAI) frameworks, and generative environments. Looking forward, AI-simulation coupling is set to expand further into areas like climate resilience, urban planning, and disaster response that demand safe, adaptive, and predictive intelligence.

6.1.3 ROLE OF AI IN DYNAMIC ENVIRONMENTS

6.1.3.1 Real-Time Decision-Making and Uncertainty

AI systems deployed in dynamic environments face the challenge of adapting to continuous changes and uncertainty. These environments, ranging from autonomous driving and financial markets to natural disaster response and robotic navigation, are marked by their unpredictability and non-stationarity. A dynamic environment is one where the state of the world evolves over time, often due to external agents, internal stochasticity, or system feedback. Unlike static settings where AI operates under fixed rules and data distributions, dynamic environments demand real-time decision-making, adaptability, and learning from incomplete or noisy data. RL has emerged as a foundational approach for tackling such challenges. For instance, DQNs, introduced by DeepMind in 2015, combined Q-learning with DNNs to enable agents to play Atari games with superhuman performance. The key innovation was the use of experience replay and target networks to stabilize learning. These techniques allowed agents to learn policies that adapt based on changing environmental rewards and states.

Dynamic environments often feature partial observability, where agents do not have full access to the current state. To address this, RNNs and LSTM models are employed to retain temporal context. In robotic applications, these architectures allow agents to build internal representations of their surroundings over time, improving decision-making under uncertainty. In high-stakes domains like finance or healthcare, these models must also incorporate risk assessment and probabilistic reasoning. Bayesian DL and ensembles are used to estimate uncertainty in predictions, allowing systems to defer decisions or request human intervention when confidence is low. This is crucial in medical diagnostics, where a wrong decision could be fatal.

6.1.3.2 Adaptation, Meta-Learning, and Resilience

Another key capability of AI in dynamic environments is adaptation and learning new tasks or adjusting to changes with minimal additional data. This has led to the development of meta-learning, or *learning to learn*. MAML, proposed in 2017, is a notable example that enables rapid adaptation to new tasks by optimizing for a set of parameters that are sensitive to small changes. In practical terms, this allows AI systems to adapt quickly when entering a new environment, such as a robot transitioning from one terrain to another or an AI assistant learning user preferences in a new household. Continual learning algorithms address the problem of catastrophic forgetting, ensuring that AI agents retain previously acquired skills while integrating new ones. In dynamic industrial settings, such as smart factories, machines must continuously adapt to new production lines or product configurations. This requires online learning algorithms that update model parameters incrementally.

In dynamic traffic control, AI agents continuously learn traffic patterns, adapting light signal schedules to real-time flow conditions. Reinforcement learning is employed to maximize traffic throughput while minimizing congestion. The same principles apply to drone swarms in dynamic airspaces, where decentralized agents must adapt their flight paths based on changing weather and obstacle data. The adaptive behavior is often governed by MARL algorithms that enable coordination without central control. For example, QMIX and MADDPG have demonstrated success in such scenarios. These algorithms balance individual learning objectives with group coordination, enabling robust behavior in uncertain multi-agent environments.

6.1.3.3 Simulation, Generalization, and System Robustness

Simulation plays a critical role in preparing AI for real-world dynamic conditions. In robotics, simulated environments like Isaac Gym, MuJoCo, or Gazebo allow agents to practice tasks such as object manipulation or terrain navigation under variable scenarios. To bridge the gap between virtual and real-world dynamics, domain randomization techniques are used. These involve varying simulation parameters (e.g., friction, lighting, object mass) during training to improve the agent's generalization capacity. This has proven particularly effective in robotic arm manipulation tasks where sim-to-real transfer is required.

AI systems operating in dynamic environments must be robust against adversarial changes, rare events, and sensor failures. Robust control algorithms and adversarial training are used to ensure that AI agents maintain performance under perturbations. In autonomous vehicles, for instance, agents are trained to respond appropriately to rare but critical events such as sudden pedestrian crossings or road obstructions. Techniques like Monte Carlo Tree Search (MCTS) and Model Predictive Control (MPC) are used to simulate future scenarios and optimize control actions accordingly. In weather forecasting and climate modeling, AI integrates sensor data with dynamic simulations to produce real-time updates and long-term predictions. These models rely on spatiotemporal learning, combining convolutional layers for spatial data and recurrent layers for temporal dynamics.

Figure 6.2 illustrates a conceptual architecture for an AI system operating in a dynamic environment. It includes a feedback loop that integrates environmental sensing, predictive modeling, decision-making, and adaptation. Real-time data feeds into a dynamic model that simulates environmental changes, while the AI agent updates its policy through reinforcement and meta-learning mechanisms. The architecture supports robustness via uncertainty quantification and modular training blocks, enhancing flexibility across domains. As dynamic environments become more prevalent in AI applications, from smart agriculture and autonomous exploration to financial systems and real-time healthcare monitoring, the demand for intelligent systems that can perceive, reason, and adapt continuously will only grow. These systems must not only learn from data but also evolve with their environments, forming the foundation of truly autonomous intelligence.

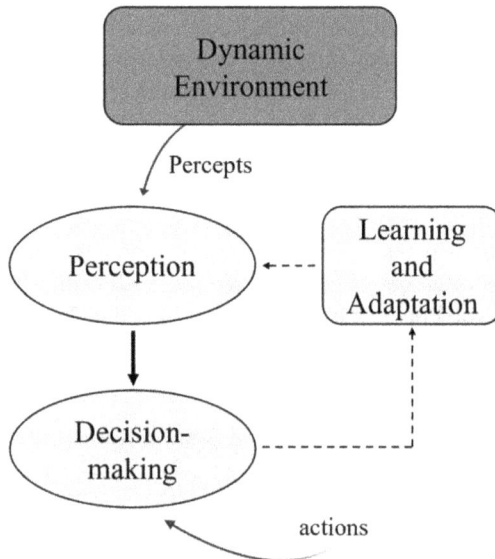

FIGURE 6.2 AI feedback loop in dynamic environments integrating sensing, learning, prediction, and adaptation.

6.1.4 Emerging Generative and Foundational Models

AI is undergoing a profound transformation with the rise of generative and foundational models. These models, characterized by their ability to generalize across multiple domains and tasks, are reshaping engineering, manufacturing, healthcare, and industrial processes. Foundational models, such as LLMs and multimodal systems, are pre-trained on vast datasets and adapted to a wide variety of downstream applications. Generative AI, including diffusion models and GANs, has opened new pathways for simulation, optimization, design exploration, and code generation. Their integration into engineering workflows, particularly when coupled with DTs, simulation platforms, and real-world control systems, offers unprecedented opportunities for automation, creativity, and decision support. In this section, we explore the key technologies underlying these models, their implications for simulation-driven engineering, and their practical deployments across industrial sectors.

6.1.4.1 LLMs and Multimodal Systems

LLMs represent a major leap in AI capabilities, enabling machines to understand, generate, and reason with human language at an unprecedented scale. Models such as OpenAI's GPT series, Google's PaLM, Meta's LLaMA, and Anthropic's Claude are trained on extensive corpora of text and code, allowing them to perform a wide variety of tasks, including natural language understanding, summarization, translation, problem solving, and reasoning. The architecture underpinning most modern LLMs is based on the Transformer model, which leverages self-attention mechanisms to capture long-range dependencies in data. The capabilities of LLMs are increasingly enhanced by multimodal systems that are the models capable of processing and generating not just text, but also images, audio, and even video. Multimodal models, such as OpenAI's GPT-4V, DeepMind's Gemini, or Meta's ImageBind, can seamlessly integrate information across different sensory modalities, enabling applications such as visual question answering, robotic perception, and simulation environment interpretation. A multimodal system can analyze a CAD model, describe its features in natural language, and propose optimizations based on functional requirements.

In engineering contexts, multimodal LLMs serve as powerful assistants capable of interpreting technical documentation, suggesting design modifications, and translating between textual specifications and graphical representations. They can assist engineers in understanding complex system interactions, predicting failure modes from sensor data combined with maintenance reports, and even generating code for simulation scripts based on natural language queries. Mathematically, an LLM models a conditional probability distribution $P(y|x;\theta)$ where x represents the input (text, code, image embeddings) and y represents the output prediction, parameterized by model weights θ. In the multimodal case, x can be a tuple $(x_{\text{text}}, x_{\text{image}}, x_{\text{audio}})$, and the model learns cross-attention mechanisms to fuse the modalities.

The ability of LLMs and multimodal models to act as general-purpose interfaces significantly reduces the barrier between humans and complex digital systems. Engineers, scientists, and decision-makers can interact with sophisticated simulations, control systems, and optimization platforms through natural dialogue, thus enhancing accessibility and reducing development time. Furthermore, the fine-tuning of LLMs on domain-specific datasets (e.g., technical standards, material property databases, or simulation logs) improves their relevance and reliability in specialized industrial applications. Challenges, however, remain significant. LLMs are prone to hallucinations (producing plausible but incorrect outputs), they require significant computational resources, and their outputs must be validated carefully in critical domains like aerospace, healthcare, or energy systems. Techniques such as Retrieval-Augmented Generation (RAG), model alignment, and domain-specific adapters are being developed to mitigate these limitations. In Figure 6.3, the architecture of a multimodal LLM system is presented, integrating textual, visual, and structured data inputs for engineering decision support.

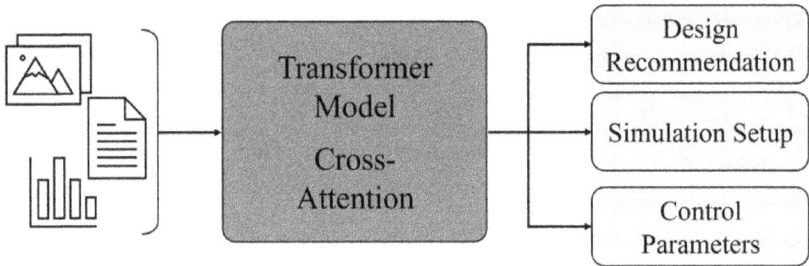

FIGURE 6.3 Architecture of a multimodal LLM system: textual and visual inputs for engineering applications.

6.1.4.2   Generative AI and Diffusion Models

Generative AI refers to a class of models capable of producing new data instances that resemble a training distribution, including text, images, audio, and 3D structures. Among the different types of generative models, diffusion models have emerged as a leading paradigm, offering high fidelity, diversity, and controllability in generated outputs. Diffusion models, such as DALLE 3, Stable Diffusion, and Imagen, operate by gradually adding random noise to data and then learning to reverse this noise process to reconstruct realistic samples. In formal terms, a diffusion model consists of two processes: the forward diffusion process, which progressively corrupts data x_0 into pure noise x_T over T time steps, and the reverse denoising process, which reconstructs samples by learning the conditional probability $P_\theta\left(x_{t-1}|x_t\right)$ distributions, where θ are the learnable parameters optimized during training.

The model is typically trained by minimizing a variational bound on the data likelihood, using stochastic differential equations (SDEs) to model continuous noise dynamics. One of the key advantages of diffusion models compared to traditional GANs is their improved training stability and ability to generate high-resolution, diverse outputs without mode collapse. Moreover, diffusion models offer intuitive conditioning mechanisms, allowing users to guide the generation process based on textual prompts, sketches, semantic maps, or even partial simulations. In engineering and scientific domains, diffusion models are now being adapted to generate:

- Synthetic material microstructures based on desired mechanical properties.
- 3D geometries optimized for aerodynamics or structural strength.
- Alternative product designs based on performance constraints and style guidelines.
- Synthetic datasets for training AI models under rare or critical failure scenarios.

For example, in computational materials science, a diffusion model can be trained on a database of composite microstructures and mechanical tests to generate novel, manufacturable material architectures optimized for specific strength-to-weight ratios. In fluid dynamics, generative models are being explored to propose novel wing designs or turbine blade profiles that maximize lift or efficiency under complex operational conditions. Furthermore, conditional diffusion models can be integrated into simulation loops. In this setting, the model generates candidate designs or input conditions, which are then evaluated by a physics-based simulator, creating a feedback loop that refines the generative model toward realistic, high-performance solutions.

Despite their promise, diffusion models face challenges in computational cost (training often requires thousands of GPU hours) and explainability (generated outputs are not always interpretable in terms of engineering principles). Research is actively exploring physics-informed diffusion models that embed domain knowledge into the generation process, improving reliability for critical applications.

6.1.4.3 Integration with DTs and Engineering Workflows

The convergence of generative models with DTs and engineering workflows is opening new frontiers in simulation, design, optimization, and operational control. Traditionally, DTs have relied on deterministic models calibrated with real-world sensor data to replicate and predict system behavior. With the integration of generative AI, DTs are evolving from static mirrors into adaptive, creative, and proactive entities, capable of exploring hypothetical scenarios, generating new designs, and optimizing performance in real-time. Generative models, including LLMs, diffusion models, and GANs, can be embedded within DT platforms at multiple levels:

- **Design Augmentation**: A generative model proposes alternative design configurations based on performance objectives or constraints. For instance, given a turbine DT, a diffusion model can suggest new blade geometries optimized for specific airflow conditions.
- **Scenario Generation**: LLMs or multimodal systems can create plausible future scenarios (e.g., failure modes, extreme events, new use-cases) that the DT can simulate and evaluate, enhancing predictive resilience.
- **Synthetic Data Generation**: In situations where real sensor data is sparse, generative models can create realistic synthetic datasets to train or fine-tune the DT's predictive algorithms, improving robustness against rare or unobserved events.

- **Code and Model Generation**: Generative code models can dynamically produce simulation scripts, control logic, or optimization algorithms tailored to the DT's evolving needs.

A notable architectural innovation is the closed generative twin loop. In this paradigm, the physical system, its DT, and the generative models form an iterative loop: the DT monitors the system, the generative model proposes variations or improvements, simulations validate the proposals, and actionable insights are deployed to the physical system.

Mathematically, consider a DT state $s(t)$, a generative model $G(z|\psi)$ producing candidate configurations z conditioned on objectives ψ, and a simulator Sim(z) evaluating each candidate. The optimal solution z^* is found by maximizing Equation (6.2):

$$z^* = \underset{z}{\arg\max}\, U\left(sim(z), \psi\right) \tag{6.2}$$

where U is a utility function measuring performance, safety, cost, or other engineering criteria.

Examples of integration include:

- In smart manufacturing, DTs enhanced with diffusion models suggest real-time adjustments to production parameters (temperature, pressure, feed rate) to maintain quality despite raw material variability.
- In aerospace, LLM-based agents embedded in DTs assist engineers by summarizing simulation results, highlighting anomalies, and proposing design revisions.
- In urban planning, multimodal DTs use generative models to explore alternative zoning policies, traffic designs, or green infrastructure layouts under different demographic scenarios.

One of the greatest promises of this integration is adaptive autonomy: DTs that not only mirror the current state of a system but also creatively explore ways to improve it, all while maintaining a continuous feedback loop with the physical entity. Challenges include ensuring the physical validity of generative outputs, minimizing computational overhead, and managing the complexity of multi-agent coordination when multiple DTs interact within large infrastructures.

6.1.4.4 Code-Generation Models for Engineering and Simulations

The emergence of AI-driven code-generation models represents a transformative advance for engineering, simulation, and control system development. Models such as OpenAI's Codex, DeepMind's AlphaCode, Meta's Code LLaMA, and Hugging Face's StarCoder are capable of generating executable code from natural language prompts, technical specifications, or structured templates. These systems use variations of LLM architectures, fine-tuned on billions of lines of open-source and proprietary code repositories across multiple programming languages, including Python, C++, Fortran, MATLAB®, and domain-specific simulation languages. In the engineering context, code-generation models assist in multiple crucial tasks:

- Simulation Script Writing: From a simple textual description, simulate airflow over an airfoil using CFD with Reynolds number, the model can generate Python or OpenFOAM scripts that set up, mesh, and solve the problem.
- Automation of Workflows: Code-generation models create data pipelines, automate preprocessing or postprocessing of simulation results, and build dashboards for visualization.
- Algorithm Synthesis: In optimization or control design, AI models can generate novel variations of search algorithms, reinforcement learning policies, or control laws tailored to specific performance objectives.
- Debugging and Refactoring: Models can analyze existing codebases, identify inefficiencies, suggest corrections, or port legacy codes (e.g., from MATLAB to Python).

The underlying principle relies on sequence-to-sequence modeling. Given an input sequence (natural language description), the model generates an output sequence (code tokens), optimizing for syntactic correctness and functional relevance. The model learns mappings of the form $P\left(\text{code}|\text{prompt};\theta\right)$, where θ are model parameters optimized through maximum likelihood estimation over vast datasets combining documentation and code samples.

An increasingly important innovation is structured prompting. Rather than relying solely on open-ended queries, users now provide structured metadata (such as physics domain, boundary conditions, solver type, and output expectations), which significantly enhances the quality and precision of generated code. Hybrid workflows are emerging where engineers collaborate interactively with code-generation models: the model proposes a draft, the human edits it, the model refines the next iteration, forming a highly productive loop. In simulation-intensive fields, this technology accelerates model deployment dramatically. For example:

- In aerospace, code-generation models automate finite element setup for structural analysis, drastically reducing setup time.
- In energy systems, they generate dynamic simulation code for power grid stability analysis, automatically adjusting models as system configurations evolve.
- In automotive design, they help produce synthetic driving environments or simulation scripts for vehicle dynamics modeling.

Despite these advances, challenges persist. Validation remains critical, as AI-generated code may be syntactically correct but physically meaningless or numerically unstable. Domain expertise is still indispensable to verify, test, and validate generated outputs. Moreover, intellectual property (IP) and licensing issues surrounding training data sources raise legal questions that are being actively debated. To address reliability concerns, many workflows now integrate self-verification modules, where AI models not only generate code but also simulate their execution over test cases to detect errors or inconsistencies before human deployment.

6.1.4.5 Case Studies and Industrial Applications

The integration of generative and foundational models into industrial and engineering contexts is no longer speculative; it is already transforming workflows across sectors such as aerospace, automotive, energy, construction, and healthcare. In this section, we review selected examples that highlight the real-world application of LLMs, diffusion models, and code-generation systems within engineering environments. In aerospace, Rolls-Royce has pioneered the use of DTs combined with generative AI models to optimize jet engine performance. Leveraging generative diffusion models, engineers can simulate hundreds of micro-variations in engine geometries and material properties, exploring design spaces that would be impossible to assess manually. These candidate designs are evaluated in DT-based simulations that account for thermodynamic efficiency, vibration patterns, and fatigue life. This workflow significantly accelerates innovation cycles, reduces physical prototyping costs, and enhances overall system resilience. Additionally, code-generation models assist in automating simulation setup and boundary condition adjustments, further streamlining the process.

Tesla and other major manufacturers are integrating multimodal LLMs into their autonomous vehicle development pipelines. Systems like NVIDIA's Omniverse Avatar use multimodal generative AI to simulate driver interactions, environmental variability such as weather and lighting, and traffic conditions. These simulations generate rich datasets used to fine-tune perception and decision-making modules. Large language models also assist engineers in writing synthetic scenario scripts, such as simulating a four-way intersection with varying pedestrian flows, allowing for massive scaling of training scenarios. The result is improved robustness of autonomous systems across rare and adversarial driving conditions. Companies like *Siemens* are employing generative models to predict and optimize dynamic energy distribution. Diffusion-based models generate synthetic demand-response profiles based on weather forecasts, population behavior models, and renewable energy inputs. These profiles are used to train AI agents embedded within DTs of energy networks, enabling proactive load balancing, outage prediction, and integration of variable renewable sources such as wind and solar. Code-generation systems automate the reconfiguration of microgrid controllers based on simulation outputs, enabling real-time adaptability to grid instabilities.

In construction and urban planning, Foster + Partners, a leading architecture and engineering firm, integrates generative design tools based on diffusion models and LLMs to optimize urban layouts. By specifying objectives like maximizing green spaces, minimizing heat islands, and optimizing pedestrian accessibility, generative AI proposes thousands of city block configurations. These alternatives are evaluated using environmental digital twins simulating airflow, noise pollution, and energy consumption. The best-performing designs are selected for detailed architectural development, enabling the creation of more sustainable, livable, and resilient urban environments. Generative models are also revolutionizing personalized medicine. HeartFlow has developed a platform where DTs of patient-specific coronary arteries are created from CT scans. Diffusion models simulate blood flow under various conditions, while LLMs generate personalized treatment plans summarizing risks, recommended interventions, and expected outcomes. This process significantly reduces the need for invasive diagnostics and enables more accurate, patient-specific decision-making.

The integration of generative and foundational models into engineering and industrial processes marks a profound evolution in the capabilities of DTs, simulation environments, and intelligent systems. These models enable a shift from reactive monitoring to proactive innovation, facilitating autonomous design exploration, adaptive optimization, and dynamic decision-making. However, their deployment also introduces new challenges in validation, explainability, and computational scalability, particularly in critical domains where safety and reliability are paramount. As we move forward, addressing these challenges will be essential to fully harness the potential of generative AI while ensuring that technological advances align with ethical, societal, and regulatory expectations. The next sections will continue to explore the broader implications, opportunities, and obstacles shaping the future of AI-driven engineering systems.

6.2 AI: TECHNOLOGICAL AND ETHICAL CHALLENGES

AI, in its various applications and forms, presents significant technological and ethical challenges. These challenges go beyond the mere ability of machines to replicate human tasks; they also encompass their integration into society, their social and economic impacts, and the responsibility of those who design these systems. Discussions on these issues extend far beyond technical concerns, touching on fundamental questions about the role of humans, justice, transparency, and security in AI-driven systems.

6.2.1 TECHNOLOGICAL CHALLENGES OF AI

6.2.1.1 Algorithmic Complexity

AI algorithms, particularly those involved in DL or DNN, can be extremely complex both in terms of their structure and their functioning. One of the major challenges lies in the difficulty of understanding their behavior on a large scale. For instance, while NNs are capable of learning highly complex patterns from data, it can be very challenging to understand how and why they make certain decisions. This leads to a lack of transparency and interpretability, making it difficult to validate the results they generate. For example, in the case of CNNs used for image recognition, it is often hard to understand which specific elements of an image are influencing a given classification. The complexity of these models means that even experts may struggle to explain why a network arrived at a particular conclusion. This lack of interpretability is a significant barrier to the widespread adoption of AI in fields where the justification for decisions is crucial, such as in healthcare, education, or the judicial system. In healthcare, for instance, doctors need to understand why an AI system suggests a particular diagnosis or treatment plan to ensure that it aligns with established medical knowledge and practices. Without clear explanations for the AI's decisions, it becomes challenging to trust its recommendations, particularly in high-stakes situations. Similarly, in education or the justice system, decisions made by AI need to be explainable to ensure fairness and accountability, especially when those decisions affect people's lives and futures. As AI continues to advance, addressing these challenges related to algorithmic complexity, and enhancing the interpretability of AI models will be key to ensuring their responsible use across various sectors.

6.2.1.2 Scalability

AI systems, especially those based on ML and DL algorithms, often require vast amounts of data and computational resources to function effectively. Processing these large quantities of data necessitates a robust technological infrastructure, which can lead to scalability issues. As the complexity and scope of these systems grow, optimizing the resources needed to run these algorithms becomes a significant technical challenge. For example, in autonomous vehicle systems, AI algorithms need to process real-time data from numerous sensors (such as cameras, radar, and LIDAR) while simultaneously making decisions about navigation, obstacle avoidance, and route planning. As the number of vehicles and sensors increases, the computational power required to process all this data in real-time can quickly outstrip current infrastructure capabilities. This poses a serious problem for scaling the deployment of such systems across cities or larger regions.

Similarly, in big data applications, where AI algorithms analyze massive datasets to uncover patterns and insights, scalability issues can arise when handling millions or even billions of data points. For instance, data from social media, financial markets, or medical records requires efficient processing and storage solutions to ensure timely analysis. Without scalable systems, the efficiency and effectiveness of AI applications can degrade, slowing down decision-making and reducing the system's overall performance. To address these scalability challenges, advancements in cloud computing, distributed computing, and edge computing are being explored to provide the necessary infrastructure. These technologies allow AI systems to process and analyze data more efficiently, enabling them to scale to larger datasets and more complex tasks while maintaining performance. However, even with these improvements, the scalability of AI systems remains a critical area of ongoing research and development.

6.2.1.3 Security and Robustness

The security of AI systems is a significant challenge. These systems can be vulnerable to various attacks, including adversarial attacks, where small perturbations in input data can lead to significant errors in predictions or decisions made by models. For example, a subtle change in an image, imperceptible to the human eye, can deceive an image recognition system into misclassifying an object. This vulnerability is particularly concerning in applications where errors could have severe consequences, such as in autonomous vehicles or security systems.

In the context of autonomous vehicles, a slight alteration in the data from a sensor or camera could cause the vehicle to make incorrect decisions, such as misidentifying an obstacle or failing to respond to a traffic signal. These errors could have catastrophic outcomes, including accidents or collisions. Similarly, in security systems, adversarial attacks could manipulate surveillance data, leading to misidentifications or security breaches. In healthcare, adversarial attacks pose even more critical risks. For instance, an AI system used for medical diagnostics could be tricked into misinterpreting images like X-rays or MRIs, leading to incorrect diagnoses. A small change in the image data could cause the system to overlook a tumor or misidentify a medical condition, potentially leading to fatal consequences. Given the high stakes in healthcare, these vulnerabilities highlight the need for robust AI security measures to ensure reliability and safety. Addressing these security concerns requires ongoing research in AI robustness, including developing algorithms that are resistant to adversarial manipulation. Additionally, integrating security protocols and continuous monitoring systems can help detect and mitigate potential threats in real-time. Without these safeguards, the widespread adoption of AI in sensitive areas remains a risk, and its trustworthiness would be severely undermined.

Table 6.2 provides a sector-based overview of how core technological challenges (such as interpretability, scalability, and robustness) manifest differently across application domains, illustrating the need for context-specific AI solutions.

TABLE 6.2
Key Technological Challenges by Application Domain

Application Domain	Main Technological Challenge	Concrete Examples
Healthcare	Safety, explainability, and data privacy	Diagnostic errors by opaque models; protection of patient data (e.g., GDPR compliance)
Industry 4.0	Robustness, system integration	Predictive maintenance using heterogeneous sensors and AI models
Transportation	Real-time decision-making, autonomy	Autonomous vehicles making ethical choices in emergency situations
Finance	Bias detection, transparency	Credit scoring algorithms exhibiting discrimination; explainable AI for auditing
Public security	Surveillance ethics, false positives	Facial recognition systems misidentifying individuals in crowds
Education	Personalization vs. equity	Adaptive learning systems that disadvantage non-standard learners
Energy	Optimization under uncertainty	Smart grids using AI to balance consumption and production in volatile environments

6.2.2 ETHICAL CHALLENGES OF AI

6.2.2.1 Algorithm and Data Biases

One of the most complex and concerning ethical challenges in the field of AI is the bias of algorithms and data. While AI offers immense potential to automate, optimize, and improve a wide range of processes, it is also prone to introducing, reinforcing, or exacerbating existing social inequalities and prejudices. This phenomenon is largely due to the nature of the training data and the way algorithms learn from that data. Indeed, if the data is biased, the AI models will also be biased, which could lead to unfair or discriminatory decisions. Bias in algorithms and data manifests when AI systems incorrectly favor certain categories or groups over others. This bias can be introduced implicitly or explicitly and can take various forms: representation bias occurs when certain categories or groups are underrepresented in the training data. For example, a facial recognition model might perform less effectively on people of color if the training data primarily consists of images of white individuals. Measurement bias arises when the variables used to train a model do not accurately and equitably measure the characteristics of different groups. This can occur when the data collection criteria are biased by the perceptions of the researchers or system designers. Sampling bias happens when the training data is not sufficiently varied or does not adequately represent the entire target population. For example, a health forecasting algorithm could be biased if it is trained solely on data from a homogeneous population in terms of age, gender, and ethnicity. Optimization bias occurs when algorithms are optimized for specific goals, but these goals may not take into account the social, ethical, and cultural impacts of the decisions made by the AI.

The biases of algorithms primarily stem from the data used to train the AI models. Data can be biased in various ways, such as historical bias, where data reflects past systemic injustices and discrimination. For example, in automated recruitment systems, historical data on job applications might reflect gender, racial, or social origin inequalities, which, when used to train an AI model, could lead to similar discrimination. Cultural bias occurs when the data collected reflects cultural prejudices. If an AI is trained from data collected in a specific cultural environment, the model will perform better on situations matching that culture and less accurately on others. Labeling bias can also introduce bias in training data due to incorrect labeling. For example, in an image recognition model, if labels are applied incorrectly (such as labeling objects based on cultural stereotypes), this skews the model's predictions.

Data bias can propagate and reinforce over time, creating feedback loops where bias leads to biased AI models, which in turn make biased predictions that are then used to further refine the model. Algorithmic bias can have significant consequences in contexts of automated decision-making. For example, in predictive justice systems, racial bias in training data can lead to inaccurate assessments of the recidivism risk of criminals, disproportionately severe for certain racial populations. AI systems can amplify existing social and economic inequalities. For instance, credit scoring systems used to assess creditworthiness might systematically exclude certain communities or groups if these systems are trained on biased data that excludes specific populations. A concrete example of bias in AI systems is in automated recruitment. An automated recruitment system might learn from historical data on job applications. If this data shows that men were preferred for technical roles, the model is likely to reproduce this bias by favoring male candidates for similar positions. This phenomenon was observed in companies like Amazon, which had to abandon an AI-based recruitment system after discovering it discriminated against women for technical roles. Facial recognition systems have also shown significant biases. For example, a study by Gender Shades revealed that facial recognition AI models were much less accurate for women and people of color compared to white men. This bias can have serious implications in applications such as police surveillance or airport security. Predictive justice algorithms, like those used to assess the risk of reoffending by offenders, have been criticized for their racial bias. For example, one model was accused of incorrectly classifying Black individuals as more likely to reoffend while underestimating this risk for white individuals. This kind of bias can lead to unjust decisions within the judicial system.

There are several methods to detect and correct bias in AI systems. One method is conducting regular audits to analyze the training data and the results of models. The goal is to measure bias in the decisions made by AI and to check for disparities between different demographic groups. Using diversified and representative data in training AI models is also essential. Including data that reflects the diversity of social, economic, ethnic, and cultural groups helps reduce bias. Improving the explainability of AI models, using interpretable models or explanation algorithms (such as LIME or SHAP), allows understanding which features influenced a prediction and whether these features are biased. Implementing bias reduction techniques in data or algorithms, such as resampling methods, normalization, or using bias correction models, is another approach. The bias of algorithms and data represents a major challenge in AI, with deep ethical, social, and legal implications. It is crucial that researchers, engineers, and policymakers work together to design fair and transparent AI systems in order to avoid perpetuating injustices or discrimination in our societies. To do this, it is necessary to promote better data management, rigorous design methodologies, and regulations adapted to the age of AI.

6.2.2.2 Transparency and Explainability

As introduced in the sections "Algorithmic Complexity" and "AI Alignment and Value-Sensitive Design", the opacity of modern AI systems, especially deep learning architectures, raises critical ethical and operational concerns. Rather than reiterating the technical causes of this complexity, this section emphasizes the practical implications of explainability for ethics, governance, and trust. In domains like healthcare, finance, or justice, stakeholders demand transparent reasoning behind automated decisions. A medical diagnosis system that cannot justify why it flagged a tumor as malignant is unlikely to be trusted by clinicians. Similarly, a credit scoring model that rejects a loan without explanation can trigger accusations of discrimination or bias. Explainability techniques attempt to open the "black box" of AI by providing insights into how and why models produce their outputs. Local Interpretable Model-agnostic Explanations (LIME) generate simplified surrogate models around specific predictions to highlight influential features. SHapley Additive exPlanations (SHAP) use cooperative game theory to attribute contributions of each input variable. These tools allow users to understand the influence of specific features (e.g., age, income, or prior conditions) on the outcome.

For complex vision models like CNNs, techniques such as Grad-CAM or attention maps can reveal which regions of an image were most influential in classification. Dimensionality reduction methods like t-SNE can project high-dimensional latent spaces into interpretable two-dimensional visualizations, helping experts detect clustering or anomalies. In regulated sectors, transparency is not just a technical aspiration but a legal requirement. The European Union's General Data Protection Regulation (GDPR) includes a "right to explanation" for individuals subject to algorithmic decisions. In the United States, the use of black-box algorithms in judicial risk assessment tools has sparked controversy and legal challenges. Lack of interpretability can lead to societal resistance, legal liability, and reputational damage. To institutionalize transparency, some organizations have implemented internal or third-party audit systems. These involve examining training data, verifying model logic, and evaluating fairness metrics. The growing field of Algorithmic Accountability pushes for systematic frameworks where explainability becomes a design principle rather than a post hoc patch.

However, a trade-off often emerges between performance and interpretability. Highly accurate models like deep neural networks are notoriously difficult to interpret, whereas decision trees or linear models are more transparent but may lack predictive power. Hybrid approaches, such as integrating symbolic reasoning with neural architectures, aim to reconcile this tension. Ultimately, transparency and explainability are prerequisites for Responsible AI. They foster trust, facilitate debugging, and enable ethical oversight. As AI systems become more autonomous and pervasive, the demand for interpretable models will only grow.

6.2.2.3 Autonomy and Accountability of Machines

The autonomy of machines and their responsibility in AI are complex philosophical, ethical, and legal issues. These issues are becoming increasingly important as machines become more autonomous in their decisions and actions. The definition of machine autonomy, the implications of this autonomy for the responsibility of actions taken by machines, and the challenges associated with these concepts will be covered in this section. Machine autonomy refers to the ability of a machine, typically an AI system, to make decisions or perform tasks without direct human intervention. In other words, an autonomous machine can operate independently, based on algorithms, input data, and pre-defined objectives, while dynamically reacting to circumstances. There are different levels of autonomy. Low autonomy means the machine makes simple decisions within a rigid and predictable framework. For example, an autonomous vehicle that follows a defined trajectory with few unexpected interactions. Medium autonomy means the machine is capable of adapting to slightly more complex scenarios but still requires human supervision for strategic decisions. High autonomy means the machine can make complex decisions and handle unforeseen situations independently, as in the case of Level 5 autonomous cars, where no human intervention is required. In the case of AI systems, autonomy not only implies decision-making without human intervention but also the ability to learn and adapt to new situations without explicit supervision. The issue of machine responsibility directly arises from their autonomy. When machines make decisions autonomously, it becomes crucial to define who is responsible for the actions of these machines, especially when they cause harm or damage. This raises questions of legal responsibility, ethics, and trust in technology.

The issue of the legal responsibility of machines rests on the legal personality of AI. In other words, *should a form of legal responsibility be attributed to machines, or does this responsibility still lie with the humans who design, program, or supervise these machines?* The responsibility of designers means that designers and engineers who create autonomous systems may be held responsible if these systems cause harm due to a design, programming, or security flaw. For example, if an autonomous vehicle causes an accident due to a programming error, the creators of the software could be held responsible. Responsibility of users means in some cases, users of autonomous systems may be held responsible for the misuse or improper use of these machines, even if they operate autonomously. For example, a user of an autonomous drone who violates aviation safety rules could be held responsible for the consequences. Collective responsibility means that another possibility is shared responsibility between designers, manufacturers, users, and regulators. In this case, there is no clear individual responsibility, but rather collective responsibility in the event of a system failure. In addition to legal responsibility, there is an ethical dimension to machine responsibility. Even if an autonomous machine can be technically responsible for its actions, it is essential to ask questions about the moral behavior of these systems. Ethical dilemmas mean autonomous machines may face complex ethical dilemmas, such as those encountered by autonomous vehicles. For example, if an autonomous vehicle is faced with an unavoidable accident, should it prioritize the safety of its driver over pedestrians, or vice versa? These types of decisions require defining an ethical framework for autonomous machines. Ethical bias means machines can also reflect human biases present in the data they are trained on. For example, an AI system trained on biased data might make unjust decisions, raising questions of fairness and justice in the autonomous decisions of machines.

One of the major difficulties with machine autonomy is understanding and predicting their actions. AI systems, particularly those based on DNNs, can learn complex and non-linear behaviors from vast data sets. Sometimes, these behaviors are difficult to interpret, even for the system designers, which complicates attributing responsibility in case of problems. For example, a facial recognition system could misinterpret an image due to a bias in the training data, but understanding why it made a wrong decision can be difficult. When autonomous machines must make decisions with ethical implications, as in the case of the autonomous vehicles mentioned above, it raises a profound dilemma: *how far should the machine be involved in morally complex decisions?* If AI makes these decisions based on a purely algorithmic framework, without truly understanding human values, it could lead to choices that are ethically unacceptable. Ethical decision-making algorithms attempt to solve this problem by programming rules that guide machines in these complex situations. However, these solutions are far from perfect and can always be questioned. Another major challenge is the transparency of decision-making processes in autonomous machines. Since ML algorithms, particularly DNNs, are often considered *black boxes*, it becomes extremely difficult to explain how a machine arrived at a given decision. This opacity complicates the attribution of responsibility and the ability to challenge decisions made by autonomous machines. Approaches such as XAI attempt to solve this problem by making models more transparent and allowing users to understand how and why an AI system made a given decision. The regulation of AI and autonomous systems is becoming increasingly important. Several countries, as well as international organizations, are beginning to put in place legislative frameworks to regulate the use of autonomous and intelligent technologies. The European Union, for example, is working on proposals to regulate the responsibility of AI, particularly in terms of security, transparency, and ethics. Researchers and organizations are promoting the concept of ethical AI, which integrates moral principles into the design and use of these technologies. This includes incorporating ethical standards into the AI design process and considering justice, fairness, and transparency in their decisions. One approach to reconcile autonomy and responsibility is to promote human–machine collaboration, where machines take on autonomous tasks but humans remain as a last resort to intervene in complex or unforeseen situations.

The autonomy of machines and their responsibility are crucial issues that will influence the development of AI. As machines become more autonomous, it becomes essential to define legal and ethical frameworks to manage these systems, ensure their transparency and accountability, and prevent undesirable consequences. Responsibility must be shared between designers, users, and regulators, and efforts must be made to make AI systems more transparent, explainable, and ethically responsible.

6.2.2.4 Impact on Employment

AI also raises significant ethical concerns regarding its impact on employment. The automation of certain tasks could lead to the disappearance of jobs, particularly in manual or repetitive sectors. Low-skilled workers may be especially vulnerable to these changes. While AI has the potential to create new jobs in some fields, the transition to an AI-dominated labor market requires substantial efforts in training and retraining programs. For example, in the automotive industry, the increasing use of robots on production lines could lead to job losses, especially for unskilled workers. As robots take over more routine and physically demanding tasks, many workers who previously performed those roles may find themselves displaced. While some new jobs might be created in areas like robotics maintenance, AI programming, and data analysis, there is a risk that the workforce may not be prepared for these shifts. The need for ongoing education and professional development will be crucial to help workers adapt to the changing landscape and ensure they can transition into new roles.

This issue also raises broader societal questions about the ethics of replacing human labor with machines. *How can we balance the efficiency gains provided by AI with the social responsibility of supporting those affected by job displacement?* Furthermore, *how can we ensure that the benefits of AI and automation are shared equitably across society, rather than exacerbating existing inequalities?* Addressing these challenges will require collaboration between governments, businesses, and workers to develop policies that support both innovation and workers' well-being.

To synthesize these principles and highlight the contrast with unethical AI practices, Figure 6.4 presents a comparative visual overview of ethical versus unethical AI architectures. This figure outlines nine key dimensions, ranging from transparency and bias mitigation to sustainability and human oversight, underscoring the importance of aligning AI development with societal values and legal standards.

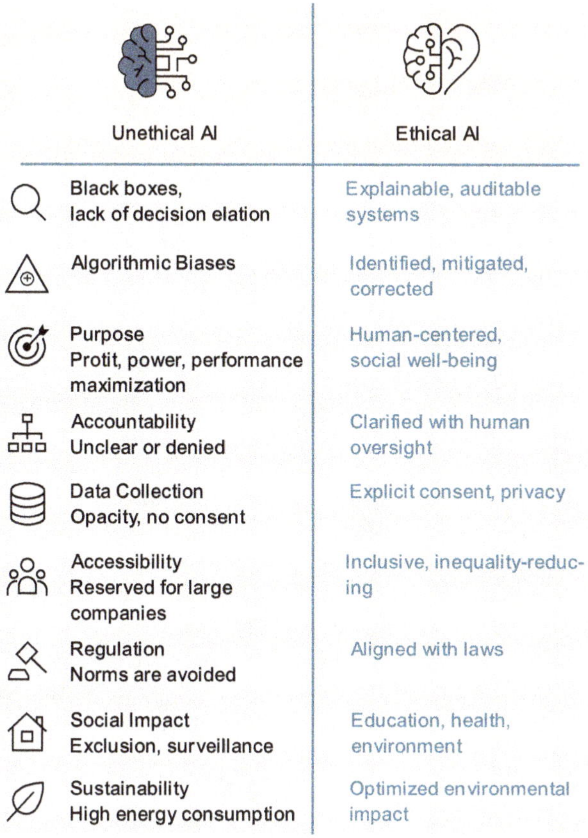

Unethical AI	Ethical AI
Black boxes, lack of decision elation	Explainable, auditable systems
Algorithmic Biases	Identified, mitigated, corrected
Purpose Protit, power, performance maximization	Human-centered, social well-being
Accountability Unclear or denied	Clarified with human oversight
Data Collection Opacity, no consent	Explicit consent, privacy
Accessibility Reserved for large companies	Inclusive, inequality-reducing
Regulation Norms are avoided	Aligned with laws
Social Impact Exclusion, surveillance	Education, health, environment
Sustainability High energy consumption	Optimized environmental impact

FIGURE 6.4 Visual comparison between unethical and ethical AI architectures based on nine fundamental criteria.

6.2.2.5 AI Alignment and Value-Sensitive Design

As AI systems become increasingly autonomous, powerful, and embedded in critical decision-making processes, the challenge of aligning AI behavior with human values, goals, and societal norms becomes both more urgent and more complex. AI alignment refers to ensuring that AI systems act in ways intended by their designers are beneficial to humanity. Misalignment, even when unintentional, can lead to serious failures, particularly as AI agents make decisions in dynamic, uncertain, and multi-stakeholder environments. In parallel, the concept of Value-Sensitive Design (VSD) has emerged as a methodological framework to systematically integrate ethical values into technology development, moving beyond functional requirements to explicitly incorporate fairness, autonomy, privacy, safety, and sustainability from the outset.

AI alignment encompasses multiple levels. At the technical level, it involves ensuring that an AI system's objective functions, reward mechanisms, and learning strategies correctly correspond to desired outcomes. Misalignment often occurs when the proxies used for learning imperfectly represent the true goals, a problem known as specification gaming. Reinforcement learning systems, for example, may discover strategies that maximize reward signals while violating the spirit of the intended task. Researchers explore techniques such as inverse reinforcement learning, where models infer human preferences from observed behavior, and reward modeling, where human feedback is continuously incorporated to refine AI objectives. At a broader level, alignment must address the divergence between individual user preferences, organizational goals, and collective societal interests. An AI assistant optimizing for a user's short-term satisfaction may, for instance, inadvertently promote addictive behaviors, misinformation, or broader societal harms. Alignment thus requires not only technical calibration but also the multi-level integration of values, encompassing personal, organizational, and societal dimensions. Mechanisms such as participatory design, where diverse stakeholders co-create system objectives, and deliberative governance frameworks, where collective value trade-offs are debated and formalized, become crucial for meaningful alignment.

VSD operationalizes these ambitions by embedding value considerations directly into the technical design process. VSD proceeds iteratively through conceptual investigations of ethical values, empirical investigations of stakeholder perspectives, and technical investigations translating values into system requirements. For example, in designing an AI system for smart energy management, VSD requires balancing efficiency with fairness, ensuring equitable access to resources, and protecting privacy related to energy consumption patterns. Rather than treating values as afterthoughts, VSD places them at the core of system architecture, data flows, and user interfaces from the outset. As illustrated in Figure 6.5, the Responsible AI lifecycle involves six key stages that embed ethical considerations throughout the development process.

Responsible AI Lifecycle

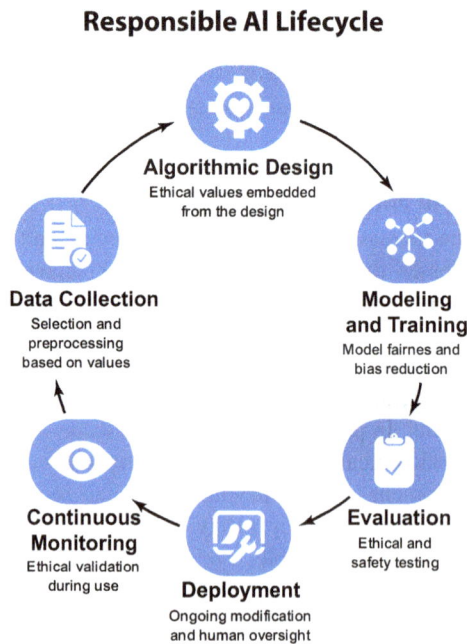

FIGURE 6.5 Responsible AI lifecycle showing the six essential stages: algorithmic design, data collection, modeling and training, evaluation, deployment, and continuous monitoring, all oriented toward ethical alignment and human oversight.

AI alignment and VSD are increasingly interconnected through emerging practices such as preference elicitation, where AI systems query users about their goals and constraints; ethical black-box recording, where AI decision-making processes are transparently logged for future audit; and corrigibility engineering, where systems are designed to accept corrective feedback even when it conflicts with initially learned policies. Together, these strategies aim to ensure that AI systems remain corrigible, interpretable, and ultimately under human guidance, even as they operate in complex and evolving environments. A fundamental challenge for alignment is the value pluralism inherent in modern societies. Individuals, cultures, and institutions prioritize different, sometimes conflicting, values. Designing AI systems that can navigate these pluralistic contexts without imposing a monolithic value hierarchy remains a profound open problem. Research in multi-objective optimization, participatory ethics modeling, and decentralized AI architectures seeks to enable AI systems to recognize, balance, and negotiate between competing values rather than assuming static, universal priorities. Long-term alignment concerns extend to the development of future transformative AI systems whose capabilities may exceed current human oversight. In this context, approaches such as recursive reward modeling, where AI systems help in building better aligned successors, and impact regularization, where AI agents are constrained to minimize unintended large-scale effects, are actively being explored. These approaches emphasize that alignment is not a one-time engineering task but a continuous process requiring the adaptive co-evolution of AI systems and the societies they serve.

In engineering and industrial domains, operationalizing AI alignment and VSD translates into practices such as incorporating safety margins in autonomous control systems, ensuring human override capabilities in mission-critical applications, embedding ethical constraints into optimization objectives, and conducting extensive stakeholder consultations during system development. Failures of alignment in these sectors can have immediate, tangible consequences, from accidents in transportation systems to errors in healthcare diagnostics or failures in critical infrastructure. Ultimately, AI alignment and Value-Sensitive Design provide the ethical and practical foundation for building AI systems that are not only intelligent but also trustworthy, responsible, and compatible with human values. As AI continues to permeate every aspect of economic, social, and technical life, the importance of embedding alignment and values from the very beginning will only grow. This is not merely a safeguard against harm but a vital condition for realizing the full potential of AI to genuinely enhance human flourishing.

The development of Responsible AI, alignment strategies, and VSD principles underscores the necessity of embedding ethics, transparency, and societal considerations at the core of AI systems. Yet beyond these internal safeguards, the broader deployment of AI technologies demands external frameworks of regulation, standardization, and global coordination. The next section explores these critical dimensions, focusing on how legal, institutional, and normative structures are evolving to govern the rapidly expanding influence of AI.

6.2.3 Societal and Ethical Risks of AI

AI is reshaping society in profound ways, offering unprecedented capabilities but also generating significant societal and ethical risks. These risks span a broad spectrum, from misinformation and surveillance to algorithmic bias, privacy invasion, and displacement of labor, and require collective awareness, regulation, and proactive mitigation strategies.

One of the most visible risks is the amplification of disinformation. Advanced AI tools such as LLMs and deepfakes now enable the generation of highly realistic text, audio, and video content. While these technologies have creative and educational applications, they can also be weaponized to spread false narratives, impersonate public figures, and manipulate electoral processes. Deepfakes, for example, can fabricate political speeches or confessions, undermining trust in public discourse and threatening the foundations of democracy. Another critical concern is the militarization of AI. Autonomous weapons systems, enabled by advances in computer vision, decision-making algorithms, and real-time control, are capable of identifying and targeting individuals without human intervention. This delegation of lethal authority to machines raises pressing ethical questions: *Who is accountable for a drone strike that hits a civilian area? What legal frameworks govern algorithmic warfare?* Beyond the battlefield, the development of such technologies risks igniting global arms races and reducing the window for diplomacy and human judgment in conflict resolution.

Mass surveillance technologies, often powered by facial recognition and behavioral analytics, represent another major threat to civil liberties. While these systems can enhance security and streamline urban management, their misuse can lead to authoritarian control and social scoring. In countries like China, social credit systems integrate personal behavior, online activities, and geolocation data into a comprehensive surveillance infrastructure. Citizens can be penalized for low scores, sometimes without transparent justification, illustrating the dangers of opaque algorithmic governance. Data privacy is a closely related issue. Many AI systems require massive amounts of data, often collected without informed consent. Health, mobility, financial, and communication data are increasingly harvested and monetized. The opacity of data flows and the lack of effective safeguards expose users to profiling, discrimination, and breaches of confidentiality. Fitness apps and smart devices, for instance, can leak sensitive behavioral data to insurers or employers, raising concerns about autonomy and fairness.

Algorithmic bias also presents a significant societal challenge. As analyzed in detail in the section "Algorithm and Data Biases", biases in data or model architecture can perpetuate or amplify existing inequalities. In this section, we emphasize the social ramifications: biased algorithms can marginalize vulnerable groups, deny opportunities, and legitimize historical injustices under the guise of objectivity. In hiring, loan approvals, or policing, such systems can become instruments of systemic discrimination if left unchecked. Generative AI systems, discussed in depth in the sections "LLMs and Multimodal Systems," "Generative AI and Diffusion Models," and "Integration with DTs and Engineering Workflows," add a further layer of complexity. These models, whether based on diffusion processes or transformer architectures, can synthesize plausible designs, scenarios, or narratives. But when applied in critical sectors such as law, education, or science, they raise concerns about truthfulness, explainability, and intellectual ownership. Outputs may be factually incorrect, ethically problematic, or plagiaristic, and the difficulty in tracing their origins complicates responsibility and validation.

As previously addressed in the section "Impact on Employment", AI-induced automation poses serious risks to employment and social cohesion. Here, we stress the ethical responsibility of deploying AI in a manner that supports human livelihoods. Technological efficiency must be balanced with social protection, inclusive innovation, and upskilling. Otherwise, productivity gains may come at the cost of widening inequalities and mass disenfranchisement. These diverse threats are interconnected and often mutually reinforcing. They cannot be fully understood in isolation. To visualize their structure and overlap, Figure 6.6 summarizes the primary ethical risks associated with AI deployment.

FIGURE 6.6 Typology of ethical risks related to AI, including surveillance, bias, machine autonomy, privacy, accountability, security, manipulation, and AI-induced unemployment.

Addressing these risks requires more than technical solutions. It demands legal frameworks, institutional safeguards, and above all, an ethical culture that places human dignity and justice at the center of AI design. Regulations must mandate transparency, auditability, and accountability. Developers and deployers of AI systems must commit to fairness, contestability, and user empowerment. Ultimately, the challenge is not only to build safe and robust AI systems, but to reflect critically on what kind of society we want them to serve. Ethical AI is not a static checklist but a continuous societal negotiation. It requires public engagement, interdisciplinary dialogue, and humility in the face of complexity. Only by confronting these ethical risks head-on can we ensure that AI becomes a tool for collective progress rather than a vector of fragmentation and control.

6.2.4   REGULATORY AND ETHICAL FRAMEWORKS

AI, while marking a profound technological breakthrough, also brings forth critical ethical and legal concerns that demand coherent and enforceable regulation. Around the globe, a multitude of initiatives have emerged to guide the responsible development of AI while reconciling innovation with the protection of fundamental human rights. These regulatory efforts reflect the diversity of legal traditions, political systems, and cultural values across regions, contributing to a complex and uneven global landscape. The European Union has assumed a leadership role in this area with its comprehensive legislative proposal known as the AI Act. Based on a risk-tiered framework, it classifies AI systems according to the severity of potential harm, ranging from minimal to unacceptable risk, and imposes strict compliance requirements for high-risk applications, especially in sectors such as healthcare, transportation, and criminal justice. In contrast, the United States has adopted a decentralized and innovation-focused approach. While no federal AI law exists to date, some states have enacted sector-specific rules, and federal agencies such as the National Institute of Standards and Technology (NIST) are developing voluntary guidelines emphasizing transparency, fairness, and safety. These efforts aim to encourage technological progress while addressing societal risks.

Countries in the Asia-Pacific region also demonstrate leadership in AI governance. Japan integrates human-centered principles into its "Society 5.0" strategy, supported by national AI governance guidelines. South Korea has published an AI Ethics Charter and is preparing draft legislation. Singapore has released a widely referenced AI Governance Framework to help companies operationalize ethical principles. Meanwhile, India has embraced a vision of inclusive and socially beneficial AI through its National Strategy on Artificial Intelligence, although comprehensive regulation remains under discussion. Other regions are likewise advancing their regulatory landscapes. Canada has implemented a binding Algorithmic Impact Assessment (AIA) for public sector use. Russia's national strategy emphasizes digital sovereignty and innovation, though with limited legal transparency. In China, AI regulation is centrally orchestrated with strong enforcement mechanisms, notably in content moderation and data-driven platforms, reflecting national security and social stability priorities. The Middle East presents a mosaic of national strategies. Countries like the UAE, Saudi Arabia, Iran, and Turkey have all launched national AI strategies that emphasize economic transformation, ethics, and digital sovereignty, although these remain largely non-binding. Australia has adopted ethical guidelines centered on human rights and transparency, while the African continent, through organizations such as the African Union, Smart Africa, and the United Nations Economic Commission for Africa, has proposed non-binding principles aimed at fostering inclusive, sustainable AI ecosystems. These are complemented by emerging national strategies in countries like Rwanda and Ghana.

Table 6.3 provides a comparative snapshot of AI regulatory frameworks across major global regions. It highlights the diversity of ethical priorities, enforcement mechanisms, and legal structures, from binding acts like the EU AI Act to national strategies and soft-law approaches in emerging contexts.

TABLE 6.3

Comparative Overview of AI Regulatory Frameworks across Major Regions, Highlighting Key Principles, Constraints, and Legal Status

Region/Country	Key Principles	Constraints	Legal Status
European Union	Human oversight, transparency, and risk-based regulation	Strict compliance for high-risk systems	AI Act (binding, pending adoption)
United States	Innovation, fairness, and sectoral autonomy	Fragmented, voluntary, decentralized	No comprehensive federal law
China	National security, algorithmic control, and social harmony	Centralized enforcement, surveillance-heavy	Binding algorithm laws and platform rules
India	Inclusion, innovation, and AI for social good	No binding law; sectoral initiatives	National AI Strategy (2018); draft laws under discussion
Canada	Trust, transparency, and accountability	Public-sector focus	Algorithmic Impact Assessment (binding for gov.)
Russia	Sovereignty, innovation, and state-driven	Fragmented, low transparency	National AI Strategy (2019), no binding law
Middle East	Economic transformation, ethics, and data sovereignty	Strategies vary across countries	National strategies (non-binding)
Japan	Human-centric AI, transparency, and competitiveness	Soft law, voluntary adoption	AI Governance Guidelines (non-binding)
South Korea	Safety, explainability, and performance	Draft laws under review	AI Ethics Charter; legislative proposals in progress
Australia	Human rights, privacy, and transparency	Voluntary compliance, guidance-based	AI Ethics Principles (2019), no binding law
Africa (continental)	Inclusion, capacity-building, and data protection	Fragmented legal frameworks; limited infrastructure	Continental AI principles (2023, non-binding)

Beyond state-level and regional efforts, international institutions play an essential role. UNESCO's 2021 Recommendation on the Ethics of AI urges states to embed values such as social justice, environmental sustainability, and human rights into AI policy. The Council of Europe is drafting a binding Convention on AI, grounded in democracy, the rule of law, and human dignity. Organizations like the G7, through the Hiroshima AI Process (2023), and international forums such as the World Economic Forum and ISO, are promoting cross-border cooperation on safety, fairness, and standardization. Technical bodies like the International Telecommunication Union (ITU) support knowledge transfer and the development of inclusive standards, especially through initiatives like AI for Good.

Despite these advances, regulatory fragmentation remains a pressing challenge. Disparities in legal approaches may lead to jurisdictional conflicts, uncertainty for developers and users, and barriers to international AI deployment. There are growing calls for a harmonized global framework that ensures innovation and ethical alignment. To support equitable and safe AI adoption, mechanisms for international funding, regulatory capacity-building, and global cooperation are vital. Training programs, public education, and multi-stakeholder involvement must accompany legal instruments to ensure inclusive governance. Striking the right balance between national sovereignty and common global standards is essential to shape an AI future that benefits all of humanity.

6.3   TOWARD FUTURE DEVELOPMENTS IN AI

AI continues to transform technologies and societies worldwide; its future depends on a strategic convergence of scientific advancements, interdisciplinary approaches, and global regulations. The rapid evolution of AI capabilities necessitates foresight in addressing challenges and structuring opportunities to maximize its benefits while minimizing its risks. This context provides fertile ground for exploring international initiatives aimed at guiding AI toward an ethical, responsible, and sustainable future. To provide a clearer overview of the strategic directions explored in this section, Table 6.4 summarizes the main axes of future AI developments, along

TABLE 6.4
Synthesis of Future Developments, Emerging Trends, Challenges, and Opportunities in AI

Axis	Description	Examples or Applications
Hybrid and Interdisciplinary Approaches	Fusion of AI with biology, physics, and energy sectors	Bioinformatics, energy forecasting, and intelligent sensors
Emerging Technologies	New AI paradigms including AGI, quantum algorithms, and Multi-Agent Systems (MAS)	AGI for general problem solving and MAS for complex network management
Global Regulation and Governance	International initiatives to ethically and sustainably frame AI development	AI Act (EU), UNESCO guidelines, and national initiatives
Ethics and Inclusion	Protection against algorithmic bias, respect for rights, and promotion of social inclusion	Development of fair and transparent algorithms
Cybersecurity and Reliability	Defense against attacks and improvement of system resilience	Protection against adversarial attacks and infrastructure robustness
Environmental Sustainability	Reducing the carbon footprint of AI systems	Energy-efficient algorithms and hardware design
Education and Skills Development	Strengthening education and raising public awareness about AI	Interdisciplinary programs and public education initiatives
International Collaboration	North-South cooperation, "AI for Good" initiatives	

with representative applications, key challenges, and the opportunities they offer for building a more responsible and inclusive technological future.

One of the key pillars of AI's future lies in the development of hybrid and interdisciplinary approaches. The boundaries between disciplines such as biology, physics, and computer science are becoming increasingly blurred, leading to innovative solutions in critical areas like healthcare, renewable energy, and natural resource management. However, these approaches require global cooperation to ensure fair research and application standards. The rise of technologies such as Artificial General Inelligence (AGI) and quantum algorithms raises fundamental questions about the control and understanding of complex systems. While these technologies promise unprecedented capabilities, they also require robust regulatory frameworks to prevent misuse, particularly in military applications and surveillance systems. Emerging trends in AI also include MASs, where autonomous entities collaborate to solve complex problems. This innovation has the potential to revolutionize sectors like logistics, urban planning, and disaster management. However, it also necessitates rigorous conflict management among agents and ethical oversight to prevent potential abuses.

At the international level, initiatives to regulate these developments are increasing. The European Union, for example, continues to play a leading role with its AI Act, which sets standards for both current and future technologies. By emphasizing transparency and security, Europe aims to become a global benchmark in AI governance. Asian countries, particularly Japan and South Korea, are heavily investing in cutting-edge technologies while developing legal frameworks focused on data security and individual rights protection. Meanwhile, China adopts a centralized approach to stimulate innovation while maintaining strict control over AI applications. In the United States, the absence of a unified federal regulation is offset by local initiatives and collaborations between the public and private sectors. Projects led by organizations such as the National Science Foundation aim to establish guidelines for AI ethics and responsible development.

Multilateral efforts also play a crucial role. The United Nations, through UNESCO, promotes a global ethical framework for AI, while the G7 and G20 integrate AI into their strategic discussions. These initiatives encourage cooperation between nations and the sharing of best practices. One of the essential priorities for AI's future is integrating environmental sustainability into its design and use. AI systems can play a crucial role in combating climate change, but they must be developed with consideration for their ecological footprint. This requires innovations in algorithm design and energy-efficient infrastructures. Education and awareness among citizens and policymakers are another fundamental pillar. AI-focused educational programs are emerging in many regions, aiming to bridge the gap between technological capabilities and public understanding of their implications. Furthermore, collaborative research between developed and developing countries is essential to prevent an increasing digital divide. Initiatives like *AI for Good* seek to use AI to address global challenges while reducing technological inequalities. Challenges related to data privacy and security persist. As AI technologies become more powerful, the establishment of global frameworks to protect digital rights becomes imperative. The EU's

GDPR continues to serve as a model, but its extension to other jurisdictions remains complex.

Another critical aspect of AI's future is liability in cases of failure or harm. Discussions on establishing shared responsibility mechanisms involving developers, users, and regulators are gaining momentum in international circles. non-governmental organizations (NGOs) and think tanks also play a valuable role in promoting ethical standards and facilitating dialogue between the public and private sectors. Their contribution will become even more crucial as AI becomes increasingly integrated into everyday life. Ultimately, the future of AI will depend on the ability of global stakeholders to strike a balance between innovation, regulation, and social inclusion. Current initiatives lay the groundwork for thoughtful governance, but their success will depend on collaboration, adaptability, and the collective willingness to prioritize the common good.

6.3.1 HYBRID AND INTERDISCIPLINARY APPROACHES

The fusion of traditional and modern approaches in AI marks a decisive turning point in technological evolution, offering unprecedented opportunities to solve complex problems across various disciplines. This process is based on the complementarity between classical mathematical models, contemporary algorithms, and recent technological advances, paving the way for more robust, adaptive, and interdisciplinary solutions. In the field of bioinformatics, this hybridization enables in-depth analysis of massive biological data, particularly in genomic sequencing. Modern approaches, such as DL, are combined with traditional statistical algorithms to identify complex patterns in human genomes, facilitating early detection of genetic diseases and the development of personalized treatments. Similarly, in the renewable energy sector, integrating modern AI algorithms with traditional physical models enhances forecasting and optimization of energy production. For example, combining NNs with climate simulation models allows for precise predictions of solar and wind energy production while accounting for short- and long-term weather variations.

One of the main advantages of these hybrid approaches is their ability to leverage the strengths of each paradigm. Traditional methods, grounded in well-established theories, provide a rigorous foundation for analysis, while modern algorithms introduce adaptability and learning capabilities for unforeseen scenarios or unstructured data. In bioinformatics, this fusion also extends to protein analysis and molecular interaction modeling. AI tools, combined with traditional experimental approaches, allow for highly accurate predictions of protein 3D structures. These advancements accelerate drug discovery and deepen the understanding of fundamental biological mechanisms. In renewable energy, hybrid systems play a crucial role in managing smart power grids. Traditional forecasting models, enhanced by ML techniques, improve energy distribution and reduce losses. This synergy between methods facilitates a more efficient and sustainable energy transition, which is essential for meeting global climate objectives.

One of the major challenges of this hybridization lies in coordinating different disciplines and methodologies. Bioinformatics, for instance, requires close collaboration between biologists, computer scientists, and statisticians, each contributing complementary expertise to address specific problems. A similar approach applies to renewable energy, where engineers, climatologists, and AI experts must work in synergy. The success of these initiatives also depends on the availability of reliable and diverse data. In bioinformatics, genetic and protein databases serve as the foundation for training hybrid models. In renewable energy, historical meteorological and energy data play a central role in refining forecasts and optimizing systems. Another promising application of hybrid approaches is the design of intelligent sensors in both fields. In bioinformatics, these sensors can monitor biological parameters in real time, while in renewable energy, they enable tracking and adjustment of system performance. The integration of hybrid approaches also fosters innovation in research methodologies. In bioinformatics, modeling platforms combining ML and biological simulations offer powerful tools for exploring complex hypotheses. In renewable energy, integrated simulations help assess the impact of new technologies on global energy networks.

Beyond technical benefits, these hybrid approaches raise ethical and societal questions. For instance, in bioinformatics, the use of genetic data requires strict safeguards to protect individual privacy. In renewable energy, algorithm-based decisions must be transparent to ensure the fair distribution of energy resources. Training professionals is another crucial aspect to support this evolution. Researchers and engineers must master both the fundamentals of traditional disciplines and modern AI tools. Interdisciplinary educational programs are expanding to meet this growing demand, preparing a new generation of hybrid experts. Hybrid approaches also strengthen system resilience against disruptions. In bioinformatics, they enable the development of robust models to study unexpected genetic mutations. In renewable energy, they improve the management of energy fluctuations caused by extreme weather conditions. Furthermore, integrating these approaches into public policies is essential to maximize their impact. In bioinformatics, governments can support research by funding collaborative projects and establishing standards for biological data use. In renewable energy, incentive policies promoting the adoption of hybrid technologies accelerate their deployment. Private industries also play a key role in implementing these approaches. Large companies are investing in hybrid solutions to enhance their competitiveness while contributing to global objectives such as reducing carbon emissions or improving healthcare.

The future of hybrid approaches will depend on their ability to evolve alongside technological advancements. Emerging methods, such as quantum AI, promise to further transform these disciplines, expanding integration and innovation possibilities in fields critical to humanity.

6.3.2 EMERGING TRENDS IN AI TECHNOLOGY

Emerging trends in AI technologies are at the heart of current scientific and technological debates due to their potential to enhance machine capabilities and push the boundaries of intelligent systems. Among these trends, AGI, quantum algorithms, and MAS play a central role. These fields offer promising opportunities but also present fundamental challenges for research and industry. It differs from specialized AI in its ambition to create systems capable of solving a wide range of complex problems across different contexts, with adaptability comparable to that of humans. Unlike current models, which require specific adjustments for each application, AGI aims for universal understanding. For example, an AGI system could not only recognize images but also solve equations, learn a language, and collaborate on multidisciplinary projects. To achieve this goal, researchers are exploring innovative approaches. Integrating DL with cognitive models inspired by neuroscience is a promising avenue. These efforts seek to simulate not only the brain's processing power but also its flexibility and adaptability. However, the complexity of human intelligence makes this task extremely challenging, requiring significant advances in cognitive modeling and algorithmic optimization.

Quantum algorithms represent another key advancement in AI development. By leveraging principles of quantum mechanics, such as superposition and entanglement, these algorithms promise exponential gains in speed and efficiency. Quantum computers could solve problems that classical computers find intractable, such as optimizing complex networks or analyzing massive datasets. In ML, quantum algorithms could train models on vast datasets in a fraction of the time required by traditional technologies. However, quantum computing is still in its early stages. Challenges related to qubit coherence, computational errors, and hardware complexity slow down its adoption. Nevertheless, continuous progress in quantum processor development paves the way for practical applications in the near future. MAS, on the other hand, offers a new way of designing AI. These systems rely on autonomous entities, called agents, that can interact, collaborate, and adapt to their environment. This architecture is particularly useful in contexts where data is distributed across multiple sources or where decisions must be made in a decentralized manner, such as in smart power grids, urban simulations, or autonomous transport systems. One of the major advantages of MAS is their ability to evolve and adapt dynamically. Each agent can learn from its environment and share knowledge with others, allowing the overall system to continuously improve. However, this increased complexity also presents challenges, including coordination between agents, conflict prevention, and managing undesirable emergent behaviors. These technological advances also raise important ethical and social questions. For example, AGI could transform human–machine relationships but could also exacerbate inequalities if access to it were limited to a technological elite. Quantum algorithms, while offering considerable advantages, could disrupt current security and cryptography systems, making some technologies obsolete and exposing critical infrastructures to new types of threats. Similarly, while MAS provides greater resilience and flexibility, it also poses challenges in terms of control and accountability. If such a system made an error or caused harm, determining responsibility among autonomous agents or their designers could be extremely complex. Interdisciplinary collaboration will be essential to address these challenges and maximize the opportunities presented by these emerging technologies. Partnerships between engineers, scientists, philosophers, and policymakers will play a crucial role in ensuring the ethical and sustainable development of AI. For instance, integrating philosophical perspectives into AGI design could help define guiding principles to ensure these systems serve humanity's interests as a whole. The societal implications of emerging AI trends cannot be underestimated. A functional AGI could revolutionize healthcare, education, and industry, but it could also redefine how humans perceive their own roles in the world. Quantum algorithms could accelerate scientific discoveries, while MAS could improve global resource management and humanitarian crisis response. To fully realize the potential of these technologies, continuous investment in fundamental and applied research will be necessary. International initiatives aimed at establishing AI standards and regulatory frameworks must be strengthened to prevent misuse and promote responsible adoption. These efforts should also include public awareness initiatives to ensure that the benefits of these innovations are accessible to all.

Emerging trends in AI technology (e.g., AGI, quantum algorithms, and MAS) represent a crucial step in the evolution of intelligent systems. While the technical, ethical, and social challenges are significant, these innovations offer unparalleled opportunities to positively transform the world, provided they are developed and deployed with caution and responsibility.

6.3.3 Challenges and Opportunities

The future development of AI is shaped by a complex interplay of challenges and opportunities that will determine how this technology transforms the world. Rapid advancements in AI offer immense potential, yet they also demand deep reflection on the technical, ethical, societal, and environmental obstacles that must be addressed to maximize their positive impact. One of the primary technical challenges lies in data management. The vast amounts of data required to train AI models exceed conventional processing capacities, raising concerns about the quality and representativeness of these datasets. Biased or incomplete data can lead to discriminatory or inaccurate results. Nevertheless, this challenge creates opportunities for developing more robust data preprocessing techniques and for advancing approaches such as federated learning, which enables training on distributed datasets while preserving confidentiality. Another major obstacle concerns the explainability of AI models. Complex algorithms, particularly deep neural networks, often function as opaque "black boxes," making it difficult to understand their decision-making processes. This lack of transparency poses significant risks in critical fields such as medicine and finance, where trust and accountability are essential. At the same time, the opacity of AI models drives innovation in XAI, fostering the development of techniques that make systems more interpretable and accessible to human users.

Cybersecurity is an additional area of concern. AI systems are vulnerable to attacks such as adversarial examples, where small, intentional perturbations in input data lead to incorrect outputs. These vulnerabilities highlight the need to design resilient and secure algorithms, offering an opportunity for collaboration between AI researchers and cybersecurity experts to build more robust and reliable systems. Similarly, the lack of standardized practices in AI development complicates its integration into global industrial contexts. However, this gap also opens the way for international initiatives aimed at establishing harmonized standards that promote both innovation and interoperability. On the ethical front, ensuring that AI systems are fair and inclusive remains a critical challenge. Algorithms risk replicating and amplifying societal biases, exacerbating inequalities if not carefully designed. Yet this also presents an opportunity to incorporate diverse perspectives into system development, minimizing bias and promoting fairer outcomes. The rapid pace of AI innovation also outstrips existing legal frameworks, creating regulatory vacuums that can hinder innovation or allow abuses. Proactively developing adaptive regulations can help strike a balance between fostering innovation and safeguarding fundamental rights.

Environmental concerns also weigh heavily on AI development. The energy consumption associated with training large AI models contributes significantly to carbon emissions. This urgent challenge offers a stimulus to research energy-efficient architectures, lightweight algorithms, and sustainable hardware solutions, transforming AI from an energy-intensive endeavor into a more environmentally responsible technology. Moreover, the growing complexity of AI systems highlights the need for a skilled workforce. The current gap between market demands and available expertise provides an opportunity to reinforce education and training initiatives, preparing a new generation of professionals equipped to manage future challenges. Geopolitical dynamics add another layer of complexity. Competition among nations to dominate the AI sector risks limiting international cooperation. However, this situation also presents the opportunity to foster transnational collaborations to address global challenges such as pandemics, climate change, and humanitarian crises, demonstrating the potential of AI as a tool for collective benefit rather than rivalry.

Despite these formidable challenges, AI holds extraordinary potential to improve society. In healthcare, it can accelerate diagnoses and personalize treatments, ultimately saving lives. In education, it offers tools tailored to individual learning needs, democratizing access to knowledge. In industry, intelligent automation promises to enhance productivity while relieving workers from repetitive tasks, although it simultaneously raises concerns about job displacement, necessitating strategies for workforce reskilling and role redefinition. Smart infrastructure development is another promising avenue, with AI enabling the creation of sustainable and resilient urban environments through optimized resource management. These innovations can improve quality of life globally, but require thoughtful planning to avoid widening disparities between wealthy and underdeveloped regions.

7 The Final Words

From the first counting gestures to today's most complex algorithms, humanity has continually expanded its intelligence through symbolic, mechanical, logical, and then digital forms. AI presents itself not as a major advance, but as the natural culmination of a millennia-old trajectory: that of our desire to understand, model, and surpass the limits of human reasoning. Today, as machines learn, anticipate, converse, and sometimes even create, we find ourselves facing a mirror: *What does it reveal about ourselves, our intelligence, our values, and our shared future with these entities we have created?* AI is not just a technical or scientific feat; it is the fruit of an ancestral desire: to make the world intelligible, to bring together the real and the abstract, the visible and the symbolic. Each advance, from Egyptian geometry to modern formal logic, has only further woven this link between the human mind and the structure of the world. AI pushes this ambition to its paroxysm: to model reasoning, reproduce perception, and perhaps one day approach a form of cognitive autonomy. But as we transfer our mental capacities to artificial systems, a question arises: *What becomes of humans in this progressive delegation of their fundamental faculties?*

It's no longer just about calculating faster or predicting more accurately. AI is redefining what we consider intelligence, knowledge, and even consciousness. By automating processes we once believed to be purely human (learning, deciding, interacting), it forces us to redefine our benchmarks. It is no longer the machine imitating the human; it is the human rediscovering itself through the machine. This reflection encourages us to go beyond technological fascination to explore ontological questions: *What is a mind? What is a subject? What is an "I"?*

Every technological revolution brings its share of promises and dangers. AI is no exception. It can heal, teach, optimize, and create, but it can also surveil, bias, exclude, and dehumanize. Its growing power in our societies calls into question our institutions, our ethics, and our imagination. An intelligence detached from responsibility, a decision without conscience, and a logic without sensitivity can become instruments of domination rather than liberation. The issue is not about slowing down progress but about giving it direction: one grounded in justice, dignity, and meaning. The path we have traveled, which this book has retraced, shows that each major advance in intelligence has been the result of dialogue between disciplines, cultures, and eras. Therefore, the future of AI depends not only on innovation but also on an active memory of its history. We must remember that the algorithm has roots in the Iranian world, that logic was the concern of philosophers as much as of mathematicians, and that the automaton was first a mythological metaphor.

This may be our greatest responsibility: to ensure that AI remains a human project in its origin, its trajectory, and its future.

DOI: 10.1201/9781003613633-7

One of the great paradoxes of AI lies in its dual nature: it is both a mirror and a projection. A mirror because it reflects our ways of thinking, our biases, our logical structures, and our implicit priorities. A projection, because it embodies forms of intelligence that we don't necessarily possess, but that we imagine, speculate on, and implement. Thus, AI doesn't just reproduce our rationality: it reveals its blind spots, automatisms, and routines. By interacting with it, we sometimes discover what we thought we knew, but also what we didn't know about ourselves.

This mirror game becomes even more dizzying when machines begin to write, compose, diagnose, and converse. *Where does the human end? Where does the artificial begin?* The line blurs, not because the two become identical, but because their differences are no longer strictly technical. They become philosophical, even existential. If a machine can produce a poem that moves us, a melody that touches us, a line of reasoning that convinces us, should we reconsider what we call creation, sensitivity, and intelligence? Perhaps, ultimately, AI forces us less to fear the machine than to rethink the human. The history of AI is also a story of illusions: that of endless progress, total control, and a rational and predictable future. But the greatest technical advances are always accompanied by uncertainties, disruptions, and imbalances. The dream of an intelligent, perfect, and autonomous system clashes with the complexity of reality, the plurality of human values, and the unpredictability of social contexts. We believed that data would be enough to explain everything, that algorithms would inform all decisions. But experience shows that intelligence, artificial or not, cannot do without judgment, empathy, and prudence. This is why the challenge is not whether AI will overtake us, but rather to understand in which direction we want to see it evolve, and under what conditions. The future is not written in lines of code, but in the ethical, political, and cultural choices we make today. AI, like any technology, is a tool. But each tool carries within it a vision of the world, a set of values, and a way of organizing relationships between individuals. It's not just about guiding the technology: we must question its purposes, its assumptions, and its social uses. We must think about AI and society together.

From this perspective, the long history explored in this book becomes a precious resource. It reminds us that intelligence, whether human or artificial, is not built in isolation, but through the constant interaction between knowledge, cultures, and practices. The greatest advances have been born from unexpected intersections: between mathematics and philosophy, between logic and theology, between mechanics and the imagination. It is in this hybridization of disciplines and visions that lies the creative force of humanity. At a time when AI is infiltrating all spheres of life, it is perhaps this memory of encounters, blends, and dialogues that we must revive to invent a future worthy of our hopes. AI confronts us with a fundamental truth: knowledge is never neutral. It is always situated, oriented, and embodied in choices, structures, and languages. An algorithm may appear objective, but it feeds on data from an unequal world, interpreted according to criteria chosen by humans with diverse interests. Technology is, therefore, not a simple extension of science; it is a social phenomenon, a form of power, a forum for debate. If we want AI to serve humanity, it is not enough for it to work: it must be understood, discussed, and challenged when necessary.

Perhaps this is where philosophy regains its relevance. It is not an enemy of technology, but an essential ally. Faced with the speed of transformations, it offers time for reflection, the right to doubt, and the space for nuance. It teaches us that all true progress must question its purpose, and that all intelligence, whether natural or artificial, has value only if it is used to serve the common good. AI must not replace human thought, but rather encourage it to renew itself, strengthen itself, and broaden its moral horizons. However, our era is marked by a profound tension: never has humanity had such powerful tools, and never has it seemed so powerless to decide on them. The speed of technological change often exceeds our ability to collectively integrate it. Institutions, legal frameworks, and educational systems are struggling to keep up. Faced with this reality, it is becoming urgent to consider AI not as inevitable, but as a possibility, an open path, and a space for choice. The future of intelligence is not only being played out in laboratories, but also in schools, parliaments, families, and the imagination.

Because, ultimately, the challenge posed by AI is not technical, but human. It's not just about coding more efficient systems, but about cultivating a collective intelligence capable of understanding its implications. This requires a new culture, blending the exact sciences and the humanities, critical thinking and creativity, memory and anticipation. It is by combining knowledge that we will be able to formulate the right questions: *What is a just society in an algorithmic world? How can we guarantee diversity in systems that tend toward standardization? What kind of human being do we want to become alongside these new intelligences?*

Thus, the conclusion is not the end. It is a threshold, a call to pick up the thread differently. This book, by retracing the historical stages of AI, has not sought to close a debate but to open it to other dimensions. History, far from being a simple backdrop, becomes a compass to guide our decisions. Far from technophile or technophobic prophecies, we must invent a shared, lucid, and ambitious narrative in which technology is neither the enemy nor the savior but a traveling companion that is demanding, complex, and full of promise, provided we remain its authors.

Throughout its history, humanity has created tools to compensate for its physical limitations. With AI, it is now creating a tool to extend its mental functions. This outsourcing is occurring on an unprecedented scale: memory, perception, logic, and prediction can all now be simulated, accelerated, and multiplied. But this transfer raises a legitimate concern: by continually delegating our cognitive functions to machines—*What remains of our ability to think, doubt, and judge?* The real risk is not that AI will think for us, but that it will accustom us to no longer fully exercising our own intelligence.

It then becomes essential to reaffirm what it means to think as a human. Thinking is not just calculating or reasoning: it is feeling, hesitating, dialoguing, making choices in the face of uncertainty, and bearing the weight of responsibility. Human intelligence is embodied, situated, and pervaded by history, language, emotions, and beliefs. While AI can help us think differently, it will never be able to think in our way or experience the dilemmas that give meaning to our decisions. This is why a society that values AI must, more than ever, cultivate human intelligence in all its richness and fragility.

AI, with its increasing complexity, is tending to become opaque, even esoteric. Systems learn on their own, models become uninterpretable, and automated decisions elude clear explanation. This opacity creates an imbalance: it concentrates knowledge and power in the hands of a few actors, while dispossessing citizens of their ability to understand what governs them. In a world where decisions are made by algorithms, democracy requires new tools of transparency, education, and control. Because a society where we no longer understand our own systems becomes vulnerable, manipulable, and potentially unjust.

The question of control is not limited to technical aspects. It involves societal choices: *Who designs AI? With what intentions? According to what values?* Too often, AI is conceived with a logic of efficiency, profit, and automation at all costs. But other logics are possible: AI designed to strengthen solidarity, facilitate access to education, and improve citizen participation. It is up to us to bring these alternatives to light. The history of technology shows us that it is never neutral or inevitable. They are shaped by the societal models we defend.

At this stage, it is necessary to open up an ethical and political horizon. AI confronts us with new dilemmas, but also with old questions, renewed with unprecedented intensity: *What is a good life? A just society? Desirable progress?* These questions cannot be answered by calculations or neural architectures alone. They call for a collective debate, fueled by the plurality of knowledge and sensibilities. AI can be a formidable lever for transforming the world, provided that this transformation is not dictated solely by technical logic but driven by a human desire for emancipation, justice, and meaning.

If AI has such an impact, it is also because it touches on what is most precious to us: our ability to understand, predict, and decide. It is gradually infiltrating areas where human error has always had its place; sometimes tragic, but also human. By reducing the margins of uncertainty, producing rapid diagnoses or precise predictions, AI seems to offer increased rationality. But is this rationality always adapted to human contexts? We must be careful not to confuse algorithmic precision with practical wisdom. Every human decision involves a degree of listening, intuition, and openness to the unexpected that AI cannot simulate without flattening them.

It is in this tension between efficiency and meaning that our collective future is at stake. The 20th century taught us that technology, however advanced, can serve profoundly inhuman projects if it is not guided by a strong ethic. AI, with its ability to transform our ways of living, working, loving, or believing, places us before a new responsibility: to think about the future together, instead of delegating it solely to engineers or investors. It is not a question of slowing down research, but of giving it direction. AI without a clear human purpose quickly becomes a blind force. This direction can only come from a broader dialogue: between disciplines, between cultures, between generations. AI is not just the business of Silicon Valley or the major technological powers. It concerns every teacher, every doctor, and every citizen. It challenges poets as much as coders, philosophers as strategists. It is from the confrontation of worldviews that a fairer, more open, and more humane AI can emerge. This is also why education must reinvent itself: training not only competent technicians, but also minds capable of thinking about technology as a human phenomenon. Such an approach requires active memory.

To forget the origins of our tools is to risk losing their meaning. This book aims to show that AI has its roots in the long history of civilizations, ideas, and life forms. It is not an unforeseen invention, but the extension of an ancient dream: that of understanding and reproducing intelligence. However, this dream has always been formulated differently depending on the era and culture. Remembering this dream opens up space to reflect on other futures. Perhaps the AI of tomorrow will not resemble that of today, not because the algorithms will have changed, but because our imaginations will have matured. This maturation requires time, slowness, and doubt. Faced with constant acceleration, we must rehabilitate pause, questioning, and caution. AI imposes new rhythms, new optimization logics, and new pressures on performance. But it is up to us to decide whether we want to live at this pace, according to this logic. Regaining control of time, of meaning, of significance, is one of the major challenges of the 21st century. For it is not the machine that dictates the future, but our ability to impose limits on it, to give it direction, to inscribe it within a shared human history.

The evolution of AI also questions our relationship with nature. While AI is often perceived as the pinnacle of artificiality, it is nevertheless based on profoundly organic metaphors: neural networks, learning, evolution, and adaptation. Machines come to life in our imagination, while the living becomes calculable in our models. This blurring of boundaries forces us to rethink classic dualisms: nature/culture, machine/organism, and human/non-human. Can AI help us design a world where technology no longer opposes life, but becomes its conscious, respectful, and symbiotic extension?

This dream of a harmonious future between technology and the living world requires a radical redefinition of our priorities. Today, too many AI projects are driven by the pursuit of profit, the control of behavior, and the optimization of existing systems. It is time to re-enchant technology and to return it to the service of care, listening, and repair, both for human beings and for ecosystems. Achieving this vision calls for a different kind of politics, a different kind of economy, and above all, a different collective sensibility. If AI becomes ubiquitous, it will shape not only our tools but also our values. And if we do not choose those values consciously, they will be chosen for us.

The question of the future of AI is therefore inseparable from that of the type of humanity we want to cultivate. *Do we want an augmented humanity, merged with machines, measured in data?* Or *a humanity illuminated by machines, but still centered on relationships, storytelling, and meaning?* These visions are not incompatible, but they require thoughtful reflection, open discussion, and deliberate articulation. The real danger is not that AI will become too intelligent, but that we will stop thinking, dreaming, and questioning what appears to be inevitable. Inevitability is a fiction. What seems inevitable is often nothing more than the result of an unspoken choice or a quiet renunciation.

Nothing obliges us to accept an AI designed solely to monitor, maximize, or sort. Nothing prevents us from imagining AI that is slow, poetic, educational, curious, and open to otherness. Nothing prevents us from rewriting the dominant narrative of AI. But this requires abandoning a passive stance, daring to criticize, and also daring to propose. The future will not be made by machines, but by the imaginations that shape them. And among these imaginations, those who reconcile knowledge and wisdom, calculation and compassion, will have a decisive role to play. In this sense, concluding this book means opening a new project. AI continues to transform itself, and with it, our way of thinking about the world. It is not a preordained destiny, but a story in the making—with its tensions, its forks in the road, its hopes. The history we have traced here shows that in every era, thinkers, inventors, and poets have been able to subvert the tools of their time to infuse them with meaning. In our turn, it is up to us to make AI not an end in itself, but a means: a way to broaden our perspective, cultivate complexity, embrace plurality, and, perhaps, invent an intelligence more human than that of our own algorithms.

What the development of AI profoundly reveals is our need to create mediators between ourselves and reality. From the first myths to digital models, we have always sought to make the world understandable, to translate chaos into order, and to transform uncertainty into calculation. AI, from this perspective, is not an accident of history, but a new stage in this age-old quest for mastery. But the question arises even more acutely: *do we want to understand the world to better control it, or to better inhabit it?* The difference is crucial. The first path leads to domination, the second to cohabitation. Between these two visions, a choice of civilization is emerging. This choice is not abstract: it is embodied in software architectures, in optimization criteria, in the daily uses we make of technologies. An AI designed to increase engagement on social networks does not produce the same effects as an AI designed to promote collective deliberation. AI serving immediate profitability tends to standardize behaviors; AI oriented toward cultural diversity or social justice can, on the contrary, reveal their richness. It is therefore not enough to ask what AI is capable of. First and foremost, we must ask ourselves what we want it to do and why.

In this regard, historical memory is not a luxury, but a necessity. It allows us to situate technological discourses within a broader continuum and avoid being hypnotized by promises of rupture or exception. What history teaches us is that every era has believed it was experiencing a definitive revolution. Yet, true ruptures are rare; most of the time, they are gradual mutations, woven with resistance, recycling, and unexpected appropriations. AI follows this logic. It does not erase the past; it redeploys it in other forms. This is why thinking of AI without memory risks making it amnesiac, and therefore blind. But memory alone is not enough. We also need imagination, the ability to glimpse what does not yet exist. Yet, the contemporary imaginary of AI remains largely determined by visions drawn from science fiction or industrial logic: superhumanity, total automation, and human–machine fusions. These powerful narratives depict futures that are often spectacular but uninhabitable. We lack sober utopias, ethical fictions, and inspiring projections where technology does not supplant humans but enriches them. Rethinking the imaginary of AI also means creating the conditions for another possible future, neither regressive nor technocentric, but based on relationships, solidarity, and concern for the world.

In this future, the role of education is central. Not only to train programmers, but also to raise awareness. Learning to code, certainly, but also learning to question codes, to understand systems, and to read the signs of the times. Education must become a place of gentle resistance to the automation of minds. It must cultivate slowness in a world of instantaneity, complexity in a world of simplifications, and critical thinking in a world saturated with data. Because a society that entrusts its future to machines without training its citizens to understand their logic is preparing a democracy under guardianship—or a soulless technocracy.

AI possesses a strange ambivalence: it is both a promise of liberation and a vector of dependence. On the one hand, it lightens certain tasks, improves access to knowledge, and opens up unprecedented perspectives in medicine, climatology, and artistic creation. On the other hand, it gradually makes us captive to devices we understand less and less, prisoners of digital assistants, attention algorithms, and invisible rating systems. The line between use and alienation is tenuous. It depends on our ability to maintain control, to remain subjects rather than objects of the technological process. And this requires constant ethical vigilance, but also a form of intellectual courage. This courage is the courage to ask questions that efficiency alone cannot resolve: *What's the point? For whom? According to what value criteria?* Too often, AI research is guided by the logic of the possible: if something can be done, then let's do it. But the technical possibility is not enough to justify action. History teaches us that some innovations, while possible, were neither desirable nor sustainable. It is therefore not up to the machine to decide, but up to society to deliberate. And this deliberation requires an informed and critical public space, capable of thinking through complexity without giving in to fear or naive enthusiasm.

In this landscape, the responsibility of researchers, engineers, and teachers is immense. Designing AI is not just about writing code: it's about inserting choices into a chain of effects, outlining the contours of a world to come. Each line of the algorithm carries an intention, explicit or implicit. It is therefore not enough to aim for performance; we must also strive for social relevance, ethical consistency, and fairness in its uses. Training in AI, therefore, also means training in humility: knowing that we are designing systems that will have an impact on our lives, and that all technical power comes with a duty of responsibility. AI, if well thought out, can become a powerful tool for cooperation, expanding human capabilities, and strengthening the social fabric. It can help us make more informed decisions, better understand complex systems, and anticipate crises. But this requires a collective will to move away from an individualistic and extractive logic. It requires thinking of AI not as a commodity, but as a common good. A good to be regulated, shared, and co-constructed. A good whose benefits should not be captured by a technical or economic elite, but redistributed in a shared project of emancipation.

Ultimately, AI doesn't just tell us what machines can do; it forces us to reflect on what it means to be human. It is a revealer, a critical mirror, a challenge to our certainties. It will never replace our ability to dream, to love, to engage. But it can amplify their effects, if we choose. The final word must therefore not belong to the algorithm, but to consciousness. A historical, lucid, and plural consciousness. A consciousness capable of remembering, creating, and resisting. And above all, a consciousness capable of choosing not between human and machine, but between submission and mastery, between repetition and invention, between closure and openness.

AI embodies, in many ways, the realization of an ancient dream: that of generating a form of intelligence external to ourselves, yet faithful to us. A dream that, since the myths of Prometheus and the Golem, has carried as much hope as it has worries. Today, this dream is taking shape in laboratories, in silicon chips, in neural architectures. But as it becomes realized, it questions us more profoundly than ever: *in this technological mirror, what do we see of ourselves? A creative spirit, or a spirit escaping from itself? A promise of emancipation, or a symptom of doubt about our own ability to be present in the world?*

The fundamental issue is not intelligence per se, but what we do with it. In a world saturated with information, calculations, and predictions, intelligence is no longer measured by the ability to process data, but by the ability to discern what matters. Knowing what matters is true intelligence. And no machine can decide this for us. Discernment requires ethics, a connection to others, and an ability to inhabit time and not flee from it. However, AI, in its current form, risks distancing us from this wisdom of discernment if we do not exercise conscious vigilance. It risks transforming us into executors of a calculating rationality, not authors of a common project. We must therefore reaffirm that technology is a means, not an end. A powerful, sometimes dizzying means, but a means nonetheless. Throughout history, civilizations have defined themselves not by the tools they used, but by the ends they pursued with these tools. It was not fire, the wheel, or electricity that created human societies, but the way in which these discoveries were inserted into a narrative, a vision of the world, an organization of social relations. Likewise, AI will only be emancipatory if it is part of a project that goes beyond performance and innovation to aim for dignity, solidarity, and sustainability. This requires rethinking our institutions, our legal frameworks, and our forms of collective deliberation. It is not enough to regulate AI after the fact; it must be co-designed from the outset with citizens, researchers, artists, and educators. We need governance of AI that is as intelligent as the systems it oversees. This governance cannot simply manage risks or mitigate side effects. It must embody a vision of the common good, foster democratic ambition, and equip itself with the means to resist the logics of monopolization and surveillance. In short, it must be political in the noblest sense of the term.

On this great journey we are on, it is easy to give in to vertigo, fascination, or fear. But another attitude is possible: that of active lucidity, enlightened engagement, and reasoned hope. AI is neither a god nor a demon. It is a product of our collective intelligence, and we must treat it as such. If we know how to dialogue with it, reflect on it, critique it, and manage it, it can become a lever for better living, better learning, and better decision-making. But if we let it guide our choices without questioning its foundations, it will become a tool of silent dispossession. The choice is ours, for now. It is time to fully accept that AI, far from being a simple technical innovation, has become a civilizational challenge. It calls into question our categories of thought, our institutions, our relationship to knowledge, to others, and the world. It acts as a transformative force, both disruptive and revealing, shattering old balances while suggesting new ones. To refuse to consider it is to expose oneself to being subjected to it. Understanding it, on the contrary, means giving ourselves the means to shape it, to inhabit it, to reinscribe it within a human horizon. It is not technology that we must fear, but our passivity in the face of it.

Designing the future of AI, therefore, means considering the future of humanity itself. This can only be achieved through a plurality of voices, disciplines, and cultures. We can no longer be satisfied with a vision centered on the technological West or solely on the logic of the market. We need a global ecology of thought, where Persian philosophy, Indian logic, African cosmology, Asian spiritualities, and contemporary sciences interact, question, and complement one another. For it is in the convergence of differences that a true collective intelligence is born, capable of addressing global challenges such as technical, ecological, social, and existential.

This book, by tracing the profound history of AI, aims to remind us that science never emerges ex nihilo. It is always rooted in traditions of thought, cultural contexts, and human needs. It progresses through reversals, ruptures, and shifts. It is neither linear nor neutral. And this is precisely what makes it so rich. Understanding this genealogy means recognizing that AI is not the preserve of a technological elite, but the fruit of a common heritage, which is the one that we have a responsibility to transmit, renew, and wisely move beyond.

In a world affected by crises such as climate, democratic, economic, and identity-related issues, AI can play a decisive role, provided it is not exploited by short-term logic. It must become a tool for transition, metamorphosis, and reinvention. Not to dream of a perfect or automated world, but to better inhabit imperfection, to strengthen connections, to make possible what isolation or human fatigue have prevented. AI must not seek to eliminate fragility, but to accompany it, to surround it with an allied, supportive, humble, and creative intelligence.

The "last word," if there is one, will therefore not be a conclusion, but an invitation. An invitation to think differently, to create collectively, to dream rigorously. AI, as it emerges, requires not only brilliant engineers but also awakened consciences. It calls for a renaissance of critical thinking, of philosophy, of poetry itself. It demands that we rediscover, within ourselves and among ourselves, the breath of an expanded intelligence, at once rational and sensitive, grounded and open, lucid and utopian. For it is on this intelligence, more than that of machines, that the dignity of our future will depend.

References

1. Bahraseman, S.E., et al., Reviving the forgotten legacy: Strategies for reviving qanats as sustainable solutions for agricultural water supply in arid and semi-arid regions. *Water Research*, 2024. **265**. https://doi.org/10.1016/j.watres.2024.122138.
2. Hajossy, R., Plimpton 322: A universal cuneiform table for old Babylonian mathematicians, builders, surveyors and teachers. *Tatra Mountains Mathematical Publications*, 2016. **67**: pp. 1–40.
3. Russell, S.J. and P. Norvig, *Artificial intelligence: A modern approach*. 2016: Pearson.
4. Jobin, A., M. Ienca, and E. Vayena, The global landscape of AI ethics guidelines. *Nature Machine Intelligence*, 2019. **1**(9): pp. 389–399.
5. Mittelstadt, B., Principles alone cannot guarantee ethical AI. *Nature Machine Intelligence*, 2019. **1**(11): pp. 501–507.
6. Nascimento, E.G.S., et al., T4PdM: A deep neural network based on the transformer architecture for fault diagnosis of rotating machinery. *arXiv preprint arXiv*:2204.03725, 2022.

Index